CYBERCOUNSELING AND CYBERLEARNING:

Strategies and Resources for the Millennium

Edited by
John W. Bloom and Garry R. Walz

Developed Collaboratively
by the American Counseling Association and
CAPS, Inc. in association with the ERIC Counseling and
Student Services Clearinghouse

CYBERCOUNSELING AND CYBERLEARNING: STRATEGIES AND RESOURCES FOR THE MILLENNIUM

10 9 8 7 6 5 4 3 2

American Counseling Association
5999 Stevenson Avenue
Alexandria, VA 22304

CAPS, Inc. in association with the
ERIC Counseling and Student Services Clearinghouse
201 Ferguson
Greensboro, NC 27402

Director of Publications
Carolyn C. Baker

Copy Editor
Lucy Blanton

Cover design by Martha Woolsey

Library of Congress Cataloging-in-Publication Data

Cybercounseling and cyberlearning : strategies and resources for the Millennium/
edited and contributions by John W. Bloom, Garry R. Walz.
    p.   cm.
    Includes bibliographical references and index.
    ISBN 1-55620-180-x (alk. paper)
    1. Counseling—Computer network resources. [1. Internet (Computer network)]
    I. Bloom, John W. II. Walz, Garry Richard.
    BF637.C6 C88 2000
    361'.06'02854678—dc21   99-088958

Table of Contents

Foreword   ix

Preface   xi

Acknowledgements   xix

About the Editors   xxi

About the Authors   xxiii

Introduction   xxxiii

Cybersampler xxxvii

PART I
Benefits and Challenges of Technology in the Millennium

Chapter 1: Paul F. Granello
Historical Context: The Relationship of
Computer Technologies and Counseling   3

Chapter 2: John A. Casey
Managing Technology Wisely:
A New Counselor Competency   17

Chapter 3: Thomas W. Clawson
Expanding Professions Globally:
The United States as a Marketplace for Global
Credentialing and Cyberapplications   29

Chapter 4: JoAnn Harris-Bowlsbey
The Internet: Blessing or Bane for the
Counseling Profession? 39

Chapter 5: Duane Brown
The Odyssey of a Technologically Challenged
Counselor Educator Into Cyberspace 51

PART II
Infusing New Technology Into Counseling,
Education, and Human Services

Chapter 6: John McFadden and Marty Jencius
Using Cyberspace to Enhance Counselors' Cultural
Transcendence 67

Chapter 7: Courtland C. Lee
Cybercounseling and Empowerment:
Bridging the Digital Divide 85

Chapter 8: Juneau Mahan Gary and Linda Remolino
Coping With Loss and Grief Through On-Line
Support Groups 95

Chapter 9: Joanna Refvem, Jean C. Plante,
        and W. Larry Osborne
Interactive Career Counseling in Middle and Secondary
Schools: Integrating the Use of the Internet Into
School Career Development Programs 115

Chapter 10: Michael K. Altekruse and Leah Brew
Using the Web for Distance Learning 129

Chapter 11: Marla Peterson
Electronic Delivery of Career Development
University Courses 143

Chapter 12: GARRY R. WALZ AND L. STAR REEDY
The International Career Development Library:
The Use of Virtual Libraries to Promote
Counselor Learning 161

Chapter 13: JACQUELINE LEWIS, DIANE COURSOL, AND
           KAY HERTING-WAHL
Electronic Portfolios in Counselor Education 171

Chapter 14: MARTY JENCIUS AND MICHAEL BALTIMORE
Professional Publication in Cyberspace: Guidelines and
Resources for Counselors Entering a New Paradigm 185

PART III
Outcomes, Achievements, and
Quandaries of Cybercounseling

Chapter 15: SUSAN X DAY AND PAUL SCHNEIDER
The Subjective Experiences of Therapists in Face-to-Face,
Video, and Audio Sessions 203

Chapter 16: KATHARINE R. COLLIE, DAN MITCHELL, AND
           LAWRENCE MURPHY
Skills for On-Line Counseling:
Maximum Impact at Minimum Bandwidth 219

Chapter 17: JANET E. WALL
Technology-Delivered Assessment:
Power, Problems, and Promise 237

PART IV
Applications of Technology in Counselor Preparation,
Professional Development, and Distance Learning

Chapter 18: JACK PRESBURY AND JOE MARCHAL
Getting Counselor Expertise Into a Computer:
A Cyberassistant for Students of Brief Counseling 255

Chapter 19: LINDA SATTEM, KATHRYN REYNOLDS, GREGORY
R. BERNHARDT, AND JEAN R. BURDESHAW
Cyberspace Education and Lifelong Learning for Professionals:
Dangerous Opportunities 275

Chapter 20: PAMELA S. LEARY
Technology and the Continuing Education of
Professional Counselors 291

Chapter 21: M. HARRY DANIELS, J. MICHAEL TYLER, AND
B. SCOTT CHRISTIE
On-Line Instruction in Counselor Education:
Possibilities, Implications, and Guidelines 303

PART V
Ethical and Professional Challenges in Cybercounseling

Chapter 22: ROSEMARIE SCOTTI HUGHES
Cybercounseling and Regulations: Quagmire or Quest? 321

Chapter 23: JEFFREY S. LOVE
Cybercounselors v. Cyberpolice 339

Chapter 24: CAROL L. BOBBY AND LUCIEN CAPONE III
Understanding the Implications of Distance
Learning for Accreditation and Licensure of
Counselor Preparation Programs 361

Chapter 25: ELIZABETH DUMEZ
Cyberpaths to Ethical Competence 379

PART VI
Envisaging the Future of Cybercounseling

Chapter 26: GARRY R. WALZ WITH CONTRIBUTIONS FROM
JOHN W. BLOOM, JAMES SAMPSON, WAYNE
LANNING, AND ROBERT CHAPMAN
Summing Up 405

PART VII
Web Site Resources

Chapter 27: GARRY R. WALZ AND JOHN W. BLOOM
Introducing the *Cybercounseling and Cyberlearning*
Web Site 417

APPENDIXES

Appendix 1: Ethical Standards for Internet On-Line
Counseling of the American Counseling
Association 423
Appendix 2: Technical Competencies for Counselor
Education Students: Recommended
Guidelines for Program Development 429
Appendix 3: Technology Standards for
School Counselors 431
Appendix 4: Technology Competencies Matrix 433
Appendix 5: Standards for the Ethical Practice of
Web Counseling of the National Board
for Certified Counselors 441
Appendix 6: National Career Development Association
Guidelines for the Use of the Internet for
Provision of Career Information and
Planning Services 445
Index 453

Foreword

I am most pleased to write this Foreword for *Cybercounseling and Cyberlearning: Strategies and Resources for the Millennium*. Early on I decided that the examination of technology and its implications for counselors and counseling would be an important theme in my presidential year. Technology is a part of all of our lives, and only through a rigorous and continuing examination of it can we make judicious use of it as counselors.

I am especially pleased with the approach taken in this publication, namely that of assisting counselors to become better informed about cybercounseling so that they can decide for themselves what their personal position is on the worth and use of cybercounseling. It will be an excellent resource for personal use as well as for stimulating discussions and interactions at meetings and conferences.

I believe the editors, John Bloom and Garry Walz, and the many excellent writers are to be congratulated for their work. Special appreciation is also due to Garry Walz for initiating the collaboration between the American Counseling Association (ACA) and ERIC Counseling and Student Services Clearinghouse (ERIC/CASS). It was a monumental effort that should have lasting benefits for both the Association and the counselors who use the publication.

I believe special appreciation is also due to Richard Yep, Executive Director of ACA, and Carolyn Baker, Director of ACA Publications, who early on saw the worth of producing this publication and actively supported it through challenging times.

A special feature of this technological initiative is a cybersection where cybercounseling resources that are a part of this publication are available on a *Cybercounseling and Cyberlearning* web site.

This site will be managed by ERIC/CASS under a grant provided by the American Counseling Association Foundation at my request. We all owe the ACA Foundation our appreciation for its help in assisting ACA to enhance its technological posture.

If you find within this publication ideas and/or resources that are useful to you, we will be most pleased. It was the desire to assist you to better understand and use technology as counselors that motivated us to develop the publication. By checking the ACA and ERIC/CASS web sites, you can learn about continuing developments related to cybercounseling.

Best wishes on your journey into cyberspace.

Donna Ford
President, ACA

Preface

CYBERCOUNSELING, CYBERLEARNING, AND ERIC/CASS

ERIC/CASS provides a compelling vantage point from which to view the helping services community, the myriad population subgroups seeking help, and the broad range of needs and concerns reflected in the types of information they seek. Counselors, parents, students, educators, and administrators in diverse settings turn to ERIC/CASS for help in locating the best available information on helping and healing. In particular, counselors on the front line, with too much to do and too little time to learn new interventions, need access to resources that they can put to use immediately.

At ERIC/CASS, we are in a unique position to identify the disparities between what people need and want and what information and resources are currently available. Traditionally, these disparities are what have moved us to undertake major new initiatives in our publications and professional services. More often than not, a compelling need cannot be adequately met by simply churning out a more sophisticated information search of different databases. Moreover, it is not resolved by multiplying the number of voices re-iterating the need and expressing uncertainty and doubt.

What is needed is a thoughtful analysis of the knowledge pertinent to specific goals and aspirations. Rarely does any one voice, or the accumulated thoughts of a particular group, suffice to illuminate the path of choice. However, even with a thoughtful analysis, we may still need to take leaps of faith to decide what to do; but it helps if we know how far we need to leap and where the best spots to land are.

Thoughtful analyses and syntheses with inspired leaps of faith are what have characterized ERIC/CASS' responses to numerous challenges that have been presented to us. By calling upon those most experienced in and committed to probing the challenges to counseling, we have put together publications that have offered newly generated ideas and courses of action. Though that which is offered may give way as new information is generated, it does provide guidance for the here and now. We are compelled to make decisions and take action now; hence it is a high priority that, while helping people to visualize the future, we also assist counselors to deal with present challenges and demands.

In previous clearinghouse projects, we have focused on implementing career development programs, introducing computers into guidance, preparing counselors as agents of change, providing new perspectives and approaches to school guidance, targeting research to counseling outcomes, providing a social action approach for counseling, empowering counselors to facilitate student learning, and using virtual libraries as springboards for new counseling practice. These are only some of the themes that have served to focus our energies over the 30-plus years of ERIC/CASS' existence.

Currently, numerous challenges expressed in gripping tones and emphasizing dire need and public concern are confronting counselors. School and societal violence, substance abuse, school-to-work transitions, and multicultural/diversity issues have impacted directly upon our profession. In today's world, concerns are voiced with a strength and immediacy seldom experienced even a few years ago. None of these concerns, however, have been expressed with more persistence and breadth than those related to technology and its impact on counseling. This is a challenge as to how each counseling professional perceives counseling and how he or she intends to use or ignore technology in all aspects of his or her work as a counselor. All counselors must come to grips with this exponentially expanding medium and decide for themselves what to do and what not to do.

Of particular importance to us at ERIC/CASS as purveyors of information and resources is the dearth of relevant resources for counselors in deciding *what to do when* in the area of cybercounseling. This void has motivated us to produce a handbook of sorts that can be used now and, hopefully, for some time to come. As a clearinghouse, we are alert for niches of need that appear in the knowledge base for counselors and counseling. Topics that are extensively covered in the literature, from which any given counselor has much to choose, have only minimal appeal to us. If it has already been said, why say it again? Proliferation of ideas and information already widely disseminated is a disservice to the intended user (a waste of his or her time!) and a foolish utilization of writing talent.

When there are compelling questions vital to the practice of counseling that have been incompletely or inadequately responded to, we take note. When we identify one of these needful niches, we have two clear options: synthesize the existing information into a form that facilitates adoption and improved practice or generate intensive and extensive information and ideas based upon an analysis of what has already been learned. Of course, in many instances we do both: synthesize the most cogent of extant knowledge and use it as a springboard to formulate new concepts and ideas worthy of tryout and experimentation.

Based upon the range and number of queries we receive at ERIC/CASS in which technology and counseling are the main drivers, we clearly see this area as a needed niche. This conclusion is further supported by the large quantity of articles identified by ERIC searches in which technology and counseling are the main subjects. Noteworthy is that although the number of articles on technology/counseling is large, the articles often fail to provide a functional bridge for counselors to move from where they are (frequently a state of concern and uncertainty) to a spirited moving forward with clear goals and directions. A large collection of disparate articles on technology and counseling, even excellent ones, do not provide a clear pathway to the future.

Based upon our analysis of user needs and desires and the availability of relevant resources, we decided to make technology and counseling as one of the top priorities for our 5-year strategic plan. It is a good fit given our past commitment to technology as well as our current use of technology to develop the ERIC/CASS Virtual Libraries for Counselors and the unique interactive database and search system, the International Career Development Library (see chapter 12). It is a topic we are fully enmeshed with both professionally and personally. A book of the magnitude of this one does not magically spring into view like a freshly activated computer. It is the result of countless interactions with knowledgeable peers, intense probing of the literature, and the tryout of ideas and plans on others. Like an older model computer, it first had to be loaded, and then a ragged image appeared with frequent starts and stops. The image of what the book should be and how it should be used is, in our perception, now of reasonably high resolution and in brilliant colors. We like it. We are prepared to own it.

WHAT'S IN A TITLE?

For us a great deal. It reveals the basic rationale and orientation of the book. It is a succinct, incisive way of expressing what is between the covers; and it also offers some revealing hints about how it can be used.

First, the terms *cybercounseling* and *cyberlearning* convey our basic belief that human services specialists are confronted by the challenge of using both computers and the Internet to offer counseling to persons without regard to time and space. Importantly, we also believe that, more so than ever before, counselors are in the learning business and can be important mediators in their clients' learning activities. Taken together, cybercounseling and cyberlearning present many new opportunities and challenges for counselors, such as reaching more clients than ever before. But is it really counseling? It seemed imperative to us that all counselors be cognizant of what challenges and opportunities the cyberage has opened up for counselors so that they might make judicious and thoughtful plans and decisions rather than faddish and politically correct ones.

Second, awareness is a necessary first step in responding to a need, but not a sufficient one. You need the means to respond as well. That is where the strategies and resources come to the fore. We believe each counselor must select a strategy for the use of cybercounseling and cyberlearning that reflects his or her beliefs and values. We see this publication with its six basic themes, as expressed in the titles of Parts I through VI, as assisting each individual to be an active participant in developing a customized strategy for becoming a counselor in a cyberworld. Clearly, however, it does not take an advocacy stance as to what part of cybercounseling and cyberlearning a person adopts as his or her own strategy of counseling. We strongly desire to influence counselors to make informed decisions about cybercounseling; but we do believe that the specifics of what to do or what not to do are the prerogative of the individual—subject, of course, to professional ethical and legal standards.

SOMETHING FOR EVERYBODY, BUT NOT EVERYTHING FOR EVERYBODY

In reflecting on what should be the contents of the book, numerous considerations came to mind. It should appeal to both technological novices and experts; serve the function of basic reference or handbook; provide basic overviews of key facets of technology and guidance; offer specific suggestions on various start-up procedures in cybercounseling; be a source of links, relevant resources, and models; and illustrate cybercounseling and cyberlearning rather than just discuss them. A rather tall order! Particularly if, as we prioritized, it is inviting and useful to persons of widely varying backgrounds.

Some suggested we do it all on-line and forget the idea of hard copy. Others saw that as limiting our audience and missing out in providing a highly flexible resource available whenever and wherever a person wanted it. In the end, we decided upon a hybrid—a hard copy format that includes a special Cybersampler providing abstracts of a dozen plus cyberresources. Four of these cyberresources are hard copy publications; the rest are on-line so that they can be visited and checked out through actual use.

There is also a special cybersection—a *Cybercounseling and Cyberlearning* web site established and maintained by ERIC/CASS (cybercounsel.uncg.edu). (See chapter 27; see also chapter 12.) The *Cybercounseling* site will provide a home for on-line cybercounseling resources and provide access to the on-line chapters of this publication. Further, individuals can both visit the site and contribute their own programs to it. ACA President Donna Ford, who made the examination and judicious use of technology in counseling a major theme of her presidency, was instrumental in obtaining a small grant from the ACA Foundation to launch the *Cybercounseling and Cyberlearning* web site at ERIC/CASS.

HOW TO USE THIS PUBLICATION
(AND AVOID GETTING LOST OR OVERWHELMED!)

The publication was designed with a three-step cycle of use in mind. This three-step approach is intended to maximize the benefits that can accrue through use of the publication, both for individuals and the helping profession as a whole.

- **Step One: Scan and Read.** We recommend that the first step in using this book be to become fully familiar with the contents. Some sections will be of more interest to you than others, but it is important that you know the organization of the book and what it contains for future reference and use. It will take some time to digest what is between the covers, so allow time for browsing and reflecting on what you read. Then zero in on the chapters that most interest you. With many of them you will want to visit web sites and examine the materials they recommend. So be near a computer you can use!

- **Step Two: Adopt and Adapt.** It is both enjoyable and professionally rewarding to apply the practices and programs presented in the different chapters. Even though you may be a "cyberregular," it will probably come as a surprise to you to see the breadth and depth of ideas and resources presented. Examine them carefully and judiciously with a view as to what to use and what to ignore. The basic question should be, How can I use what I see to augment and enhance my counseling? It need not be adoptions of whole programs, but rather of small segments you can integrate into your teaching and/or counseling.

- **Step Three: Share Your Experiences and Insights.** As you develop your own customized cybercounseling and cyberlearning practices, think of what you are especially proud of and pleased with that you can share with others. There is great satisfaction in sharing what you have developed or refined so that others may profit from your insights and experiences. It is also a great way to extend your own learning. It can even lead to a stimulating network of like-minded colleagues!

Have an idea or want more information on submitting materials? Just give us a call at 1-800-414-9769 or e-mail us at ericcass@uncg.edu. In any case, John and I would love to hear from you. Hug us or slam us—virtually, that is. But don't ignore us!

Garry R. Walz

Acknowledgements

The following persons deserve special recognition for their efforts in making this publication possible:

- Donna Ford, President, American Counseling Association, for enthusiastically incorporating the idea of the publication into her presidential theme.
- Richard Yep, Executive Director, American Counseling Association, for his interest in and support of the publication throughout its development.
- Carolyn Baker, Director of Publications, American Counseling Association, for merging the multiple efforts into a compelling final product.
- Thomas Clawson, Executive Director, National Board for Certified Counselors, for his leadership in drawing the attention of counselors to the importance of examining the impact of cyber-counseling upon the counseling profession.
- Jillian Barr Joncas, Assistant Director for User Services, ERIC Clearinghouse on Counseling and Student Services, for facilitating the communication between Indianapolis, Greensboro, and Washington, DC.
- Joy Rose, Secretary, Graduate Studies Office, College of Education, Butler University, Indianapolis, Indiana, for helping keep a lid on things at Butler!
- Last, but of particular importance, the numerous contributors to this book for their dedicated work that has—despite numerous challenges—produced a body of superior articles.

About the Editors

John W. Bloom is a professor of counselor education in the College of Education at Butler University in Indianapolis, Indiana. As a member of the Board of Directors of the National Board for Certified Counselors, he helped draft NBCC's Standards for the Ethical Practice of Web Counseling in 1997. Correspondence should be addressed to Butler University, 4600 Sunset Avenue, Indianapolis, IN 46207, (317) 940-9490, or via the Internet at jbloom@butler.edu.

Garry R. Walz is director of the ERIC Counseling and Student Services Clearinghouse at the University of North Carolina at Greensboro, North Carolina, and professor emeritus of the University of Michigan. He is a past president of the American Counseling Association (ACA) and the Association for Counselor Education and Supervision (ACES) and past chair of the Counseling and Human Development Foundation. He is a recipient of the ACA Gilbert and Kathleen Wrenn Humanitarian Award and the National Career Development Association Eminent Professional Career Award. Correspondence should be sent to ERIC/CASS, 201 Ferguson Building, University of North Carolina at Greensboro, P.O. Box 26171, Greensboro, NC 27402-6171, (800) 414-9769, or via the Internet at gwalz@aol.com or ericcass@uncg.edu.

About the Authors

Michael K. Altekruse is professor and chair, Department of Counseling, Development, and Higher Education at the University of North Texas in Denton, Texas. Dr. Altekruse has developed three WWW courses and recently received a grant to develop four more courses leading to career counselors' certification. Correspondence should be addressed to Department of Counseling, Development, and Higher Education, P. O. Box 311337, Denton, TX 76203-1337, (940) 565-2910, or via the Internet at altkrs@coefs.coe.unt.edu or altkrs@unt.edu.

Michael Baltimore is an associate professor in counselor education in the Department of Counseling and Clinical Programs at Columbus State University, Columbus, Georgia. He is co-founding editor of the peer-reviewed, web-based *Journal of Technology in Counseling*. Correspondence should be addressed to Department of Counseling and Clinical Programs, 4225 University Avenue, Jordan 104, Columbus, GA 31907, (706) 568-2222, or via the Internet at baltimore_michael@colstate.edu.

Gregory R. Bernhardt is dean of the College of Education and Human Services at Wright State University in Dayton, Ohio. Correspondence should be addressed to WSU, Dayton, OH 45435, or via the Internet at gregory.bernhardt@wright.edu.

Carol L. Bobby is the executive director of the Council for Accreditation of Counseling and Related Educational Programs

(CACREP). She is past chair of the Association of Specialized and Professional Accreditors (ASPA) and is the current chair of the Center for Quality Assurance in International Education (CQAIE). Correspondence should be addressed to CACREP, 5999 Stevenson Avenue, Alexandria, VA 22304, (703) 823-9800 Ext. 301, or via the Internet at <u>CACREP@aol.com</u>.

Leah Brew is a doctoral student in the Department of Counseling, Development, and Higher Education at the University of North Texas in Denton, Texas. Ms. Brew is currently working at the university. Correspondence should be addressed to Department of Counseling, Development, and Higher Education, P.O. Box 311337, Denton, TX 76203-1337, (940) 565-2910.

Duane Brown is a professor at the University of North Carolina at Chapel Hill in Chapel Hill, North Carolina. Correspondence should be addressed to 620 Barbury Drive, Chapel Hill, North Carolina 27514, (919) 942-0950, or via the Internet at <u>dbrown@email.unc.edu</u>.

Jean R. Burdeshaw is director of internal communication at the NCR Corporation in Dayton, Ohio. Correspondence should be addressed to NCR, 1700 South Patterson Boulevard, Dayton, OH 45479, (937) 445-1109, or via the Internet at <u>jb129524@ exchange.daytonoh.ncr.com</u>.

Lucien Capone III is university counsel for the University of North Carolina at Greensboro. He is also chair of the UNC Computer Law and Internet Legal Issues Committee (CILIC). Correspondence should be addressed to P.O. Box 6170, Greensboro, NC 27402-6170, (336) 334-3067, or via the Internet at <u>l_capone@office.uncg.edu</u>.

John A. Casey is an associate professor in counselor education in the Department of Counseling and Educational Psychology at the University of Nevada, Reno. He is a former chair of the Association for Counselor Education and Supervision Technology Interest Network. Correspondence should be addressed to Mailstop 281, Reno,

NV 89557-0213, (775) 784-6637 x2065, or via the Internet at jcasey@unr.edu.

Robert Chapman is coordinator of the Alcohol and Other Drug Program at LaSalle University Counseling Center in Philadelphia, Pennsylvania. Correspondence should be addressed to La Salle University Counseling Center, 1900 West Olney Avnue, Philadelphia, PA 19141-1199, (215) 951-01355, or via the Internet at chapman@lasalle.edu.

B. Scott Christie is in private practice at Family Counseling and Consulting in Medford, Oregon. His doctoral thesis, *Distance Clinical Supervision in Cyberspace: A Qualitative Study*, was completed in 1998. Correspondence should be sent to 2468 Springbrook Road, Medford, OR 97504, (541) 734-9395, or via the Internet at riskies@grrtech.com.

Thomas W. Clawson is executive director, National Board for Certified Counselors, Greensboro, North Carolina. He lived in Europe for 8 years and worked in five countries and has presented at numerous international conferences. Correspondence should be addressed to NBCC, 3-D Terrace Way, Greensboro, NC 27403, (336) 547-0607, or via the Internet at clawson@nbcc.org.

Katharine R. Collie is a professional artist and a doctoral researcher at the Institute of Health Promotion Research at the University of British Columbia in Vancouver, British Columbia. Her research focuses on art-based psychosocial treatments for people with life-threatening illnesses, in particular computer-supported treatments for people with mobility limitations. Correspondence should be addressed to Institute of Health Promotion Research, 2206 East Mall, Room 324, UBC, Vancouver, BC V6T 1Z3, Canada, (604) 222-1219, or via the Internet at kcollie@interchange.ubc.ca.

Diane Coursol is a counselor educator at Minnesota State University, Mankato. Correspondence should be addressed to MSU 52/P.O.

Box 8400, MSU-Mankato, Mankato, MN 56002-8400, (507) 389-5656, or via the Internet at diane.coursol@mankato.msus.edu.

M. Harry Daniels is professor and chair of the Department of Counselor Education at the University of Florida in Gainesville. He is an active member of the Association for Counselor Education and Supervision Technology Interest Network. Correspondence should be addressed to Department of Counselor Education, 1215 Norman Hall, P.O. Box 117046, Gainesville, FL 32611, (352) 392-0731, or via the Internet at harryd@coe.ufl.edu.

Susan X Day is an assistant professor at Iowa State University in Ames, Iowa. She received her PhD in counseling psychology from the University of Illinois at Urbana-Champaign in 1999 and has published articles in the *American Psychologist, Psychological Science*, and the *Michigan Quarterly Review*. Correspondence should be addressed to Psychology Department, Lagomarcino Hall, Iowa State University, Ames, IA 50010, (515) 232-8363, or via the Internet at sxday@iastate.edu.

Elizabeth DuMez is former manager of the National Association of Social Workers (NASW) Office of Ethics and Professional Review. Correspondence may be addressed to 3837 North Upland Street, Arlington, VA 22207, (703) 241-0824, or via the Internet at bethdumez@erols.com.

Juneau Mahan Gary is coordinator of and assistant professor in the counselor education program in the Department of Special Education and Individualized Services at Kean University in Union, New Jersey. She teaches graduate counseling courses and, in counseling, helps clients cope with issues of loss and bereavement. Correspondence should be addressed to Kean University, 1000 Morris Avenue, Union, NJ 07083, (908) 527-2523, or via the Internet at Juneaux@Juno.com.

Paul F. Granello is an assistant professor in counselor education in the School of Physical Activity and Educational Services at the Ohio State University in Columbus, Ohio. He has a doctoral specialty in computer technology and statistics and has written software and developed web pages. Correspondence should be addressed to 288 Arps Hall, 1945 North High Street, Columbus, OH 43210, (614) 688-4931, or via the Internet at granello.2@osu.edu.

JoAnn Harris-Bowlsbey is executive director of the Career Development Leadership Alliance, a nonprofit organization dedicated to training counselors in technology-driven ways; a professor at Loyola College in Baltimore; and a special consultant to Nippon Manpower in Japan. She is a pioneer in the field of computer-based career planning systems, a past president of the National Career Development Association, and a recent recipient of its Eminent Professional Career Award. Correspondence should be addressed to Loyola College in Maryland, 4501 North Charles Street, Baltimore, MD 21210, (410) 840-4734, or via the Internet at bowlsbey@erols.com.

Kenneth E. Hartman is associate professor of instructional technology at Widener University, Philadelphia. He is creator and director of the National Technology Institute for School Counselors and author of the *Internet Guide for College-Bound Students*. Correspondence should be addressed to Widener University, Philadelphia, PA 19013, (610) 499-4000, or via the Internet at ken.e.hartman@widener.edu.

Kay Herting-Wahl is a counselor educator at Minnesota State University, Mankato. Correspondence should be addressed to MSU52/ P.O. Box 8400, MSU-Mankato, Mankato, MN 56002-8400, (507) 389-5658, or via the Internet at kay.wahl@mankato.msus.edu.

Rosemarie Scotti Hughes is dean of the School of Counseling and Human Services at Regent University in Virginia Beach, Virginia. She is a member and vice chair of the Virginia Board of Licensed Professional Counselors, Marriage and Family Therapists and Substance Abuse Professionals. Correspondence should be addressed to 1000 Regent University Drive, CRB 215, Virginia Beach, VA 23464-9865, (757) 226-4255, or via the Internet at rosehug@regent.edu.

Marty Jencius is an assistant professor in counselor education in the Department of Counseling and Clinical Programs at Columbus

State University, Columbus, Georgia. He is co-founding editor of the peer-reviewed, web-based *Journal of Technology in Counseling*. Correspondence should be addressed to Department of Counseling and Clinical Programs, 4225 University Avenue, Jordan 120, Columbus, GA 31907, (706) 568-2222, or via the Internet at jencius_marty@colstate.edu.

Wayne Lanning is associate dean for graduate studies, College of Education, Oklahoma State University, Stillwater, Oklahoma. Correspondence should be addressed to Oklahoma State University, Stillwater, OK 74078-4033, (405) 744-8976, or via the Internet at wl@okstate.edu.

Pamela S. Leary is recertification administrator with the National Board for Certified Counselors in Greensboro, North Carolina. She has been a national leader in the continuing education field for 7 years. Correspondence should be addressed to 3-D, Terrace Way, Greensboro, NC 27403, (336) 547-0607, or via the Internet at leary@nbcc.org.

Courtland C. Lee is Dean of the School of Education at Hunter College in New York. He is past president of the American Counseling Association. Correspondence should be addressed to Hunter College, 695 Park Avenue, 1000 W, New York, NY 10021, or via the Internet at colee@shiva.hunter.cuny.edu.

Jacqueline Lewis is a counselor educator at the University of New England in Australia. Correspondence should be addressed to Department of Health Studies, UNE, Armidale NSW 2351 Australia, 02-6773-3665, or via the Internet at jlewis6@metz.une.edu.au.

Jeffrey S. Love is an attorney with the firm of Lane Powell Spears and Lubersky LLP in Portland, Oregon. He was a featured speaker at the 1998 Annual Conference of the American Association of State Counseling Boards, received his JD from the University of California at Berkeley in 1987, and is a member of the Oregon and California bar associations. Correspondence should be addressed to 610 SW Second Avenue, Portland, OR 97204, (503) 778-2139, or via the Internet at LoveJ@lanepowell.com.

Joe Marchal is a professor of integrated science and technology at James Madison University in Harrisonburg, Virginia. He teaches courses in artificial intelligence and intelligent systems. Correspondence should be addressed to Integrated Science and Technology and Computer Science, JMU, Harrisonburg, VA 22807, or via the Internet at Marchajh@jmu.edu.

John McFadden is Benjamin E. Mays Professor in the Department of Educational Psychology at the University of South Carolina in Columbia, South Carolina. He is author of *Transcultural Counseling: Bilateral and International Perspectives*. Correspondence should be addressed to Department of Educational Psychology, USC, Columbia, SC 29208, (803) 777-7797, or via the Internet at jmcfaddden@ed.sc.edu.

Dan Mitchell is co-founder and senior therapist with Therapy Online, an Internet-based counseling service in Vancouver, British Columbia. He has also been practicing as an addictions counselor with the British Ministry for Children and Families for the past 9 years. Correspondence should be addressed to 2864 Munday Place, North Vancouver, B.C., Canada V7N 4L2, (604) 726-7389, or via the Internet at mitchell@therapyonline.ca.

Lawrence Murphy is co-founder and senior therapist with Therapy Online. He has worked as a therapist for 7 years and is presently employed in health promotion and substance abuse prevention in southern Ontario. Correspondence should be addressed via the Internet at research@sympatico.ca.

W. Larry Osborne is an associate professor at the University of North Carolina at Greensboro. He authored *Career Development, Assessment, and Counseling: Applications of the Donald E. Super C-DAC Approach* and is the recipient of the 1998 American Counseling Association Research Award. Correspondence should be addressed to

Counseling and Educational Development, 220 Curry Building, University of North Carolina at Greensboro, Greensboro, NC 27412, (336) 334-3430, or via the Internet at wlosborn@uncg.edu.

Marla Peterson is professor of counselor education and counseling psychology at the University of Tennessee, Knoxville. She is the co-host for the International Counselor Network (ICN) and is a charter member of the Technology Committee of the American School Counselor Association. Correspondence should be addressed to 239 Claxton Addition, College of Education, University of Tennessee, Knoxville, TN 37996-3440, (424) 974-5131, or via the Internet at Peterson@utkux.utcc.utk.edu.

Jean C. Plante is a school counselor at Walkerton Middle School in Winston-Salem, North Carolina. She is a recent graduate of the University of North Carolina at Greensboro, having received her master's in counseling, school track, with an emphasis in middle schools. Correspondence should be addressed to jcplante@yahoo.com.

Jack Presbury is a professor of psychology at James Madison University in Harrisonburg, Virginia. He has prepared school and community counselors for nearly 30 years. Correspondence should be sent to Department of Psychology, MSC 7401, Harrisonburg, VA 22807, (540) 568-6114, or via the Internet at presbujh@jmu.edu.

L. Star Reedy is Internet special project manager at the ERIC Counseling and Student Services Clearinghouse, Greensboro, North Carolina. Correspondence should be addressed to the International Career Development Library via e-mail at icdl@uncg.edu.

Joanna Refvem is a school counselor at Mount Airy Middle School in Mount Airy, North Carolina. Correspondence should be addressed to 725 Cross Creek Drive, Mount Airy, NC 27030, (336) 789-1822, or via the Internet at jobabes@infoave.net.

Linda Remolino is a school counselor at Wayne Hills High School in Wayne, New Jersey. She hosts two on-line support groups for loss. Correspondence should be addressed to Wayne Hills High School, 272 Berdan Avenue, Wayne, NJ 07470, (973) 633-3101, or via the Internet at Remofami@aol.com.

Kathryn Reynolds is an education and human services librarian in the Paul Lawrence Dunbar Library at Wright State University in Dayton, Ohio. Correspondence should be sent to Paul Lawrence Dunbar Library, Wright State University, Dayton, OH 45435, (937) 775-3516, or via the Internet at kathryn.reynolds@wright.edu.

James Sampson is professor and co-director, Center for the Study of Technology in Counseling and Career Development, Florida State University, Tallahassee, Florida. Correspondence should be sent to University Center, Suite A4100, FSU, Tallahassee, FL 32306-2490, (850) 644-2490, or via the Internet at jpsampso@garnet.acns.fsu.edu.

Linda Sattem is a Licensed Professional Counselor in private practice in Dayton, Ohio. Correspondence should be addressed to 1608 Wimbleton Avenue, Fairborn, OH 45324, (937) 878-7110, or via the Internet at LLS1952@aol.com.

Paul Schneider is completing a predoctoral internship in counseling psychology at the University of Texas Medical Branch in Galveston, Texas. He has been involved with distance technology at the University of Illinois for more than 5 years and has worked in web design, computer instruction, and distance learning. He was chair of the opening symposium for the American Psychological Association's 1999 Telehealth Miniconvention. Correspondence should be addressed to 3002 69th Street, B2, Galveston, TX 77551, or via the Internet at p-schne@uiuc.edu.

J. Michael Tyler is counselor education program leader at Florida Gulf Coast University in Fort Myers, Florida. He is also a member of the ACES Technology Interest Network. Correspondence should be addressed to 10501 FGCU Boulevard, South, Fort Myers, FL 33965-6565, (941) 590-7792, or via the Internet at jtyler@fgcu.edu.

Janet E. Wall is assistant vice president of ACT in Hunt Valley, Maryland. Correspondence should be addressed to Education Technology Center, Executive Plaza I, Suite 200, 11350 Mc-Cormick Road, Hunt Valley, Maryland 21031, (410) 584-4000, or via the Internet at wall@act.org.

Introduction

The new millennium has dawned with all its attendant challenges and responsibilities. If the previous millennium is any indicator, expecting the unexpected will be our norm, particularly as it applies to the challenges and responsibilities related to the application of emerging technologies to the behavioral health professions.

The previous century saw numerous events of a technological nature that forever changed the landscape of the world. Among these—as selected and ranked by American journalists and scholars and reported by the Associated Press—were the following:

18. Soviets launch Sputnik, first space satellite (1957);
28. Television debuts in the United States at New York World's Fair (1939);
31. Mass-marketed personal computers launched (1977);
32. World Wide Web revolutionizes the Internet (1989);
40. First regular radio broadcasts begin in America (1909);
42. ENIAC becomes world's first computer (1946);
43. Regular television broadcasting begins in the United States (1941);
51. U.S. scientists patent the computer chip (1959);
52. Marconi transmits radio signal across the Atlantic (1901);
92. Pathfinder lands on Mars, sends back photos (1997), and
97. Bill Gates and Paul Allen start Microsoft Corp. to develop software for Altair computer (1975). ("Atomic Bombing," 1999)

This handbook describes current practices as we begin the new millennium that will, in turn, give us a window to the behavioral health professions of the future. We already know that many of the initial fears associated with development of the computer technologies in the 1980s and 1990s have proved unfounded or at least minimized. We now know both intuitively as well as empirically that people can counsel effectively without visual input even as the lack of visual input is about to become a technological moot point for cybercounselors. We also know that distance education in the behavioral health professions and beyond holds much promise as an answer to many accessibility issues facing higher education today.

Therefore, this book explores issues and practices of cybercounseling, cybereducation, and so much more. It makes more than a perfunctory scratch on the surface of technology as it impacts cybersupervision, cyberresearch, cyberethics, and cyberassessment. Responsible practitioners who have risked for the present and the future present their findings in traditional and innovative ways. This hard copy text not only presents the printed word but gives the reader links to the latest web sites that substantiate and validate their work. Furthermore, readers are encouraged to access a special ERIC/CASS cybersite that contains another comprehensive set of works, including PowerPoint presentations and direct links to web sites (see chapter 27). The ERIC/CASS cybersite is intended to be an evolving, fluid site in which additional documents can be posted in a time frame much more efficacious than that permitted by traditional hard copy journal publications.

It is our hope that this publication and its attendant web site instill a sense of pride in the extensive accomplishments of behavioral health professionals across the world who are or now can be linked with each other in very real virtual ways. Readers of this publication can contribute empirical and anecdotal information to formal and informal researchers across the globe so that solutions to today's technological glitches are but days and weeks away from becoming a reality rather than months or years. More than this, we see professional turf boundaries melting away as the school psychologist in Georgia e-mails the counsellor (yes, two l's) in Vancouver with a new idea, and the social work educator in Arizona "instant messages" a colleague in China with the answer to a long-standing professional concern.

If, on the basis of the previous paragraphs, the reader is contemplating giving up her or his quest for new technological insights because this all seems too high tech or too nerdy or too avant-garde, please know that neither of the co-editors of this publication could ever have imagined the spectrum of concerns that were addressed in the manuscripts we received. Neither could we fully understand nor do we really want to understand all the technologies and all the applications being presented here. As we ponder over this introduction, we are reminded of how formidable, even intimidating, many of the manuscripts were on first reading.

We also want to be respectful of those who may be using this publication as their first step into the world of technology in counseling and have had little or no exposure to "what's out there." For those people we are featuring a list of hard copy publications and web sites that have already become "must reads" or "must visits." Identified by Bloom and Walz, this "Cybersampler" contains illustrative and useful start-up resources. We are hopeful that pursuing these resources will be both stimulating and motivating to further immerse yourself in this publication.

John Bloom
October 1999

REFERENCE

Atomic bombing of Japan tops century's news. (1999, February 24). *The Indianapolis Star*, p. A12.

Cybersampler

PUBLICATIONS

We urge you to read and browse this cybersampler. Some of the resources may be of little interest to you, but others may catch your fancy and provide the inspiration needed to take your own technology skills to the next level.

1. **Introduction to the Internet: Opportunities and Dilemmas.** Wilson, R. F., Jencius, M., & Duncan, D., 1997, *Counseling and Human Development, 29*(6), 1–16. The authors describe many Internet services and how these various services may be of value to counselors and educators. Pitfalls and ethical problems that must be addressed as counselors attempt to reap the benefits of Internet communication are presented also.

2. **Counseling on the Information Highway: Future Possibilities and Potential Problems.** Sampson, J. P., Kolodinsky, R. W., & Greeno, B. P., 1997, *Journal of Counseling and Development, 75,* 203–212. In 1996 Sampson, Kolodinsky, and Greeno investigated the status of counseling services being offered on the Internet. Their research formed the basis for some of the first ethical standards to appear in the professional literature.

3. **Ethics in Technology.** Peterson, D. B., Murray, G. C., & Chan, F., 1998, in R. R. Cottone & V. M. Tarvydes (Eds.), *Ethical and Professional Issues in Counseling* (pp. 196–235), Columbus, OH: Merrill. Peterson, Murray, and Chan present the most complete examination of ethical, legal, and profes-

sional issues to date. They address topics such as the ethical management of electronic media, on-line forums of counseling, computer-assisted assessment, computer-assisted counselor-assisted counselor education, ethical use of software, technological counseling interventions for people with disabilities, and a four-level model of ethical practice and technology.

4. ***British Journal of Guidance and Counselling,*** 1998, 26(1). This special issue contains articles by Dan Murphy and Lawrence Mitchell (When Writing Helps to Heal: E-mail as Therapy), John W. Bloom (The Ethical Practice of Web Counseling), Storm King and Stephan Poulos (Using the Internet to Assist Family Therapy), and others.

WEB SITES

5. **National Board for Certified Counselors** (NBCC, 1998) http://www.nbcc.org.

   • **Standards for the Ethical Practice of Web Counseling:** In 1997, the board of directors of the National Board for Certified Counselors adopted the first set of ethical standards to guide the practice of web counseling or on-line therapy.

   • **Core Standards for Internet Mental Health Practice** (Bloom, J. W., & Sampson, J. P., Jr., 1998): In January 1998 the National Board for Certified Counselors convened a Bilateral Internet Mental Health Practice Forum in Bethesda, Maryland, and established a compelling agenda for the future of Internet mental health practice. Participants agreed to develop core standards intended to protect clients receiving mental health services on the Internet, to give mental health care professions a common ground, and to provide a basis for review of professional standards, clinical standards, and the need for Internet mental health practice guidelines by professions and government agencies. Posted at http://www.career.fsu.edu/techcenter/standards.html.

6. **The Counselor Education Resource Center** (CERC) (Sabella, 1998) http://coe.fgcu.edu/faculty/sabella/cerc/index.htm. Russ Sabella, counselor educator at Florida Gulf Coast

University, has created a site that contains links to over 300 counseling-related sites, course syllabi submitted from counselor educators all over the world, and a listing of counseling-related listservs as well as other counseling resources such as papers and instruments. Additional information can be found in Sabella's 1999 text, *School Counselor.COM* (Minneapolis, MN: Educational Media Corporation).

7. **Therapy Online** (Murphy & Mitchell, 1998) http://www.therapyonline.ca. Dan Mitchell and Lawrence Murphy, on-line therapists with master's degrees in counseling from the University of British Columbia in Vancouver, Canada, have established a web site that can serve as a model for those seeking best practices in web counseling.

8. **Mental Health Net** (Grohol, 1998) http://www.cmhc.com/guide/cyber and **Psych Central** (Grohol, 1998) http://www.grohol.com. John Grohol is a Columbus, Ohio, on-line psychologist, author, and director/webmaster of both Mental Health Net and Psych Central. Trained and educated as a clinical psychologist at Nova Southeastern University, he now acts as a patient advocate, mental health educator, and on-line services innovator. Mental Health Net presents a comprehensive guide to on-line therapy resources and is organized into three separate sections: Disorders and Treatments, Professional Resources, and Reading Room. Psych Central is an index for psychology, support, and mental health issues, resources, and people on the Internet.

9. **CyberTowers** (Mahue, 1998) www.cybertowers.com. Cyber-Towers is a collaborative effort combining the resources of Marlene M. Mahue, a web developer and editor-in-chief of the WWW e-zine, *Self-Help & Psychology Magazine* with the resources of a large staff of html programmers. This site contains information about the CyberTowers Professional Center, a web location for professionals and executives wishing to establish an on-line presence. CyberTowers also contains information about distance learning, telehealth, risk management, and self-help and psychology.

10. **Metanoia** (Ainsworth, 1998) http://www.metanoia.org. Martha Ainsworth, a consultant in computer communications who works in cyberspace, provides communications support (web

sites, Internet conferencing, print design) for nonprofit organizations and individuals. *Metanoia* is a Greek word meaning to face a new direction, and new directions can be found at the links to, for example, having my own web site, information on "Internet Therapy," check therapists' credentials (developed in partnership between Metanoia and Mental Health Net), the International Society for Mental Health Online, and feeling suicidal.

11. **ERIC Clearinghouse on Counseling and Student Services** (ERIC/CASS) http://www.uncg.edu/edu/ericcass/. This site is home to a wide variety of resources and services developed by ERIC/CASS for counselors and other human services specialists. In particular it offers full-text counseling-relevant digests, information on new counseling resources, and hot links to two major on-line counseling resources: the International Career Development Library (see no. 12) and the ERIC/CASS virtual libraries. The virtual libraries provide full-text documents on critical counseling topics such as conflict resolution, substance abuse, learning and achievement, and cultural diversity. In addition, the ERIC/CASS site serves as a gateway to the full spectrum of resources developed by the U.S. Department of Education, the National Library of Education, and the full ERIC system, including the capability to conduct on-line searches of the entire ERIC database.

12. **International Career Development Library** (ICDL) http://icdl.uncg.edu. This is a unique, interactive database. Developed and managed by ERIC/CASS and the National Occupational Information Coordinating Committee, the web site provides a wide range of career-relevant resources and services such as customized searches, full-text document retrieval, topical discussions, training registries, and links to other web sites.

13. **America's Career Kit** http://www.ajb.org. Offered by the U.S. Department of Labor, this resource includes three tightly integrated web sites to support job seekers and employers as they navigate the job market. These sites include

- **America's Job Bank** (AJB) providing hundreds of thousands of job openings daily and powerful resume building, posting, and searching services;
- **America's Career InfoNet** offering customer-driven access to national, state, and some local labor market information regarding projected growth, comparable wages, and selected job attributes (skills, tasks); and
- **America's Learning Exchange** (ALX) connecting people to the training and education they need to enhance their skills and compete in a dynamic market.

PART I

Benefits and Challenges of
Technology in the Millennium

1

Historical Context: The Relationship of Computer Technologies and Counseling

PAUL F. GRANELLO

Computers are not new. They have been around for over half a century. ENIAC, a huge machine that used vacuum tubes, was invented in 1946 (Fargis & Bykofsky, 1989). The relationship between computers and counseling is not new, either, and has existed for decades. However, the impact and focus of computer technology on counseling, and in wider sense psychotherapy, has changed over time. As we look forward as a profession to the future of the computer-counseling relationship, it may serve us to first briefly look back. This reminiscence will help us orient ourselves before looking into a future with its many possibilities. It will also help us to remember that as counselors we have a unique role in society: to advocate for technology that enhances rather than degrades the human condition (Fromm, 1968). It is within this context that this chapter reviews the evolution of the relationship between computers and counseling—both the delivery of counseling treatments and the education and training of future counselors.

THE 1950s AND 1960s: MAINFRAMES, MINIS, AND COMPUTER AS THERAPIST

Mainframe computers were around during the 1950s but were very expensive and only available to the government and to large universities. Computational time was a scarce resource, and emphasis was placed on efficient use of computer time. Computer programming languages were designed for efficient use by the ma-

3

chine rather than the convenience of the human user. These limitations restricted the development of computer applications for
counseling. However, during the 1950s theorists like B.F. Skinner
and Norman Crowder developed ideas about programmed instruction that are the historical antecedents for the modern computer-
aided instruction and web-based distance education that are
currently in vogue (Niemiec & Walberg, 1989).

In the early 1960s minicomputers came to replace mainframes.
In 1962 Digital Equipment Corporation produced the first mini-
computer. Minicomputers utilized the integrated circuit that had
been invented in 1959 at Texas Instruments. They were smaller
than mainframes, more powerful, and more affordable (Fargis &
Bykofsky, 1989). Access to computers became a more plentiful resource, and more user-friendly programming languages were developed, including BASIC, PASCAL, and specialized programs for
computer-aided instruction called PLATO and ILLIAC. Thus it is
really in the 1960s that the relationship between computers and
counseling and psychotherapy began in earnest.

COUNSELING THERAPY

Early efforts at integrating computers with psychotherapy aimed
at producing computer programs that could emulate a human therapist. One example is ELIZA, a famous early program developed by
Joseph Wizenbaum in 1966 that allowed people to talk to it as they
could with a real counselor in therapy (O'Dell & Dickson, 1984).
The program was based on the reflective qualities of Person Centered Therapy promoted by Carl Rogers, and it is still available today
on the World Wide Web (www-ai.ijs.si/eliza-cgi-bin/eliza_script). Another example, developed by Colby, Watt, and Gilbert (1966), intended to conduct a therapeutic dialogue with the user. The theory
embodied in the program was that of psychoanalytic free association. Both program examples had several flaws. One of the most
important of these was the computer's inability to process "natural
language." Computers have a hard time understanding what people
mean when they use colloquialisms such as "The audience gave the
musician a hand." In this case, the computer has to know that in
the context of a musical performance *giving a hand* does not literally mean a human appendage but rather applause (Sharf, 1985)!

After these initial attempts at developing computer therapists, researchers concluded that the computer had serious limitations and, as a tool for providing therapy, could probably not replace counselors in the near future.

COMPUTER-AIDED INSTRUCTION (CAI)

In addition to the interest in using computers for counseling interventions, there was a developing interest in using computers to deliver education and training programs. International Business Machines Corporation (IBM) was influential in the early development of CAI and by 1959 had developed the first program for teaching mathematics. In 1963, in cooperation with Stanford University, IBM released COURSEWRITER, the first programming language for CAI, complete with an entire elementary curriculum (Niemiec & Walberg, 1989). Another leader in the development of CAI was the Computer Education Research Laboratory (CERL), which worked closely with Control Data Corporation to develop PLATO (Programmed Logic for Automatic Teaching Operations). PLATO became the most widely used instructional program in both the United States and Europe and was primarily directed at college-level instruction (Niemiec & Walberg, 1989). PLATO was significant to the computer-counseling relationship because it represented the development of a programming language for nonprogrammers by allowing experts from diverse disciplines to put their course content onto computers without needing to be programming experts.

In the counseling and psychotherapy world, the end of the 1960s led to a call for more accountability from the profession for demonstrating the efficacy of the many theories that had been proposed during the decade. The mantra became, What works for whom and under what conditions? This movement in the profession created an interesting spin-off dynamic within the counseling-computer relationship. Because the logical and intuitive methods by which human counselors worked in counseling were poorly understood, representing them as a computer process was not possible. It was hypothesized that efforts to articulate clearly the counseling treatment process so that it could be programmed for the computer might lead to improved understanding of the process itself, and thus to advances in technique and theory (Wagman & Kerber, 1984). Just as in many other areas of society during the 1960s, the computer-counseling relationship was one of experimentation, which led to an understanding that the computer could not readily replace therapists.

THE 1970s AND 1980s: MICROCOMPUTERS FOR EVERYONE (WHAT CAN I DO WITH IT?)

Computer technology took giant strides forward in the 1970s and 1980s with the advent of the microcomputer. Although predictions of paperless offices have never come to pass, the microcomputer has changed society, moving us from the industrial age to the information age. Computing power has increased steadily from the first microcomputer in 1973 thoughout the 1980s and 1990s with concurrent reductions in cost. During the 1970s and 1980s computer access became a relatively plentiful resource in the United States, with many schools and public libraries equipped with computers. Although counselors were first predicted to be resistant to using microcomputers, this has proven not to be the case. Computer use by counselors and psychotherapists grew considerably during the 1980s (Cairo & Kanner, 1984), and with increased counselor access to computers, the questions became, How can they be used? and What are the ethical issues that arise from those uses? (Engels, Caulum, & Sampson, 1984).

COUNSELING INTERVENTION AND SERVICE MANAGEMENT

During the 1970s and 1980s, as the number of practitioners grew, numerous applications for the computer were developed for a variety of counseling activities including counseling interventions, personality testing, career guidance, and client data management for program evaluation (Alpert, Pulvino, & Lee, 1984). Counselors and psychotherapists realized that the computer could not handle therapeutic work like a human therapist but could perhaps play an adjunctive role to therapy. Therapists began to use the computer to work with a client's specific treatment problem when a corresponding well-defined treatment strategy could be employed (Wagman & Kerber, 1984). Two examples were notable. The first, the PlatoDCS system (Wagman & Kerber, 1978), used the PLATO language for a dilemma counseling system that could be used with clients who felt "caught" when making a decision between two adverse consequences. This program provided the client with a structured model for solving dilemmas (Wagman & Kerber, 1984). The second example, MORTON (Selmi, Klein, Greist, Jonhson, & Harris, 1982), was designed to use a cognitive therapy approach to work with clients with mild to moderate depression. The program was highly educational in nature and focused on teaching clients to identify underlying cognition, which may lead to depression. Both programs demonstrated the efficacy of using computers as adjuncts to counselors when the computer task was well defined in areas such as cognitive psychotherapy, therapeutic games, biofeedback, and behavior therapy (Lawrence, 1986; Matthews, DeSanti, Callahan, Koblenz-Sulcov, & Werden, 1987). Programs such as these, however, are still not commonly used by clinicians in the field.

During the 1980s, the use of the computer as an adjunct to therapy significantly affected the counselor activities of client assessment and career counseling. Today, virtually all major assessment instruments for vocational guidance and personality testing are available in computer-administered or scored formats (Ben-Porath & Butcher, 1986; Jackson, 1985). Testing represents a structured event that computers handle well, freeing up clinician time and facilitating scoring of instruments. The educational components of vocational guidance are also delivered well by a computer because they are primarily informational. Several major systems have evolved, including CIS, SIGI Plus, and Discover (Kapes, Moran-Mastie, & Whitfield, 1994). Sampson et al. (1994) have provided a useful comparison of 15 computer-assisted guidance systems.

The later part of the 1980s saw the development of managed behavioral health care and the use of proprietary computer databases to track service delivery to clients by third-party funding sources. Many counselors saw this information collection as burdensome and threatening, possibly due to the one-way nature of the process, perceptions concerning violations of the traditional client counselor confidentiality ethics, and the feeling that the information was often used to deny treatment to the client more for the purposes of cost containment than client care. Suddenly, computers were being used to assist outsiders to regulate our profession. Many counselors

reacted against technology, feeling that they should not have to justify themselves or demonstrate their effectiveness, that what they
did was not quantifiable or programmable. The ascendancy of cognitive therapy that occurred during the 1980s was promoted by the
computer-counseling relationship, and by the third-party managed-
care funders looking for "critical pathways" of care that could make
counseling a predictable and therefore "capitated" process. Therapy
decisions needed to be as clear cut as the *Diagnostic and Statistical
Manual of Mental Disorders* (American Psychiatric Association,
1980, 1994) decision trees (which resemble computer algorithms)
made them appear. The accountability press of the 1980s wanted
mental health treatments to have predictable outcomes, to serve as
data in a computer program.

Counselor Education and Supervision Applications

Using the computer for counselor training was explored during
the 1980s, both in terms of the development of new software programs and investigations into the pedagogy of teaching with computers (Hosie & Smith, 1984; Phillips, 1983). By 1984 *Counselor
Education and Supervision* devoted a special issue to computers
and counselor education. Explorations into developing computer
applications for counselor training included those for acquisition of
facts, development of skills, personal and professional development, exam administration, statistical analysis for research, and supervision (Froehle, 1984; Lee & Pulvino, 1988; Phillips, 1984a,
1984b; White, 1988).

Let us examine one of these areas—the development of student
skills—in which applications were explored. One of the tasks confronting a counselor trainee is to learn to distinguish among the array of presenting behaviors of clients and to select an appropriate
response given any one particular constellation of behaviors. Simulation has long been employed in counselor training efforts through
role-play and modeling. The idea of having a computer that could
simulate a client for student practice before working with a real
client seemed appealing. The computer could allow the instructor
to control the information that the student was given, including a
specific diagnosis, or set of demographic features. Client 1 was an
example of a simulation program in which several emotional and

demographic factors could be manipulated for the student to get a variety of practice in diagnosis (Hedlund, Vieweg, & Cho, 1987). This simulation training had the advantage of allowing several student counselors to work with the same computer client and then discuss with each other their approaches. In addition, the same student could work with the same computer client in a trial-and-error fashion without the relationship variables changing. Some of the drawbacks of working on simulations are, of course, the lack of nonverbals (although this can be overcome with today's technology) and a lack of random or intuitive behavior on the part of the client.

The Great Therapists Program (Halpain, Dixon, & Glover, 1987) was an example of a program related to the process of modeling responses for students. It provided the student with a client statement, allowed the student to type in his or her response, and then displayed a response from a master therapist from three different counseling orientations for the student to compare to his or her own response. The program was promoted as a method for students to learn how to apply a theory to client statements. Another example was the SuperShrink program (Lowman & Norkus, 1987), an educational simulation of clinical interviewing with the student as interviewer and the computer as client that allowed the student to question the computer client. Research on the SuperShrink program found support for the position that students prefer educational simulations that require more active involvement of the kind required by real settings even though they may also require more effort and be more frustrating. Research also found that students enjoyed the problem solving or investigatory nature of working with simulations that allowed them to question the computer (Lowman & Norkus, 1987).

The types of computer-simulation training programs that moved the computer-counselor relationship beyond simulation to consultation (and may be the shape of things to come) were Expert Systems, artificial intelligence computer programs that represented the decision-making processes of an expert, such as a master counselor. The U.S. Navy, for example, developed CATCEC (Computer Supported Assessment and Treatment Consultation for Emotional Crises) in the 1980s for use on nuclear submarines (Lichtenberg, Hummel, & Shaffer, 1984). The program was an expert consultation system for assisting a non-mental-health-expert to assess and treat emotional and behavioral emergencies in a remote area such as a submarine where a counselor is not available. The program made suggestions based on information provided by the consultee and could adapt its line of questioning based on the information provided. The potential of such expert systems programs was immense. In such a program, students could interact with a computer client who could adapt and respond to their line of questioning, similar to how a real client is affected by a counselor.

In addition to application development, during the 1980s counselor educators also began to investigate the pedagogy of teaching with computers. Several important questions had to be answered concerning the application of computer technology to training counselors. Was there any advantage of using computers, other than the novelty of the technology, over traditional methods of teaching? If computer-assisted instruction had some benefits over traditional methods, Which students benefited the most? and When and for what courses should the technology be implemented during counselor training programs? Several studies found that computer-assisted instruction did have positive impacts on students in relation to learning basic reflective skills (Alpert et al., 1984), retaining career information (Cairo & Kanner, 1984), and improving self-awareness (Matheson & Zanna, 1988). Further, the effects of computer-based instruction were found to be significantly better for low achievers, possibly due to the individualized pace that computer-assisted instruction provides the student (Skinner, 1990). In addition, a literature review on the effects of personality factors in human and computer interaction found that introverts perform better on computer-aided instruction tasks (Pocius, 1991). Counselor educators were beginning to examine the most effective methods for implementing computer-assisted instruction in their programs.

In 1988, Lambert wrote an article entitled "Computers in Counselor Education: Four Years After a Special Issue" as a follow-up to the 1984 special issue of *Counselor Education and Supervision*. He realistically identified many obstacles that impeded the further development of computer technology within the counseling field. For example, many faculty remained untrained and inexperienced in computer use and were unaware of potential benefits derived from computer use in training. In addition, the uniqueness of some counseling courses prevented use of off-the-shelf software, and customized applications were expensive or time consuming to manufacture. For these reasons, Lambert concluded that the widespread use of computer applications for counselor training had yet to occur. Many of the problems identified by Lambert have persisted into the 1990s.

THE 1990s AND BEYOND (HEY, THIS INTERNET THING IS IMPRESSIVE!)

Interest seemed to wane in computers during the early 1990s, as indicated by a drop in computer-related articles in scholarly journals. As the 1990s have progressed, however, technological changes have occurred again and breathed new excitement into the computer–counseling relationship. The boom in Internet access and use, first in academic circles and then with the general public, has created an entire new chapter in the computer–counseling relationship. For the first time in the history of the computer–counseling relationship, the number of individuals involved with computers has grown from a small elite to a large cohort. Although beyond the scope of this chapter, the potential impact of the Internet and the World Wide Web on counseling is enormous and warrants brief illustration. Virtually all of the major counseling professional organizations have established web pages for their memberships. ERIC/CASS has established a virtual library from which the full text of articles can be downloaded to a counselor's personal computer, making access to vast amounts of information easier than ever. Counseling therapies are already being delivered on-line, and yet more information on psychological topics is available to any consumer who has a web browser. Many new ethical and professional regulation questions have sprung up since the development of web counseling.

Counselor educators have also discovered the Internet. Listservs, such as ICN (International Counseling Network) for practicing counselors, CESNET (Counselor Educators and Supervisors Network) for counselor educators and supervisors, and COUNSGRADs (Counseling Graduates) for counselor education graduate students, have become popular means of professional communication. The advent of the World Wide Web has opened up the field of CAI and made the computerization of course content (web-authoring) easier and easier for the layperson. As a result, more and more counseling courses are being developed as computer mediated or as part of distance education projects. It is now possible to do live streaming video on the web, thus enabling a counselor educator to model techniques to students around the world.

Many limitations face the computer–counseling relationship today, however. These include the ability of counselors and faculty to be trained in web page development, the ability to find funds to research the best methods of providing instruction via the Internet, and the ability of students to access the information. Many students are limited by the bandwidth (the amount of information) they can download or process though a phone cable. Ethical considerations about use of student or client information stored in computers or about providing counseling across governmental jurisdictions are also caveats.

The past has taught us that technological limitations are usually not long lasting in the field of computers. In fact, it is usually difficult to keep up with the pace of change. The future holds many possibilities. For example, super simulations could immerse clients or students in virtual reality worlds for treatment or instruction (Rothbaum et al., 1995), or artificially intelligent consultation systems could work as assistant therapists in suggesting treatment techniques and tracking client progress. Whatever the future may hold, we can expect that the interface between the counseling profession and computer technologies will continue to expand and develop—as it has since computers were first invented.

CONCLUSION

There has been a growing relationship between the profession of counseling and computers over the last four decades (Mruk, 1989). However, not until the 1990s has the number of counselors and counselor educators involved with using computers grown to represent the actual adoption of the technology by the profession. Computers have been used in creative ways both to assist in treating clients and to help educate new counseling professionals. In looking to the future, computers will, in all likelihood, continue to have an impact not only on our profession but also in a wider sense on our culture and human identity itself. To date, the pace of development of computer technologies has seemingly outpaced our profession's ability to research its application adequately and answer important ethical questions concerning its use. Dehumanizing or humanizing the computer forces us to take a new look at what it means to be human, and at the possibility that thinking machines may lead us to new insights into what it is to think and feel as a human being. Counselors are socially sanctioned healers and as such may have a role that goes beyond simple use of a technology; thus they may have a role in understanding the impact of that technology on society. Because humans like to apply anthropomorphism to machines, we must be careful in the future not do the reverse and apply mechanomorphism to our clients and students (Caporael, 1986). Perhaps the greatest challenge to our profession in the future is not only to exploit the benefits of the computer–counseling relationship but also to advocate for the use of computer technology by the society as a whole in ways that protect—rather than diminish—human freedom and dignity.

REFERENCES

Alpert, D., Pulvino, C. J., & Lee, J. L. (1984). Computer-based accountability: Implications for training. *Counselor Education and Supervision, 24,* 212–221.

American Psychiatric Association. (1980). *Diagnostic and statistical manual of mental disorders* (3rd ed.). Washington, DC: Author.

American Psychiatric Association. (1994). *Diagnostic and statistical manual of mental disorders* (4th ed.). Washington, DC: Author.

Ben-Porath, Y. S., & Butcher, J. N. (1986). Computers in personality assessment: A brief past, an ebullient present, and an expanding future. *Computers in Human Behavior, 2,* 167–182.

Cairo, P. C., & Kanner, M. S. (1984). Investigating the effects of computerized approaches to counselor training. *Counselor Education and Supervision, 24,* 212–221.

Caporael, L. R. (1986) Anthropomorphism and mechanomorphism: Two faces of the human machine. *Computers in Human Behavior, 2,* 215–234.

Colby, K. M., Watt, J. B., & Gilbert, J. P. (1966). A computer method of psychotherapy: Preliminary communication. *Journal of Nervous and Mental Diseases, 142,* 148–152.

Engels, D. W., Caulum, D., & Sampson, D. E. (1984). Computers in counselor education: An ethical perspective. *Counselor Education and Supervision, 24,* 193–203.

Fargis, P., & Bykofsky, S. (Eds.). (1989). *The New York Public Library desk reference*. New York: Webster's New World, Simon & Schuster.

Froehle, T. C. (1984). Computer-assisted feedback in counseling supervision. *Counselor Education and Supervision, 24*, 168–175.

Fromm, E. (1968). *The revolution of hope, toward a humanized technology*. New York: Harper & Row.

Halpain, D. R., Dixon, D.N., & Glover, J.A. (1987). The great therapists program: Computerized learning of counseling theories. *Counselor Education and Supervision, 27*, 255–260.

Hedlund, J. L., Vieweg, B. W., & Cho, D. W. (1987). Computer consultation for emotional crises: An expert system for "nonexperts." *Computers in Human Behavior, 3*, 109–127.

Hosie, T. W., & Smith, C. W. (1984). PILOTing courseware. *Counselor Education and Supervision, 24*, 176–181.

Jackson, D. N. (1985). Computer-based personality testing. *Computers in Human Behavior, 1*, 225–264.

Kapes, J. T., Moran-Mastie, M., & Whitfield, E. A. (Eds.). (1994). *A counselor's guide to career assessment instruments*. Alexandria, VA: National Career Development Association.

Lambert, M. (1988). Computers in counselor education: Four years after a special issue. *Counselor Education and Supervision, 28*, 100–109.

Lawrence, G. H. (1986). Using computers for the treatment of psychological problems. *Computers in Human Behavior, 2*, 43–62.

Lee, J. L., & Pulvino, C. J. (1988). Computer competency: A means for learning to be a better counselor. *Counselor Education and Supervision, 28*, 110–120.

Lichtenberg, J. W., Hummel, T. J., & Shaffer, W. F. (1984). CLIENT 1: A computer simulation for use in counselor education and research. *Counselor Education and Supervision, 24*, 155–166.

Lowman, J., & Norkus, M. (1987). The SuperShrink interview: Active versus passive questioning and student satisfaction. *Computers in Human Behavior, 3*, 181–192.

Matheson, K., & Zanna, M. P. (1988). The impact of computer-mediated communication of self-awareness. *Computers in Human Behavior, 4*, 221–233.

Matthews, T. J., DeSanti, S. M., Callahan, D., Koblenz-Sulcov, C. J., & Werden, J. I. (1987). The microcomputer as an agent of intervention with psychiatric patients: Preliminary studies. *Computers in Human Behavior, 3*, 37–47.

Mruk, C. J. (1989). Phenomenological psychology and the computer revolution: Friend, foe, or opportunity? *Journal of Phenomenological Psychology, 20*, 20–39.

Niemiec, R. P., & Walberg, H. J. (1989). From teaching machines to microcomputers: Some milestones in the history of computer-based instruction. *Journal of Research on Computing in Education, 21*(3), 263–276.

O'Dell, J., & Dickson, J. (1984). ELIZA as a "therapeutic" tool. *Journal of Clinical Psychology, 40*, 942–945.

Phillips, S. D. (1983). Counselor training via computer. *Counselor Education and Supervision, 23*, 20–28.

Phillips, S. D. (1984a). Computers as counseling and training tools. *Counselor Education and Supervision, 24,* 130–132.

Phillips, S. D. (1984b). Contributions and limitation in the use of computers in counselor training. *Counselor Education and Supervision, 24,* 186–203.

Pocius, K. E. (1991). Personality factors in human-computer interaction: A review of the literature. *Computers in Human Behavior, 7,* 103–135.

Rothbaum, B. O., Hodges, L. F., Kooper, R., Opdyke, D., Williford, J. S., & North, M. (1995). Virtual reality graded exposure in the treatment of acrophobia: A case report. *Behavior Therapy, 26,* 547–554.

Sampson, J. P., Jr., Reardon, R. C., Wilde, C. K., Norris, D. S., Peterson, G. W., Strausberger, S. J ., Garis, J. W., Lenz, J. G., & Saunders, D. E. (1994). Comparison of the assessment components of 15 computer-assisted career guidance systems. In J. T. Kapes, M. Moran-Mastie, & E. A. Whitfield (Eds.), *A counselor's guide to career assessment instruments* (pp. 373–379). Alexandria, VA: National Career Development Association.

Selmi, P. M., Klein, M. H., Greist, J. H., Johnson, J. H., & Harris, W. G. (1982). An investigation of computer-assisted cognitive-behavior therapy in the treatment of depression. *Behavior Research Methods and Instrumentation, 14,* 181–185.

Sharf, R. S. (1985). Artificial intelligence: Implications for the future of counseling. *Journal of Counseling and Development, 64,* 34–37.

Skinner, M. E. (1990). The effects of computer-based instruction on the achievement as a function of achievement status and mode of presentation. *Computers in Human Behavior, 6,* 351–360.

Wagman, M., & Kerber, K. W. (1978). *Dilemma counseling system.* Minneapolis: Control Data Corporation.

Wagman, M., & Kerber, K. W. (1984). Computer-assisted counseling: Problems and prospects. *Counselor Education and Supervision, 24,* 142–167.

White, M. J. (1988). A computer-administered examination in professional ethics. *Counselor Education and Supervision, 28,* 116–120.

2

Managing Technology Wisely: A New Counselor Competency

JOHN A. CASEY

On Thursday, July 29, 1999, Mark Barton, an Atlanta stock market day trader apparently upset over $105,000 in stock losses, opened fire in two brokerage offices, killing 9 people and wounding 13 others before taking his own life. The shootings took place in the offices of All Tech Investment Group, a firm that offers on-line Internet stock market trading to anyone who puts up at least $50,000 in equity to open an account.

Day trading is predicated on profit taking with large amounts of money and minimal shifts in stock prices. It has been characterized as "intense, volatile, and risky" and "at the center of the stampeding bull market that's mesmerizing Americans—sometimes at great financial and emotional cost" ("Day Trading," 1999). To cope with the stress inherent in day trading, All Tech employed a corporate psychotherapist to help traders. But that was not enough to stop Mark Barton.

Mark Barton's case is far more dramatic than most, but many of the stress factors that precipitated his violent outburst are becoming more and more everyday occurrences. The benefits of using technology to gain advantage—and the risks encountered by doing so—are becoming more and more a part of the human experience in this technological era.

Although technology has dramatically changed our way of life, the question remains: Are we better off, as individuals and as a society, with what people indiscriminately refer to as technological advances? The question was probably asked as early as the 15th century when Benedictine monks woke to the sound of newly invented clock bells, replacing the more natural rhythm of the morning sunrise. The question has also probably been asked as each new technology was invented, whether the Model T (and its pollution and the 1920s version of road rage), electricity (with its electrocutions and unsightly wires), or the telephone (with its recorded message menus or its autodial telemarketing).

Some innovations have had severe and disastrous results. Early enthusiasm over the discovery of asbestos, silicone implants, and the pesticide DDT faded when their unintended, harmful side effects became known. In 1999, the gasoline additive MTBE was legally mandated for use by the state of California as an air pollution deterrent. Soon, however, MTBE became the catalyst for closure of one third of the wells in the Lake Tahoe basin as it was discovered to be a carcinogen that had leached its way into the state's drinking water supply.

Are we better off? The accelerated emergence of technologies in the last half of the 20th century has made the question even more pertinent. As more and more of our daily lives depend upon microchip-enabled media such as computers, fax machines, cell phones, e-mail, and the Internet, our lives have paradoxically become both more simplified and more complicated. Although these inventions are purported to save time, we now try to accomplish more tasks or acquire more electronic "toys" as a result. One result is that the United States now has longer work hours and less leisure time than any other industrialized nation.

If counseling and guidance professionals are to improve the mental health of individuals and society, then they must carefully examine the relationship between mental health and technology. Indeed, healthy management of technological tools may be one of the most critical competencies a counseling professional can model and teach. The purpose of this chapter is not to provide all of the answers but to stimulate the discussion with some relevant perspectives in relation to awareness of technology's benefits and limitations and our growing need to manage technology wisely.

STEP ONE: DEVELOPING AWARENESS

Guidance and *counseling* have been defined as the processes of helping people make important choices that affect their lives in both values and changes (Gladding, 1996). We make choices daily about our values and behavior in the use of technology, sometimes consciously, sometimes unconsciously. We choose to answer a telephone, log on to the Internet, respond to an e-mail, subscribe to a listserv, send a fax, or watch television.

How can counselors begin to help people make their choices wisely? A first step in the process is awareness. Becoming aware that we are indeed making a choice to use (or not use) a particular technology, coupled with awareness of the potential benefits and limitations of using that technology, can lead to a healthy questioning of the relative worth of each technological tool in a given time and place.

AWARENESS OF BENEFITS

Technology's benefits have increased rapidly and include psychological benefits.

Expanded Benefits at Faster Speeds

The widespread benefits of technological innovation have been many. They include financial gain to many in technology-rich nations, increased access to information, increased speed of information access, democratization of information access, increased learning acquisition, increased productivity, increased leisure, increased choices, increased motivation for learning, increased mobility, reduction of routine tasks, and increased connectedness with less isolation.

Psychological Benefits

Another benefit, psychologically, might be intensified emotional relationships. Gergen (1991) speculated that technology can intensify the emotional level of many relationships by changing the traditional community patterns of communication. Without technology, traditional relationships in traditional communities move toward a moderate leveling of emotional intensity, as married couples might replace "exciting romance" with "comfortable depth." Moreover, in traditional face-to-face communities, there is a high degree of informal surveillance, in which gossip and community norms keep novel and/or deviant behavior in short supply. With technology, however, Gergen observed that neither of these constraints operate. Thus with expanded telecommunications and travel options, the once quiet evening at home is now replaced by a parade of faces, information, and intrusions.

> One can scarcely settle into a calming rut, because who one is and the cast of "significant others" are in continuous motion. Further, because relationships range far and wide, largely through various electronic means, they cannot easily be supervised by others. (pp. 60–61)

With a broader pool of relationships to draw upon in cyberspace, it is not surprising that some find stronger relationships in their cyber-community that in their geographically proximate neighborhoods.

The autonomy offered by technology may encourage more risk taking. Some clients are more encouraged to seek counseling through the Internet, choosing to avoid resistance associated with more traditional face-to-face encounters. The use of e-mail in one case allowed a Latino university student to bypass likely prejudice by Anglo vineyard owners when he conducted informational career interviews on vitacultural careers through e-mail (Casey, 1998). The student was likely to have been denied access to the owners had he made the requests in person; using e-mail, however, he was issued numerous invitations for onsite visits.

Awareness of Limitations

The limitations of technology do not always present themselves amidst the initial excitement over innovation. Alfred Nobel's enthusiasm with his discovery of dynamite only later turned sour when its destructive capability with weapons became evident.

Volti (1988) contended that "one of the most pleasant myths about technology is that it can work its wonders without altering existing social arrangements." Indeed, the social and economic landscape has been dramatically altered.

The Technogap

One example of the technological age's dramatically altered landscape is the polarization of the technogap between the haves and have nots (Casey, 1998). As the creators of technology create more power, wealth, and leisure for themselves, the users of technology are left with even less power, wealth, and leisure. This has occurred both within the population of technology-rich nations as well as between nations that have and have not benefited from technology.

Loss of Worker Security

Another example of the technological age's dramatically altered landscape is the decline of security in the workforce. Technological tools allow fewer people to do the same work at more efficient speeds with less need for midlevel hierarchy. Thus midlevel workers are often the first casualty in corporate mergers, relocation, and downsizing. As a result, job insecurity and an ongoing need for reinvention have become survival skills for the vast majority of workers (Feller, 1997; Rifkin, 1995).

Indeed, the changing nature of the workforce due to technology has led to paradoxical dilemmas. Strikes for higher wages by farm workers have been an economic catalyst to invent new technologies for planting and harvesting. Fierce strikes by labor organizations over job protection against outsourcing or global relocations have led to more robotic replacements.

Less Skilled Workers

Work tasks that used to require specialized knowledge now utilize technology to make the end user interchangeable. For example, a company of temporary workers now exists to supply "overflow" telephone operators when the help lines for companies like Microsoft become overloaded. These overflow operators, who are not trained technical employees, use a computer screen tutorial to ask certain questions of the caller and, depending on the response, go through a "menu tree" of further questions and responses leading to help-line suggestions. (When all else fails, the operator is instructed to inform the caller to "turn off the computer for 20 minutes and then, if still not working, call back.")

Likewise, in the world of managed care for mental health insurance, minimally trained phone receptionists are prompted to ask selected questions when prior approval for health care is requested. The level of professional (master's or doctoral) approved for referral is dependent on key words the patient states to indicate level of severity of his or her problem.

Decreased Benefits

The benefits of employing part-time, interchangeable, low-level employees are numerous. The wage scale can often be less than $10 per hour. With laws requiring that health benefits be provided to workers who are employed over 19 hours per week, companies can save the cost of benefits by employing more part-time employees. Alternately, contracting out for temporary employees previously employed in-house can also eliminate the cost of benefits. These trends have given rise to a dramatic increase of workers who work two or three part-time jobs and who comprise a large number of the working poor. The largest employer in the world is now a temporary agency called Manpower.

The fear that the interchangeability of workers and the elimination of the middle man will spread into higher education has been voiced by David Van Nuys (1995) in an on-line treatise entitled *Distance Learning and the Demise of the Professoriate*. Van Nuys, a self-described technophile who has designed and taught a course, "Computer Applications in Psychology," has warned that "the Costco-ization of American education" will be appealing for those who want to minimize cost and maximize convenience by offering courses that provide credits and degrees via distance education—and, in the process, lose the essence of the pedagogy. "We are living in a time of minimal specification" (Van Nuys & Gomes, 1995).

Health Problems

Health problems have perhaps been the largest negative side effect of the technological era. Direct problems, such as physical pain from prolonged activity on a keyboard, have spawned new industries. We have products that promise ergonomic aid, laws that mandate ergonomic safety, medical specialists to treat repetitive stress injuries (such as carpel tunnel syndrome), and attorneys who specialize in prosecuting offending companies that fail to prevent injuries or fail to support its victims in the aftermath.

Indirect health problems can also be traced to technology-related stress. Muscular, digestive, and cardiovascular systems can all be affected. Early warning signs, gone unheeded, can develop into long-term and even life-threatening illnesses.

Four out of 10 Americans view their jobs as the largest cause of stress in their lives, according to a report released in 1999 by the National Institute for Occupational Safety and Health. The report also noted that 75% of employees believe today's worker has more on-the-job stress than workers in the previous generation ("The Pressure Cooker," 1999).

Addiction

One population that seems particularly vulnerable to the health risks of technostress are those with Type A behaviors (Friedman & Rosenman, 1974) and those with a tendency toward either obsessive compulsive behaviors and/or addictions. College and community mental health centers report a dramatic rise in clients who report moderate or severe computer addiction. Computers offer a strong magnet with their immediate gratification and immediate reinforcement. Young (1996), in a study of 496 heavy on-line users, suggested that Internet addiction is similar to gambling addiction because it involves failed impulse control without involving an intoxicant. According to this study, the use of the Internet can disrupt an individual's academic, social, financial, and occupational life as do other well-documented addictions such as pathological gambling, eating disorders, and alcoholism.

Individuals who have few or no social skills find refuge in the closed world of computer addiction. The high degree of control that comes from writing computer code, controlling a mouse and keyboard, or, for that matter, controlling channels with a television remote control offers a safe haven for those who find human interaction stressful. Howard Besser (1995), who studied the social impacts of the Internet, stated that the pull of interactive media is more powerful than television or old-style video games, not unlike the pull of gambling. A sedentary lifestyle and/or desensitization to the human experience are two additional complications associated with technology addiction.

Computer addiction takes a heavy toll on health, school, and work. It also exacts a toll on marriages and families. Maya Sullivan has emphasized that

> [computer addicts] are so drawn to the on-line world that they spend as much as 40 hours a week compulsively tapping away on a computer keyboard. Unwilling to pull the electronic plug, they lose sleep, forget to eat, leave the dishes unwashed, shirk work and even neglect their children. ("Virtual World," 1996)

In Silicon Valley, California, marriage and family therapists have developed practices that specialize in technology-related disorders. The intense pressure to meet a deadline, develop a new product quickly, stay ahead of the competition, or meet stockholders' expectation for quarterly profits add pragmatic rationalizations for the addict.

Decreased Leisure

Technology has challenged traditional notions of leisure. The average work week during the 1990s has lengthened in the United States to well beyond the traditional 40 hours for full-time employees. It is not uncommon to find a new breed of worker who is willing to work overtime for added income for months or years, only to take an extended vacation of months and years and then return to a new job at a new company. Recognizing the high level of transience and low level of loyalty, employers have replaced traditional retirement plans with transportable pensions whereby the employee can remove accumulated contributions from their prior employer and roll them over into the next employer's pension program.

Another effect of technology on leisure has been the blurring of the boundaries between work and play. Workers check their e-mail while traveling on vacation; they also play computer games and send e-mail jokes while on the job. Cell phone users respond to work issues while having a meal or backpacking in the mountains. Telecommuting has emerged as one answer to traffic congestion. Controls on the use of intrusive technologies are developing: concerts now begin with a request that pagers be turned to pulse mode; states are discussing traffic laws restricting the usage of cell phones.

Multitasking

Performing multiple tasks concurrently, once the bane of only those labeled Type A, has become so common that multitasking is actually assigned to many workers, adding to everyday stress. Answering a phone with a headset or speakerphone while using hands on a keyboard or cash register is commonplace. Monitoring thousands of stocks simultaneously using sophisticated software is now expected of any financial adviser. And with market trading now including round-the-clock global monitoring of the markets in Tokyo, Frankfurt, London, and New York, there seems to be little respite from stress other than exhaustion or death. The New York Stock Exchange, in 1999, has decided to extend its hours to accommodate west coast traders (and, not incidentally, compete for market share against west-coast-based NASDAQ companies).

STEP TWO: MANAGING TECHNOLOGY WISELY

Becoming aware of the benefits and pitfalls created by technological innovation is only a first step. A necessary sequel is changing cognitive and behavioral strategies to manage personal use of technology wisely and then, after modeling wise technology usage, infusing the teaching of wise technology management into counseling activities with clients.

Consider the following guidelines as starting points for evaluation and application:

1. **Keep an internal locus of control around the use of technology.** It is easy to jump into many new technologies because of peer pressure or market hype. Resist. Ask if the new technology is really necessary. Many upgrades of software and hardware are intended to enrich the producer, not the consumer. If you can accomplish tasks reasonably well given current computer configurations, sit back and enjoy them.

2. **Choose appropriate technologies wisely.** You can be far more efficient and effective with judicious use of technology.

Knowing how to tap into a database effectively, for example, can save days, weeks, months, or even years of time.

The operative word here is *appropriate*. Sometimes using a lower tech photocopier accomplishes the same result as scanning a photo into digital format, opening it up through photo editing software, and printing it out on a laser printer. Similarly, a simple overhead transparency can sometimes accomplish the same result as transporting a laptop and projection system. If you are using instant messaging on your computer screen to exchange words with a person nearby, a phone call or even personal visit may be more efficient.

3. **Draw boundaries around your use of technology.** If your goal is to have leisure, resist the urge to turn on the cell phone. It may be wiser to check your messages on e-mail or voice mail only at selected times of the day, not as they arrive. Technology is a tool, not a lifestyle, so keep it balanced with exercise, spirituality, friendship, humor, relationships, and other essential elements of life (E. Rust, personal communication, July 8, 1999).

   Risk a little techno-ridicule once in a while. Although some of us have learned ways to discourage telephone solicitors, we still feel compelled to read and answer every e-mail we get or to copy friends we haven't seen in years with the most trivial messages.

4. **Do not measure your worth on the basis of what skills or competencies the person next to you possesses.** "Many times in putting this publication together I've thought about all the things I can't do, or haven't done, or choose not to do, which makes me feel totally incompetent. I've never downloaded any free software, I've never played games other than Solitaire, I've never entered a chat room, I break out in a sweat every time I have to call the Help desk, etc. However, I also know that others consider me a computer guru; it is all a matter of perspective" (John Bloom, personal communication, June 5, 1999).

5. **Monitor your impulse control, need for immediate gratification, and fascination with new technologies.** Internet/World Wide Web communication, coupled with faster connections and faster computer processing rates, have enabled instantaneous connectivity to take place. It can be a seductive

process, especially when graphics, sound, and other multimedia enhancements offer multisensory gratification. But we must neither confuse form with substance nor let form subtract from substance.

CONCLUSION

The benefits of technology are the driving force behind its innovation, but the costs associated with it are often evident only as the new technologies come on line. Tragic incidents, like the Barton shootings in Atlanta, can be important wake-up calls for counselors to examine closely how the human interface with technology must be cautiously approached.

Technology has changed our way of life. It offers us tools that have both benefits and limitations. If counseling and guidance professionals are to improve the mental health of individuals and, ultimately, our society, we must carefully examine the nature of our technology usage. Awareness, modeling, and teaching of wise technology usage strategies are recommended steps in the process.

REFERENCES

Besser, H. (1995). From Internet to information super highway. In J. Brook & I. A. Boal (Eds.), *Resisting the virtual life: The culture and politics of information* (pp. 59–70). San Francisco: City Lights Press [On-line]. Available: http://www.gseis.ucla.edu/~howard/papers/brook-book.html.

Casey, J. A. (1998). Technology: A force for social action. In C. C. Lee & G. R. Walz (Eds.), *Social action: A mandate for counselors* (pp. 199–211). Alexandria VA: American Counseling Association.

Day trading: Intense, volatile, and risk. (1999, July 30). *USA Today* [On-line]. Available: http://www.usatoday.com/news/ndsthu09.htm. (Note that a $1 fee has been created since this article was accessed on the web, should the reader want to download the article.)

Feller, R. (1997). Redefining "career" during the work revolution. In R. Feller & G. Walz (Eds.), *Career transitions in turbulent times* (pp. 143–154). Greensboro, NC: ERIC Counseling and Student Services Clearinghouse.

Friedman, M., & Rosenman, R. H. (1974). *Type A behavior and your heart.* New York: Knopf.

Gergen, K. J. (1991). *The saturated self.* New York: Basic Books.

Gladding, S. (1996). *Counseling: A comprehensive profession* (3rd ed.). Englewood Cliffs, NJ: Prentice-Hall.

The pressure cooker: Is the fast pace of business getting you steamed? (1999, July 5). *Reno Gazette-Journal*, p. B1.

Rifkin, J. (1995). *The end of work: The decline of the global labor force and the dawn of the postmarket era.* New York: Putnam.

Van Nuys, D. (1995). *Distance learning and the demise of the professoriate* [On-line]. Available: http://www.sonoma.edu/psychology/VanNuys/Distance.html.
VanNuys, D., & Gomes, M. (1995, April). *The dawn of Costco U: Feminism and the dark side.* Paper presented at the meeting, The Virtual Campus: Developing Feminist Perspectives, San Luis Obispo, CA [On-line]. Available: http://www.sonoma.edu/psychology/VanNuys/Distance.html.
Virtual world can take a toll on reality. (1996, August 10). *San Jose Mercury News*, p. 1.
Volti, R. (1988). *Society and technological change.* New York: St. Martin's Press.
Young, K. S. (1996, August). *The emergence of a new clinical disorder.* Paper presented at a meeting of the American Psychological Association, Toronto, Ontario, Canada.

ADDITIONAL RESOURCES

- Internet Addiction Diagnosis and Support Group (http://www.cybernothing.org/jdfalk/media-coverage/archive/msg01305.html)
- Internet Addiction Overview (http://webreview.com/wr/pub/96/04/08/tipsheet/index.html)
- Mental Health Discussion Page (http://webreview.com/wr/pub/96/11/29/hour/index.html)
- Hochschild, A. (1989). *The second shift.* New York: Avon Books.
- Hochschild, A. R. (1997). *Time bind: When work becomes home and home becomes work.* New York: Metropolitan Books.
- Rubin, L. B. (1994). *Families on the faultline: America's working class speaks about the family, the economy, race, and ethnicity.* New York: HarperCollins.
- Schor, J. B. (1991). *The overworked American.* New York: BasicBooks.

3

Expanding Professions Globally: The United States as a Marketplace for Global Credentialing and Cyberapplications

THOMAS W. CLAWSON

Americans usually assume that globalization means taking our ideas, values, services, and products to the international marketplace. Although this could mean profitable sales, in professions such global offering is more likely to mean expanding the human capital interested in the discipline of the profession.

For a variety of reasons, the most important being the United States' longitudinally strong economic status, we maintain a trade imbalance of more imports than exports. Thus it is logical to predict that the United States' attempt to globalize professions may well result in the same trade deficit that now exists with tangible goods such as automobiles or coffee. With this prediction assumed true, this chapter explores how the United States may become a marketplace for offshore credentialing.

Because I am quite versed in the U.S. profession of counseling, it is this discipline that is most often cited for the purposes of this publication. And because counseling lends itself, for better or worse, to cyberapplications, perhaps this scenario will be a wake up call and a new way of thinking for the helping professions.

In a speech I presented to the sixth annual international conference of the Center for Quality Assurance in International Education (CQAIE) (www.cqaie.org) in Washington, D.C., May 1998, I outlined some ideas I have formed regarding the process of bringing service organizations and even new disciplines into the U.S. mainstream. The advent of the World Wide Web has made this feasible because professional organizations are historically low budget operations. Now the large population of the United States with its large number of Internet users is more a market *for* the world than *to* the world.

In the monograph, *The Foundations of Globalization of Higher Education and the Professions* (Lenn & Miller, 1999) I wrote about this subject. CQAIE is quite interested in the effects of cybercommunication upon higher education and the professions. CQAIE has allowed me to excerpt many ideas from my May 1998 speech as recorded in the monograph.

The Center for Quality Assurance in International Education was founded as a collaborative activity of the U.S. self-regulatory community through its participating associations and recognized accrediting and competency assurance bodies. Established in 1991 and located in the National Center for Higher Education, the center is a focal point for discussion and collaboration both within the United States and between the United States and other country associations concerned with issues of quality and fairness in the international mobility of students, scholars, and professionals; credentialing and recognition of programs; and international educational linkages. It facilitates the comparative study of national quality assurance mechanisms in higher education in order to strengthen and improve efforts with each country and promote mobility among national systems. The center's services and program fall essentially into four categories: (1) providing strategic planning and assistance with the development and implementation of accrediting, licensing, and certification programs outside the United States; (2) assisting other countries in the development of quality assurance systems for higher education and the professions; (3) monitoring quality issues relative to the globalization of U.S. higher education and the professional sectors; and (4) serving as secretariat for the Global Alliance for Transnational Education (GATE) (www.edugate.org).

In 1998 a sign of financial mergers of the 1980s taking on a global perspective of immense proportions was reported:

Daimler-Benz & Chrysler Announce the World's Largest Merger!

In an age of so many corporate mergers and acquisitions, we take this news with resignation that if it is not good—at least it is the general nature of business today. Yet in 1979, Chrysler was near bankruptcy, and a tax-supported loan from the United States bailed out Chrysler (and Chairman Lee Iacocca) to become a renewed national commodity. This was in an era of "Buy American" and "don't let Japan and Europe put our workers out of business."

In 1980 merger of Daimler-Benz and Chrysler would have been thwarted or stopped by public outcry and/or government intervention. Recently, reporters have noted that there has been neither a U.S. government nor popular response—Why? Because globalization is now a forgone conclusion.

I want to introduce an idea that may be unique to readers. That is, as we look at the world of professions and the globalization of professions, we often realize that Americans play a role in taking their professions abroad. I agree, but suggest that for a variety of reasons, Americans have not excelled in globalizing professions. Certainly, they have their strong points in law, accounting, architecture, nursing, engineering, and others, but they lag behind many countries as exporters of services. The reason America is not an exporter has many facets.

Be assured this is not America bashing. Some of my best friends are American, but because we Americans have a habit of talking about ourselves, I want to relate some secrets that could put us in our proper place, that is, in our proper place in the world community of professions. So while pointing out an opportunity for other nations' professionals to flourish here in the United States, I think that American professionals will benefit from bringing professions here. And I think that for all the expertise we own here, we must first understand professions around the world before we can successfully integrate and later export our ideas productively.

Following are some historical reasons why American professions on the whole need education and planned action from those who could make vast gains by establishing your professions in the United States. Although they are not complete, they are meant to stimulate your ideas that may lead to bringing professions to the United States.

- We teach once we have expertise, and once the cycle of being expert begins, then it is hard to be a student. It can give us a bad reputation for one-sided thinking.
- We have been called upon after wars to "export expertise." It is a habit to respond; we are not as good at spreading our word when not asked.
- There is a natural recalcitrance toward the United States that levels the playing field. Suspicion of U.S. imperialism, as faulty as the idea is in professions, gives other countries an advantage of early trust.
- We are weak at languages because of our history of mass immigration and educational priorities.
- Our economy has been so good for the past 40 years that we look to the home front, not to foreign expansion.
- Our professional workforce is university based, and U.S. universities do not export much. In fact, they compete.
- We have a market available to cultivate, yet we have not seen ourselves as a "developing nation."

I propose that now is the time for offshore professions to come to the United States with aspirations of introducing their style of education, professional practice, professional societies, and regulatory practices.

Why could such a scheme work?

- Americans are especially intrigued with foreigners and foreign language because we do not travel widely. And when we do, we do it briefly and without much cultural immersion. Further, we do not emigrate. Very few Americans need to emigrate, nor do we seek change offshore. And as a whole we shy from language development. It simply is not a priority. Therefore, as a country, we think that multilingual people must be more clever than we are.
- Importation of professional societies and their trappings should have little resistance because it has not been a threat—while the United States *is* resisted elsewhere.
- The Internet, satellites, and travel make it easy to avoid regulation.
- Education is available for export to the United States. Foreign degrees are recognized and often sought.

- We have 23,000 associations and room for more. Foreign professional associations could be a niche market.
- Association management companies can alleviate corporation problems; foreign associations could be managed by U.S.-based entities.
- Many credentials are being created globally with a small-to-large market here in the United States.
- American economy has two waves of professionals:

  1. Baby Boomers who are ready to spend and are having crises of aging. Baby Boomers are so named from the boom, explosion, of births after World War II.
  2. Generation X and Boomer Echoes who will be the next wave.

  These are the next two generations. Both groups are susceptible/receptive to new ideas.

- Foreign contact raises the chance of foreign travel and living. Therefore, professionals, especially those who are maturing, will see foreign associations as a way to explore the world in the safety of like-minded professionals.

I recently spoke at a conference of the (U.S.-based) National Organization for Competency Assurance (NOCA) with an audience of some 300 people from 170 professional certifying bodies. When I asked them how many were currently practicing or considering near-future global expansion, 90% gave positive responses. However, with further investigation, I found few succeeding and few with viable plans. My conclusion is that the world need not be preparing itself for an onslaught of U.S. professional expansion.

CUSTOMIZING GLOBALIZATION TO PROFESSIONS

My interest in global credentialing began in 1981 when I started an 8-year odyssey of teaching in and administering a Boston University graduate program in Germany, Great Britain, Belgium, Italy, and Spain. Although 95% of my students were Americans associated with the military or diplomatic missions, the remaining 5% were nationals of European countries and presented a new challenge—credential review and explaining the U.S. system. Articulating degrees was then and is now a major obstacle in cross-cultural education.

I found that merely working in the U.S. environment does not prepare us for "translating" what we do and how we are trained. To this end, I recently completed a document for the United States Information Agency that discussed the problems that professionals face when they attempt to bring their expertise from a foreign country to the United States. Among the areas I covered for those professionals to review were education, experience, and transferring skills. I started by defining terms for those not familiar with our systems, such as *certification, credential, accreditation, licensure, registry, federal,* and *national*.

In helping foreign émigrés, I suggest checking to see if their profession is properly listed in the *Occupational Outlook Quarterly* (U.S. Department of Labor, 1994) and with the Bureau of Labor Statistics (http://www.stats.bls.gov). I also suggest contacting any government's embassy to find out where their labor statistics are kept. Further, the immense resources of the World Wide Web should become a staple of international movement of professions.

Living and working in Europe for 8 years and working in five countries, I got to know lots of professionals and talked to many about moving to all points in the world. Little did I know that their wrestle with our maze of credentials was met with equal consternation from the agencies that would later be befuddled by their potpourri of degrees, diplomas, and credentials. Now we all have our share of needs to master confounding issues of international credentialing of professionals no matter where we are from. As professionals with global expertise, we have two mandates:

1. **Instructing our members of professions with strategies for finding regulations and proper credentials in foreign countries, and in the same view, knowing who we, as professionals, should turn to as foreign counterparts** (National Center for Competency Assurance, 1996). For example,

   • the U.S. Chamber of Commerce is one place where professionals from all countries go around the world to convene and interact;

- most embassies and consulates of nations have a series of trade-related programs; and
- most international corporations have programs to help with offshore transitions.

2. **Instructing foreign applicants in how to translate their portfolios into meaningful host-style applications** (Gorlin, 1994). At the same time, we face the problem of being able to understand foreign equivalency, even when materials are translated into our language. For example, a professional friend was chagrined when a British student showed up at his university for a "course." When he realized she had moved (with furniture) to the United States to take what she called a course, he found that her British concept of a course was of an entire course of study or master's degree—as opposed to a class. If we cannot translate well in the same language, imagine the avenues of possible error with the scores of languages we will soon face.

A CHECKLIST FOR CUSTOMIZING GLOBALIZATION TO A PROFESSION

Keep the following thoughts/ questions in mind in considering the three questions in this checklist:

- Are global regions considered?
- What education and training is needed in your profession?
- What trade/service/industry is affected at home and abroad?

1. What does your profession have to offer
   - to new countries?
   - to other professionals?
   - to similar professions?
   - to a world community?

2. By going global, can your profession expect to gain
   - prestige?
   - financial benefit?
   - higher service to populations?
   - guild gains?

3. With globalization, can your profession (in your country) lose

- local prestige?
- change of education/training norms?
- financial risk of exploring offshore markets?
- loss of time in exploring regulatory restrictions?

CONCLUSION

Of course, there is no way to guess correctly what will happen with the globalization of professions, but I will make some assumptions as follows. Travel and communications have changed the course of history so drastically that watching the effect on product industries should give rise to a pattern that service (professional) industries will take. Knowledge is the most flexible commodity to transfer globally. A hundred years ago, professional conferences were necessary because there was no way quickly to get information to many in the same profession. Now conferences are not necessary, but they are important in connecting real people to ideas. The international nature of conferees, of information exchange, and of service professionals' mobility points toward constant widening of linkages among professionals.

At the same time, the widening impact of Internet use will no doubt affect professional movements. The positive effect is, of course, the instant exchange of information. The negative effect could be the disintermediation of service providers. That is, the change or elimination of intermediate suppliers of services like hospitals and architecture firms to direct market access for anyone with Internet access. Professionals may be put in a position of direct marketing all services.

Immigration and emigration of professionals will continue to grow, not just with the rise of international mergers but also with the idea that the world is a smaller, more easily accessed place. There will be more comfort and ease seen in crossing borders as professionals.

The increase in global product trade will pull service (professional) trade along with it. And the opening of new markets in China, Africa, South America, and other places will increase demands for trade. Although it may not be fortunate, it is evident that developing nations will model education and training after current schemes. That will take more professionals abroad to exchange education, and it will unify professional ideologies. This alone could be the most influential part of unifying professions. For as countries develop professions, surely international ties will abound.

Surely the Internet or World Wide Web will be a most viable and stimulating force for globalization of all professions.

REFERENCES

Gorlin, R. (1994). *Codes of professional responsibility* (3rd ed.). Washington, DC: Bureau of National Affairs.

Lenn, M., & Miller, B. (1999). *The foundations of globalization of higher education*. Washington, DC: Center for Quality Assurance in Higher Education.

National Organization for Competency Assurance. (1996). *Certification: A NOCA handbook*. Washington, DC: NOCA.

U.S. Department of Labor. (1994). *Occupational outlook handbook, 1997–98*. Washington, DC: U.S. Government Printing Office.

4

The Internet: Blessing or Bane for the Counseling Profession?

JoAnn Harris-Bowlsbey

The phenomenal growth in the use of the Internet in the past 5 years has revolutionized work tasks in hundreds of occupations. Consider the impact of the Internet on book stores, real estate agencies, travel agencies, banks, institutions of higher education, libraries, and retail stores, to name just a few affected occupational settings. Counselors must also adequately recognize the potential impact of the Internet on counseling and related professions—especially career counseling—and invest the energy necessary to make that impact positive because it appears that impact is inevitable.

This chapter examines expectations we might have as a profession about the Internet phenomenon and looks to the history of computer-based career planning systems for relevant questions we might ask. Further, it notes challenges that should be foremost in our minds and concludes with possible solutions for managing this transition.

GREAT EXPECTATIONS

The Internet offers the profession an impressive array of possible blessings, including most obviously, the potential to reach immensely greater numbers of clients with counseling and information services. Currently, 50% of American homes have access to the Internet either because homeowners have paid an access fee through a commercial service provider or because they have acquired Internet service free or for a reduced charge through a library or educational institution. Another significant percentage has gained Internet access through their place of employment. Public libraries have acquired the hardware and connections, thanks, in part, to a billion dollar gift from the foundation of Microsoft's chair, Bill Gates, resulting in provision of free access to their clientele. If Gates' predictions in *The Road Ahead* (1996) come true, there will be a continuing decline in the cost of hardware and access to the Internet, making its use in American homes as common as that of the television set. Thus one great expectation has been that the Internet will quickly become a universally available highway, with affordable tolls, over which to send and receive assessment, information, and counseling support.

I am fortunate to have been one of those very early developers, in the late 1960s, of computer-based career planning systems. In the early years, I predicted that by 1987, 80% of American homes would have computers, and along with other early developers, I dreamed about the possibility that computer-based career planning systems would have early, wide, and almost universal acceptance. As a matter of fact, that did not happen.

Another logical expectation was that counselors, and those who manage counseling services, would add the Internet as an additional powerful tool to their quiver of services, as they did earlier with assessment and computer-based systems. As a young developer of computer-based systems, I had this expectation as well. However, what I learned in 1968, and continue to learn in 1999, is that a large proportion of counselors still do not embrace technology with open arms. Embracing it means having interest in technology, possessing a set of skills to deal with it, and having the imagination to develop modes of providing service that combine high touch and high tech. My sense is that for many warm, caring individuals with the mean Holland code of SEA (social, enterprising, and artistic), the embracing of technology remains foreign and uncomfortable!

In the 30 years that have rolled by since the release of the first computer-based career planning systems, there has been increasing acceptance of technology and, for some, the development of skills to use it effectively. Perhaps this history has laid a foundation that will allow the acceptance and productive use of the Internet to advance at a much faster pace.

Yet another logical expectation has been that individuals who take advantage of technology-driven services will enjoy positive effects from their use. These include increased self-efficacy, improved decision-making skill, easier identification of alternatives available in given situations, and better-informed decision making because of the world of information at their fingertips.

Thirty years of using computer-based systems have indeed had positive effects including increased self-efficacy and increased decision-making skill, increased awareness of the need to plan ahead and increased knowledge about specific occupations, and greater specification of career goals (Taber & Luzzo, 1999). However, these effects have not accrued at the rate or magnitude of early expectations.

Still another expectation about the use of the Internet and other computer-driven technologies has been that the role of the counselor can and will improve for the better. In this case, *better* means that highly trained professionals can be freed from routine tasks such as schedule changing, information dissemination, and report generation so that the saved time can be used to meet with clients and address specific problems that a computer cannot serve well. Though this has been a persistent expectation since the beginning of the use of technology in guidance, there is very little evidence that this expectation has been met.

Are there Internet characteristics that make these expectations more likely to come true than has been the case with stand-alone and networked computer-based systems? Perhaps. First, the Internet has an uncanny appeal at this time in history, and many are inclined to think the Internet is good simply because of its snowballing track record. Second, Internet services on the whole remain free of charge, whereas the high cost of developing, maintaining, and marketing earlier computer-based systems, combined with their limited market, resulted in relatively high annual user fees. Third, Internet capabilities are far more expansive, both in the sense of their outreach and in the sense of their nature, which includes use of multimedia, e-mail, video conferencing, transmission of databases, and multiple linkages to other rich resources on the Internet.

GREAT QUESTIONS

The history of computer-based systems and the capabilities of the Internet combine to help us formulate the questions that we, as a profession, need to be asking. If we can formulate the really relevant questions, we are much more likely to be able to find answers for them. Here are the ones I want to pose:

- Do we believe that parts of our work with clients who present different kinds of problems and concerns can be handled as effectively utilizing technology as we currently do with traditional face-to-face interventions? If so, what concerns should be matched with which technological interventions?
- If we can design technology-driven activities and services to perform those tasks, how will we use the time that is saved—to serve more clients, to provide more in-depth assistance to the ones we are already serving, or to take on more tasks that are at the periphery of our calling?
- Assuming that some tasks can be defined that the computer does as well or better than we humans do, how should human counselors support or provide follow-through for those tasks?
- Knowing that individuals have different learning styles, different levels of readiness for receiving counseling services and information, and differing levels of acceptance of technology, how will we identify clients for whom providing services in a technology-driven way will be a disservice, or at best a waste of resources, until issues have been resolved that serve as barriers?
- In a cyberworld where free is considered to be good, how do we develop and sustain high-quality services for which little or inadequate revenue is being generated?
- How do we recruit counselors and counselor educators (whose basic personality type draws them to work with people in real-time, face-to-face, empathic ways) who have skills in program or web site design so that the materials we use are developed by individuals with appropriate credentials and so that programs of service are developed that move between technology and human support in seamless and complementary ways?
- How do we change the curriculum of preservice and in-service education for counselors to provide training in use of technology,

both as cognitive content and as an area in which there is a practicum?

- How do we evaluate services that combine technology and human support? Over the years we have found it extremely difficult to define the outcomes we desire, construct instruments or methods to measure them, and get enough researchers and subjects to apply this measurement. As subjects in cyberspace are more difficult to identify and research, and even more difficult under distance conditions, how will we succeed in knowing if services are improved or denigrated through incorporation of technology?

Though it is likely that there are many more questions that could be asked, these are central and sufficient to occupy our attention in the short range.

GREAT CHALLENGES

Assuming that we could find good answers to the questions just posed, the profession's entry into virtual counseling will still be fraught with tremendous challenges. There are specific challenges for the development and quality of web sites, for clients, and for counselors.

In the development of web sites, the challenges relate to disjointedness and quality. Though there are hundreds of web sites that provide some assistance or information related to topics in the purview of guidance, these sites are entirely disjointed. There is no master plan that has organized guidance services in some way and then addressed the components in detail. The typical client is unable to sequence the pieces (such as taking an interest inventory before selecting titles of occupations for which to get descriptions, or using an activity to determine the criteria desired in a job before searching an extensive job bank) and is thus faced with a smorgasbord of possibilities that have no known sequence or relationship to one another. At this stage of the development of guidance activities and information on the Internet, a client needs a knowledgeable counselor to identify helpful sites and to help the client apply their content to the decision making at hand.

Professional standards related to quality for web site development and use of these sites with clients are just emerging. With a few notable exceptions, professionals are not reviewing sites against criteria; and no professional organization is acknowledging sites with a seal of approval. With the exception of sites developed by college and university counseling and career centers, most sites are being developed by individuals or organizations that do not possess expertise in our field. The myriad of web sites have widely varying quality, and there is no way to help the consumer decide which are worthy of time and attention.

The second group of challenges relates to interaction with clients. Because users of web sites or cybercounseling are typically not in face-to-face contact with a counselor, it is difficult to assess the readiness or capability of a client to profit from technology-driven service. The guidelines adopted by the National Board for Certified Counselors (NBCC, 1998; see Appendix 5) state that a counselor must talk with a potential client by phone in order to assess this readiness. Guidelines adopted by the National Career Development Association (NCDA, 1997; see Appendix 6) indicate that the counselor must do periodic monitoring of the client's progress by telephone or videophone teleconference. Phone conversation may be helpful. Use of video conferencing, at a time when it is more commonly available for all, may be more effective because some nonverbal cues will also be available. The same guidelines indicate that it is unethical for a counselor to provide cybercounseling to a person whom he or she assesses as unlikely to profit from treatment in this mode and that the client should be referred to a geographically close counselor for face-to-face counseling.

It is difficult at best, even when counseling is being provided face-to-face, to evaluate its effectiveness or the degree that it has helped clients meet goals that they and the counselor have mutually set. This problem is exacerbated in cyberspace. The relationship with the client is tenuous and electronic, and it is easier to terminate in midstream. The goals set for the relationship are restricted. In a service mode that is badly in need of evaluation, the chances for success are significantly lower than in face-to-face mode.

Another difficulty related to the client is that we know far too little at this time about how to provide cybercounseling or simply human support to activities completed or information gained via the Internet. We do not know whether synchronous or asynchronous e-mail interaction is more effective, whether addition of audio and/or video to counselor-client interactions makes them more effective, or whether individuals with different personalities or learning styles are more likely to profit from assistance in this mode than others.

The third group of challenges relates to counselors who will work with clients in technology-driven modes. We do not know what the ideal Holland or Myers-Briggs Type Indicator code is for an effective cybercounselor. Because we do not know this person's characteristics, selection criteria at the preservice training level may be inadequate or incorrect. Clearly, those who specialize in cybercounseling need preservice and in-service training that is significantly different from that needed by those who specialize in traditional, one-to-one counseling. How can those who need to change counselor education programs acquire a sufficient level of knowledge to be able to do so? How does a cybercounselor achieve a positive, trusting relationship with a client? How do techniques such as reflection, questioning, and encouraging translate into e-mail communication? How are important tasks such as problem identification and goal setting accomplished in a technology-driven context?

POSSIBLE SOLUTIONS

Many challenging questions and needs have been raised, and with the speed at which technology is moving, we as a profession need to find answers and solutions quickly. Here are some of my ideas about ways in which useful solutions could be identified.

It seems critically important that the American Counseling Association and its related entities should take the lead in facing and finding solutions to these challenges. A first task is to expand the ethical guidelines that have to date been developed by the National Career Development Association, the National Board for Certified Counselors, and the International Association of Educational and Vocational Guidance (IAEVG). Though these guidelines together form a very good basis, they are not yet complete or sufficient. By means of an appointed task force with broad representation, ACA could further develop these guidelines and publicize them broadly to its own members, schools and universities, publishers of material in the field, and the general public. Further, the association could be mindful of legislation that needs to address a variety of ethical concerns related to the Internet and could promote wording that addresses those concerns.

A second task for ACA and its collaborating entities is to develop more comprehensive and definitive standards for web sites that are used for cybercounseling or guidance and career information. These standards need to include

1. requirements related to the credentials of developers and a requirement that developers must state their credentials;
2. the methods of screening clients who will be supported by distance technology;
3. characteristics of assessment instruments whereby results can be released directly to clients without counselor intervention;
4. methods and criteria for referral of cyberclients to on-site counselors; and
5. methods by which counselors will support clients at a distance.

Standards should also include specifications for user interface, response time, use of multimedia assets, and confidentiality of records. Given the immensity of this task, it might be organized from one source that can delegate specific parts of the task to entities within the whole having the greatest expertise in these parts.

Once standards for quality web sites are developed, the professional associations should develop a structure for reviewing them in order to rate them—or to certify them or not certify them—as quality sites. Further, ACA and its entities should mount a publicity campaign to inform developers about the standards, to inform consumers about them, and to attempt to enforce the standards.

These kinds of activities will help solve the problems of development, critical review, and certification of web sites and services in our field. They do not address the problem of getting a broad base of the current and future members of the profession trained to work effectively in cyberspace. Solving this challenge requires changes in preservice and in-service counselor education programs. The curriculum required for training in counseling must be reviewed and expanded to include the new technologies. Experiences provided through supervised practicum need to include cybercounseling and use of web sites in conjunction with one-to-one and group modes of service.

Changing counselor education curriculum is a significant challenge. Though many institutions of higher education are optimally equipped from a technical point of view to deliver instruction in distance-learning modes, one nagging problem has been to get faculty members comfortable in developing courses in this mode and in providing student learning experiences in a very different way. If this is true of faculty members in general, it may be doubly true of counselor educators. Faculty members entered their profession because of a love of dealing directly with students. They are unlikely, especially if beyond the age of 30, to make an easy transition to the cyberworld. In order to change this scene it may be necessary for accrediting bodies or curriculum-approval organizations to require changes in curriculum and in modes of delivering that curriculum.

Just as counselor training programs currently offer specialties in mental health counseling, school counseling, family counseling, and the like, they should also offer a specialty in technology-enhanced counseling. It will be critical that at least one faculty member in the department be knowledgeable and enthusiastic in this area, that students experience some of their own mentoring and course work in this medium, and that they have supervised practicum in cybercounseling and guidance.

These thoughts trigger others about the selection of students into counselor training. Those who will succeed best in cybercounseling and guidance are likely to have different personality characteristics than those who favor and succeed in face-to-face counseling. It is likely that this new breed of counselors have Holland codes of RSE (realistic, social, enterprising) or ISE (investigative, social, enterprising), and thus different ways need to be developed to attract and select these candidates.

Similarly, vigorous attention should also be given to in-service training of counselors. Because those who are certified or licensed have to maintain continuing education, there could be an additional requirement that some of this training be in the area of delivering service by technology. That, of course, begs for the development of this curriculum, which might be optimally delivered as web-based training in order to introduce counselors to this medium.

I have spoken of the responsibilities of professional associations, certifying and accreditation bodies, and institutions of higher education in helping the profession to use new technologies ethically and effectively. There is also a significant role for government agencies and other funding sources. Because the norm has been set that most services are free of charge on the Internet, tremendous funding is needed for development of high-quality web sites. It is impossible to develop high-quality services and maintain them without a revenue flow. At the beginning of computer-based career guidance systems, for example, there was very significant funding from state and federal sources and from charitable foundations. The revenue flow for web counseling and guidance has to come only partially from client fees and largely from external funding and perhaps some advertising of products we feel comfortable listing for our consumers. Funding could also support the revision of counselor education curriculum and aggressive in-service training—a model that was forged in 1958 with funding from the National Defense Education Act, which provided training for a generation of counselors.

External funding should also be used for research in this field. As already mentioned, research related to the optimal combination of types of service, characteristics of those who will profit from these methods, and effectiveness of cybercounseling and guidance will be both difficult and expensive. It will be more cost-efficient if a large-scale research program can be coordinated from one source rather than having multiple, small research studies.

These methods combined might make an important impact on the need to develop standards, monitor web sites, train and retrain counselors, and conduct research in this new method of service delivery. Another method that might be extremely useful at this time could be a summit conference to which professionals knowledgeable in these technologies were invited for a think-tank activity of several days. Such an activity could be structured in a way that focused major attention on these and other crucial issues and developed a summary of best thinking on these matters as well as a suggested plan for future action.

CONCLUSION

This chapter has reviewed some of the expectations and hopes that we hold for the expansion of counseling and guidance services to a large and geographically distributed population in need of them through the use of distance technology. At the same time, it has reviewed the challenges of making this leap into cybercounseling and guidance and some of the critical questions that the profession should be asking. Finally, it has proposed some possible ways to take the next steps in developing ethics and standards of quality and engaging in new areas of counselor training and research.

REFERENCES

Gates, W. (1996). *The road ahead.* New York: Penguin Books.

National Board for Certified Counselors. (1998). *Standards for the ethical practice of web counseling.* Greensboro, NC: Author.

National Career Development Association. (1997). *Guidelines for the use of the Internet for provision of career information and planning services.* Columbus, OH: Author.

Taber, B. J., & Luzzo, D. A. (1999). *A comprehensive review of research evaluating the effectiveness of DISCOVER in promoting career development* (ACT Research Report 99.3). Iowa City, IA: ACT.

5

The Odyssey of a Technologically Challenged Counselor Educator Into Cyberspace

DUANE BROWN

In 1982 my wife both surprised and frightened me with a gift: a brand-new, state-of-the-art computer. Her intent was aimed at least partially at helping me with one of the essential aspects of my work—my writing. However, I have long suspected that my wife's secondary motive was to spare my long-suffering secretaries from the horrors of interpreting my handwriting in draft after draft of articles, chapters, and books. I saw her purposes, agreed with them, and set my course toward computer literacy. It was to be a longer voyage than I envisioned.

The fright I experienced when I received my wife's gift was stimulated by one piece of the hardware: the keyboard. I had not taken typing in high school or elsewhere because I did not wish to become a secretary. In fact, my visceral reaction to clerical duties is so strong as to evoke anxiety and nausea whenever I engage in them. My concept of hell is to have my Self-Directed Search misinterpreted by Lucifer and be sentenced to an eternity of typing, filing, and mutilating data and information. Nevertheless, I screwed my courage to the sticking point and ordered a software program called Typing Tutor. After installing this substitute for a business education teacher, I dutifully awoke each morning to practice my typing for 30 minutes or so. Soon I was so discouraged that my self-esteem was at an all-time low. I had been utterly defeated by a piece of software that kept telling me that I was making more mistakes than I had words on the paper and that my speed, when normed on a group of average 7-year olds, was one standard deviation below the mean!

I vowed not to be defeated by something that could be placed on a floppy disk, however, and went in search of a typing class taught by a real teacher. I enrolled in a continuing education typing class at the local high school, purchased the book, and set out to conquer typing. It did not work. My fingers strayed too far from the home keys and refused to work in a rhythm that produced words that remotely resembled those that appeared in any known dictionary. Also, I kept noticing that in terms of speed I was last in the class. I dropped out and sold the computer for half of what my wife had paid for it. I decided that improving my handwriting was easier than learning to use a computer.

The Awakening

Fast forward to 1987 and I was still without a computer. I also found myself confronted with an interesting conundrum. How could I keep detailed records, file flawless reports in a timely manner, and maintain my "handwritten copy to secretary—typewritten copy to me—edited copy to secretary—final report to me" approach? At the time, my wife and I were offering weekend fearful-flyer seminars for American Airlines, and our manager expected a report on Monday mornings. Our manager graduated from the Stanford University MBA program, and she knew a thing or two about report writing. She suggested that we purchase a computer. When I protested that I could not type, she observed, "you don't need to be able to type to use a computer, although it helps." "Really!" I exclaimed. She then explained the hunt-and-peck system she used, and I realized that I could indeed "type." I then purchased a computer while fending off the "I told you so comments" from my spouse. The 286 computer that I purchased had no mouse and was as slow as molasses by today's standards. But the results of my work came so quickly and so neatly that I felt like a caveman who just invented the wheel. In fact, my vision of myself as a Neanderthal was not far off the mark. Unfortunately my satisfaction with my newfound technological prowess was so delusional that I ignored the development of the 386 and 486 computers until the university installed a 486 in my office. I also ignored campus rumblings about another phenomenon: the Internet.

The Epiphany

In 1996 the University of North Carolina at Chapel Hill completed the installation of a fiber optic network, and my computer was connected to the university Intranet as well as the Internet. The faculty of the School of Education and I were told that all internal communication would come to us via e-mail. I refused to accept this idea, partially because my computer was out of order, and partially because I did not wish to change. The result was that I missed the note telling me that textbook orders were due and that I needed to sign up for a parking sticker. Realizing that I was about to be without many of the essentials a professor needs in order to do his or her job (actually almost losing my parking place was the biggest jolt), I acquired a password and opened my e-mail. The computer screen blinked to life with the notation, "You have 1,336 new messages." I was astounded, and my first inclination was to erase all 1,336 messages and start from scratch. However, my computer, which seemed to be getting smarter all the time, would not allow me to erase the messages except one at a time. To my delight I found some precious kernels of information among mostly chaff. I learned that a professor from Japan had heard one of my presentations and was interested in discussing some of my work. An old lost friend wrote that he had discovered my e-mail address and wondered how I was doing. A former student had a position open and wondered if we had students who might be interested. Amazingly, 20 or so of the 1,336 messages dealt with vital "stuff." Even more surprisingly, I could respond using my now well-developed hunt-and-peck approach to the keyboard. E-mail has potential!

Within a week of opening my e-mail at the university, I contacted an ISP (Internet service provider) and gained access to the Internet both at home and at the university. My first efforts at surfing the net were conducted at home with no particular purpose. On one occasion I typed in career development and hit enter. My poorly designed search yielded over 1 million matches. As I began to explore some of these matches, an almost childlike wonder replaced the skepticism that I had about the utility of technology and what can be found in cyberspace. The potential of the computer and the Internet as a communication tool, a means for self-instruction, and a tool for teaching others seemed limitless. Technology made my reports neater, freed my secretary from the misery of interpreting my handwriting, and made me a better informed professor. However, I had only begun to realize the potential of the Internet as an educational tool.

HOW I LEARNED TO ACCOMMODATE CYBERSPACE, TECHNOLOGY, AND COUNSELOR EDUCATION

In 1998 the School of Education hired a new dean. She immediately declared that one of her points of emphasis would be distance education. My concept of distance education at the time was what I practiced at Iowa State University (ISU) and West Virginia University (WVU). Distance learning at WVU and ISU involved getting into a car, driving 50 to 150 miles, teaching a class, and returning to campus dead tired. The new dean made it clear that this old-fashioned idea of distance learning was not what she had in mind. Distance learning was to involve video conferencing and web-based training. Video conferencing was not a new idea to me because some professors in the School of Education had telecast courses to other sites such as Charlotte, NC, with considerable success. Furthermore, video conferencing was not as threatening to my concept of counselor education as web-based training because video conferencing is conducted in real time, is face-to-face, can involve student-to-student interaction, and involves student-professor interaction that is not greatly different from what happens in a typical classroom. The fact that 25 to 300 miles of geography separates students and professors poses certain barriers to the instructional process. However, with the development of powerful computers equipped with ProShare® that allow one-on-one and small-group face-to-face interactions, many of these obstacles can be overcome. Even persistent reports from other counselor educators that students who participate in a video-conferencing course often complain of the lack of direct contact with the professor did not dampen my optimism about the potential of video conferencing. I believed then, and continue to believe, that the problems that people experience with video conferencing stem primarily from lack of experience and in no way lessen the potential of this technology to reach audiences otherwise unreachable. At this point, I have not taught my first course using video conferencing, but I am not greatly concerned about the outcomes of the courses I will teach in the near future.

In 1998, however, web-based training still seemed like an unlikely instructional choice for counselor education courses. My view of web-based training was not unlike that of the professor who was asked why she was participating in a web-based training design course. She answered facetiously, "I'm interested in designing an impersonal counselor education program." The concept of a counselor education student taking a course with nothing more than an on-line set of directions and a computer to guide the learning process was so unacceptable I discarded it completely in the initial design of an off-campus program in school counseling. I drew my conclusions solely based on my biases—and then decided that perhaps I should be a bit more open-minded and do my homework. My exploration of web-based training continues to this day, but what I have done to this point has consisted of three phases.

The first phase of my exploration of web-based training I call the "informal Wally Hannum" phase. Dr. Hannum is a professor of instructional technology in the School of Education at the University of North Carolina at Chapel Hill. For the modest price of a lunch, he gave me an informal lecture on the perils and promises of web-based training and some material to read that he had prepared for publication. I emerged from our luncheon with one piece of priceless advice. Dr. Hannum suggested that anyone intending to use technology in the instructional process should first consider what his or her objectives are and then select the best instructional methodology to achieve those objectives. What he did not say, but was obvious to me, was that rejecting the use of technology without fully considering its potential as an instructional tool is folly.

My next task was to read the material that was provided to me during my luncheon meeting with Dr. Hannum. In this material he listed, among other things, the advantages and disadvantages of technology as an instructional tool. Hannum (in press) grouped drawbacks into three categories: logistical, instructional, and economic. The logistical advantages of web-based training involved ease of scheduling courses for program administrators, increased flexibility for students because they can decide when to engage in the learning process, ease of access to other information such as journal articles on the Internet, and the relatively small effort required by professors to update courses. A major instructional advantage of web-based training includes the possibility of coordinating a number of instructional approaches such as video and audio segments and text to achieve specific learning objectives. Other instructional advantages of web-based training are that students control all aspects of the course including the pace, have the opportunity to review prerequisite material before proceeding with the learning process, and can review material and repeatedly practice skills to enhance their mastery. The primary economic advantage of web-based training is that information can be delivered at lower cost to both students and universities because of reductions in travel cost for students and facilities costs for universities. I was surprised to learn that web-based training does not seem to reduce faculty costs. Hannum indicated that initial web-based training course preparation time and time needed to provide oversight of the learning process during the delivery of a web-based training course varies little from traditional instruction.

Web-based training also has disadvantages. From a logistical point of view, the inability to use lengthy video clips because of the time it takes to download them stands as a major disadvantage. Assessment of the outcome of web-based training also poses logistical problems. Although examinations can be placed on-line, students cannot be monitored as they take the examination. This forces instructors to either vary their evaluation efforts or to ask students to come to a centralized location to take examinations. The major instructional limitation of web-based training for counselor education is that the development of counseling skills may not be possible, but this is by no means a certainty. Another instructional limitation of web-based training occurs whenever the material being delivered requires that it be learned in sequence. There are no assurances in these courses that students follow the prescribed sequence, particularly when some of the elements in the sequence are boring or more difficult. The fact that web-based training requires the use of e-mail, chat rooms in real time, and asynchronous or threaded chat may also be a disadvantage of this instructional approach. Students must learn to use them in order to maximize their learning, and the acquisition of these skills may be daunting tasks for some students. However, learning these skills may also be an advantage to students in the long term. Standards adopted recently the Association for Counselor Education and Supervision (ACES, 1999a; see Appendix 2) make it clear that counselor education students need to learn these and other technical competencies.

One of the major economic disadvantages of web-based training is that initial course preparation probably takes longer than the preparation of a course that is to be delivered using a traditional format. Moreover, Hannum (in press) was of the opinion that the cost advantages that normally accrue through the use of web-based training are lost when group size falls below 12, although he offered no empirical support for this position. My own limited experience suggests that Hannum is on target with his observation that web-based training courses require more preparation time than traditional courses, but there are several applications of web-based training in counselor education courses that should not be overlooked. (The applications will be discussed later.)

The second, more formal phase of my exploration of web-based training began after my initial discussion with Dr. Hannum and my examination of the materials that he provided. I felt reassured that web-based training has possibilities for offering courses and portions of courses to students. I attended a series of formal presentations that dealt with courseware, that is, software packages that can facilitate the process of preparing web-based training courses. I also delved into areas such as the newly approved ACES standards for distance learning (ACES, 1999b).

During the formal learning stage of my orientation to web-based training, I learned, among other things, that courseware packages are not the same. Some, particularly Blackboard.com, have a number of features that simplify the preparation of courses. I was particularly delighted to find that I could use my word processing program to prepare lessons and then cut and paste them into the various Blackboard.com modules. Blackboard.com will also administer tests that have been placed in a course, make them available at specified times, score tests and place the results in a virtual grade book, and keep track of student involvement during on-line chats. Perhaps more importantly, students who provide incorrect responses to test questions can be directed to material within the course that provides the correct information. Although I have not mastered Blackboard.com or any other courseware package, after 12 hours of training I can perform most of the essential tasks needed to prepare an on-line course.

The most important thing I learned during the more formal part of my introduction to web-based training is that I do not have to learn computer languages or new technological skills in order to develop on-line courses. I still do not know what *html* means, let alone possess the ability to use it to prepare an on-line course. Software developers have "dumbed down" computer languages, and now I can better understand and use them. Additionally, I learned to show my ignorance, which was undoubtedly obvious anyway, and ask questions. I know that one of the seminar leaders was a bit frustrated with me when I insisted that he sit with me while I learned to design a particular aspect of my course. In some ways I am in the same place with my ability to design web-based training courses as I was nearly 18 years ago with my typing course: last in the class. However, I have now written several publications, including this one, with my hunt-and-peck method of typing, and I am confident that I can use my course design skills to craft new learning experiences.

The third phase of my exploration of web-based training was to complete the design of my first web-based training course, a project that was begun in one of the seminars I attended. I concluded that the best time to work on the design was when I was teaching the course traditionally. I also decided that it might be a good idea to pilot test some of the units so that student feedback could be obtained. Students enjoyed the unit on designing programs to prevent sexually transmitted diseases (STDs) but hated the test that covered this area. They liked the unit because it included many links to web sites filled with interesting information, pictures, and stories. Although I have never been able to develop an objective test that students liked, the nature of the feedback that I received on this test made me think momentarily that my role in life is to torment students. In retrospect I may have made an error by giving students a series of exercises to complete using the information on the web sites that were included in the unit. Although I did not specify as much, I believe that students concluded that if they answered the questions and completed the exercises they would be prepared for the examination. The answers to questions on the test could be found in the assigned web sites but were not necessarily related to the assignments. I concluded that next time I must be more specific. Others who are engaged in web-based training have told me that one of the most difficult aspects of designing a web-based training course is being explicit enough that even the student with the lowest ability to follow directions can complete the assignment successfully. I now fully understand why they made this observation. I also understand the need to pilot test modules and assignments before incorporating them into courses for which students pay hard-earned money.

WHERE I AM IN LATE 1999

My bias is still that much of what we teach in counselor education must be taught professor to students using either traditional methods or video conferencing regardless of whether the courses are on or off campus. For example, it is hard for me to imagine teaching an entire group process or counseling techniques course using web-based training, but I am open to the idea that the knowledge and skills needed in these areas can be taught using video conferencing. However, I am convinced that much of the didactic content that counselor educators teach, including counseling and career development theory, measurement theory, social and cultural foundations, and professional issues can be taught as well using web-based training courses as they can using traditional approaches. I am also convinced that some of what we teach can be better taught using web-based training. Web sites provided by the U.S. Department of Labor (http://www.dol.gov/) and the Bureau of Labor Statistics (http://www.stats.bls.gov) can help students find and use occupational information and obtain projections about occupational growth and decline. Clearinghouses such as the one developed by ERIC/CASS—International Career Development Library (ICDL) (http://icdl.uncg.edu/reference.html) (see also chapter 12)—can help students acquire information about professional organizations, conduct literatures searches using ERIC databases and on-line journal articles, and access America's Career Kit, which includes America's Job Bank, America's Talent Bank, America's CareerInfonet, and America's Learning Exchange. Students can file electronic resumes and conduct job searches in cyberspace using America's Job Bank, learn to identify educational opportunities using America's Learning Exchange, or access important sources of occupational information such as the *Occupational Outlook Handbook* (U.S. Department of Labor, 1994) from ICDL. ICDL also provides links to other learning houses such as The Riley Guide and What Color Is Your Parachute? Job Hunting Online, both of which contain a wealth of resources regarding the job search. As the title International Career Development Library suggests, links are also provided to information about occupations in a limited number of other countries such as Canada and New Zealand.

Using on-line resources can be incorporated into a traditional course in the form of outside assignments. However, in web-based training courses they can inserted into text, hyperlinked to web sites, and thus incorporated into the learning process instantaneously. Students can also be introduced to inventories such as the Career Key (Jones, 1997) that was designed to measure Holland's (1997) constructs. Students can take the inventory on-line and learn how their results can be linked instantaneously to the information found in the *Occupational Outlook Handbook*. Web sites focusing on the prevention of drug use, problem pregnancies and STDs, and child abuse offer rich sources of information on these topics that may not be available in textbooks. School violence holds center stage in American education today, and the Internet offers a variety of sources that can assist school counselors to reduce violence in their schools. School counselors can also find a storehouse of financial aid information, data about community and 4-year colleges, and a wealth of other information for students who expect to attend a postsecondary institution. The list of uses of web-based training, whether incorporated into on-line lessons or assigned as part of traditional courses, is endless.

Recently we have embarked upon an attempt to design a virtual career development laboratory. This laboratory will allow on and off campus students to explore occupational information not available on the Internet, view samples of tests and inventories, access directories of web sites, explore computer-assisted career guidance systems, and receive instruction on the use of complex systems such as O*NET. The effectiveness of this laboratory is unknown at this time. However, its conceptualization was stimulated by my exploration of the potential of web-based training, and the result may be that both traditional and on-line instruction will be enhanced.

The use of web-based training is constrained by traditional thinking. Tom Hohenshil (1999) reported to our faculty that one of the first things he had to do was discard the ideas that web-based training should parallel traditional instructional processes. When counselor educators design a traditional course, they begin by considering the objectives they hope to accomplish and then choose learning experiences that will achieve their purposes. Does this sound familiar? It is identical to the advice I received from Dr. Hannum in my introduction to distance learning. Typically, professors select from strategies such as lecture/discussion, simulations, role-plays, case study analyses, research papers, in-class presentations, projects, and discussion/study groups. Web-based training offers the instructors the same range of options. Lectures can be inserted into lessons as text or audio clips, chat rooms can replace discussion groups and question and answer sessions, simulations can be inserted, and case studies can be analyzed and discussed. Currently, web-based training does not provide opportunities for role-playing, but computers equipped with video cameras will allow students to form linkages in cyberspace and avail themselves of this opportunity.

It is also worth noting that one of the limitations of web-based training noted earlier—the limitation on the use of videotapes as an instructional modality—will soon be eliminated. The use of video is currently restricted because of narrow band technology and slow modem speed that slows the downloading time and delays transmission. Frankly, I cannot define bandwidth, but I know that narrow band technology will be replaced by wide band technology in the very near future, and the faster modems are already available. The result is that extensive use of videotape in web-based training will soon be possible.

Some of the most exciting applications of technology for counselor educators have nothing to do with web-based training courses or traditional uses of video conferencing. Available technology offers counselor educators the opportunity to enhance the quality of field activities such as supervision and staffing. John Galas, who is a member of the counselor education faculty at the University of North Carolina at Chapel Hill, has worked with professors from school psychology and school social work programs to bring students from the three programs together to staff their clients and draft treatment plans for them. What is unique is that the professors are on the University of North Carolina at Chapel Hill campus and the students are in a field setting. Moreover, it is now possible through the use of computers equipped with Proshare® to view a counseling session in progress and to conduct individual and group supervision sessions with students at off-campus sites while remaining on campus.

Information that can be incorporated into the counseling process is available on-line and is more up-to-date than much of the information currently used for bibliography (Srebalus & Brown, in press). Students headed for private practice can be taught how to use the Internet as a marketing tool, and school counselors can learn how to use their own web sites to disseminate information to parents and students. Students should learn to apply these skills as portions of their field experiences. Also, as already noted, on-line tests and inventories can be used to facilitate the counseling process in many instances.

CONCLUSION

Will high tech replace high touch? I do not believe that it will. However, caring and concern can be demonstrated in a number of ways including the efficient use of the client's time, providing services using modalities that are suited to the client's preferences, and using approaches that are culturally sensitive. Technology can and should be used to enhance the services that we provide to clients. Similarly, counselor educators have an obligation to continue to explore effective and efficient means of preparing professional counselors. The ACES (1999b) *Guidelines for On-Line Instruction in Counselor Education* (http://www.chre.vt.edu/1-s/thohen/ACEWEB.htm) under the course quality section suggest that distance learning approaches "must offer, at a minimum, an equivalent opportunity to that provided in a traditional course" (p. 10). This of course assumes that traditional approaches to training counselors are the best way to facilitate the training process. The ACES guidelines, which cover numerous concerns that must be addressed in the design and delivery of on-line courses, are the proper starting point as we consider the use of web-based training, video conferencing, and other approaches to training. However, these standards should not be the last word on distance learning or training in general. I foresee a time when we will conclude that technological approaches and use of the resources available in cyberspace may be superior to traditional approaches in teaching certain skills and facts. It has taken me 18 years to reach this point, and I am excited about testing this, my most recent hypothesis about technology and cyberspace.

Finally, I offer the following advice to counselor educators who are relative newcomers to web-based training, video conferencing, and the concept of distance learning:

1. Keep an open mind about the use of on-line courses and video conferencing as instructional tools. They will not replace some of the instructional methodologies that we now employ, but they have a place in counselor education programs.
2. Travel to an institution that uses web-based training or video conferencing as instructional approaches or hire a consultant to discuss the potential of distance learning with your faculty.
3. Keep abreast of the new developments in the delivery of information via the Internet. Wide band technology and faster modems will allow us to use videotape on an unlimited basis in our instruction.
4. Software programs such as ProShare® coupled with video cameras mounted on computers will allow us to converse with students who are off campus. This development, along with the development of higher speed computers, provides counselor educators with the potential to provide distance supervision that may be superior to the supervisory methods we employ today.
5. Enroll in a continuing education course or workshop with a knowledgeable professional. Although some people have designed courses and experiences without instruction, at this point

in time this is an unnecessarily stressful approach to designing distance learning courses. Available courseware makes the design of web-based training courses quite simple.

6. Stay abreast of the developments of clearing houses such as ICDL. The information contained on these web sites and the links to other databases greatly ease the process of accessing data.

7. Encourage doctoral students who are in need of research projects to conduct evaluation studies and empirical tests of the relative value of distance learning. Do not encourage them to conduct the mostly meaningless surveys that solicit the opinions of counselor educators about the value of distance learning in counselor education. I suspect that most counselor educators are like me, unable to give an informed opinion regarding the true worth of distance learning at this time.

REFERENCES

Association for Counselor Education and Supervision. (1999a). *Recommended technical competencies for counselor education students.* Alexandria, VA: Author.

Association for Counselor Education and Supervision. (1999b). *Guidelines for on-line instruction in counselor education.* Alexandria, VA: Author [On-line]. Available: http://www.chre.ut.edu/l-s/thohen/aceweb.htm.

Hannum, W. (in press). *Web-based training: Advantages and disadvantages.* In B. Kahn (Ed.), *Web-based training.* Beverly Hills, CA: Sage.

Hohenshil, T. (1999). *Designing distance learning courses.* Workshop delivered at the University of North Carolina at Chapel Hill, Chapel Hill, NC.

Holland, J. L. (1997). *Making vocational choices: A theory of vocational personalities and work environments.* Odessa, FL: Personality Assessment Resources.

Jones, L. K. (1997). *The career key.* Raleigh: North Carolina State University.

Srebalus, D. J., & Brown, D. (in press). *Counseling in a multicultural society.* Boston: Allyn & Bacon.

U.S. Department of Labor. (1994). *Occupational outlook handbook, 1997–98.* Washington, DC: U.S. Government Printing Office.

PART II

*Infusing New Technology Into
Counseling, Education, and Human Services*

6

Using Cyberspace to Enhance Counselors' Cultural Transcendence

JOHN MCFADDEN AND MARTY JENCIUS

D eveloping cultural competence is part a lifelong process for the mental health professional that includes awareness, knowledge, acquisition, skill development, and continuous inductive learning (Lum, 1999). As part of professional development, mental health practitioners seek exposure and experiences that add to their development of a diverse worldview (Sue & Sue, 1999). For those interested in developing cultural competence, the Internet provides an adjunct to traditional learning methods. Available to the professional at the click of a mouse is a massive collection of information regarding other cultures. Culturally isolated mental health professionals can use the borderless matrix of cyberspace to gather information and get exposure to people of other cultures. The stylistic model (McFadden, 1999) provides a comprehensive framework by which the mental health professional can organize cultural resources in cyberspace. This chapter provides direction in how to add the additional tool of cyberspace technology to the mental health professional's repertoire of skills.

In the new millennium, the need for culturally competent mental health professionals includes those who are technologically competent (Rotter, McFadden, Lee, & Jencius, 1999). Both fields, multicultural counseling and technology, are relatively youthful movements in the mental health field. Both paradigms, although not intrinsically connected, will find themselves coalescing in the new millennium as the need for global connectedness increases.

The authors of this chapter suggest that professionals looking to explore technology enter that paradigm with a transcultural framework with which to map cyberspace. The premise of the stylistic model and dimensions expressed by the model gives the mental health professional a robust foundation by which to proceed.

The stylistic model (McFadden, 1999) for transcultural counseling was developed to assist mental health providers in formulating a graphic framework to promote their specific counseling theory and technique. Therefore, this model could be described as eclectic in nature as it allows for numerous approaches to be applied. In order for counselors to advance change and growth in their clients, a clear understanding and acceptance of their own culture is essential. In other words, historical self-understanding is a prelude to comprehending other cultures, particularly in consideration of the broadening of an individual's worldview. McFadden's stylistic model is predicated on this premise and suggests self-reflection, heritage insight, historical linkages, interdependent connections, and individual imagery—all of a cultural nature. Adapting from Cross (1971), such cultural insight could lead individuals to achieving a stage of internalization in which they have inner security, satisfaction with self, great love and compassion for oppressed people, and participation in the community for the purpose of making it better—that is, they have a collectivistic orientation.

STRUCTURE FOR STYLISTIC COUNSELING

The graphic configuration in Figure 6-1 shows a modified frontal view of McFadden's stylistic model (McFadden, 1999) for counseling. It reflects three primary dimensions: cultural-historical, psychosocial, scientific-ideological. These dimensions are designed to facilitate understanding of dynamics that impact on counselor-client interaction, moving through the model in an ascending manner, from cultural-historical through psychosocial, to scientific-ideological. Thus the cubical descriptors are hierarchical in nature.

According to McFadden (1999), the model

- provides foundation for hierarchical movement—vertically, horizontally, and diagonally;
- is composed of a series of cubical descriptors;

Figure 6-1
Stylistic Counseling Model

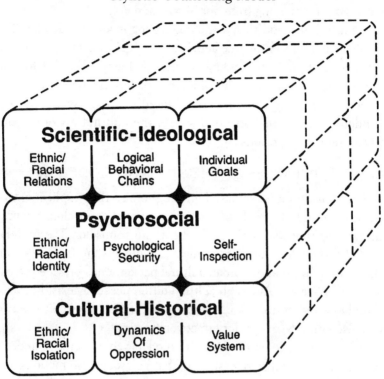

- is universal in its approach as it permeates various segments of society, encompassing all clusters of cultural, ethnic, and racial groups and immigrants;
- proclaims the need to engage minority clients relative to their specific cultural orientation and social perspectives; and
- has implications for use across gender, sexuality, disability, and economic categories.

The foundation of the stylistic model is the cultural-historical dimension. It pertains directly to the history and culture of a given group. Of particular significance is how that nationality, race, ethnic group evolved culturally and what various circumstances impacted them.

The mesodimension, identified as psychosociological, can be defined as that aspect of human behavior that directly impacts on the psychological and sociological development of individuals. It can be noted that there is a variety of stimuli throughout our lives that represent social forces that contribute to our rational or irrational behavior, often emerging from our history and culture.

A third dimension to stylistic counseling is known as scientific-ideological, representing the action phase. It is considered to be the most concrete in transcending cultures and very adaptable for use in cyberspace. The extent by which counselors can determine their effectiveness with this model is related to what extent they ascended vertically or horizontally from the cultural-historical and psychosocial dimensions.

PREMISES OF THE STYLISTIC MODEL

The stylistic model is based on the premise that implications of culture are multilayered and that transactional counseling requires uncovering those layers by both client and counselor. The foundation of the model, the cultural-historical dimension, is founded on the assumption that our broad cultural backgrounds provide the basis for who we are. Although cultural differences may exist between the client and counselor, awareness of parallels between the two can also enhance counselor effectiveness.

Another premise upon which this model is constructed includes a psychosocial dimension, assuming that our social interactions and psychological responses to them are indeed relevant. It is incumbent upon counselors to be familiar not only with the culture of their clients but also with the structure of their thinking and behavior because social paradigms greatly influence individuals and groups.

The third premise for the stylistic counseling model reflects motivations of clients that drive their aspirations toward achievement, action, and fulfillment. This is where counselors and clients develop strategies and solutions. Stylistic counseling on this dimension can be realized as being very effective because of its holistic approach in seeing each client as a unique cultural entity.

Toward advancing premises for the stylistic model, McFadden (1999) has developed a set of 12 principles of stylistic counseling as follows:

1. Stylistic counseling proposes a model for formulating an individual counseling program compatible with the counselor's ori-

entation and conducive to meeting the needs of clients effectively.

2. Stylistic counseling suggests that cubical descriptors of a person's behavior are hierarchical in nature.
3. Stylistic counseling is an approach to helping others that integrates the cultural-historical, psychosocial, and scientific-ideological dimensions of human behavior.
4. Stylistic counseling is an approach to helping others that integrates the cultural-historical base as the foundation for effective helping relationships.
5. Stylistic counseling states that an individual's psychosocial experiences are inherent factors that affect the individual's perception of self and others.
6. Stylistic counseling encourages implementation of an active dimension to the helping professions through clear articulation at the scientific-ideological level.
7. Stylistic counseling requires that the counselor develop a genuine concern and commitment to the client's best interest regardless of cultural differences.
8. Stylistic counseling requires that the counselor develop an ability to open and maintain effective cross-cultural channels of communication.
9. Stylistic counseling requires that the counselor develop the attitude that each client in a counseling situation has a cultural experience unique to the client.
10. Stylistic counseling requires that the counselor develop an active awareness of his or her own attitudes and feelings toward minority individuals and groups.
11. Stylistic counseling requires that the counselor's role become that of an agent and helper within the scope of the client's frame of reference.
12. Stylistic counseling requires that the problem be redefined with emphasis placed on societal responsibility for human dignity and enhancement.

Technology is a new medium that gives counselors access to other cultures and enhances the capability of cultural transcendence. In relationship to the stylistic model, technology can enhance the aforementioned premise of the model. Cyberspace contains resources that can assist counselors in becoming aware of parallels and diversities between the culture of the counselor and client of a different culture. Counselors are free to explore, using the Internet's search resources, a variety of information posted on various ethnic and cultural groups. From these resources the counselor can gain some idea about clients' structure of thinking, incentives for aspiration, and a variety of problems that they confront. Although these experiences are most likely not representative of the intensity or quality of the experience that can be gained by direct contact with a given culture, cyberspace provides another medium by which counselors can increase their multicultural understanding within the premise of the stylistic model.

The stylistic model's three dimensions provide a framework by which to classify cyberspace cultural content. Digital content found in cyberspace could be assessed for the stylistic dimension(s) that it impacts. If the content teaches the counselor about the culture of others, then the content is impacting on the cultural-historical dimension. It is possible to find speeches, essays, and other forms of cultural communication and expression on the Internet to depict this. The content might be described as impacting also on the psychosocial dimension of the stylistic model. Forums that discuss the regional, national, and international environments of a culture are prevalent on the Internet. The recent war in Kosovo with extensive coverage found about the refugee crisis on the Internet is an example of cyberspace action targeting the scientific-ideological dimension of the ethnic Albanians. In this case, the dimensions of the stylistic model had content areas that crossed over into other dimensions. Although the world was transfixed by the immediate plight of the refugees (scientific-ideological), we were also becoming more aware of the cultural-historical aspects of that part of the world.

Cyberspace's potential impact from a stylistic framework is governed to a degree by what information is delivered on the Internet. The Internet has become a viable resource of current information about the world. It is a fluid, ever-changing resource, often without order, censorship, or scholarly academic scrutiny (Wilson, Jencius, & Duncan, 1997). Although it is difficult to assess what cultural information is on the net, some assumptions based on the exposure of this chapter's authors can be implied. Because of the immediacy of information available from the Internet, it appears to emphasize the scientific-ideological dimension of the stylistic model. Perhaps this emphasis is an artifact of the consumer demand for up-to-the-minute information from the Internet. As more and more of the world's culture becomes digital, we can anticipate that the other dimensions of the stylistic model will grow in resource material. In the future we may see more of the psychosocial and the cultural-historic dimensions represented on the Internet. It may be safe to assume that the Internet will only grow larger. Technology will have a greater impact on how we perform our tasks as mental health professionals. In addition, we will continue to progress in the development of the culturally competent counselor. Both paradigms of culture and technology will further converge in the new millennium.

CONVERGING PARADIGMS

The level of development each paradigm brings to the mix will limit the convergence of technology and multicultural counseling. Competencies in multicultural counseling have been developed for the profession (Arredondo et al., 1996) and directly impact the process of counselor education through infusion in training programs. Counselor educators have recently begun to address the need for counselors to develop technology skills that they will use as part of their training in the new millennium. The Association for Counselor Education and Supervision's Technology Interest Network has developed *Recommended Technical Competencies for Counselor Education Students* (ACES, 1999b; see Appendix 2). These 12 competencies are directed at counseling students and establish the first level of technology skills that a counselor may need to be technologically competent. The guidelines are absolutes, in that counselors are expected to master these competencies. The ACES competencies do not take into consideration that technology competency is a developmental process (Rosen & Weil, 1995) but establish expected outcomes from a counselor's education. Jencius (1999) has begun to address the movement of technology skill acquisition to a developmental approach with the technology competencies matrix.

The matrix (available at http://coe.colstate.edu/matrix.htm; see Appendix 4) utilizes the 18 International Society for Technology in Education (ISTE) standards as a guideline for expected outcomes for counselors learning technology (ISTE, 1997). Since ISTE standards have been adopted by the National Council for Accreditation of Teacher Education (NCATE), we should begin to see these standards being woven into counselor education programs. Offsetting the ISTE competency standards in the technology competencies matrix is a developmental axis that uses the stages of skill development proposed by Ivey and Ivey (1999) including identification, basic, active, and teaching mastery. This developmental axis gives the user of the matrix discrete tasks to progress from having no technology skill on an ISTE standard to achieving the ISTE standard fully. Currently, the second author of this chapter is working on a self-assessment, based on the technology competencies matrix, that assists helping professionals in determining areas of growth and strategies to achieve technology competencies.

The helping professions are moving technology to a larger framework by developing standards of practice for web counselors, creating professional association committees, and developing guidelines for on-line instruction. The National Board for Certified Counselors has established *Standards for the Ethical Practice of Web Counseling* (1997b; see Appendix 5). Although the web counseling standards do not address diversity issues directly, the guidelines refer the counselor to the NBCC *Code of Ethics* (1997a), which does address the need for respecting diverse cultures (Sec. A #13). In addition to NBCC setting web counseling standards, the American Counseling Association has established a committee to look at the cybercounseling issue. The committee and this publication, *Cybercounseling and Cyberlearning: Strategies and Resources for the Millennium*, are products of ACA's looking seriously at the use of computers in counselor development. The Association for Counselor Education and Supervision's Technology Interest Network has developed a set of on-line course guidelines (ACES, 1999a; see Chapter 21). These guidelines not only address the need to consider diversity in the aspect of the student taking the course (Guideline 8) but also model acceptance as a way of working as a counselor. Each of these three initiatives moves cybercounseling to a larger framework that will have a direct impact on the training and practice of the multicultural counselor in the new millennium.

With all the emphasis on technology infusion into multicultural counseling, technology is not the great cultural equalizer. We know that there are cultural differences in access to technology and cultural preferences regarding technology. An example of cultural access differences to the Internet is a recent study by the U.S. Department of Commerce, National Telecommunications and Information Administration (NTIA) (1999). The study, entitled *Falling Through the Net: Defining the Digital Divide*, drew attention to the differences in access to the Internet across cultures. According the to the U.S. study, Caucasians are twice as likely to have Internet access as African Americans or Hispanics. Asians/Pacific Islanders are reported to have a higher percentage of their homes accessing the Internet than any other cultural group. Regardless of income level, those living in rural areas lag behind urban areas in Internet access; some urban areas are 50% more likely than rural areas to have access. Brosnan and Wanbil (1998) pointed to differences between the United Kingdom and Hong Kong in attitude and gender responses to computer usage. In the United Kingdom, male survey respondents held more positive attitudes and less anxiety than females. This trend was reversed in Hong Kong respondents. In Durndell, Cameron, Knox, and Stocks (1997), Romanians had far less experience with computers than Scottish students and were also far more positive about using them.

Despite differences in access and attitudinal reactions to computer use, technology holds the possibility of assisting counselors in their own multicultural development. The Internet is a new, rich, fluid medium that allows for global linkages never previously imagined. In the case of the counselor trainee, homogeneity of culture within a specific geographic location restricts access to other cultures. Given the open forum of the Internet, it is possible to connect with people from other cultures in a global manner. Despite the cautions needed in making acquaintances on this Internet, culturally enriching connections are possible. While trying to work the bugs out of an Internet video conference session, the second author of this chapter received a helping hand with the technology from a businessman in Chile. He was kind enough to help with the setup and even pointed his camera out his office window to show a view of his city. This experience may have not been a cultural immersion experience, but it was a serendipitous exposure not easily obtained without the medium of the cyberspace.

The goal of enhancing multicultural understanding in counselors through technology infusion is a legitimate one. Roblyer, Dozier-Henry, and Burdette (1996) suggested goals for students in the classroom that also apply to counselors in training. The goals include making students (counselors) aware of cultures other than their own, creating an interest in communicating with people different from themselves, and teaching that even with the most distant peoples we have more in common than we think. Other goals that Roblyer et al. believed are too ambitious for technology to handle with multicultural education include accepting learning from and appreciating people with different value systems, beliefs, and behaviors. These goals, according to Roblyer et al., require deeper study and interpersonal experiences with other cultures beyond those that Internet contacts can generally provide.

So how do we move from being cultural-techno neophytes to mental health professionals who use cyberspace to augment our cultural transcendence? Morse and Layne's (1997) model *Beyond Chalk* has application in the way it divides learning environments by time and place variables. The traditional classroom is time and place dependent. Counselors have prescribed classes that meet at prescribed times. Moving toward using cyberspace for cultural understanding, the counselor might wish to first explore time-independent/place-dependent digital resources like CD-ROMs. An example of a time-independent/place-dependent digital resource is the National Occupational Information Coordinating Committee's (NOICC) Interactive CD-ROM on Exploring Career Development, which was developed in collaboration with the University of South Carolina's Career Development Training Institute (CDTI, 1995) in a team effort that included this chapter's lead author. The content of this resource can impact the scientific-ideological dimension of the stylistic model. An example of a time-independent resource that can impact the cultural-historical dimension is *Microsoft's Encarta Africana* (1999), an encyclopedia of African American history and culture. Other time-independent/place-dependent resources are listservs and newsgroups. These offer a large spectrum of stylistic dimensional representation that capture individual or multiple dimensions based on their topic content. In addition to time-independent/place-dependent resources are time-dependent/place-independent resources such as scheduled Internet chat rooms and video conferences. These often require some advanced technology skills and planning on the part of the mental health professional. A further learning environment is provided by time-independent/place-independent resources that include those on the World Wide Web, many of which cross multiple stylistic dimensions.

PUTTING IT ALL TOGETHER

So how does the mental health professional interested in developing a culturally competent practice begin to use the Internet? One strategy is for the practitioner to utilize the process for exploring the Internet as suggested by Wilson, Jencius, and Duncan (1997). Cyberspace changes rapidly, and with it many resources change. Thus the strategy presented here is to indicate how to locate the resources, in lieu of simply giving lists of resources. By looking at the various resources on the Internet and by organizing the resources using a stylistic framework, greater exposure to diverse cultures can be obtained. Along with all the possibilities of the Internet comes a word of caution. With the increased possibilities of the Internet come some increased risks. Cyberspace allows for anonymity, and hence some individuals use it to deceive unwary Internet travelers. It is recommended that the mental health professional not divulge information that could cause potential personal risk.

USING E-MAIL

E-mail is most mental health professionals' introduction to cyberspace. Finding others of diverse culture with whom to develop a pen pal relationship is not easy. Given the concerns about deception on the Internet, the use of conventional methods to make initial contact with people before pursuing an e-mail relationship to discuss cultural issues is recommended. Developing professional contacts with people from other cultures and then carrying those relationships onto cyberspace is the preferred strategy. Counselor educators may link students with reliable associates of differing cultures. Mental health practitioners can work with colleagues to link them with reliable contacts among people from other cultures.

Using Newsgroups

The Internet newsgroup is a collection of electronic text posts to a central server that stores the posts and responses in a fashion that allows for public retrieval based on topics. The process is asynchronous, wherein posts to the newsgroup are stored, are available to anyone, and can be responded to by anyone. Newsgroups are organized by topic, and it is from their organizing scheme that most Internet browsers and their mail clients have a configuration for searching and retrieving newsgroups. The first task is to retrieve a list of newsgroups that are related to culture. Simply putting the keyword *culture* in the newsgroup search engine (as part of your news reader) retrieves some 300 newsgroups including alt.culture. African.American.history, alt.culture.us.Hispanics, soc.culture. Iranian, and soc.culture.south-africa. The caveat holds that these newsgroups are open to the public and that thus some posts are interesting, some posts are junk, and some posts are meant to inflame others who have an interest in the group. Nevertheless, by sorting through some of the posts, wonderful information about a culture can be found.

Using Listservs

An Internet listserv is a group of subscribed members around a particular topic that post e-mail to a central site with a copy bounced to every member of the group. Some groups are moderated, and the mail is edited by a listowner before it goes out to the whole group; others are unmoderated, leaving the posts to flow freely. Listservs differ from newsgroups in that newsgroups have all the posts housed at a server and users must retrieve them, but listservs are distributed automatically as part of their software. The easiest way to find lists to which to subscribe is to use the World Wide Web's Liszt search engine at http://www.liszt.com. This mega search engine for Internet lists asks users to enter a keyword, and then gives users listservs that match their keyword. Entering the word *native*, for example, retrieved some 42 lists that matched that keyword. The Liszt search engine then directs users to find more information about the list by sending e-mail to the list's information archive through the listserver. For example, one list retrieved under the *native* search was NATIVE-L, described as being "aboriginal peoples: news and information." Information is included on how to further subscribe to the listserv of your interest.

Using Chat Rooms

Chat rooms are synchronous text-based dialogues between two or more people who are connected by using the same server reflector. There is stand-alone software for using chat rooms and servers dedicated to chat functions, but with the onset of java, script-based chatrooms are being included in a web-based format. Chat rooms are probably the part of cyberspace that draws the greatest amount of controversy. Stories of illegal and illicit cyberrelationships are offset by stories of happy life partners meeting in chat rooms. Brought into question is the larger issue of the genuineness of the relationship, of whether people can have true contact using cyberspace. Using what we grew up with as defining relationships, the Internet does meet the three dimensional in-the-room qualities of those relationships. Given that what we consider to be a relationship has changed over the last millennium, cyber-relationships may be just another shift in how we view human contact. Chat rooms hold the potential for contact with people of other cultures—with the warning that they also hold the potential for abuse. The authors of this chapter recommend that serious mental health professionals wishing to use chat rooms look for some professional affiliation that is sponsoring the chat room as at least the first line of scholarly defense. General chat rooms open to the public often turn into a free-for-all of greetings and innuendos. From a counselor education viewpoint, chat rooms have been used extensively to supplement class meetings and as an economical way to bring outside experts into the classroom (Rotter et al., 1999). Because chat rooms are prevalent and spontaneous in their content and development, one way to find them is to use a WWW browser search for chat. This will generate a site list of chats that are available.

Using Web Sites

Internet Web sites are generally static graphic-based documents with hyperlink capability. Hyperlinks allow for a document at one site to link the user to an unlimited number of other sites. As scripting web pages has become more sophisticated, the web is incorporating more of the content from other cyberspace resources in a web-based format. E-mail, newsgroups, listservs, and chatrooms, including other resources not described here (such as Gopher and FTP), are being incorporated into a web format so mental health professionals seeking to enter cyberspace can do so on one web platform.

The centerpiece of the web is the browser/search engine. As noted earlier, search engines use keywords entered by the user to search and retrieve links to web sites that contain those keywords. Becoming schooled in the use of the Internet browser and a variety of search engines will enhance searches for information that can enhance cultural understanding. Popular search engines include Yahoo at http://www.yahoo.com, Infoseek at http://www.infoseek.com, Northern Lights at http://www.nlsearch.com, Lycos at http://www.lycos.com, and Alta Vista at http://www.altavista.com. Because search engines are portals for many into cyberspace, the creation of search engine sites is booming, so much so that the current generation of search engines include meta-engines. Meta search engines are engines that combine the searches of multiple sites into one search. Popular meta-engines are Dogpile at http://www.dogpile.com, Metacrawler at http://www.metacrawler.com, Internet Oracle at http://www.searchgateway.com, and Savvy Search at http://www.savvysearch.com. Mental health professionals looking to use the web for culture-based resources could provide keywords to such engines and then direct themselves to the web pages of interest. For example, another search for *native* located web-based culture information on Nativeweb: Resources for Indigenous Cultures Around the World at http://www.nativeweb.org. The site contained links to message boards (newsgroups) and links to other indigenous peoples' organizational sites.

Using Video Conferencing

Computer video conferencing is the process of transmitting and receiving simultaneous video and audio across cyberspace using computer cameras and microphones. This is a new technology, and exploring this technology requires some sophistication with the equipment. The process has been used experimentally for distance learning (Rotter et al., 1999) and for studying its efficacy as an adjunct for supervision (Baltimore, Jencius, & Iris, 1999). The authors of this chapter used this technology for the purpose of having the lead author as an invited presenter in the second author's multicultural counseling class. Students responded well to having exposure to an expert and the author of their textbook. As this technology becomes easier to use, the possibilities of linking audio and video for the purpose of joining differing cultures are easier to see.

Cyberspace is not devoid of pitfalls. Mental health professionals need to be aware of issues that limit the use of cyberspace in developing cultural understanding. These issues include

- **limited access:** As mentioned earlier, there is great disparity across cultural groups between those who have access to cyberspace and those who do not. Only a small sample of any particular culture may be reached, and many cultures are not being equally represented in cyberspace.
- **limited scope:** The nature of the information available in cyberspace is limited to that information that someone chooses to submit. It is false to assume that what is in cyberspace is representative of the whole culture.
- **limited contact:** Cyberspace is currently limited in what it can provide toward real contact with cultures. Cyberspace only can act as an adjunct to direct experience with other cultures. Wise mental health professionals will continue actively to seek positive direct experiences with other cultures as part of their development toward multicultural wisdom (Hanna, Bemak, & Chung, 1999).

CONCLUSION

Given the possible connections that cyberspace provides to mental health professionals, how do we begin the process of technology infusion into culturally competent practice? The first suggestion is that mental health professionals need to aspire to be a model for others. Before we can model appropriate use of technology to help in understanding cultures, we need to understand it and practice it ourselves. The second is that we should enter cyberspace with a framework by which to understand cultures. The stylistic model presented in this chapter provides a good framework by which to organize cultural information in cyberspace. Once such a cultural framework is used, we can explore cyberspace using the systematic process described in this chapter, moving from time- and place-dependent strategies to time- and place-independent strategies. A third suggestion is that we keep both feet planted firmly in midair. Cyberspace is a new and fluid environment. Use of scholarly skepticism will aid in discerning the worthy material found on the Internet. A final suggestion is that we seek the support of other colleagues and work cooperatively with other professionals who are exploring the mixing of these two paradigms, cyberspace and culture. Cyberspace provides us with the tools to do such cultural collaboration with colleagues on a worldwide platform.

REFERENCES

Association for Counselor Education and Supervision, Technology Interest Network. (1999a). *Guidelines for on-line instruction in counselor education.* [On-line]. Available: http://www.chre.vt.edu/f-s/thohen/ACESWEB.htm.

Association for Counselor Education and Supervision, Technology Interest Network. (1999b). *Recommended technical competencies for counselor education students.* [On-line]. Available: http://www.chre.vt.edu/f-s/thohen/competencies.htm.

Arredondo, P., Toporek, R., Brown, S., Jones, J., Locke, D. C., Sanchez, J., & Stadler, H. (1996). *Operationalization of the multicultural counseling competencies.* Alexandria, VA: Association for Multicultural Counseling and Development.

Baltimore, M., Jencius, M., & Iris, K. (1999, April). *Supervision and the Internet: Efficacy and uses of video conferencing.* Paper presented at the American Counseling Association 1999 World Conference, San Diego, CA.

Brosnan, M., & Wanbil, L. (1998). A cross-cultural comparison of gender differences in computer attitudes and anxieties: The United Kingdom and Hong Kong. *Computers in Human Behavior, 14*(4), 559–577.

Career Development Training Institute. (1995). *Exploring career development* [CD-ROM]. Columbia: University of South Carolina, Department of Educational Psychology.

Cross, W. E. (1971). Negro-to-Black conversion experience: Toward a psychology of Black liberation. *Black World, 20,* 13–27.

Durndell, A., Cameron, C., Knox, A., & Stocks, R. (1997). Gender and computing: West and East Europe. *Computers in Human Behavior, 13*(2), 269-280.

Encarta Africana [Computer software]. (1999). Redmond, WA: Microsoft.

Hanna, F. J., Bemak, F., & Chung, R. C. (1999). Toward a new paradigm for multicultural counseling. *Journal of Counseling and Development, 77*, 125–134.

International Society for Technology in Education. (1997). *National standards for technology in teacher preparation* [On-line]. Available: http://www.iste.org/Standards/index.html.

Ivey, A., & Ivey, M. B. (1999). *Intentional interviewing and counseling: Facilitating client development in a multicultural society* (4th ed.). Pacific Grove, CA: Brooks/Cole.

Jencius, M. (1999). *Technology competencies matrix* (Columbus State University, College of Education Technology Committee) [On-line]. Available: http://ccp.colstate.edu/jencius/matrix.htm.

Lum, D. (1999). *Culturally competent practice: A framework for growth and action.* Pacific Grove, CA: Brooks/Cole.

McFadden, J. (1999). *Transcultural counseling* (2nd ed.). Alexandria, VA: American Counseling Association.

Morse, L. C., & Layne, R. G. (1997). Beyond chalk: Teaching with technology. In J. A. Chambers (Ed.), *Selected papers from the Eighth National Conference on College Teaching and Learning.* Jacksonville, FL: Florida Community College at Jacksonville.

National Board for Certified Counselors. (1997a). *Code of ethics* [On-line]. Available: http://www.nbcc.org/ethics/nbcc-code.htm.

National Board for Certified Counselors. (1997b). *Standards for the ethical practice of web counseling.* [On-line]. Available: http://www.nbcc.org/ethics/wcstandards.htm.

Roblyer, M. D., Dozier-Henry, O., & Burdette, A. P. (1996, May–June). Technology and multicultural education: The "uneasy alliance." *Educational Technology*, pp. 5–13.

Rosen, L. D., & Weil, M. M. (1995, Fall). Tips for mental health professionals to merge on-line. *Treatment Today*, pp. 48–49.

Rotter, J., McFadden, J., Lee, R., & Jencius, M. (1999, April). *The infusion of technology in counselor education programs.* Paper presented at the American Counseling Association 1999 World Conference, San Diego, CA.

Sue, D. W., & Sue, D. (1999). *Counseling the culturally different: Theory and practice* (3rd ed.). New York: Wiley.

U.S. Department of Commerce, National Telecommunications and Information Administration. (1999, July 8). *Falling through the net: Defining the digital divide* [On-line]. Available: http://www.ntia.doc.gov/ntiahome/fttn99/contents.html.

Wilson, R. F., Jencius, M., & Duncan, D. (1997). Introduction to the Internet: Opportunities and dilemmas. *Counseling and Human Development, 29*(6), 1–16.

7

Cybercounseling and Empowerment: Bridging the Digital Divide

COURTLAND C. LEE

In the United States, the country with the greatest gap in wealth between rich and poor of any industrialized nation, basing the opportunity for quality mental health and educational services on access to the new network technologies is potentially to consign many to marginalization and disenfranchisement. This chapter addresses a major issue that must be considered with respect to cybercounseling: ensuring equal access to counseling and related services via network technologies. A troubling scenario as we enter the 21st century is that those with access to computers and other means of technology are positioned to take advantage of cybercounseling and thereby benefit from quality mental health and related services on-line, while those without such access are at risk for receiving lesser services. This is underscored by recent data from the U.S. Department of Commerce (1999) that revealed that households with incomes of $75,000 and higher are 20 times more likely to have access to the Internet than those at the lowest income levels, and more than 9 times as likely to have a computer at home. Additionally, Whites are more likely to have access to the Internet from home than Blacks or Hispanics have from any location. Significantly, regardless of income level, Americans living in rural areas are lagging behind in Internet access. Indeed, at the lowest income levels, those in urban areas are more than twice as likely to have Internet access than those earning the same income in rural areas.

Given these data, it is imperative that, as cybercounseling continues to evolve as a viable service delivery mode, those professionals who have access to and make extensive clinical and educational use of computers act so that network technology becomes a tool of empowerment, not disenfranchisement. It is also imperative that equal access becomes an integral part of this mode of service delivery.

Guidelines are provided in this chapter for ensuring equal access to the technology for cybercounseling. It starts with some reflections on the traditions of mental health and related professions with respect to power and access. Next, the promise of cybercounseling with respect to human empowerment is considered. The chapter concludes with guidelines to ensure equal access to cybercounseling.

THE TRADITION OF MENTAL HEALTH PROFESSIONS: ISSUES OF POWER AND ACCESS

There is little doubt that mental health and related professions have a distinguished history and tradition of helping individuals solve problems and make decisions related to academic, career, and personal-social issues. The services represented by counseling and related disciplines have proven to be helpful to scores of people. However, it has been passionately argued over the past two decades that the nature of these same professions has been an oppressive and sociopolitical process with respect to large and diverse segments of the population. This argument has been voiced through a number of perspectives including the multicultural (Lee, 1997; Sue & Sue, 1990), the feminist (Cook, 1993; Smith & Siegal, 1985), and the social justice (Katz, 1985; Lewis & Arnold, 1998). The basic argument from these perspectives is that many groups of people are inappropriately served or are underserved in mental health and related systems.

It has been asserted that the scope and practice of mental health and educational professions tend to be gender-, race-, and class-biased. Within the traditions of these professions, the ideal consumer of mental health services tends to belong to the groups in society with the privileges of gender, race, and class. This consumer has often been referred to as the YAVIS (young-attractive-verbal-intelligent-successful) client. This is an individual who, more often than not, has voluntarily sought the services of a mental health professional for help with problem resolution or decision making. Implicit in the profile of such a client is the fact that he (or possibly she) generally has the financial and related resources to access the best possible counseling or other psychoeducational services available.

Large segments of the population have traditionally not fit the so-called YAVIS profile, however. For these people, access to and provision of quality mental health or educational services has been problematic. When these services are considered in culturally, socially, or economically diverse contexts, it has often been the case that service provision is a forced rather than a voluntary experience. This experience is often with an insensitive or unresponsive representative of the vast social welfare system. Unfortunately, the odds are often extremely high that many individuals without a degree of cultural, economic, or social privilege will not have access to quality clinical services. Therefore, rather than being an empowering factor in many people's lives, counseling and related services become disenfranchising. Counseling contributes to further cultural, economic, or social marginalization for scores of client groups.

Given this tradition, as cybercounseling continues to evolve, several intriguing and important questions need to be considered. Will cybercounseling as a therapeutic or educational resource be empowering or disenfranchising? Will cybercounseling be available only to those individuals whose social and economic status and privilege afford them access to the technology for quality cybercounseling? The answers to such questions lie at the very heart of the issue of equal access.

CYBERCOUNSELING AND
THE PROMISE OF HUMAN EMPOWERMENT

Empowerment has become an increasingly popular construct in counseling and education. In counseling it has been defined in the following manner:

Empowerment is the process by which people, organizations, or groups who are powerless or marginalized (a) become aware of the power dynamics at work in their life context, (b) develop the skills and capacity for gaining some reasonable control over their

lives, (c) which they exercise, (d) without infringing on the rights
of others, and (e) which coincides with actively supporting the
empowerment of others in their community. (McWhirter, 1994,
p. 12)

As a tool in this important process, cybercounseling offers the
potential for providing new ways to promote intrapersonal and
interpersonal skills. The computer and its inherent technological
capacity presents an opportunity to provide services to people who
have traditionally been ill-served in counseling in a number of innovative ways. Cybercounseling holds the promise of new ways of
helping people become aware of power dynamics in their lives and
develop new life skills. It also is a potentially potent force in helping groups of people maximize their collective potential.

For example, with computer technology counselors now have the
ability to offer services to areas chronically underserved by mental
health professionals. Sitting at a computer terminal, a counselor in
a large urban area can now offer his or her services to clients
in remote rural areas where social services have historically been
inadequate.

Additionally, cybercounseling holds the potential of affording
clients greater control over choice of the therapeutic setting. An economically disadvantaged inner-city client, for example, may be able
to sit at a computer terminal in his or her own home, a public library,
a school, or a place of worship and interact with a counselor in an office miles away. Rather than having to meet with a counselor in the
often alienating and intimidating confines of the professional office,
the client could engage in the therapeutic process in the comfort and
perceived safety of familiar and validating surroundings.

Such potential for new types of distance relationships via computer technology opens up new vistas for promoting human empowerment at both the intra- and interpersonal level. This is
particularly true for those who have been marginalized due to social
and/or economic circumstances.

Computer technology holds great promise for increasing self-
esteem among those whose life circumstances have impacted negatively on how they have come feel about their self-worth. Likewise,
cybercounseling can be a major vehicle by which clients may be in-

troduced to new academic, career, or personal-social decision-making models. Exposing a client to the World Wide Web, for example, could possibly provide him or her with crucial information vital to an important life decision.

Significantly, the very process of using and potentially mastering computer technology may increase a client's self-efficacy. Developing the competencies to engage as a client in cybercounseling may go a long way to help shape an individual's sense of environmental mastery. This, in and of itself, is potentially empowering for people whose life circumstances have socialized them to be intrapersonally reactive as opposed to proactive.

Similarly, cybercounseling can play a crucial empowering role at the interpersonal level. Computer technology may promote skills in setting boundaries, becoming more assertive, and communicating more effectively.

In addition to empowerment at the individual level, emerging computer technology has great potential at the group level. Cybercounseling may prove to be a potent tool in the process of organizing and educating groups of traditionally disenfranchised clients for social action and systemic change. It has been asserted that problematic client behavior can often be traced to the negative effects of environment on cognitive and affective functioning. Client issues, therefore, are often merely reactions or symptoms to deep-seated problems in the social environments in which people must interact. A counselor, therefore, may need to become an agent of social change and intervene not only at an individual level but at a system-wide level as well. Either in partnership with and/or for clients, a counselor in such a role challenges cultural, social, historical, or economic barriers that stifle optimal mental health and human development. Such a professional should have two important goals in the counseling process: to help clients understand problem causation by recognizing the influence of the social context on human development, and to help empower clients by assisting them in developing and implementing strategies to eliminate or reduce systemic discrimination or oppression in all of its forms (Lee, 1998).

A counselor networked electronically with a group of educated and organized, hence empowered, clients represents a potent force to combat marginalizing and oppressive forces. Imagine helping to educate economically disadvantaged women and men about changes in welfare laws and then organizing them to make their voices heard in state legislatures about how those changes could negatively effect their ability to care for their children via a listserv and by collecting background information from the World Wide Web!

The potential of technological networking for human empowerment is predicated on the assumption that computer hardware and software are universally accessible. However, this is currently not the case. Social and economic disparities exclude many individuals from access to the important technology that makes cybercounseling a reality. Counselors and related professionals, therefore, face a challenge: ensuring that cybercounseling does not become a part of the tradition of socioeconomic bias and cultural privilege that has often unequally stratified the scope and quality of mental health and educational services.

Ethical practice dictates that counselors provide for equal access to computer applications in counseling services. To do less will be condoning or engaging in discrimination against those whose social or economic status preclude ready access to computer technology (see the ACA *Code of Ethics and Standards of Practice*, 1997). The next section provides guidelines for ensuring equal access to the network technologies for cybercounseling.

GUIDELINES FOR CYBERCOUNSELING: ENSURING EQUAL ACCESS

In discussing guidelines for equal access to cybercounseling, this mode of psychoeducational intervention must be viewed from a broader perspective. Efforts to ensure such access should be guided by some basic interconnected principles. First, cybercounseling should be considered merely one of a variety of service delivery modes. Second, used ethically, and possibly in conjunction with more traditional forms of intervention, this methodology can potentially enhance a professional's ability to meet the needs of clients. Third, regardless of cultural, economic, or social background, it is important to remember that cybercounseling is not for every client.

Guided by these principles, counselors and their colleagues in related professions will have to step out of their traditional roles and become advocates for social action to ensure equal access to cybercounseling (Casey, 1998). The following guidelines are closely linked and focus on the goal of providing equal access to computer applications in counseling and related services.

- **Community audit:** Counselors should conduct an audit of their community, assess where the digital divide exists, and investigate which individuals or potential client groups have limited or no access to computer technology.

- **Partnerships:** Following an audit, counselors should form consultative relationships with key players in their community that could partner with each other to make technology hardware and software available to those with limited access. These players might include schools, community organizations, and selected businesses. For example, a counselor might consult with a computer firm and work with them on initiatives to make hardware, software, and educational/technical assistance available pro bono to schools, religious institutions, or other centers of community activity in economically disadvantaged areas.

- **Education:** When necessary, and as appropriate, counselors should help clients and/or potential clients develop the competencies necessary to take advantage of cybercounseling. The acquisition of the awareness, knowledge, and skills for computer literacy should be incorporated into educational or career exploration and planning.

- **Governmental advocacy:** In order to ensure equal access to computer technology, a supportive policy framework is needed at all levels of government. Legislation and government policies must be sensitive to social and economic inequities with respect to network technologies. Counselors should advocate at all levels of government, therefore, to raise awareness and increase legislative involvement to ensure that crucial network technology is available to all. Socioeconomic status should not automatically exclude people from access to technology that, in large measure, has become basic to a decent quality of life. For example, counselors may need to work to ensure that laws and policies regarding Internet access do not become exclusive to those individuals with the financial resources to take advantage of such services.

CONCLUSION

As helping professions enter the 21st century and nascent network technologies realize their full potential as therapeutic and educational modalities, it is an ethical and moral imperative that the digital divide be bridged. It is important that those in counseling and related fields take active steps to ensure that cybercounseling is available to all clients regardless of their social or economic status. The issues of access and privilege that have traditionally divided client populations into the "haves" and the "have nots" must not be allowed to stifle the vast clinical and educational potential of network technology. All people who seek help, regardless of their demographic realities, should be able to find the on ramp to the information superhighway.

REFERENCES

American Counseling Association. (1997). *ACA code of ethics and standards of practice*. Alexandria, VA: Author.

Casey, J. (1998). Technology: A force for social action. In C. C. Lee & G. R. Walz (Eds.), *Social action: A mandate for counselors* (pp. 199–212). Alexandria, VA: American Counseling Association and ERIC Counseling and Student Services Clearinghouse.

Cook, E. P. (Ed.). (1993). *Women, relationships, and power: Implications for counseling*. Alexandria, VA: American Counseling Association.

Katz, J. H. (1985). The sociopolitical nature of counseling. *Counseling Psychologist, 13*, 615–624.

Lee, C. C. (Ed.). (1997). *Multicultural Issues in counseling: New approaches to diversity* (2nd ed.). Alexandria, VA: American Counseling Association.

Lee, C. C. (1998). Counselors as agents of social change. In C. C. Lee & G. R. Walz (Eds.), *Social action: A mandate for counselors* (pp. 3–14). Alexandria, VA: American Counseling Association and ERIC Counseling and Student Services Clearinghouse.

Lewis, J. A., & Arnold, M. S. (1998). From multiculturalism to social action. In C. C. Lee & G. R. Walz (Eds.), *Social action: A mandate for counselors* (pp. 51–65). Alexandria, VA: American Counseling Association and ERIC Counseling and Student Services Clearinghouse.

McWhirter, E. H. (1994). *Counseling for empowerment*. Alexandria, VA: American Counseling Association.

Smith, A. J., & Siegal, R. F. (1985). Feminist therapy: Redefining power for the powerless. In L. B. Rosewater & L.E.A. Walker (Eds.), *Handbook of feminist therapy* (pp. 242–249). New York: Springer.

Sue, D. W., & Sue, D. (1990). *Counseling the culturally different: Theory and practice* (2nd ed.). New York: Wiley.

U.S. Department of Commerce, National Telecommunications and Information Administration. (1999). *Falling through the net: Defining the digital divide.* Washington, DC: U.S. Government Printing Office [On-line]. Available: http://www.ntia.doc.gov/ntiahome/fttn99/contents.html.

8

Coping With Loss and Grief Through On-Line Support Groups

JUNEAU MAHAN GARY AND LINDA REMOLINO

The death of a loved one is a natural and inevitable life experience. Those who must cope with the loss of a loved one experience a wide variety of grief reactions that are normal and expected,
yet difficult and painful to experience. The grief reactions encompass psychological, physical, and social aspects of a person's life
(Rando, 1988).

Typically, people discuss their grief reactions and their passage
through the phases of grief (although they generally do not label the
reactions or phases as such) with someone they know or do not discuss their grief reactions at all. Discussing reactions with good listeners who have "been there" enables people to resolve issues and
complete the grief process, thus paving the way for healing, rather
than suffering in silence and suppressing feelings. Empathic listeners with words of encouragement and an accepting approach can
improve the griever's clarity of thought and encourage creative
problem-solving abilities that promote healing (Fleming, 1990).

What happens to the griever, though, after the empathic listeners
have helped as much as they can or have implicitly communicated
that the grieving period should be over and that life must go on?
The griever can join a traditional, face-to-face support group or join
an on-line support group. Current computer technology now enables people to discuss issues of grief and loss with others as well as
exchange information, resources, and services from the comfort of

their homes through on-line support groups. On-line support groups can provide a level of safety, control, comfort, and anonymity for members to share their stories, pain, and healing with others in a public forum that is also private because members converse with each other from their homes or from other safe places such as a library computer terminal. In the United States, support groups, either traditional or on-line, are one of the few places where grief can be expressed openly and publicly (Golden, 1999).

This chapter first looks at the grief and healing process and at the on-line support groups available to ease the process. The chapter then examines one such support group. Discussions of the ability to provide immediate responses to traumatic events as well as other benefits and limitations of on-line support groups conclude the chapter.

GRIEF AND HEALING

The grief process is typically a nonlinear, repetitive, and painful process to transcend. It involves adaption to many changes over time, is marked by repetitive cycles of progression followed by stagnation or regression, yet is necessary to complete in order for the griever to heal. The ultimate goal in completing the grief process is to confront grief reactions and to adapt to change. Many authors have proposed various phases of grief that the griever must transcend, but in general, there are three broad phases of grief: avoidance, confrontation, and reestablishment (Rando, 1988).

Grieving is generally perceived as an emotional process that involves feelings, thoughts, and attitudes. In addition to the emotional aspect of grief, there are also the physical and behavioral aspects, culminating in the three aspects of grief (Rando, 1988):

- **Psychological/emotional reactions** include fear, anxiety, loss of faith, disbelief, depression, guilt, confusion, search for meaning, despair, relief, hallucinations, dreams/nightmares, lack of concentration, and anger.
- **Physical/health symptoms** include changes in eating and/or sleep patterns, weight increase or decrease, crying, fatigue, increased risk for illness, muscle weakness, and oversensitivity to noise.

• **Behavioral responses** include diminished interest in usual activities, acting out, and withdrawal from and/or rejection of support systems.

The griever is often assisted through the grief and healing process by his or her support system, but ultimately the griever must complete the journey alone. Others can and do help, but they may be unaware of the type and extent of emotional support needed, may be limited by myths about grief and death, may be afraid to express their own feelings, may be uncomfortable listening to the expression of feelings by others, or may experience familial or cultural taboos about open discussions about grief or death. The griever may need to turn to support groups for acceptance and understanding.

Traditional support groups are effective in assisting many people to express feelings and improve coping strategies, but they also have obstacles that limit their efficacy. They usually require that services be available in the member's geographic area, that everyone convene at the same time, that issues of cultural stigmatization and social status about seeking support external to the family be resolved so as not to interrupt attendance, that membership fees be paid (which may be prohibitive for some), that obstacles (such as being housebound due to physical, medical, or caregiver limitations) be overcome, or that transportation arrangements be made (Weinberg, Uken, Schmale, & Adamek, 1995). Although face-to-face support groups help many, they are not a panacea.

ON-LINE SUPPORT

Many on-line support groups are perceived by their members as being helpful, validating, and supportive (Spinney, 1995; Weinberg, Schmale, Uken, & Wessel, 1995; Weinberg, Uken, et al., 1995; Zinn, Simon, & Orme, 1997), although current research on the efficacy of on-line support groups is limited. An on-line support group for loss helps to reduce members' feelings of isolation and their sense of feeling overwhelmed, which are common reactions during the grieving process. Participation also gives members the opportunity to review their lives, complete unfinished business, "let go," reconcile relationships with others, work through the phases of grief, and move on as they reenter daily life (Rando, 1988). Weinberg, Uken, et al. (1995) noted the importance of having members who are in different phases of coping ability in order to maximize group support. Members in an early phase of grief can share their anxieties while members in a later phase can offer support and problem solving. In addition to the favorable reactions of members to on-line support groups, Weinberg, Uken, et al. (1995) identified three of Yalom's (1995) therapeutic factors (i.e., instillation of hope, group cohesion, and universality) as contributing to an on-line support group's perceived helpfulness.

On-line support groups are a relatively new and growing component of the larger field of cyberservices for mental health. On-line support groups can be accessed through use of a computer and modem in conjunction with comprehensive Internet service providers (ISPs), such as Prodigy, America-On-Line (AOL), and CompuServe, through Internet portals (e.g., Yahoo) or through specific web sites (e.g., www.death-dying.com). Table 8-1 provides a sample of web sites for loss and grief issues. Kotecki and Chamness (1999) have offered a tool to evaluate the quality of web sites. Each comprehensive ISP, portal, or web site sets its own standards regarding training of hosts, crisis management, regulations, disclaimers, quality control, and procedures.

On-line support groups are based on the tenets of traditional support groups. Both types of support groups encourage members to express concerns, emotions, and ideas; offer advice and support; ask questions; and share information in an anonymous setting. On-line support groups offer many features of traditional support groups (Weinberg, Uken, et al., 1995), but do so using cybercommunities or chat rooms in which people participate in self-help and support groups. Like traditional support groups, on-line support groups can range from serving as one therapeutic component of a comprehensive mental health system to serving as the sole support system.

In particular, on-line support groups for loss assist members in facing the void left by the loss of a loved one. Support is offered as members adjust to significant changes and major stressors in their lives. Facing holidays and special occasions are considered difficult for most members, especially if this will be their first occasion or holiday since the loss of a loved one (Weinberg, Schmale, Uken, &

Table 8-1
Sample of Web Sites for Loss and Grief

www.azsids.org	www.kn.pacbell.com
www.crisissupport.org	www.ourhouse-grief.org
www.death-dying.com	www.petloss.com
www.evergreenhealthnet.org	www.rc.net
www.familiesandsurvivors.com	www.rivendell.org
www.grief.org.au	www.seattlewidowed.com
www.griefsupport.org	www.shiningsouls.com
www.growthhouse.org	www.survivingsorrow.org
www.hospicenwo.org	www.taps.org
www.infomrt.com	www.webhealing.com
www.inforamp.net	www.worldmemorial.com

Wessel, 1996). Likewise, those who are terminally ill and/or their loved ones face similar anxieties if they anticipate that approaching holidays and special occasions may be the last ones they celebrate together.

A GLIMPSE INSIDE ONE ON-LINE SUPPORT GROUP FOR LOSS

This section contains a description of the experiences of one of this chapter's authors who hosts an on-line support group for loss issues. Most members focus on grief issues, including death from a terminal illness or coping with the death of a loved one. Members correspond anonymously using contrived screen names (i.e., pseudonyms) and receive immediate feedback, support, advice, and/or information. They take turns communicating with each other in a manner similar to a face-to-face support group. In spite of the lack of physical interaction and the lack of nonverbal communication among members in on-line support groups, limited expressions of emotions are conveyed symbolically, visually, and in shorthand as illustrated in Table 8-2. Members can communicate with the whole room or converse with an individual as others follow the dialogue on their computer screens.

This on-line support group for loss is in real time, is text based, and meets for 1 hour per week at a specific time. The scheduled

Table 8-2
Cybershorthand and Symbolic Expression of Emotions

Emotions	Symbols
Frown	:(and ☹
Hug to others	{{{{{{}}}}}}
Hug to the entire room	{{{{{room}}}}}
Hug and kiss	{}&**
Smile	:) and ☺
Shorthand	**Symbols**
Cursing	&!$#*%
Laughing out loud	LOL
Long time, no see	LTNS
Yelling	Capitalize word (e.g., he HATES that)

meeting time encourages consistent participation. Most members attend regularly while a few attend intermittently. Well-established and stable on-line support groups can create a sense of community as well as create lasting and intimate relationships with others whom they will never meet face-to-face, yet from whom they can seek support in times of despair and isolation. The bonds of this cybercommunity can become so intense in on-line support groups for loss that in extenuating circumstances a private session can be arranged. In one example, two members, both in the final stages of terminal illnesses, requested that the host facilitate their final and private good-byes.

Hosts, sometimes called community leaders, are resource persons, rather than on-line counselors or mental health experts. Counseling, as in e-counseling, is not permitted because a human services degree is not a requirement to host. Hosts use human relations skills to assist members to express feelings, and they disseminate information. Training for hosts is described at the end of this section. As a resource person, the host makes referrals to helplines, hospice services, books, cassettes/CDs, crisis centers, other on-line support groups, traditional support/self-help groups, and/or mental health web sites. Most hosts are not paid, but some are compensated with free ISP services.

Prior to each session, the host selects a specific topic designed to promote intimate dialogues and self-disclosure. The quality of each session is different and is based on the composition of the group, each member's grief reactions, relevance of the topic, and members' pressing issues. At times, members' needs may differ from the preselected topic, and the host must be flexible in order to meet the group's immediate needs. Topics discussed in typical sessions include phases of grief, death of a child, predominant emotions during each phase of grief, helping caregivers to assist aging and/or ailing parents or other relatives, physical changes during grieving, issues of terminal illness, helping others through the grieving process, and helping grieving children. The excerpt included here represents a typical session from the on-line support group for loss hosted by one of the authors of this chapter. In this session, members are discussing coping with an approaching holiday season. It illustrates the types of experiences shared by members and demonstrates the individual and group support and expressions of emotion within an anonymous environment. Sessions are fast paced and sometimes contain grammatical and spelling errors. The session has been edited for ease of comprehension. What follows is what members see on their individual computer screens:

Host:	*Welcome to our chat! Join us as we discuss the losses in our lives.*
Question:	Would you like me to go over some tips for getting through the holiday season?
Member 1:	Yes, please.
Member 2:	Yes, host, please do.
Member 3:	Yes.
Member 4:	Yes, I seem to have lost my coping skills.
Host:	*Understand your grief; you have to be ready for the holidays . . . Accept that they will be hard and you will feel your loss . . .*
Member 1:	The support that I used to have . . . it's gone . . . comfort is gone . . . I've isolated myself for years.
Member 3:	Member 1, you have us . . . we're support for you.

Member 5:   {{{{{{{{{Member l}}}}}}}}}}

Member 6:   I found that just getting out at Christmas and giving of yourself and getting involved comforts me. . . .

Host: *Consider this . . . Are all the traditions you celebrate during the holidays really traditions or just things that you've done in a certain way that really hold no significance for you? This may be a good time to give that some thought. . . . Can you change anything? Maybe it would help.*

Member 2:   Well, I don't do anything traditional so that I am not taken back to ugly times.

Member 6:   Nothing specifically traditional, just flow with it. . . .

Member 7:   I can't change...family doesn't know my grief.

Host: *Prepare yourself for the holidays by taking an extra effort to take care of you! Pamper yourself; do some "selfish things" . . . . be gentle with you!*

Member 1:   That's good.

Member 5:   Sometimes I find that I have to just put my feelings aside and just go on.

Member 3:   For now . . . I've been renting a lot of movies that hold my attention and eating only my favorite foods and I try to find things that make me laugh . . . I've been doing a lot of laughing. . . . I find this really healing.

Host: *Laughter is great medicine :)*

Member 6:   I can't laugh, I can't cry either, I feel numb.

Host: *Numbness is a very normal part of the grieving process. . . . {{{{{{Member 6}}}}}}}*

Member 2:   {{{{{{Member6}}}}}}}

Member 3:   I can relate, Member 6.

Host: *A neat idea . . . How about celebrating the life of the one who you've lost? . . . Create a treasure box?*

Member 7:   How host?

Member 6:   You've got my interest.

Member 1:   Can you explain host?

Host: *A treasure box is a box that you get from the grocery store. Decorate it with wrapping paper. Have each member of the family write down two or three of their best memories of the loved one. Put the remembrances in an envelope and put it into the box. Place a keepsake that you have of that person in the box too. Don't share anything yet! Designate a certain time of the day of your holiday to all gather around the box. Withdraw them one by one and share with the group. Save the funniest ones for the last and this will be a heart-rending experience. You can be assured of ending it with some laughter.*

Member 2: Hey, I like that.

Member 3: Just the thought of it is making me cry :(

Member 6: I want to be strong again :((

Host: {{{{{{{Member 3}}}}}}

Member 5: {{{{{Member 3 & Member 6}}}}} you will be again. . . .

Host: *Remember tears are liquid emotion . . . they are healing . . . it's okay to cry . . . you are watering the flowers in your soul.*

Member 8: Host, I would then water the flowers of more than my soul, I could sustain a rainforest LOL.

Member 7: Me too.

Member 9: I don't know how to get there . . . I can't cry . . . I want to . . . maybe something is wrong with me. . . .

Host: *Please always remember that there is no time limit on grief . . . everyone grieves in their own way and in their own time frame.*

Host: {{{{{{{{{Room}}}}}}}}}

Member 10: Do you have to do the treasure box just during the holidays or can you do it . . . Like at birthdays or anniversaries . . .?

Host: *It can be done anytime that you wish . . .*

Member 2: I don't think I can do it. . . . I'm not there yet.

Member 3: Maybe someday I can. . . .

Hosts are selected without regard for professional credentials because they are not offering counseling services. Although some hosts are human services specialists, others are not. Prospective hosts are screened on-line to determine their interpersonal skills and their ability to facilitate group discussion. Once selected, hosts are trained on-line. AOL's training of hosts, for example, consists of the Virtual Leaders Academy and Community Leaders College. Training stresses group facilitation skills, computer literacy, and enforcement of an AOL Terms of Service agreement. Training modules focus, for example, on the role of the host, crisis management, chat room behavior, and referral skills. Training is completed on-line and follows a prescribed and sequential list of courses. Each course is scheduled for 2 to 3 hours and concludes with an examination. Experienced hosts mentor newly trained hosts before they host alone. Continuing education on-line is required every 6 months and is monitored by a volunteer training coordinator.

Hosts ensure that communication remains focused on the topic and that ground rules—such as (1) remain anonymous, (2) take turns, (3) remain focused on the topic, (4) abstain from harassment (e.g., personal criticism, cursing, or name calling), and (5) maintain confidentiality—are observed. Violators of the ground rules can be sanctioned. Although violators are rare in on-line support groups for loss, violators are a common nuisance in other types of on-line support groups (e.g., Adult Children of Alcoholics—ACOA—or open chats for general mental health issues). Violator sanctions vary by ISP. Each ISP's Terms of Service contract outlines appropriate on-line behavior and explains how violations are handled.

IMMEDIATE RESPONSE TO GRIEF ON-LINE

Traumatic events that were once considered local dramas acquire national and international significance as a result of instant and extensive news coverage. Extensive media coverage of events such as the numerous school shootings and their resulting deaths between 1997 and 1999 illustrates this point. These traumatic events produced a range of emotional reactions in victims and television viewers, including anger, anxiety, depression, and fear. Noteworthy is the role that the Internet is playing in helping people to cope immediately with tragedies involving death such as the recent school shootings. For instance, many ISPs immediately responded by establishing on-line support groups devoted specifically to a school shooting. People went on-line to try to understand the numerous school shootings, to reach out to others, to learn how to make schools safe, to cope with school violence, to handle grief reactions, and to recognize danger signs of violence in high-risk youth.

AOL, for instance, responded to the Columbine High School shootings by offering an immediate service that included dialogues with grief specialists to help people cope following the shootings. Specifically, in the afternoon and evening of the shootings, AOL News sponsored two 90-minute Live News Chats. An AOL News moderator queried participants and posed their questions in text-based format through the Internet to grief specialists in other states, including one of the authors. Participants were able to read the responses of the grief specialists and pose additional questions. At this early stage of the unfolding tragedy, questions tended to be informational (i.e., seeking answers), and comments tended to be emotional and typically expressed anger and denial (i.e., "it shouldn't happen in a place like this"). Because the tragedy was occurring during the Live News Chats, AOL News provided visual news bulletins simultaneously.

Once the shock wore off and the grieving began, on-line support groups were overwhelmed in the days and weeks following many of the school shootings. New members, either from the local area of the shootings or from among television viewers, joined veteran on-line support group members to seek support and to express anger, outrage, and other emotions. Dialogues were strained, and many members seemed to experience inhibition when disclosing intimate feelings. The sessions required strong facilitation skills by the host to encourage participation. Perhaps the strain was partially due to numbness caused by the current trauma, new members' lack of familiarity with the mechanics of on-line support groups, awkwardness about the on-line support group interactive process, or feeling overwhelmed by the wide range of emotions expressed on-line. For veteran on-line support group members who were already coping with a loss, the school tragedies or other traumatic news events can resurrect previous and unresolved loss issues and unrelated grief issues.

BENEFITS OF ON-LINE SUPPORT GROUPS FOR LOSS

The benefits of on-line support groups as they address the issues of loss and grief include increased access, the ability to meet specialized needs, and universality.

On-line support groups for loss bring support and camaraderie to people for many reasons and in different ways. Although everyone will face a loss or will grieve the death of a loved one, such intimate and honest dialogues and expressions of grief can be stigmatizing. Relatives and neighbors may be overwhelmed and avoid the subject, pushing the frustrated and grieving person into isolation. Loss support groups validate each member's feelings and facilitate an open and intimate discussion. Furthermore, they are an alternative to traditional support groups and enable people to seek support from a variety of perspectives when feeling vulnerable, when in need of a great deal of support, or when relatives, friends, and the local community are unable to offer support.

On-line support groups reduce the sense of isolation and loneliness, a predominant reaction for most people in the midst of the grief process. Moreover, they offer support for those who reside in underserved locations, for those who are housebound, for those seeking anonymity, or for those who might otherwise grieve alone and not seek a face-to-face support group or support person (Finn, 1996; Spinney, 1995; Weinberg et al., 1996).

SPECIALIZED ON-LINE SUPPORT GROUPS

Some loss groups may need to be age- and/or gender-specific or focus on specific needs or characteristics of loss (Koocher, 1996). Specialized on-line support groups can be formed more successfully than traditional support groups that are limited by geographic boundaries. Possible topics could include death of a child, needs of survivors of homicide or suicide, death or incapacitation from a school shooting, and spiritual or cultural issues of death. Hosts, with a professional expertise in a specific issue of loss, could facilitate these on-line support groups to discuss specialized issues and concerns.

Teens and children may need age-specific groups in order to discuss loss issues based on their maturational level (Bacon, 1996; Koocher, 1996). They may be encountering their first experience with death without a frame of reference or with limited coping skills. Moreover, they may be uncomfortable seeking help from adults or may be unable to relate to adult issues about loss in adult on-line support groups. Similarly, adults may encounter difficulty helping teens and children cope with grief. In the school shootings, for instance, teens and adolescents were directly confronted with death and mortality. Teens in other schools not directly impacted by a school shooting have gone on-line to express fear about the implications of the school shootings and concern about the possibility of violence occurring in their own schools.

A youth can access on-line support groups as long as a parental security block has not been imposed. The parents, however, should be aware of their child's Internet use and should be encouraged to capitalize on the youth's participation in on-line support groups to strengthen communication within the family.

In response to the needs of teens, On-Line Psych (through AOL), for example, has trained teens as peer hosts. However, they tend to focus on developmental issues that teens face, such as individuation and separation, rather than on loss issues in particular. Very mature teens might co-host teen on-line support groups for loss, offering teen members an alternative to talking to parents, teachers, or counselors. Most importantly, teens need someone with whom they can communicate honestly and openly about their fears, concerns, and mortality.

UNIVERSALITY AS A CURATIVE FACTOR

Others struggle, too, and this is not always evident to grieving people who tend to isolate themselves. Universality unites people as they share similar thoughts, feelings, fears, and/or reactions (Yalom, 1995) with their cybercommunity. As people share and support others, they realize that grief is normal, they feel validated, and they heal as they complete the grief process.

LIMITATIONS OF ON-LINE SUPPORT GROUPS FOR LOSS

Limitations include anonymity breaches, differing stages and phases, difficulties in crisis management, hoax perpetration, limited feedback, and unanswered ethical and legal concerns.

ANONYMITY BREACHES

Members must consider the risks of a breach in anonymity before joining an on-line support group and are advised to limit the disclosure of personal and identifying information during the registration process. In spite of computer security procedures, anonymity and confidentiality can be breached and dialogues may be intercepted (Lee, 1998; Newman, 1997).

The host should take steps to ensure the anonymity of each on-line support group member as well as the confidentiality of group dialogue by discouraging the exchange of identifying information. Grieving members who are often lonely and feel isolated or desperate may attempt to continue conversations with specific members at the conclusion of an on-line support group session. Personal communication between members without a host facilitating is discouraged as it can culminate in the exchange of identifying information, thus placing a vulnerable member at risk for cyberstalking as well as at risk for his or her physical safety and privacy. Additionally, the host fosters anonymity by sending referral and other requested information to a member's e-mail address rather than to a residence.

For most on-line support group members, anonymity is preferred. It enables them to discuss personal issues and ideas that they would not talk about with someone who knew them. For men in particular, anonymity provides a vehicle to discuss their personal feelings because they may not consider it "the thing to do" or the male way to handle problems (Spinney, 1995). For reticent adolescents, Zimmerman (1987) found that on-line communication among adolescent group members tended to be more expressive and more intimate in comparison to face-to-face adolescent group communications.

Differing Stages of Group Development and Phases of Grief

On-line support groups for loss are open continuously to new membership. Fluctuations in membership, which occur in face-to-face support groups as well, make it difficult for on-line support groups to maintain the working stage of group development for extended periods (Corey & Corey, 1997). Group cohesion is also diluted by each member's individual grief reactions, resulting in a diverse membership that needs support throughout the grief process. These limitations reduce the efficacy of on-line support groups as a sole support source for some members. On-line support groups can be an additional support within a comprehensive human services support system for those members who are vulnerable or need additional assistance.

Difficulties in Crisis Management

The successful resolution of an emotional crisis in cyberspace is a challenge. Issues of limited feedback and the lack of identifying information complicate the assessment and referral process, making a referral difficult and awkward, especially when the host is unaware of the member's geographic location and specific needs. In the case of suicide ideation, for instance, crisis referral in cyberspace may necessitate that the host instruct the member to disconnect from the on-line support group and dial 9-1-1.

In on-line support groups for loss, members tend to build a sense of community through the sharing of grief and the support extended to each other. They tend to be sensitive and supportive in crises by expressing concern for and anxiety about each other when a member uncharacteristically alters established behavior patterns on-line and may have been hospitalized or have expired. The host must remain alert to such crises and to other transitional issues as they relate to terminal illness, suicidal thoughts (which can reflect a desire to join a deceased loved one), or death.

Hoaxes

People with unscrupulous motives can deceive an on-line support group. Loss on-line support groups, in particular, do not attract many hoaxes. The reverent respect for loss may be one explanation; another may be the heightened awareness of the violator's own mortality. Hoaxes tend to occur because members are anonymous and lack an emotional commitment to the cybercommunity. Hoaxes are most commonly perpetrated by new members, and they are most obvious when a member expresses horrific or multiple losses or unbelievable experiences (however, on occasion, such experiences or losses are truthful). In a hoax, details are usually scarce and inconsistencies emerge. An experienced host may suspect a ruse but be unable to decipher the truth. The host should continue to support the member while listening for inconsistencies before confronting and referring the violator to the ISP Terms of Service agreement. ISPs typically lack strong consequences to punish the violator, other than placing limits upon the violator's ISP services in order to enforce appropriate behavior.

LIMITED FEEDBACK

Spinney (1995) observed that on-line support groups enable members to "hide" emotionally and interpersonally behind computer screens. The absence of face-to-face contact obscures vocal intonations and verbal and nonverbal cues, including body language and expressions of emotion. Although a member may initially feel uncomfortable with limited emotional and visual feedback, such discomforts may, in time, be overcome. Those with cultural or familial barriers that inhibit open discussions about death or emotional expressions of grief, or those with interpersonal difficulties, may perceive decreased intimacy, reduced intensity, and less personal feedback as an incentive to participate in an on-line support group. They may not feel pressured to take personal and interpersonal risks as they might in face-to-face support groups (Weinberg, Schmale, et al., 1995). Moreover,

> seeing your problems expressed as words typed on a computer screen can be therapeutic in itself. . . . There is no small talk. Somebody will come straight in and say "I'm feeling like crap, I want to die, tell me why I shouldn't." (Spinney, 1995, p. 38)

The lack of interpersonal pressure may increase self-confidence and self-disclosure, thereby helping members to help themselves and each other.

ETHICAL AND LEGAL CONCERNS

The hosting of and participation in on-line support groups raise some ethical and legal questions that currently remain unanswered. Jurisdiction is unclear and confusing because on-line support groups function without regard to geographic borders or local or national laws, making traditional mechanisms of resolution unsatisfactory for legal liability, dispute resolution, discipline, and other human services issues (Drucker, 1990; Lee, 1998; Spinney, 1995). Some questions to consider include the following:

- Should volunteer hosts, who may or may not be human services specialists, be required to comply with mental health mandatory reporting statutes (e.g., suspected or acknowledged child abuse) or with duty-to-warn statutes?
- How should these mental health statutes be enforced in cyberspace when there are no geographic boundaries or cyberspace governing agencies?
- Could an on-line support group member seek redress from an incompetent host if the host is anonymous to members?

Future revisions of mental health laws and ethical standards should include cyberspace mental health services and on-line support groups. Revisions will require the inclusion of all human services disciplines and national and international perspectives regarding standards, role, training, monitoring, and supervision of human services and nonprofessional hosts. Special attention should be given to enforcement issues in cyberspace (Bloom, 1997; Lee, 1998).

CONCLUSION

Death and the grieving process affect people directly and indirectly, in a myriad of ways, as the result of events ranging from the death of a relative or friend to a tragedy such as a school shooting. On-line support groups provide an alternative to traditional support groups by linking grieving people who seek support, especially if support is not available in their local community. Furthermore, on-line support groups can reduce the sense of isolation caused by geographical or physical/medical constraints and increase feelings of validation. Although preliminary research on the efficacy of on-line support groups suggests positive effects, on-line support groups are not appropriate for everyone and should not be considered a panacea. Some members may need additional medical and/or human services assistance as they progress through the grieving process.

This chapter has examined the function of one on-line support group for loss as well as discussed the benefits and limitations. On-line support groups and mental health web sites are viable and appropriate referral sources for those experiencing grief and other types of emotional distress. When the effective use of on-line support groups is understood and incorporated within the human services profession, human services specialists, talk show hosts, media health correspondents, and morticians will be able to recommend on-line support groups as easily as they promote counseling, traditional support groups, self-help books, CDs, and cassettes.

REFERENCES

Bacon, J. (1996). Support groups for bereaved children. In C. Corr & D. Corr (Eds.), *Handbook of childhood death and bereavement* (pp. 285–304). New York: Springer.

Bloom, J. (1997). NBCC web counseling standards. *Counseling Today, 40*(5), 6.

Corey, M., & Corey, G. (1997). *Groups: Process and practice* (5th ed.). New York: Brooks/Cole.

Drucker, S. (1990). Legal and ethical implications of mediated therapeutic communication. In G. Gumpert & S. Fish (Eds.), *Talking to strangers: Mediated therapeutic communication* (pp. 200–213). Norwood, NJ: Ablex.

Finn, J. (1996). Computer-based self-help groups: On-line recovery for addictions. *Computers in Human Services, 13*(1), 21–39.

Fleming, P. (1990). Software and sympathy: Therapeutic interaction with the computer. In G. Gumpert & S. Fish (Eds.), *Talking to strangers: Mediated therapeutic communication* (pp. 170–183). Norwood, NJ: Ablex.

Golden, T. (1999). Healing and the Internet. In S. Bertman (Ed.), *Grief and the healing arts: Creativity as therapy* (pp. 343–348). Amityville, NY: Baywood.

Koocher, G. (1996). Pediatric oncology: Medical crisis intervention. In R. Resnick & R. Rozensky (Eds.), *Health psychology through the life span: Practice and research opportunities* (pp. 213–225). Washington, DC: American Psychological Association.

Kotecki, J., & Chamness, B. (1999). A valid tool for evaluating health-related WWW sites. *Journal of Health Education, 30*(1), 56–59.

Lee, C. (1998). Counseling and the challenges of cyberspace. *Counseling Today, 40*(10), 5.

Newman, R. (1997). Confidentiality threat transcends technology. *Monitor, 28*(5), 38.

Rando, T. (1988). *Grieving: How to go on living when someone you love dies.* Lexington, MA: Lexington Books.

Spinney, L. (1995, December). A virtual shoulder to cry on. *New Scientist, 148,* 36–40.

Weinberg, N., Schmale, J., Uken, J., & Wessel, K. (1995). Computer-mediated support groups. *Social Work With Groups, 17*(4), 43–54.

Weinberg, N., Uken, J., Schmale, J., & Adamek, M. (1995). Therapeutic factors: Their presence in a computer-mediated support group. *Social Work With Groups, 18*(4), 57–69.

Weinberg, N., Schmale, J., Uken, J., & Wessel, K. (1996). On-line help: Cancer patients participate in a computer-mediated support group. *Health and Social Work, 21*(1), 24–29.

Yalom, I. (1995). *The theory and practice of group psychotherapy* (4th ed.). New York: Basic Books.

Zimmerman, D. (1987). A psychosocial comparison of computer-mediated and face-to-face language use among severely disturbed adolescents. *Adolescence,* 22(88), 827–840.

Zinn, I., Simon, V., & Orme, J. (1997). From on the couch to on-line: Evaluating Internet support groups: A research study. *New Technology in the Human Services, 10*(3), 2–9.

9

Interactive Career Counseling in Middle and Secondary Schools: Integrating the Use of the Internet Into School Career Development Programs

JOANNA REFVEM, JEAN C. PLANTE, AND W. LARRY OSBORNE

Information is exploding in every area of life. Adolescents and the school professionals who help them have the arduous task of deciphering a mountain of data during their pursuit of career goals and dreams. Within the school setting, counselors can facilitate the process through dialogues in individual and group counseling sessions, but this is only the beginning of the process.

Understanding and incorporating the use of the Internet in a school career development program is necessary for retrieving current information. Though traditional methods of finding information need not be abandoned, useful and user-friendly interactive computer programs exist that can guide students, parents, and counselors through the vast and complicated world of career information. Counselors must have an understanding of adolescent career development and an ability to facilitate access to the information and promote it, both via traditional sources and the Internet. This chapter discusses the current state of career planning, with a focus on adolescent career exploration and current resources in use, and then describes Career Explorer, an interactive program that uses the Internet, and its implementation in middle and high schools throughout the state of North Carolina. An appendix lists helpful web sites for career information.

CAREER PLANNING FOR THE 21ST CENTURY

The current concept of career planning incorporates many changes that have evolved throughout the last few decades and are clearly a result of the phenomenal growth of technology, increased longevity, and a global society. Counselors today act as human development change agents (Carr, 1996) and as technological guides during the career planning process, which includes decisions about how generally to live one's life. According to Herr and Cramer (1996),

> Careers are unique to each person and created by what one chooses or doesn't choose. They are dynamic and unfolding throughout life. They include not only occupations but prevocational and postvocational concerns as well as how persons integrate their work life with other life roles: family, community, leisure. (p. 32)

Sorting through information useful for making informed decisions about one's life then becomes important. Students must develop good communication skills, including use of the Internet, and then sort and apply the information by using effective decision-making skills to produce a personal plan for the future.

Adolescent Career Exploration

Career counseling in middle and high school is tailored to the unique characteristics of adolescents during those tumultuous years when they begin to learn more about themselves. Part of the adolescent's search for identity is the keen desire to explore interests, abilities, and new experiences, and to find satisfaction. Stevenson and Carr (1993) pointed out that adolescents are inexperienced, undergoing tremendous personal change. Many are facing for the first time complex decisions about the reality of work in relation to their own lives. In searching for ways to reach these young students, counselors can provide access to the Internet to enable students to make the link between school and work.

Position on the economic spectrum and cultural background influence students' understanding of the world of work. Schmidt (1999) reminded us that "The textbooks and multimedia avenues chosen to illustrate career choices must depict a variety of nontraditional occupational opportunities for women and men, as well as the career integration of people from all cultures" (p. 244). Interactive computer programs allow unlimited possibilities for students seeking to incorporate who they are into the world of work.

Goals for career counseling in middle and high school are defined by the *National Career Development Competencies* (National Occupational Information Coordinating Committee [NOICC] 1998). These guidelines describe competencies that provide a framework for planning, implementing, and evaluating a comprehensive middle or high school guidance program. The three categories of self-knowledge, educational and occupational exploration, and career planning combine to promote the growth of a student's self-concept and understanding of school-to-work transitions, and also help students incorporate knowledge and understanding into a plan for the future.

CURRENT RESOURCES IN USE

Herr & Cramer (1996) highlighted numerous vehicles for gathering career information: printed matter (e.g., career publications), audiovisual media, interviewing representatives from various careers, role-playing, field trips, and direct experience. Traditional means of delivering job and occupational information include noninteractive media such as the U.S. Department of Labor's *Dictionary of Occupational Titles* (*DOT*) (www.onetcenter.org), which lists 12,741 jobs, and *Occupational Outlook Handbook* (*OOH*) (http://stats.bls.gov/ocohome.htm), which furnishes global information on future predictions for jobs and occupations. Though available directly over the Internet, these sources are best used in conjunction with other career research tools.

The National Occupational Information Coordinating Committee, established by Congress in 1976, coordinates the collection and use of current, valid, comprehensive career information to be used in workforce development and career preparation at the national and state levels (Lester, 1996). NOICC, together with its state counterparts, the state occupational information coordinating committees (SOICCs), have worked with public and private sources to create computer-based career information delivery systems. Accessible on the Internet, these agencies contribute a base of information and links to other sites that further enhance career knowledge. For additional information about other career information delivery systems, visit the web site of the Association of Computer-Based Systems for Career Information (ACSCI) (www.acsci.org).

Career Explorer (Bridges, 1998), discussed later in this chapter, is linked through the North Carolina SOICC homepage. Other computer-based career information delivery systems include Discover II (see Lewis-Clark State College's web site www.lcsc.edu/CDS/discover.htm) and CHOICES, both of which actively engage students and adults who are seeking an overall system to create a total picture of their career and educational options. DISCOVER II is based on Super's developmental stages (Osborne, 1996) and Tiedeman and O'Hara's decision-making model, along with the data-people-things orientation of the *DOT* (Herr & Cramer, 1996). Both DISCOVER II and CHOICES (using different formats) offer interest, skill, and value assessments along with educational and occupational information. However, although useful and available, these programs are limited in their ability to provide the level of current information available through interactive computer programs. The goal in this chapter is to preview Career Explorer, which is an interactive resource that can be integrated into a middle/high school career planning program and that can stimulate adolescents to explore and seize ideas that motivate them to reach out for new experiences and knowledge.

LET'S GO SURFING: INTERNET ACCESS THROUGH CAREER EXPLORER

Establishing rapport and building a relationship are key first steps for school counselors working with adolescents and their career aspirations. Mitchell, Levin, and Krumboltz (1999) proposed that career counselors adopt a "planned happenstance" (p. 116) approach whereby the counselor helps clients "generate, recognize, and incorporate" (p. 117) chance events into their career development. Rather than waiting for life to happen to them, clients should be challenged to prepare for the unplanned so that action can be taken when the unexpected happens. Tapping into the natural desire adolescents have for exploration and utilizing the increasingly available access to the World Wide Web seem both prudent and necessary in the information gathering process. With its unlimited volume of data, the Internet is a place where adolescents may experience the unexpected and, with help, can make use of the information gathered.

There is no question that, even though readily available, acquiring and using information gathered via the Internet can be both overwhelming and time consuming. The sheer volume of data is more than any one individual can navigate without help. Programs exist and are developed daily that aid in this search. Many of these can be accessed through NOICC (www.noicc.gov) and SOICC (the NOICC site has access to a SOICC page for each state).

One such program is Career Explorer (Bridges, 1998), currently in use throughout the state of North Carolina. This program provides one of the most extensive and interactive frameworks for use of the Internet in career counseling in the schools. In particular, the program appeals to students and teachers by connecting career information to interests and education. School counselors can provide help to both students and staff, both in personal use of the information and application to subjects covered in the classroom. Additionally, the program as utilized in North Carolina schools aligns closely with the *National Career Development Competencies for Middle/Junior and High Schools* (NOICC, 1998), reviewed earlier in this chapter. The temptation when logging on to the Internet is to jump from site to site, seeking just the right information. The beauty of this program is that once students have used some of the basic tools, links are provided that are an appropriate match for their research.

The content of Career Explorer is written in a style that appeals to adolescents, with new articles appearing daily. The program offers a variety of interactive services, allowing both teachers and students to request information. Articles not only cover basic education, salary, and outlook but also contain interviews with people working in those careers. In addition, learning activities for the classroom are linked to the careers featured each day. Professionals (teachers) also can benefit from use of a variety of lesson plans and an on-line course on career development.

This type of program provides the interactive ability to upgrade or adapt material based on requests from adolescents themselves. Through e-mail, students can ask questions about occupations featured or those they have merely heard about. The combination of student access and ready availability to the Internet provides a continuously customized resource for students, teachers, and counselors.

STUDENT ACCESS

Daily news, interest inventories, interviews with professionals in various careers, and access to college web sites are among the many resources that attract students to this program. Every day a new occupation is highlighted with complete information regarding responsibilities, availability, compensation, and future outlook. For example, on June 7, 1999, one of the occupations highlighted was plastics engineer. Students were provided with a detailed description of the history of plastics, use of plastics in our society, and outlook for jobs (with reference to the *Occupational Outlook Handbook*). Students had the opportunity to play the role of a plastics engineer, with a typical decision-making problem faced in that job. They also could practice interoffice memo writing, again playing the role of the plastics engineer. Feedback and examples of both were included. In addition, there was an interview with a plastics engineer with e-mail access allowing students to interact with that representative.

E-mail also provides a way for students to request information on new or unusual occupations from Career Explorer staff. Once a student has utilized the research and other tools, Career Explorer provides links to sites such as college web pages and the College Board (for SAT information) as students contemplate their next step. With undoubtedly little time available each day to make use of this information, students can store information in their own "locker" at the Career Explorer site. Continuity is maintained, and both student and counselor can monitor progress toward stated career goals.

TEACHER INVOLVEMENT

Incorporating career information into education can be complicated and time consuming. The information provided in the Daily News feature of Career Explorer often provides a related math or

English activity/problem teachers can use in the classroom. Referring to June 7, 1999, and the plastics engineer, a math problem was
presented in which students were asked to assume the role and respond to a request by an operations manager to calculate the effi-
ciency of a flow rate gauge used in a plastics plant. The problem,
questions, and solution were all provided for use individually or in
the classroom.

Peer interaction on-line and learning modules provided by
Career Explorer enable teachers to enhance career training in the
classroom. And for those teachers so inclined, an on-line 12-week
training course on career development is available. Some school
districts in North Carolina have considered the possibility of offering continuing education credit for completing this course.

SCHOOL COUNSELOR AS COORDINATOR/CONSULTANT

Often students visit the counseling office in a school to discuss
career goals/concerns/interests with a school counselor. Individual
and group counseling will remain the hallmark of the school counselor's function, yet providing access to information also is a vital
responsibility. By creating a career center where a program such as
Career Explorer is a key fixture, time and resources are conserved
as the counselor implements the guidelines provided, as discussed
in the next section. Whether the counselor meets with students individually, provides orientation to the career center, or consults
with teachers regarding classroom modules, Career Explorer provides a framework for learning.

Herr and Cramer (1996) warned that "indiscriminate use of the
computer may not be appropriate" and that "individuals must be assisted through a variety of techniques to use data in a personally
meaningful manner" (p. 642). The National Career Development
Association (NCDA, 1999) has developed *NCDA Guidelines for
the Use of the Internet for Provision of Career Information and Planning Services* (see Appendix 6). Career Explorer meets or exceeds
several purposes of Internet-based career services suggested by the
NCDA, including delivery of information about occupations, providing on-line searches of occupational databases, and delivering
interactive career counseling and career planning services. The
NCDA guidelines cover many aspects of services provided by ca-

reer counselors over the Internet and should be reviewed prior to implementing an Internet-based career development program. Every counselor must view any helpful computer program as a resource to aid in his or her function as a counselor. The career planning journey by adolescents must be guided by counselors, teachers, and parents alike, and no machine, even if it has interactive capabilities, can compensate for the value of personal input.

IMPLEMENTING CAREER EXPLORER

In August 1997, the North Carolina State Occupational Information Coordinating Committee (NCSOICC, 1998) (www.esc.state.ns.us/soicc/index.htm) agreed to launch a pilot program featuring Career Explorer (Bridges, 1998). In collaboration with the North Carolina Department of Public Instruction and the Commission on Workforce Preparedness/Job Ready, NCSOICC developed a series of minipilots that covered the theme areas of career centers, individual counseling, classroom instruction, and professional development. In addition, a detailed outline was developed describing how the minipilots relate to National Career Development Competencies (NOICC, 1998) for both middle/ junior high and senior high. Theme areas and sample activities were as follows:

- **For the career center theme area:** Activities utilized Career Explorer's Daily News service, subject-specific career services using Career Explorer resources, and a dynamic career center project to increase participation in the school career center as a one-stop location for career information services. For example, strategies for use of the Daily News service included leaving copies of the Daily News page on the staff room table or placing it in selected teachers' boxes, placing a daily copy on selected bulletin boards in the school, and/or selecting one part of the Daily News to feature in the daily announcements. Use of the Daily News service met or exceeded the National Career Development Competencies of understanding the effect of growth and development and understanding the need for positive attitudes toward work and learning (high school); and of knowledge of the importance of growth and change; skills to locate, understand,

and use career information; and knowledge of different occupations and changing male/female roles (middle/junior high).

- **For the individual counseling theme area:** Minipilots included use by the school counselor of an informational interview and development of career research workshops. Strategies for the informational interviews included focusing on key life questions (What do you want from your life? What do you have to offer the world?) and then using results of this interview with Career Explorer's Career Research Tool. Logistics included selecting a target group of students to interview, and helping them translate their interests, skills, and personality style into the Career Research Tool, with an agreement from each student to research for at least 1 hour. Informational interviewing meets many National Career Development Competencies for both high school and middle/junior high school including skills to locate, evaluate, and interpret career information; skills to make decisions; and skills in career planning (high school); and understanding the relationship between work and learning, and knowledge of different occupations and changing male/female roles (middle/junior high).

- **For the classroom instruction theme area:** Units included Career Research (grades 10–12), Decision-Making Training (grades 7–10), Career Planning (grades 9–12), and Daily Career Current Events (all grade levels). For example, Daily Career Current Events focused on providing career-related information in a classroom. Strategies included printing copies of the Career Explorer Daily News for 20 consecutive days, with an evaluation at the end of that period regarding change in specific knowledge and career alternatives. In two participating classes, students took a pretest (simply writing 50 careers on piece of paper in 5 minutes) and then a posttest at the end of 20 days with the same exercise plus classroom discussion. Students also were encouraged to visit the Career Center during the 20-day period. For all grade levels, this activity promoted the National Career Development Competency of skills to locate, evaluate, and interpret information.

- **For the professional development theme area:** Activities included 1-minute updates for professionals, peer interaction on-line, and an on-line professional development course. The peer interaction activity promoted discussions with other career professionals, either by utilizing expert advice provided by Career Explorer staff, or the teacher-to-teacher feature in which comments, questions, and responses are posted on a virtual bulletin board. A coordinating staff member encouraged other teachers to post messages to the bulletin board over the pilot period, and also solicited questions related to career development to submit to the career expert service. This type of activity allowed teachers and other staff members to become involved with the program in order to take full advantage of the resources offered, and also to increase understanding of student experience with the program.

With time, other programs like Career Explorer will be developed and implemented as interactive career counseling gains popularity. Every day counselors, within the school setting as well as community-based agencies, must seek to maintain their awareness of new career resources and developments.

CONCLUSION

There is no question that professionals and students need help in the process of gathering, deciphering, and then utilizing career information. As we enter the 21st century, counselors are in a significant position to access and facilitate use of all sorts of career information, and they must be technically prepared to orient students, teachers, and parents to the vast opportunities that the future holds. Programs like Career Explorer provide a one-stop service for all aspects of this process. Every day new information becomes available, and as Mitchell, Levin, and Krumboltz (1999) have discussed, being prepared for the unexpected promotes individual development and career decision making. Mitchell et al. have encouraged the notion of open-mindedness in their model, which fits well with a program like Career Explorer. Who knows what will be discovered tomorrow? The future can become an adventure to look forward to instead of a decision-making time to dread.

That said, developing and implementing this type of program into a school development program can be costly both in human and financial resources. Computers with Internet access need to be available. Counselors and teachers interested in career development must commit extra hours and energy to all phases of such a project. Licensing agreements can become costly and may conflict with previous financial commitments. All these obstacles can and must be addressed.

In spite of these hurdles, centralizing career services in the school setting seems both logical and achievable. Career Explorer is currently used in 45 American states and 7 Canadian provinces, providing access for more than 2 million middle and secondary schools. This type of program clearly has widespread appeal. Shedding methods and procedures that are quickly becoming outdated and utilizing the ever-changing sources of information via the Internet depict the nature of the new millennium. Counselors will hear few arguments from adolescents who are always eager to explore, question, experiment, and eventually establish themselves in the world.

REFERENCES

Bridges, Inc. (1998). *Career Explorer* [On-line]. Available: http://bridges.com.
Carr, J. V. (1996). Comprehensiveness of career planning: The third C—Comprehensiveness. *Journal of Career Development, 23*, 33–43.
Herr, E. L., & Cramer, S. H. (1996). *Career guidance through the life span: Systematic approaches* (5th ed.). Boston: Scott, Foresman and Company.
Lester, J. N. (1996). Turbulence at the (Gallup) polls. In R. Feller & G. Walz (Eds.), *Career transitions in turbulent times* (pp. 193–204). Greensboro, NC: ERIC Counseling and Student Services Clearinghouse.
Mitchell, K. E., Levin, A. S., & Krumboltz, J. D. (1999). Planned happenstance: Constructing unexpected career opportunities. *Journal of Counseling and Development, 77*, 115–124.
National Career Development Association. (1999). *NCDA Guidelines for the use of the Internet for provision of career information and planning services* [On-line]. Available: http://ncda.org. See also Appendix 6.
National Occupational Information Coordinating Committee (NOICC). (1998). *National career development competencies* [On-line]. Available: http://www.noicc.gov/files/ncompete.html.
North Carolina State Occupational Information Coordinating Committee. (1998). *North Carolina Career Explorer: A career development Internet program* [On-line]. Available: www.esc.state.ns.us/soicc/index.htm.

Osborne, W. L. (1996). Donald E. Super: Yesterday and tomorrow. In R. Feller & G. Walz (Eds.), *Career transition in turbulent times* (pp. 67–75). Greensboro, NC: ERIC Counseling and Student Services Clearinghouse.

Schmidt, J. J. (1999). *Counseling in schools: Essential services and comprehensive programs* (3rd ed.). Boston: Allyn & Bacon.

Stevenson, C., & Carr, J. (1993). *Integrated studies in the middle grades: "Dancing through walls."* New York: Teachers College Press.

Appendix
Helpful Web Sites for Career Information

- Association of Computer-Based Systems for Career Information (ACSCI) (www.acsci.org/). This professional association focuses on the advancement and delivery of career information.
- DISCOVER II (www.lcsc.edu/CDS/discover.htm). This site at Lewis-Clark State College provides access to information about DISCOVER II, a computer-based career information delivery system.
- *Dictionary of Occupational Titles* (*DOT*) (www.onetcenter.org). The *Dictionary of Occupational Titles* is in the process of becoming the Occupational Information Network (O*NET). This site provides access to this network with its comprehensive databases of worker attributes and job characteristics.
- National Career Development Association (NCDA) (http://ncda.org). The NCDA has developed guidelines for the use of the Internet in the delivery of career counseling services. See Appendix 6.
- National Occupational Information Coordinating Committee (www.noicc.gov/). This site provides access to SOICC home-pages for each state. In addition, numerous other links to career information are provided.
- North Carolina State Occupational Information Coordinating Committee (NCSOICC) (www.esc.state.nc.us/soicc/index.htm). This site contains detailed information about Career Explorer and its use in the state of North Carolina.
- *Occupational Outlook Handbook* (*OOH*) (http://stats.bls.gov/ocohome.htm). This site, part of the Bureau of Labor Statistics web site, allows users to do keyword and index searches in the *OOH*.
- State Occupational Information Coordinating Committee (SOICC) (www.noicc.gov/). The site for each SOICC is linked through the NOICC site as already noted.

10

Using the Web for Distance Learning

Michael K. Altekruse and Leah Brew

Student enrollment is a concern for most universities. Due to the increase in college enrollment and decreased state funding for higher education, many believe that on-line courses are a cost-effective means of meeting instructional demand (California Educational Technology Initiative, 1998; Starr, 1997).

The University of North Texas (UNT) administration began to encourage the use of distance education to increase student enrollment and to help meet present student demand for classes because the administration believed that using the web for instruction was a way to reach more students, could be more cost effective for many students, and could increase student enrollment. The administration also believed that other universities offering web-based courses might create competition for student enrollment and that the university needed to be a pioneer in this form of instruction.

Before the counselor education program faculty at UNT was willing to offer counseling courses on the web, however, they had to be convinced that web-based instruction offered methodology that was equal to or better than that available in the regular classroom. In short, could students learn as much through the web-based course as they could as students sitting in a traditional campus classroom? Although there is little research on web-based instruction, a study by Stocks and Freddolino (1998) has shown the on-line educational experience, as measured by grades, to be comparable to on-campus classes. Consistent with other findings

(Keating & Hargitai, 1999), Internet students found the flexibility of the course a positive feature but the lack of face-to-face contact a negative feature.

ADVANTAGES AND UNIQUE
FEATURES OF WEB COURSES

Before deciding to set up the program's first web course, advantages and disadvantages had to be weighed. Because web-based instruction was so new, many so-called advantages were based only on theory and conjecture. This chapter's authors investigated these hypotheses in their first course and developed a list of advantages and disadvantages of web instruction based on what they learned.

The belief that web-based instruction could reach more students and make education more accessible is still unproven, yet many advantages and unique features of web-based instruction were found to exist. One advantage is that students with access to the World Wide Web at home can explore exciting and diverse web sites without having to come to campus. In the comfort of their own home, they can also receive credit for many courses. They can use the web to conduct research at leading university library sites throughout the world including

- **the UNT University Library** (http://www.library.unt.edu/): The most obvious resource for supplying the information needs of students and faculty is their own university's library system. The physical forms of that collection are well known. Most faculty are skilled users and guides, but not all are familiar with gaining electronic access to these resources.
- **electronic journals:** This is a new medium. Some journals are only published on the web while other journals are published in hard copy and then placed on the web. Recent issues of the American Counseling Association's *Journal of Counseling and Development* are available to association members at http://www.counseling.org/journals/default.htm and an extensive listing of electronic journals and periodicals can be found at http://psych.hanover.edu/Krantz/journal.html#psychjournal.
- **gopherspace:** This is a way of navigating the net that has been popular since 1992. Its strengths are ease of navigation, index-

ing, and ease of downloading. Its chief weakness is that it handles images with great difficulty, and thus is limited mainly to text.

- **newsgroups (also known as Usenet):** These are the Internet equivalent of clubs or conversation groups. Their strength is size (many thousands of such groups exist), and their weakness is lack of focus.
- **the World Wide Web:** Booming in popularity since the introduction of Mosaic in 1993, the web offers easy access to images and sound (even motion pictures!) as well as text, and powerful links within documents to specific places in other documents. For example, many national organizations such as the American Counseling Association (http://www.counseling.org), the National Association of Social Workers (http://www.naswdc.org), and the American Psychological Association (http://www.apa.org) have web sites with information on purchasing books, accessing electronic journals, membership, and ethical guidelines.

Another advantage of using the web is the ability to provide links to materials elsewhere on the web. The user can point expressly to a specific resource or to pages that gather and organize a wide range of materials. This is an especially valuable way to get at nascent "libraries" on the World Wide Web where individuals have taken responsibility for keeping an eye out for materials in a specific field and keeping links to them up to date. An example may be seen on http://www.med.nyu.edu/Psych/src.psych.html, which is a page of Internet sources for mental health professionals. Another page that represents a nascent library and that is a source for counselor education syllabi is at http://coe.fgcu.edu/faculty/sabella/cerc/index.htm.

In the Dallas/Fort Worth metroplex, it is becoming more difficult for students to get to the University of North Texas campus. Internet and web courses are in great demand when distance from campus or ease of getting to campus is an issue. Courses that can be taken without a long drive are inviting to many students.

A web course can be straightforward, like a correspondence course on the web, or it can feature movies, live lectures, and endless links to various relevant sources. Only imagination and finances limit a developer. The more the web course can offer the student, the better. Both information and technology resources change so rapidly that new features can be added to the web page daily.

Features that can be utilized on the actual web-based course to increase the appeal of the course include

- **video:** Professors can create videos of themselves covering certain parts of a course, or existing videos can be integrated on to the web page for the student to view at his or her convenience.
- **CD ROMS:** CD ROMS can be integrated and linked from the web course to provide additional information or to provide audio and videos that are difficult to set up or view on some web pages.
- **interactive teaching:** Professors can provide live lectures while the students watch on their computers at home and can have icons representing each student to watch on their monitor. Students can interact with professors by letting the professor know when they have a question by using the icon. Professors can then call on students for questions and can provide individualized responses. Teachers can also ask questions and get responses from all students by utilizing the e-mail capacity during live teaching sessions.
- **audio:** This feature is especially beneficial when integrated with computer presentation software such as PowerPoint. It simulates a live lecture.
- **computer presentations:** Presentations that have already been created for class can be transferred as an additional form of media for the web class.
- **linking:** The ability to link to other sites that are relevant to the topic on the web class is easily integrated.
- **graphics:** Using graphics is a method for making the web class more interesting.
- **movies:** Movies that are part of other software packages or portions of existing videos can be added.
- **themes:** Visual artistic themes material, such as triangles to present new ideas or the color red to indicate important ideas, can make it easier for students to understand the flow of ideas.

Features for professors who make the use of the web to teach courses in counseling include

- **testing, auto-scoring, and grading:** Such programs as WebCT (Dabbagh & Schmidt, 1998) provide a testing program whereby tests taken by students are scored immediately for the students, and results are placed in the professor's electronic grade book.
- **scheduling test dates and times:** Tests can be taken anytime the student is ready or can be scheduled at a specific time and date.
- **test formats:** Tests can be in multiple choice, short answer, or essay form, and students can take the tests right on the net. In addition, tests can be developed to be power or timed tests.
- **test bank of questions:** The program can randomly select different questions for each student and place the questions in a different order.
- **student tracking:** The professor can determine how much time a student has spent on the web page and what they did on the page.
- **enrollment:** Student enrollment is more flexible.
- **travel:** No faculty travel is necessary, whereas in other forms of distance learning, travel is required. This also saves significant funds for the university.
- **multiple models:** Flexibility in how many interactions each professor wants to maintain on the web can be determined. For example, a professor can have no interaction with the student or can require a weekly chat room.

Features for the student provided by web-based courses include

- **practice tests:** Students can take practice tests that give immediate feedback with reasons why their answers are right or wrong.
- **unanswered test questions:** Students can review to see which questions were not answered during testing.
- **in-class e-mails:** An e-mail system is set up on the web page for all class members. They may communicate with each other or with the professor in this private e-mail system.
- **class chat rooms:** Different types of chat rooms are available for class members.

- **web calendar:** Calendars can be set up with due dates for papers and test dates so that the student can find out how much work is required at a glance.

DISADVANTAGES OF WEB COURSES

There are disadvantages of teaching over the web. Some courses are not appropriate for the web, such as most of the counseling courses that have a strong experiential component. However, some argue that most courses could be taught on the web, including such courses as counseling practicum, because it is possible to have live supervision on the web by using small cameras to see the student and the supervisor. The counseling videotape recording can then be reviewed, and the student and supervisor can see each other during the supervision process.

Other specific disadvantages include

- **technological failures:** For example, a student is unable to get into the course, the computer shuts down in the middle of the test, or the links are no longer hot. Of course, sometimes technological failures also happen when using technology in regular classroom teaching.
- **software upgrades:** Recently UNT upgraded WebCT to a new and better version. Problems caused by this change included totally changing quizzes so students had problems with access, grading the quizzes wrong, and providing the same questions more than once.
- **students cheating:** The developer has no idea who may be really taking the course. If a student wants to have someone else do the work, all he or she has to do is provide this person with any safeguards that have developed, including a password.
- **lack of human contact:** Even with a 100% web course, it is recommended that an instructor meet with his or her students at least once to show students how to use the web for maximum learning.
- **student motivation:** Students must completely rely on self-discipline to complete the coursework. As a result, the lead author of this chapter gives more incompletes for his web course than any other course he has taught.

- **boringness:** Web courses are often just not as interesting as experiencing an excellent live teacher.
- **home PC limitations:** Most web courses need the latest browsers and equipment to run well. Also, if the student has hardware problems on the day of testing, the student must have quick and easy access to an alternate computer or risk not taking the test.
- **course changes:** Web course changes are both costly and time consuming.
- **testing problems:** It is possible for students to miss clicking the answer and saving it, and never know the answer they chose was not saved unless they check their work. Also, when using timed tests, if an error occurs, the timer continues even if the student cannot.
- **writing tests:** This is difficult and time consuming for web courses.
- **link changes:** The only way to monitor link changes is when students discover they cannot use a link or go through a laborious process with a program like Front Page.

DEVELOPING A WEB CLASS

There are two kinds of information on the Internet that can be used in teaching: what already exists and what can be created. What is there already is what has been put on the web by various authors. It takes a little exploring to find what is out there and filter it for classroom use, and it takes a lot of work to prepare original materials for a web course.

Some professors develop a 100% web course. In such a course students may never see their instructor. All correspondence, assignments, activities, and requirements are guided through the web. An example of a 100% web course is the Ethical, Legal, and Professional Issues in Counseling course developed by the lead author of this chapter. This course is protected by the University of North Texas and can only be accessed through a user ID and password. Only students who register for the class are given a user ID and password.

A 100% web course requires a great deal of work in the development stage and constant monitoring and maintenance. In developing the ethics web course, it was necessary first to study all university policies regarding the use of the web for teaching. Because this was a pioneer effort, policies were being developed at the same time the course was being developed. Some of the original guidelines have since been changed, and the new policies actually make the process much easier.

Other course configurations may include a combination web course with required classroom attendance, a professor just using a page as resource for a class, and a web page with only a course syllabus. An example of a combination configuration is when instructors require the students to attend the first class (to show the students how to use the course on the Internet), the last class (to return any paperwork that may have been required), and each exam (to reduce the ability for students to cheat). The professor can also require the Internet class as an additional resource to the book and lectures. The web page with a course syllabus is best utilized to advertise class requirements so students can know in advance what to expect during the course.

Policies Affecting Web Course Development

Policies that affect the development of any kind of web course include those concerning

- **contact hours:** When the ethics course was first developed, the university required the same requirements for a web course as a regular on-campus course. Consequently, a course with 15 modules that required the student to spend 3 hours per module was developed. This met the university policy of 45 contact hours for this 3-semester-hour class. This is no longer a requirement.
- **software access:** Web page developers have a choice of software to use in their development of their course or they can use the web language, html. The ethics web course used software that translates to html that also aids in providing images and links. There are many programs to use, but many universities have adopted a standard that they expect most developers to use at that university. More help will be received if the software is compatible with the university. Presently the standard at UNT is Microsoft Front Page. The ethics page, originally developed with

Netscape Gold, was easy to convert to Front Page and then to continue its development with Front Page. Front Page has the advantage of easy development because it writes in a manner similar to Microsoft Word or PowerPoint.

- **university technological limitations:** A web course can be as sophisticated as the developer's imagination. However, the university may not have the equipment or the expertise to help to meet the developer's desires. For instance, the ability to stream video into the web page requires sophisticated equipment.

- **course management tool:** At the University of North Texas, the university has adopted Web CT as their course management tool because, at the time, it was the only course management tool developed by university instructors for Internet class instruction. What was developed in Front Page was transferred to WebCT. The course can be developed in Web CT. However, it requires expertise in html language. Tasks are required that must be developed on WebCT. WebCT is where quizzes and examinations are developed, and videos, audios, and all communications are incorporated. A developer must be familiar with the course management tool with all of its advantages and disadvantages before developing a course.

- **course ownership:** Who owns the course, the developer or the university, and can the professor take the course to a new university if he or she decides to leave? This is a question that may want to be answered before developing a course. The development of a course is a great deal of work.

- **effect on teaching load:** While developing the course, will the professor be given a reduced teaching load or graduate student help? Once the course is on-line with students, will this be part of the professor's teaching load? These are questions that may also need to be answered before beginning the development process. Maintenance of the course requires nearly as much time as a traditional course because of upgrades in equipment and software that create problems, constant removal of dead links, and constant searching of new links to add to the page.

- **graduate school policies:** At UNT, a student may not be able to take any course unless he or she has been admitted to the graduate school. Many potential students show an interest in one of the ethics course, for example, but do not take the time to be admitted to graduate school.

RECOMMENDATIONS FOR PREPARING TO DEVELOP A WEB COURSE

If a decision has been made to develop a web course and preparation has been adequate for the development, the following recommendations may be helpful.

Learn More About Web Site Development

Books to learn how to develop a course for the web are available. However, the developer must be computer and web literate to learn all that is needed to know about web development through books. There are also sites on the web that teach web-page development and that include templates for page development. (See, for example, http://www.nevada.edu/~ces/webpage/weblearn.html.) The templates are good, but a site that uses them will not be unique and will not reflect the developer's personality.

What can be most helpful is to attend a course, workshop, or presentation on web development. Most universities usually offer courses for Front Page and other authoring programs. The lead author of this chapter has attended all web-related presentations at the American Counseling Association Annual Conference and has found most very helpful for obtaining new ideas.

Contribute to the Ongoing Development of a Web Site

Some universities provide web course developers for professors. The professor provides the material; the developer places it on the web. This is very helpful, but does not help in the continuing maintenance that is required for each page and that is best done by the person who knows the content of the page. Use the technician, but learn from him or her so that the page can be maintained after he or she moves on.

Search for Relevant Links to Course-Related Sources

The strengths of a web-based course include the tremendous resources available on-line that can be linked to the page. However, the search can be awkward and extremely time consuming. Keating and Hargitai (1999) have suggested a more efficient approach to researching on the web. Because web searches are based on Boolean logic, which refers to the logical relationship among search terms and works on a process of inclusion, exclusion, and substitution, using the words *AND* and *NOT* between keywords will go a long way toward limiting a search. For example, *counselor education and supervision* will yield all pages listing these three nouns. *Counselor AND education NOT supervision* will yield only pages listing *counselor* and *education*. Many search engines now use implied Boolean plus (+) or minus (−) search operators to denote AND and NOT. Therefore, a query for the example just given will look something like this: +counselor+education−supervision. Quotation marks around proper names and exact titles will yield more exact results. A search for counselor education will yield results for counselor education, counselor, and education. A search for "counselor education" will only yield results for counselor education.

E-mail listservs such as CESNET (Counselor Education and Supervision Net) and ICN (International Counseling Network) are also great resources for web sources. Anyone can join these listservs by following these processes:

- For International Counseling Network, go to http://members. home.comruste/icn.html.
- For CESNET-L, which is an active listserv for counselor educators and supervisors, subscribe by sending a message to listserv@vm.sc.edu that says "subscribe CESNET-L" and includes your first and last names.

Contact Textbook Publishers

These publishers may have counselor education course material already developed to accompany their textbooks. Before choosing a textbook for a specific course, check to see what audiovisual material the publisher has for the course and if the publisher has developed anything for web-based learning. Publishers on-line include

Addison Wesley Longman;
Allyn & Bacon;
Archipelago;
Bedford, Freeman & Worth Publishing Group;
Cambridge Physics Outlet;

Course Technology;
Harcourt College;
John Wiley & Sons;
McGraw-Hill Ryerson;
Pearson Education;
Prentice Hall and Pearson Professional;
Reference and Technology Imprints;
South-Western College Publishing and Wadsworth Publishing;
Thomson Learning, including its publishing company, Brooks/Cole; and
W. W. Norton & Company.

Web sites that list books that can be purchased include

Accelerated Development (www.taylorandfrancis.com);
AGS (American Guidance Service) On-line Store (www.agsnet.com);
American Counseling Association (www.counseling.org) and (www.counseling.org/resources);
Brooks/Cole-Wadsworth Publishing Company (www.wadsworth.com);
Merrill Education (www.merrilleducation.com); and
Research Press (www.researchpress.com.)

Explore Course Design With Care

There are many choices for a course design. Remember that pages need to be attractive and inviting, that students need to feel good about the web page and the course, and that design goes a long way in setting a positive mental attitude. A criticism of the first UNT course on ethics was that it looked overwhelming. A student would look at one of the modules and either not sign up for the course or drop the course. In addition, meeting with each student was necessary before they began to explore how best to use the resources available. Books are available on web-based course design. Two of the best are *The Wired Professor* (Keating & Hargitai, 1999) and *Building Learning Communities in Cyberspace: Effective Strategies for the On-Line Classroom* (Palloff & Pratt, 1999).

CONCLUSION

It seems that that the most frequent arguments for web-based instruction are its ability to reach students and its potential for course enrichment. The practice of providing live instruction on the web that can be accessed by the student later for study also has great potential. The use of the web to access current resources is cited as one of the greatest advantages of the web for instruction. With all of the advantages of web-based instruction there are drawbacks, however. There is nothing like live contact in counseling courses. The need for the counseling instructor to listen to verbal responses while assessing nonverbal responses has not been duplicated in web courses. For counselor education, web-based instruction will probably always be second best to live instruction.

Note that new upgrades and new features are available today that were not available during the writing of this chapter. Therefore, it is important to keep up to date on technological advances.

REFERENCES

California Educational Technology Initiative. (1998). *Technology in higher education: Opportunities and threats* (EDRS MF01/PC01). Los Angeles, CA: Gallick, Susan.

Dabbagh, N. H., & Schmitt, J. (1998). Redesigning instruction through web-based course authoring tools. *Educational Media International, 35*(2), 106–110.

Keating, A. B., & Hargitai, J. (1999). *The wired professor.* New York: New York University Press.

Palloff, R. M., & Pratt, K. (1999). *Building learning communities in cyberspace: Effective strategies for the on-line classroom.* San Francisco: Jossey-Bass.

Starr, R. M. (1997). Delivering instruction on the World Wide Web: Overview and basic design principles. *Educational Technology, 37*(3), 7–15.

Stocks, T. J., & Freddolino, P. P. (1998). Evaluation of a World-Wide-Web-based graduate social work research methods course. *Computers in Human Service, 15*(2-3), 51–69.

11

Electronic Delivery of Career Development University Courses

Marla Peterson

Dictionaries define prudent as "being wisely cautious in practical affairs" and "careful in providing for the future." Both of these phrases seem appropriate when discussing the use of electronic technology for delivering instruction on career development. Technological advances continue to make an array of instructional approaches possible, but many questions remain as to how prudent it is to use some of these technologies.

University course content must drive the technology. Once this is internalized, university faculty members and educational publishers will find ways to use appropriate technology that will enhance teaching-learning processes and materials. However, the flexible faculty member and the flexible publisher must also enter the electronic teaching world with a healthy amount of flexible skepticism. An oxymoron? No! It is simply being prudent. This should become more apparent as the findings of two recently released landmark reports on distance education are examined for implications that affect career development courses and materials.

Preservice counselor education programs usually include two courses on career development theory, research, information, and practice. Often theory and research are addressed in one course and career information and career counseling practices are included in another. As the World Wide Web burgeoned with sites devoted to career information and when many groups, including the Federal government, turned to the Internet for delivery of

143

career-related information, it became apparent that the old didactic occupational information courses needed to be transformed into electronically enhanced career and educational information systems courses. Once electronic enhancement of face-to-face instruction occurs, it is tempting to move to the delivery of courses through distance education means.

Two landmark documents on distance education were issued in April 1999. One, *What's the Difference?*, was prepared for the American Federation of Teachers and the National Education Association by Phipps and Merisotis, staff members at the Institute for Higher Education Policy. The Phipps and Merisotis document focused on a review of contemporary research on the effectiveness of distance education in higher education. The second document, *The Virtual University and Educational Opportunity*, authored by Gladieux and Swail (1999) of the College Board, discussed issues of equity and access. Both documents have implications for counselor educators who are wrestling with the changing environment of electronically enhanced instruction.

How is distance education distinguished from electronically enhanced face-to-face instruction? Phipps and Merisotis cautioned that

> Because the technology is evolving, the definition of what distance learning is continues to change. Distance learning generally includes "synchronous communication," which occurs when teacher and student are present at the same time during instruction—even if they are in two different places—and "asynchronous communication," which occurs when students and teachers do not have person-to-person direct interaction at the same time or place. (1999, p. 11)

In this chapter, *distance education* refers to teaching/learning that takes place when the learner is at a distance from the originator of the teaching material. *Face-to-face instruction* is used to describe situations in which both students and instructors are present in the classroom. Both distance education and face-to-face approaches can be electronically enhanced by a variety of media: video conferencing, audio conferencing, videotapes, audiotapes, television, telephone, computer software, fax, print, and the Internet. Courseware programs and WWW-based platforms such as those developed by eCollege.com (www.ecollege.com) and Black-Board, Inc. (www.BlackBoard.com) enable faculty members to develop courses that can incorporate any of the aforementioned technologies.

This chapter describes both near-term and long-term possibilities for electronic syllabus development and then examines how the two recent studies on distance education may guide the prudent use of technology.

UNDERSTANDING THE NEAR-TERM POSSIBILITIES

The syllabus example presented in this section illustrates some of the instructional approaches that are possible when constructing a career development course syllabus with these new courseware programs. The syllabus example also sets the context for examining what role flexible skepticism and prudence might play in the use of technology. The example is based on the use by this chapter's author of the CourseInfo system published by BlackBoard, Inc. Five years ago when this chapter's author first designed an electronic syllabus, the syllabus consisted mainly of links to key WWW sites. With the advent of new authoring programs, the possibilities have expanded. (Readers who wish to view the syllabus that this chapter's author developed with CourseInfo may obtain permission by sending a request to peterson@utkux.utcc.utk.edu.)

When students enroll in the course that was developed, they see a page that includes the following navigation areas:

Announcements	Assignments
Course Information	Communication
Staff Information	External Links
Course Documents	Student Tools

The instructor has access to all of these areas and a control panel that is not accessible to the students. The instructor can elect to activate, deactivate, and modify most of the student areas. The control panel includes a quiz generator, assessment tools, an on-line gradebook, and a course statistics field. To enable readers to think about what other possibilities might exist for using these courseware features in a career and educational information systems course, a brief overview of student areas and key instructor areas, along with course examples, follows.

ANNOUNCEMENTS

This area is used to display announcements, updates, and reminders. This area always appears when the student accesses the course. The instructor can use this area for items like reminding students to bring two disks to every class meeting, alerting the class that a state department of education representative will visit the class, and telling students she will be 10 minutes late so class members should proceed with an on-line assignment.

COURSE INFORMATION

This area is used to display general information about the course: course description from the graduate catalog; prerequisites; and times, locations, and information for lecture components. The lecture component can be expanded, for example, to include on-line activities and assignments that are linked to key WWW sites that support the content to be learned. In this course, a folder has been created for each class meeting. The contents of a folder for one class meeting are shown in Table 11-1 and include an activity/assignment that requires students to read key statements related to career development ethics, policies, and standards.

STAFF INFORMATION

Specific information about staff or faculty who are involved with the course can be placed in this location. Possibilities to insert for personalizing the course include pictures of the instructor and any graduate assistants or staff who support the course, career development background of the instructor, certification and licensures, teaching philosophy, and hopes and expectations for the course.

Table 11-1
Sample Course Folder Contents

Course Title: Career and Education Information Systems
Meeting #2: Ethics/Policies/Standards

Links and Documents	Class Activities/Notes
NCDA Guidelines for Use of the Internet http://ncda.org/polweb.html	Complete appropriate section of worksheet that will be electronically activated in class.
NCDA Guidelines for the Preparation and Evaluation of Career and Occupational Information Literature http://ncda.org/polinfo.html	Complete appropriate section of worksheet that will be electronically activated in class.
NCDA Guidelines for the Preparation and Evaluation of Video Career Media http://ncda.org/polvideo.html	Complete appropriate section of worksheet that will be electronically activated in class.
NCDA Career Software Review Guidelines http://ncd.org/polsoft.html	Let's discuss.
NCDA Career Development Policy Statement http://ncda.org/polcd.html	Covers K-Adult.

continues

Table 11-1—*continued*

NOICC Career Development Competencies http://www.noicc.gov/	Covers K-Adult.
Career Development Domain of Tennessee School Counseling Program: A Framework for Action	Covers K–12. Copy can be found by clicking on "Course Documents."
Internet Acceptable Use Policies K–12 http://falcon.jmu.edu/ ~ramseyil/netpolicy.htm	See Assignment 1 below.

Assignment 1	Select one school district's Internet Use Policy Statement that you think is particularly good. Come to class prepared to discuss good points in the statement and points that might need to be added to cover use of Internet for career development purposes.
Assignment 2	Practice the Page Composer skills that you learned last week at the first class meeting.

COURSE DOCUMENTS

This content-specific area is used for the majority of information that is to be delivered to the students on-line: course outlines, handouts, lecture materials, and related readings. In this course, the course outline and related links are located at the Course Information location, and handouts only are placed at the Course Documents location. This demonstrates that the instructor has considerable latitude in determining what is included in each location. Handouts can be easily located, and there are no last-minute dashes to the copier. Handouts include examples of elementary school, middle school, high school, and adult career development activities that are WWW-based. All students must create similar activities, so they appreciate receiving examples of the instructor's expectations for their creative work.

ASSIGNMENTS

The assignments area is designed to hold course assignments, tests, and surveys. In this course, assignments are included in the folders created for each class meeting and placed at the Course Information location. Tests that are administered during class meetings are activated at this Assignments location at the time the test is to be administered. Instructors who choose primarily to use performance-based assignments might still find this site useful for the administration of a pretest to assess knowledge of career development WWW sites. In this course, a pretest in multiple-choice format is administered at the first class meeting. The test includes actual logos and other graphics from WWW sites such as America's Job Bank, NOICC, NCDA, and various college search systems. The students find this pretest format to be motivational. They want to log on to these sites and see what they contain. When students answer an item incorrectly, they are able to see the correct answer immediately. Viewing the correct answer is, however, at the option of the instructor. The instructor can also see detailed results that display each question and if the student got the question right or wrong, elect to give feedback or a remediation statement if an essay question format is used, permit students to complete practice exercises without recording a student name or grade, and permit the student to take the assessment many times without entering the grade in the gradebook.

COMMUNICATIONS

Features at this area include e-mail, calendar, chat room, discussion board, and digital dropbox. Once students have registered for the course, the instructor can set up customized e-mail for all students, all student groups, single students, and single/select groups. In this course, students sometimes work in teams to develop career development activities for various clusters of occupations. It is very simple to send electronic messages to every member of a group. Students find the calendar a useful place for locating assignment deadlines. If the instructor chooses, students can send written assignments via the digital dropbox. This tool is used to exchange files between a single student and the instructor. With the digital dropbox, students upload a file, such as the plan for a comprehensive career development program they prepared in a word processing format, and send it to the instructor. The instructor's dropbox includes a list of the transmitted files by student name, link name, file size, and date the file was sent. The features of chat rooms and discussion boards can be confusing. The synchronous nature of the chat room enables multiple users to participate at the same time, whereas with the asynchronous discussion board students do not have to be available at the same time to have a discussion. In this course, the chat room and discussion board are not yet fully exploited. Creative instructors might use these features to

Invite several employers to talk with the class regarding hiring practices.	Chat Room
Assign each student a WWW career development site to review and post a summary for all students to read.	Discussion Board
Pose a career counseling ethical dilemma and ask students to post responses that are supported by guidelines of appropriate professional associations.	Discussion Board
Ask students to examine the home of a major national corporation. Designate a time when students will discuss how this site might be used by students/ clients for an electronic field trip.	Chat Room

EXTERNAL LINKS

This area is used by instructors to provide links to key WWW sites. In this course, the instructor places three categories of WWW site links at this location: professional associations/career development groups (American Counseling Association, American School Counselor Association, National Career Development Association, and National Occupational Information Coordinating Committee); on-line assistance for development of home pages; and examples of home pages developed in previous semesters. The technology has now become so easy to use that every student is required to develop a career development home page for a target group of choice. The home pages are premiered at a "Night of Stars." Students are highly motivated to do a good job because they know they can elect to load their work on the Internet. The instructor links their work to the course syllabus that will be used in subsequent semesters. The home page development assignment is a very practical one, which has resulted in development of home pages for area schools and agencies and the Dual Career Office, the College of Arts and Science Advising Center, and the Upward Bound Program at the University of Tennessee.

STUDENT TOOLS

This area is used by students to access a series of tools that they can use to do things like check grades and manage the student home page. The use of this feature is highly dependent upon the type of grading practices used by the instructor.

UNDERSTANDING THE LONG-TERM POSSIBILITIES

Technological advances have greatly simplified the procedures that are used to author electronic syllabi and have created avenues for new instructional methodologies. The components of the electronic syllabus discussed in the preceding section are representative of current technological developments that can enhance instruction. But how will electronic instruction be affected by future technological developments?

One thing is fairly certain. What is written today about the use of technology may need to be modified in 6 months. Counselor educators who develop an electronic syllabus can be in a continuous mode of transitioning from one format to another if they wish to take advantage of new capabilities that become available. It has been the experience of this chapter's author that each time an electronic syllabus has been modified the steps and processes for doing so have become easier. *With instructors having to spend less time on learning the technology, in the future they must place more emphasis on the quality of the content and the appropriate mix of technology mediums, instructional techniques, and instructors.* Richard Lewis, interim president of the United States Open University, a new sister institution of the British Open University (www.open.ac.uk), has indicated that the United States is not very good at distance education. "They get hooked on one model as the answer. First it was television. Now it's the Net" (Blumenstyk, 1999, p. A36).

In addition to determining the appropriate mix of technology mediums and techniques, there is another type of mix that is possible: a mix of instructors. Career development courses of the future might well include combinations of university-based instructors from multiple institutions and practitioners, particularly those who use and have developed WWW sites. University courses may include links to and mixes of portions of other courses. For example, those who prepare elementary teachers might link to that portion of a career development course that deals with elementary students. The long-advocated integration and infusion of career development concepts into the total school curriculum might have a greater chance of taking place.

A development that needs to be monitored closely is on-line access to software. Colleges, universities, and schools are already accustomed to purchasing site licenses for software that can be loaded on their servers and thus are available to a number of faculty members. In the future, institutions may be paying fees to applications service providers who will make a variety of software available on the WWW. It is now possible, for example, to run PC programs such as Corel's WordPerfect and Microsoft Office on Internet servers instead of personal computers. Already, some companies have "developed technologies that allow simple terminals, old PCs and Apple Computer Inc.'s Macintosh systems to tap into PC programs over the Internet or corporate networks, ending the need for companies or other organizations to run desktop software or upgrade machines" (Clark, 1999, p. A6). If machine upgrades become less necessary, this could have a significant impact on increasing the number of classrooms in which electronically enhanced instruction can take place.

It is well known that the WWW shatters geographic barriers. It is technically possible to develop an electronic syllabus for a career and educational information systems course and offer the course anywhere in the world via the Internet. There are problems with the quality of video material, but these problems will eventually be overcome. Beyond questions associated with technical considerations are those associated with whether it is prudent for colleges and universities to invest resources in technology, reduce the number of faculty members needed to teach courses, and reduce counselor education programs by forming distance education consortia. For some fascinating viewpoints on how on-line courses can change the role of faculty, consult *Digital Diploma Mills: The Automation of Higher Education* by David F. Noble (1999). He warned that university administrators may be using technology to discipline, deskill, and displace labor.

BEING PRUDENT: GUIDANCE FROM TWO STUDIES

Certainly counselor educators are receiving guidance from within the profession as they determine how technology can be used to enhance the preparation of counselors. However, sometimes it is also helpful to examine statements from other disciplines. Findings and recommendations from two April 1999 studies on distance education can be instructive. What these findings and recommendations might mean for electronically enhanced career development courses is explored in this section.

FINDINGS FROM *WHAT'S THE DIFFERENCE? A REVIEW OF CONTEMPORARY RESEARCH ON THE EFFECTIVENESS OF DISTANCE LEARNING IN HIGHER EDUCATION* (PHIPPS & MERISOTIS, 1999), WITH IMPLICATIONS FOR CAREER DEVELOPMENT COURSES

Finding: **Research has tended to emphasize student outcomes for individual courses rather than for a total academic program.** *Implications:* Career development courses that

feature didactic rather than clinical instruction have been the first
to be electronically enhanced. As other counselor education didactic courses make use of interactive technology, and if clinical instruction is added to this mix, ways must be found to assess the
performance of practicing counselors who are graduates of programs in which they have been prepared by a cluster of electronic
courses.

The Council for the Accreditation of Counseling and Related
Education Programs (CACREP) should monitor progress of the
Federal Government distance education demonstration effort that
began in 1999 and that may involve as many as 50 institutions over
a period of 3 years. The purpose of the demonstration is to help determine (a) the most effective technologies for delivering quality
education via distance course offerings, (b) statutory and regulatory
requirements that should be altered to provide greater access to
high-quality distance education, and (c) appropriate federal assistance for students enrolled in distance education. To what extent
will the demonstration involve courses for counselors? To what extent will both program and course evaluations be conducted?

Finding: **Research does not take into account differences
among students.** *Implications:* Career development theory and
content have long recognized that individuals differ in their interests, values, skills, and abilities. Much research remains to be done
on preferred ways of acquiring career information and on career information processing patterns.

Finding: **Research does not adequately explain why the
dropout rates of distance learners are higher.** *Implications:*
Counselor educators must be clearly cognizant of this fact if and
when well-intentioned individuals make suggestions to collapse
certain counselor education courses and even entire programs into
a distance education consortia configuration. It may well be, however, that career and educational information courses could serve as
a fertile ground for experimenting with formats that will decrease
dropout rates. If a career development course offered via distance
education was constructed as a personal information journey, it
could be a source of data on whether a course that focuses on personal meaning has higher retention rates than courses that do not
use such an approach.

Finding: **Research does not take into consideration how the different learning styles of students relate to the use of particular technologies, and research focuses mostly on the impact of individual technologies, rather than on the interaction of multiple technologies.** *Implications:* The newest WWW-based courseware programs feature multiple technologies. Increasingly, it will be a question of which technology is the best for particular content for a particular learner. The courses offered by the British Open University (www.open.ac.uk) often include a mix of media and materials and are expensive to produce. One course was designed by a 40-person course team and will be among the first seven offered in the United States. The materials for this course "include four books, several study guides, five specially produced half-hour television shows, and a set of audiotapes" (Blumenstyk, 1999, p. A 36). A support system of approximately 7,000 tutors provides face-to-face tutorials, but some tutors "rely heavily on e-mail and telephone to reach students, especially if face-to-face meetings are impractical" (Blumenstyk, 1999, p. A37). Of the more than 300 courses developed by the Open University, only 6 are designed to be completely Internet based, and these are primarily in the area of computing and information technology.

Finding: **Research does not include a theoretical or conceptual framework.** *Implications:* It is the theoretical or conceptual framework for distance education research that is under discussion here. The preparation of career counselors requires both didactic and clinical instruction. It is in the clinical arena that those who prepare counselors can make a major contribution in building research models. For example, do research designs adequately address whether didactic instruction learned through electronically enhanced means contributes to building better clinical skills?

Finding: **Research does not adequately address the effectiveness of digital "libraries."** *Implications:* This finding relates to several concerns that are also being addressed by ACA, NCDA, ACES, and ASCA. The WWW is a very open system with no quality control in terms of what types of career information and career development sites are constructed. Many sites are developed by self-proclaimed career development experts with little background in career development theory or experience in working with the target audience for which the site was developed. Some responsibility rests with federal and state government offices that have awarded money for the development of such sites. Counselor educators who develop electronic syllabi should include links to sites that represent the highest ethical and content standards of the profession. They should not be reticent to point out shortcomings of sites that are not based on sound career development theory and that do not reveal the credentials of the site owner/developer.

There are thousands of career information sites on the WWW. Notable gains have been made in cataloging and organizing adult career development sites. There is still a great deal of work to be done in organizing sites by other age/developmental levels.

The corporate world could make a major contribution toward advancing the quality of digital library career information for elementary, middle, and high school students if they teamed with career development professionals to build career development awareness and exploration activities on their home pages. Some have already done so, but in the absence of such activities, counselors can create them.

RECOMMENDATIONS FROM *THE VIRTUAL UNIVERSITY & EDUCATIONAL OPPORTUNITY* (GLADIEUX & SWAIL, 1999), WITH IMPLICATIONS FOR CAREER DEVELOPMENT COURSES

Recommendation: **Place access at the core of systems design.** *Implications:* A system must take into consideration both human and material resources. The Gladieux and Swail study reported that a "digital divide" is being created in that the distribution of computers is "highly stratified by socioeconomic class" (p. 17) and that there are wide disparities in access to computers by income, race/ethnicity, and educational attainment. The digital divide grows even greater if counselors do not have access to equipment and the skills to help clients access job openings, college admissions, financial aid, and other types of career and educational information. New counselor education graduates and experienced counselors who do not receive such preparation are at a serious disadvantage. Further, they may place their clients at a serious disadvantage. Perhaps there is a digital divide in the preparation of counselors. Some university counselor education programs may have far greater access to computing resources than others.

Recommendation: **Keep the promise of technology in perspective.** *Implications:* Technology can assist in locating career and educational information, but clients must act on the information. Although technology can help prompt actions, it often takes face-to-face human interaction to help clients sort information, rehearse actions, and follow through to achieve personal goals. High dropout rates in distance education courses point to the fact that there is much work to be done in terms of finding techniques to retain students in such courses and of determining the proper mix of face-to-face and remote instruction.

Recommendation: **Learn from the distance-learning pioneers.** *Implications:* Faculty members at universities like Virginia Tech where a distance education career development course is being offered and the University of Tennessee where the first WWW-enhanced career development course was developed can provide valuable insights in terms of designing instructional activities that seem to work in graduate courses. British Open University personnel have valuable information to share in terms of emphasis that is placed on team approaches to course development, course development costs, and the proper mix of face-to-face versus remote instruction.

Recommendation: **Take action to narrow the digital divide.** *Implications:* The digital divide between trained and untrained counselors should be a particular focus of university counselor educators. Here are some straightforward suggestions: Support counselor educator colleagues who want to learn new technologies. Convert occupational/career information courses to WWW-based courses. Advocate for access to computer classrooms; teacher educators need access to computer classrooms and so do counselor educators. Ask counselor education interns to assist practicing counselors in learning how to use the WWW.

Recommendation: **Monitor progress toward equal access.** *Implications.* Technology gives learners more control over where, when, and how they learn—but who will have that control? In a time when 40% of classrooms in schools with the highest concentration of poor students (measured by percentage of students eligible for free or reduced-price lunch) have Internet access, compared to more than 60% of classrooms in schools with the lowest concentration of poor students (U.S. Department of Education, 1999), and when half the schools that are connected to the Internet are connected only at the library/media center or principal's office (Quality Education Data, 1998), counselors must become advocates for equal access to technology. Counselors work with all students, and they are in a position to make strong arguments as to why they need technology to help students enter further education and employment settings. It seems reasonable, then, that counselor educators who prepare individuals who work with all students must advocate for access to computing resources that support instruction.

CONCLUSION

There is little doubt that advances in technology have opened many new possibilities for delivering instruction. Even though the content of courses that deal with career and educational information seems to be a natural fit for electronically enhanced instruction, those who prepare counselors need to be aware that there is a lack of quality research on the effectiveness of distance education, and that technology is creating a digital divide.

Can counselor educators stand back and wait for the research evidence to accrue? Professional judgment based on the ethical considerations and the standards of the profession will guide decisions as to what content will be delivered by what means. In making those judgment calls, counselor educators can take partial comfort in the fact that technology opens the doors for learners to tell us how they learn best. When students drop out of distance education courses at high rates, it may be that they are saying that they want technology to complement but not supplant face-to-face interaction with instructors. It may also reflect that not enough time has been spent in designing and authoring material contained in the course.

Can counselor educators stand back and wait for adequate access to become available? Counselor educators and counselors must help students and clients learn how to negotiate the career information digital world.

This chapter concludes where it began: Be wisely cautious in practical affairs. Be careful in providing for the future. Be prudent.

REFERENCES

Blumenstyk, G. (1999, July 23). Distance learning at the Open University. *The Chronicle of Higher Education*, pp. A35–A37.

Clark, D. (1999, July 21). Software is becoming an on-line service, shaking up an industry. *The Wall Street Journal*, pp. A1, A6.

Gladieux, L. E., & Swail, W. S. (1999). *The virtual university & educational opportunity.* Washington, DC: College Board [On-line]. Available: www.collegeboard.org.

Noble, D. F. (1999). *Digital diploma mills: The automation of higher education* [On-line]. Available: http://www.journet.com/twu/deplomamills.html.

Phipps, R., & Merisotis, J. (1999). *What's the difference? A review of contemporary research on the effectiveness of distance learning in higher education.* Washington, DC: Institute for Higher Education Policy [On-line]. Available: www.ihep.com.

Quality Education Data. (1998). *Internet usage in public schools 1998* (3rd ed.). Denver, CO: Author.

U.S. Department of Education. (1999). *Internet access in public schools and classrooms: 1994–98* (Issue brief, NCES 1999-017). Washington, DC: National Center for Education Statistics.

12

The International Career Development Library: The Use of Virtual Libraries to Promote Counselor Learning

GARRY R. WALZ AND L. STAR REEDY

Counselor effectiveness is strongly influenced by the counselor's ability to access and utilize quality information. Traditionally, the major source of information regarding counseling for use in counselor preparation and continuing professional development has come from books and journals. With the advent of the Educational Resources Information Center (ERIC) in 1966 and the establishment of one of the clearinghouses with a primary focus on counseling (ERIC Counseling and Student Services—ERIC/CASS), counselors were able to access relevant counseling resources from a national education database. This provided them the opportunity to search (both manually and by computer) not only journal and book literature but also "fugitive" literature that became available in full text on microfiche.

A common practice for counselors pursuing a project or doing a literature review for an advanced degree was to use one of the commercial services (e.g., DIALOG or BRS) to search the ERIC database. They selected descriptors from the ERIC Thesaurus and submitted them to a trained search specialist. About 10 days later, they received a computer printout of the annotations/abstracts of relevant journal articles and ERIC documents. They then went to a library with an ERIC microfiche collection and viewed the full text of the documents on a microfiche reader. For access to the full text of any journal article, they had to locate the journal itself.

In retrospect, this system seems somewhat tedious and limiting, but at the time it vastly expanded a counselor's ability to identify and retrieve resources relevant to his or her interests. However, with the exception of some special categories (e.g., ERIC Digests On-line), counselors still had to go physically to a library to obtain the full text of the documents of interest to them. With the advent of the Internet, counselors are now able to conduct their own on-line searches, providing them with immediate identification of resources.

In the 1990s, the Internet made possible the virtual library, or a library without walls. In a virtual library a user experiences ". . . collections of information as though physically in the library" (Saunders, 1992). In its true form, a virtual library provides the effect of a library that ". . . is a synergy created by bringing together technologically the resources of many, many libraries and information services" (Gapen, 1992).

It is as if individuals can transpose themselves into a super library where they can easily examine huge holdings on any variety of topics. And what makes the holdings of the bulging shelves so attractive is that not only can in-house collections be searched, but also distant collections of resources can be accessed—collections ordinarily not available except through the use of indexing sites such as Yahoo or (what seems a tedious process today) interlibrary loans.

THE DEVELOPMENT OF THE
COUNSELING VIRTUAL LIBRARIES

After examining the concept of the virtual library, it became apparent to ERIC/CASS that it was worthy of experimentation and that ERIC/CASS should proceed to develop a number of virtual libraries on topics of high criticality for counselors (Walz, 1997). It appeared that it was possible to design a series of virtual libraries that were responsive to the special information needs of counselors and could exhibit some distinguishing characteristics that would make them particularly attractive to counselors. The design ERIC/CASS developed was built around seven distinguishing characteristics:

1. **Resources are available in full text and can be easily downloaded.** An important priority is to include only docu-

ments that, because of their high quality, counselors will want to download for their files and/or distribute to clients and students. The key factors here are that the documents be immediately downloadable (no trip to the library required) and that they be in the public domain or possess a copyright release so that they can be copied and distributed without limitation.

2. **The libraries target critical, high priority counseling topics.** ERIC/CASS's intent is to keep each library at a manageable size by focusing on topics that lend themselves to being adequately covered by relatively few documents as opposed to large, unwieldy collections. Quantity is accomplished by hot linking to other web sites and collections.

3. **The libraries require no special skills to search and use.** By building on traditional library indexing and retrieval methods that users are familiar with, ERIC/CASS has made the libraries both inviting and rewarding to use. Typical indexes include such functional categories as specific populations, resources for parents, practitioner role, and age/grade level.

4. **Libraries are regularly updated.** ERIC/CASS's goal is to review and update each library every 2 to 4 weeks by adding new resources and purging outdated ones. The dates when they were last updated are indicated, and the home page of each library contains a notice of any particularly useful new items that have been added. Again, the intention is to make each library familiar and comfortable by simulating through electronic means the features of a proactive onsite library.

5. **Each library includes a frequently asked questions (FAQ) section.** This feature demonstrates to users that their responses to the libraries are important to the developers. When done in a thoughtful manner, the FAQs can become a proactive form of elevating the level of information-seeking skills of the users.

6. **Virtual libraries for counselors are introduced on the basis of a clear demonstrated need.** The decisions regarding topics for the virtual libraries are dependent upon input from Central ERIC, the U.S. Department of Education, professional associations, and ERIC/CASS advisory groups. The libraries are also time limited, that is, if a given library is infrequently used or

support for its continuance is lacking, its resources are incorporated into another virtual library.

7. **New acquisitions for the virtual libraries are aggressively sought from multiple sources.** Inclusion of a document in a virtual library typically results in wide international exposure for the author and provides experienced or new authors an excellent medium for sharing their ideas.

Using these listed characteristics as guiding principles, 10 topical virtual libraries have been introduced and are currently functioning. These are Career Development (ICDL), Student Achievement, Cultural Diversity, Conflict Resolution, School Violence, Bullying in Schools, Depression and Suicide, Substance Abuse, Youth Gangs, and Juvenile Boot Camps. All can be accessed at www.uncg.edu/edu/ericcass/libhome.htm.

It is a source of considerable pride for ERIC/CASS that two of the libraries (Youth Gangs and Juvenile Boot Camps) have been selected for the StudyWeb Excellence Award. Although these two have been singled out, ERIC/CASS believes that the awards apply to all of the libraries and are in recognition of the soundness of the original design. Subsequent positive user feedback and the number of "hits" by users confirm the usefulness of the libraries to counselors of varying positions and in different settings.

A career development library was one of the first and most highly regarded virtual libraries to be developed. The positive response to it was instrumental in a decision to upgrade it to a larger and more sophisticated web site, the International Career Development Library, which is described in the next section.

DESIGN AND IMPLEMENTATION OF THE INTERNATIONAL CAREER DEVELOPMENT LIBRARY

After approximately 2 years of experience with the counseling virtual libraries, ERIC/CASS joined with the National Occupational Information Coordinating Committee (NOICC) to design and implement a unique library for career development specialists. Juliette Lester, executive director of NOICC, and James Woods, NOICC information specialist, saw early on the potential of a virtual library for career development and were vital participants in its development. Important ongoing contributions have also been made by Burt Carlson and Roberta Kaplan, both of NOICC. The vision was to develop a web site that was unusual in the quality and quantity of free, on-line career development resources it offered to career specialists representing a broad array of positions and levels, such as career planning specialists, NOICC/SOICC personnel, counselor educators, state career guidance supervisors, and school counselors. It was designed to be a frequently used resource for career specialists to broaden their career development knowledge and competencies to better serve a wide variety of clients.

FEATURES OF THE ICDL

The International Career Development Library (ICDL) is a free, on-line collection of full-text resources for specialists in the field of career development. The ICDL is an on-line library that was developed based on a library model and offers electronic versions of such features as a library card, a card catalog, a reference room, and the ability to browse the stacks.

The ICDL web site (http://icdl.uncg.edu) features seven main sections: Search, Papers and Commentary, Document Submission, Reference Room, Training Center, Member Services, and What's New. Comments and questions related to any section can be sent by e-mail to icdl@uncg.edu.

Search

The main feature of the ICDL is the Search, which serves as the library card catalog. This catalog provides access to the ICDL database via a customized search engine developed for the ICDL. There are three approaches to the search:

- The Complete Catalog Search is a search engine that scans the abstracts of all holdings in the library. This search allows the user to customize retrieval for specific author and date.
- The Free Text Search is a search engine that scans the full text of all html documents in the library.
- The Scroll and Search is a list that provides access to the ICDL database by the arrangement of all holdings in a comprehensive index list. This search allows the user to browse the stacks of the library.

Papers and Commentary

Another prominent feature of the ICDL is the Papers and Commentary section. This is an on-line forum for presenting and discussing information and ideas of interest to career specialists. New papers, contributed by a range of career development experts, are posted periodically. This feature includes options to read and respond, read commentary from colleagues and the author, print papers or save them to be read off-line, and respond by posting comments to the on-line discussion.

Before a paper is removed from active debate, its author has an opportunity to respond to readers' commentary. The papers, as well as the accompanying comments, are then issued as a publication and archived in the ERIC database and the ICDL permanent collection.

Reference Room

The ICDL Reference Room provides a comprehensive list of links to career-related resources beyond the library. Links include on-line professional journals and publications, libraries and research centers, professional associations and organizations, and web sources on job search and career planning.

Training Center

The ICDL Training Center section features an on-line training registry of instructors prepared to offer training in career-related programs. Information for paraprofessionals employed in workforce or career development programs who are interested in earning credentials as a Career Development Facilitator (CDF) is provided. Also provided is access to the registry (maintained by the National Career Development Association) of qualified instructors prepared to offer the course.

Member Services

The ICDL Member Services section features the ICDL Library Card, which provides special privileges and access to select library features such as

• permitting the user to post comments regarding papers published in the Papers and Commentary section of the library;

- registering the user to receive e-mail notification when new papers are posted for discussion on the ICDL Papers and Commentary; and
- registering the user for e-mail notification of the ICDL database updates in any of 15 established areas of interest.

Document Submission

The ICDL Document Submission section welcomes materials of interest to practitioners in career counseling and guidance, educators, researchers, librarians, and others working in the field of career and workforce development. To facilitate contribution to the ICDL database, selection criteria and submission requirements are outlined on-line.

The simple two-step process for contributing to the database is explained. Document submission requires (1) an electronic (or paper) copy of the document and (2) a signed ICDL Reproduction Release.

Also in this section are answers to FAQs such as the following:

- What are the ICDL selection criteria?
- What are the advantages of having a document in the ICDL database?
- What does it cost?
- Are there any forms to fill out?
- Where do I send my document?
- How will I know if my document has been accepted?
- How long does it take to get a document into ICDL?

What's New

The ICDL What's New section highlights information that is new and noteworthy. Section features typically include New Paper Postings, Future Paper Postings, Recent Acquisitions, and Calls for Proposals.

FUTURE DEVELOPMENT OF THE ICDL

The ICDL is a work in progress. Though fully functional well before the Millennium, it is planned that the system will grow in size and features in the months ahead. Some of the insights that

ERIC/CASS has accrued to date follow. ERIC/CASS believes they are important not only to the future development of the ICDL but also to all who are engaged in comparable systems development.

- Building a database of essentially original and full-text materials that are available for downloading and reproduction is very desirable but difficult to implement. The ability for users to build their own "book" through personal selection of documents is attractive, but locating and obtaining publication clearance for each document is difficult. It is important to establish ongoing acquisition agreements with relevant organizations for building databases of sufficient quality and quantity.

- The ICDL type of web site is well suited to offering training modules for users. The modules can be of two types. The first type assists the user to better understand and use the system (library). Few users, for instance, are very experienced in strategizing sophisticated searches using Boolian logic, that is, combining terms with *and*, *or*, and *not* commands. The second type addresses topical or subject areas such as building portfolios. Modules of both types serve to orient users to the library as an ongoing source of professional development. Both types, however, should carry CEUs to motivate people to use them.

- Two of the most innovative features of the ICDL are the Papers and Commentary section, which offers users the opportunity to post their comments regarding a featured paper, and the personalized e-mail notices of new documents in members' areas of interest. Both of these features are enthusiastically viewed by ICDL users. In actual practice, it takes considerable "pump priming" to get users involved in using the new features, even highly desirable ones. Desirability apparently is often not a sufficient reason for using an innovative web site feature.

- Certain features are almost universally requested. Special collections where documents of a particular type are located on a special "shelf" or section of the library are frequently requested. Even though a good search can provide a comparable clustering of documents, the special collection feature is still positively viewed. It may also stimulate submissions so that a given person's work is contained in a collection of comparable work by others.

- It appears that a particularly useful way to popularize a special counseling resource is under the auspices of various sponsoring groups that offer training in the implementation and use of the new system. A special workshop for users offered in conjunction with a board meeting or as part of a larger training initiative seems to be an excellent way both to motivate and stimulate persons to use the new resource for upgrading their counseling knowledge.

- On-line virtual libraries that target specific counseling topics, such as career development and student achievement, are well received by counseling and career professionals. Practitioners and educators alike respond positively to both the database variety with sophisticated search strategies (e.g., the ICDL) and the menu-driven variety with collections of documents that are extensively cross-referenced but grouped in key categories such as age/grade level and type of problem (e.g., the ERIC/CASS Virtual Counseling Libraries). A key variable in the frequency and breadth of use appears to be the extent to which professional leaders and educators support and promote them. Demonstrations and presentations at national conference and workshops have been shown to increase the regular use of and positive response to them.

CONCLUSION

Early signs are that the technical challenges posed by developing a web site with many innovative technological components can be more readily accomplished than motivating persons to use the system—even when the system is perceived as useful and desirable. This suggests that a new technologically driven innovation will not be adopted and used based solely upon its apparent merits. It requires numerous initiatives to acquaint people with the innovation and to prepare them to use it. This result is consistent with a body of research on adoption and utilization of innovations, but is easily downplayed in the enthusiasm over the attractiveness of a new technology.

The original planning, which emphasized both meeting the technical challenges of developing an innovative virtual library and promoting its use through professional contacts and support, appears fully justified. Future efforts need to focus on installing new features as well as informing and motivating counselors to use the system.

REFERENCES

Gapen, D. K. (1992). *What is a virtual library?* Unpublished executive summary for Computers in Libraries '92 Conference.

Saunders, L. M. (1992). The virtual library today. *Library Administration and Management, 6*(2), 66–70.

Walz, G. R. (1997, Fall). Virtual libraries: A new resource for career counseling. *AVA Guidance Division Newsletter.*

13

Electronic Portfolios in Counselor Education

Jacqueline Lewis, Diane Coursol, and Kay Herting-Wahl

From ATM cards to the Internet, technology is now an integral part of life and work. Like most professions, the counseling field is also feeling the impact of technological innovations. Today, clients meet with their counselors in cyberspace as they engage in web counseling, and supervisors and supervisees maintain contact with each other through the Internet. This unprecedented evolution of technology has led to some concern over the ramifications for the counseling profession (Lambert, 1988). As we move into the new millennium, the profession must evaluate the role of technology in counseling and its implications for the future.

Acknowledging these developments, the counseling profession recognizes the need to ensure that counselors are technologically proficient. The electronic portfolio is one means to provide counselors with the opportunity to develop technological competencies. Today, it is used increasingly in K–12 settings (Bushweller, 1995; Golomb, 1996; Milone, 1995; Mohnsen, 1997) and in higher education (Holt, Ludwick, & McAllister, 1996; Richards, 1998; Riggsby, Jewell, & Justice, 1995).

This chapter first describes the concept, applications, development, and technological requirements for electronic portfolio development. It then discusses a model for infusing an electronic portfolio project into a graduate curriculum to prepare counselors to work more effectively in an increasingly technological environment. The chapter also examines implications of electronic portfolios for learning and for the new millennium. An appendix provides a list of web sites that have information about the electronic portfolio process.

THE CONCEPT OF THE ELECTRONIC PORTFOLIO

An electronic portfolio is a collection of selected documents that illustrate an individual's competencies, skills, and accomplishments in a consolidated technological format (Bushweller, 1995; Richards, 1998; Tuttle, 1997). Like the traditional portfolio, counselors can document their professional skills and progress for supervisors, record their professional development, and emphasize specific skill areas for potential employers.

Some counseling training programs have already begun to incorporate the traditional portfolio (Carney, Cobia, & Shannon, 1996). Baltimore, Hickson, George, and Crutchfield (1996) as well as Carney et al. have suggested that portfolios are a means of encouraging counselors to assess their own development, of promoting collaboration among students and faculty, and even as a form of performance assessment. These authors have indicated their belief that portfolios provide a more comprehensive picture of counselors' professional growth and development. The electronic portfolio incorporates all these elements. The multimedia format of the electronic portfolio allows for the inclusion of different types of documentation that attest to an individual's professional achievements. So it is possible to include text, graphics, and video and audio materials (Milone, 1995; Tuttle, 1997). The electronic portfolio can provide a more comprehensive and vivid representation of a counselor's educational experience and training during his or her graduate program or professional career (Lewis, Coursol, & Wahl, 1998).

For counselors, the electronic portfolio can effectively document individual counseling and other professional skills. Counselors may include a variety of materials such as certificates, plaques, statements of their philosophy and goals, developmental guidance plans, handouts developed for presentations, treatment plans (with all identifying information removed), records of practicum/internship hours and work experience, certificates of special training, and national and state licensures. It is also possible to include individuals' reflections on how these experiences have promoted their professional development. The electronic format enables counselors to demonstrate the performance of these skills visually through video clips of counseling sessions (simulated to protect client confidentiality) or scanned photographs of professional accomplishments.

Unlike the traditional portfolio, the documentation in an electronic portfolio can be arranged so as to maximize its impact on the reader. In the traditional portfolio it is not always possible to include materials like a video clip at the appropriate point in the binder. In fact, a statement that informs the reader to watch the videotape is usually included. This can be inconvenient for the reader who may choose to view the material later, outside its specific context. Such an arrangement can detract from the power of the portfolio. In the electronic portfolio, these materials are incorporated synergistically into the product for the reader to view for greatest effect.

APPLICATIONS OF ELECTRONIC PORTFOLIOS IN COUNSELOR EDUCATION

For counselors, the electronic portfolio can have a number of different applications. The manner in which the electronic portfolio is used depends on individual or programmatic needs. For example, the electronic portfolio may be used as a

- **professional development portfolio:** This is a way counselors can document their progress throughout their graduate program and career. Counselors can maintain a professional development portfolio containing examples of their work in courses, their internship experiences, and their work experience. They can also include their reflection of how these experiences have impacted their professional growth and development.
- **clinical skills portfolio:** This is a means of documenting a counselor's growth in the area of clinical skills. Counselors can maintain a clinical portfolio that contains samples of their work in or with various training or internship sites and agencies. They can also chronicle skills in specific areas such as career counseling, assessment, marriage and family counseling, or multicultural counseling.
- **career portfolio:** With the electronic career portfolio, counselors can present their skills, experiences, and competencies to

future employers in a real and powerful way. The electronic career portfolio can be customized to the requirements listed in the position description.

- **performance assessment portfolio:** This is an alternative method for assessing students' knowledge, skills, and ability to translate theory to practice. Such a portfolio may contain information on the student's progress over time in coursework, clinical experiences, research, and specific areas established by the department. Students may also want to document skills in the eight core areas identified by the Council for the Accreditation Counseling and Related Educational Programs (CACREP, 1994). It is critical that departments establish clear evaluation criteria and make every attempt to maintain adequate validity and reliability for this process.

THE DEVELOPMENT AND ORGANIZATION OF THE ELECTRONIC PORTFOLIO

The development and organization of the electronic portfolio is a dynamic and evolving process. For counselors, the planning and preparation can begin early in their graduate experience. In an ideal situation, counseling students are introduced to the concept and purpose of the electronic portfolio during the first semester, in introductory classes, and encouraged from the outset to think about their entire graduate experience within the context of electronic portfolio development.

An important first step in the development of the electronic portfolio is the identification of the purpose of the portfolio. Clearly articulating the aim of the portfolio is key because this determines the organization and selection of materials to be included in the final product. Therefore, thinking about the purpose of the electronic portfolio and its target audience carefully from the outset is important.

Once the purpose of the electronic portfolio is clearly defined, the next step is to consider its organizational format. The organization of the portfolio should be linked to the purpose of the electronic portfolio. In fact, the purpose determines how the counseling skills, competencies, and experiences are presented within the electronic portfolio. If the objective is to chronicle skill development, a skill-based portfolio that shows skill growth and development over time may be appropriate. Creative portfolio organization is critical as the presentation of the materials dramatically impacts how the electronic portfolio will be evaluated.

When the organization of the electronic portfolio has been determined, then the selection of the appropriate materials can begin. Materials selection should be undertaken with care. The random inclusion of materials without any thought as to their association with the purpose of the portfolio will detract from the effectiveness of the final product. When selecting materials for inclusion in the portfolio, it is imperative that counselors at all times protect client confidentiality. The selected materials are then transformed into an electronic format for incorporation into the electronic portfolio. This transformation process usually involves word processing and scanning materials into a digital format. In this way readers of the electronic portfolio have both a pictorial and written representation of the counselor's experience.

TECHNOLOGICAL REQUIREMENTS

Electronic portfolios require the hardware and software that is often available at most institutions of higher education and in many organizations or agencies today. The hardware requirements include a computer with multimedia capabilities, a scanner, digital or video camera, and a microphone. The scanner transforms documents and photographs into digital format so that they can be encompassed into the electronic portfolio. With a video or digital camera, counselors can record samples of their clinical skills and related professional experiences. With a microphone, audio recordings can be made of counselors' reflections on their professional development or of references' statements.

An essential step in electronic portfolio development is the selection of an appropriate software package. Several multimedia software packages with audio and video capabilities are available, such as Hyperstudio (1998) and PowerPoint (1998). Hyperstudio is often used for the development of electronic portfolios. However, it is also possible to use a readily available software program like PowerPoint, one of the most popular software presentation programs today.

The electronic portfolio can be stored in a variety of mediums such as a floppy disk, super disk, zip disk, jazz disk, or a writable CD. Two things to consider when choosing a storage format are the size of the portfolio and the ability to update the portfolio throughout one's professional career. With the expanding role of the World Wide Web, it appears pragmatic to consider making the electronic portfolio accessible through the Internet. To place the electronic portfolio in cyberspace, the document must be saved in html format, something that is possible in PowerPoint.

A MODEL FOR INFUSING ELECTRONIC PORTFOLIOS INTO THE CURRICULUM

In the 1999 spring semester, the Department of Counseling and Student Personnel at Minnesota State University, Mankato, introduced an electronic career portfolio project in the internship classes for second year students in the three tracks of school counseling, community counseling, and student affairs. These classes were selected because the smaller class size made it possible to provide individualized instruction and assistance to students.

The project involved two phases: faculty training and student instruction. Phase one involved training the faculty who taught the internship classes to use PowerPoint as an electronic portfolio development tool. The first step required introducing faculty to the concept, purpose, and uses of the electronic portfolio. As part of this training, the faculty were shown a presentation on electronic portfolio development and an example of an electronic career portfolio. They were then provided with a packet of materials that contained an outline of the PowerPoint presentation on electronic career portfolio development that was shown to them, a handout describing the electronic career portfolio project, a handout that provided step-by-step instructions on how to use PowerPoint to create an electronic career portfolio, and a student evaluation form for the electronic career portfolio project. The faculty were taught to use a digital camera and a flatbed scanner to transform documentation such as photographs and certificates into a digital format for inclusion into the electronic career portfolio.

Phase two was student instruction. Students were introduced to the development of an electronic career portfolio and were shown an example of a career electronic portfolio. Faculty also demonstrated to the students how to use PowerPoint to create an electronic career portfolio. In addition, the students were provided with the handouts that were shared earlier with the faculty. To support students in their initial attempts, class time was set aside during which students could begin the development of their electronic career portfolios. This allowed the faculty to provide students with individualized attention based on their needs and level of technological expertise. Throughout the semester, the project directors were available to faculty and students for consultation and instruction.

A unique aspect of this project was the decision to use PowerPoint to develop the electronic career portfolio. PowerPoint was chosen intentionally to demonstrate that sophisticated technological resources were not required for the creation of electronic portfolios. This project showed that electronic career portfolios could be created with a program to which most people have access. It was advantageous to choose a software program that faculty and students were familiar with as it allowed their attention to focus on the creation of the electronic portfolio rather than on the technical aspects of the software package.

Because the purpose of the electronic career portfolio project was to facilitate the job search process, the following organizational format was recommended:

- introduction/copyright statement;
- academic preparation;
- professional skill areas;
- awards and certification;
- conferences and presentations;
- professional affiliations; and
- references.

These categories were selected based on the skills and competencies typically expected of counseling professionals.

The introduction/copyright statement indicated that the portfolio was the individuals' unique work, personal, and not to be copied without permission. The next two sections, academic preparation and professional skill areas, demonstrated the skills and competencies possessed by individuals that are critical to the profession. The awards and certifications section provided documentation of professional skills and abilities acquired in addition to academic preparation. This allowed individuals to demonstrate areas of specialization that are most consistent with professional growth objectives. Documentation of conference and presentation attendance and of professional affiliations provided additional evidence of the individuals' commitment to professional growth. References, the final section, supported claims of expertise and experience from people who were involved with the professional development of counselors. Thus statements of support could be incorporated through video or audio format into the electronic portfolio. With the stroke of a mouse the potential reader could hear direct feedback and observations about the individual.

It is important to note that these categories were suggestions intended to provide some initial structure for the organization of the electronic career portfolio. Students were encouraged to design and present their electronic career portfolio in a professional but personally unique manner.

At the end of the semester, students handed in their electronic portfolios to the faculty instructor and received feedback. Based on the feedback, students made revisions to their product. Two weeks after the semester ended, an e-mail was sent out to all students informing them that they had the option of having their portfolios placed on the web. Those students who chose this option then linked their portfolios to the departmental web page in a read-only format. This format ensured that no information could be copied off the Internet. Examples of these portfolios can be found at www.coled.mankato.msus.edu.

Faculty reactions and support for the electronic career portfolio project were very positive. The faculty were especially appreciative of a means for infusing technology into the curricula in a way that encouraged students to reflect upon their graduate experience. Students were appreciative of the chance to learn and practice the use of technology. They were also pleased to have a tangible product to take with them as they embarked in the job search process.

THE LEARNING IMPLICATIONS
OF THE ELECTRONIC PORTFOLIO

The electronic portfolio has several advantages in addition to those offered by the traditional portfolio for counselors. Obvious advantages include cost-effectiveness, reader convenience, visual demonstrations of skills, and audio-based references. However, the electronic portfolio can also facilitate the learning process in several significant ways. In graduate training programs, electronic portfolios offer a significant way to infuse technology into the curriculum. The experience makes students more technologically proficient as they learn about multimedia software programs, digital and video cameras, and scanners. In turn, this experience prepares them to deal effectively with emerging technological developments throughout their professional careers.

The process of developing an electronic career portfolio increases insight and a sense of ownership among counselors for their professional development. As they choose what to include in their electronic portfolios, there is a greater sense of proprietorship over their professional development. Through reflection on their graduate and work experiences, counselors acquire a better understanding of the relationship between their learning and the world of work.

Electronic portfolio development also prepares counselors for the job search process. Smith (1996–97) recommended that job seekers develop career portfolios to compete effectively in the job market. Developing the electronic career portfolio teaches counselors about their skills and abilities, promoting greater professional maturity. In turn, counselors can interview more effectively because they can discuss their professional competencies in a mature and insightful manner (Golomb, 1996; Sherbert, 1996–97). Besides, the versatile format of the electronic portfolio allows it to be adapted easily to the requirements of a variety of employment opportunities.

Although the electronic portfolio offers many advantages to counselors in a highly mobile and fast-changing world, it does have limitations. Perhaps one of the most immediate concerns is the security of personal information. There is concern that an individual's personal information can be easily copied. This concern is heightened when the portfolio is available on the Internet. One way to guard against the unauthorized copying of information is to save the electronic portfolio in a read-only format when distributing it to potential employers. Security issues on the Internet can be addressed through the use of encryption procedures often in place at most higher education institutions.

Another limitation is the accessibility of technological hardware and software. The reality is that the availability of technological resources may vary from institution to institution. However, this limitation is likely to decrease as technology and electronic portfolios become more common.

IMPLICATIONS FOR THE NEW MILLENNIUM

The electronic portfolio is one way to adapt the emerging technological innovations to the field of counseling. With its versatile format, counselors can harness the potential of one of the fastest developing and dynamic technologies of the decade, the Internet. This alliance between the electronic portfolio and cyberspace provides several advantages to counseling professionals including virtually unlimited worldwide access to employment opportunities, a forum to market counseling services to potential clients, and a cost-effective medium to reach previously untapped audiences.

CONCLUSION

The electronic portfolio, a novel concept in counselor education, is an attempt to prepare future counselors for an increasingly technological world. Not only does an electronic portfolio infuse technology into the curriculum, but it also promotes professional development among counselors. As a cutting-edge innovation, the electronic portfolio prepares counselors for the challenges of the new millennium.

REFERENCES

Baltimore, M. L., Hickson, J., George, J. D., & Crutchfield, L. (1996). Portfolio assessment: A model for counselor education. *Counselor Education and Supervision, 36,* 113–121.

Bushweller, K. (1995). The high-tech portfolio. *The Executive Educator, 17,* 19–22.

Carney, J. A., Cobia, D. C., & Shannon, D. M. (1996). The use of portfolios in the clinical and comprehensive evaluation of counselors-in-training. *Counselor Education and Supervision, 36,* 122–132.

Council for Accreditation of Counseling and Related Educational Programs. (1994). *CACREP accreditation standards and procedures manual.* Alexandria, VA: Author.

Golomb, K. G. (1996). A work in progress. *Learning, 25,* 50–52.

Holt, D. M., Ludwick, K., & McAllister, P. (1996). Lone Star 2000: Documenting successful school or university teaching and learning. *T.H.E. Journal, 24,* 77–81.

Hyperstudio [Computer software]. (1998). El Cajon, CA: Roger Wagner.

Lambert, M. E. (1988). Computers in counselor education: Four years after a special issue. *Counselor Education and Supervision, 28,* 100–107.

Lewis, J., Coursol, D., & Wahl, K. H. (1998). *Electronic portfolios: Counselor education in cyberspace.* Paper presented at the Annual Meeting of the North Central Association of Counselor Educators and Supervisors, Kansas City, MO.

Milone, M. N., Jr. (1995). Electronic portfolios: Who's doing them and how? *Technology and Learning, 16,* 28–36.

Mohnsen, B. (1997). Authentic assessment in physical education. *Learning and Leading With Technology, 24,* 30–33.

PowerPoint [Computer software]. (1998). Redmond, WA: Microsoft.

Richards, R. T. (1998). Infusing technology and literacy into the undergraduate teacher education curriculum through the use of electronic portfolios. *T.H.E. Journal, 25,* 46–50.

Riggsby, D., Jewell, V., & Justice, A. (1995). *Electronic portfolio: Assessment, resume, or marketing tool?* Paper presented at the Association of Small Computer Users in Education, North Myrtle Beach, SC. (ERIC Document Reproduction Service No. ED387115)

Sherbert, S. (1996–97). Portfolio development: A journey from student to professional. *Career Planning and Adult Development Journal, 12,* 35–39.

Smith, C. (1996–97). What do employers want? How can a portfolio help? *Career Planning and Adult Development Journal, 12,* 47–53.

Tuttle, H. G. (1997). Electronic portfolios tell a personal story. *Multimedia Schools, 4,* 33–37.

Appendix
Electronic Portfolio Resources

A search of the World Wide Web revealed a number of web sites that have information about the electronic portfolio process. (One way to generate a list of such sites is to type in search terms such as *digital portfolio* or *electronic portfolio* using a search engine of your choice.) The majority of the web sites listed here contain information about the use of the electronic portfolio in K–12 or in programs of teacher education. They were selected based on their ability to describe the electronic portfolio development process or to provide examples of electronic portfolios.

- *College of Education*, Minnesota State University, Mankato (http://www.coled.mankato.msus.edu)
- *Creating Digital Portfolios* by Arnie Abrams, Southern Oregon State College (http://www.wce.wwu.edu/necccd/necchtml/proceeds/abrams/proceed.htm)
- *Electronic Portfolios* (http://www.esc20.net/techserv/workshops/portfolio/default.html)
- *Electronic Portfolios* by Yolanda Abrenica (http://edweb.sdsu.edu/courses/edtec596r/students/Abrenica/Abrenica.html#how)
- *A Guide to the Development of Professional Portfolios in the Faculty of Education* (http://www.edu.uleth.ca/fe/ppd/contents.html)
- *Sample Teaching Portfolios* (http://www.utep.edu/~cetal/portfoli/samples.htm)
- *Student-Created Electronic Portfolios* (http://www.7oaks.org/port/Default.htm)
- *Student Electronic Portfolios* by Thomas Arbruster (http://jrti.berk.tec.wv.us/portfolio/Port_intro.htm)
- *Student Portfolios* (A Collection of Articles) (www.business1.com/iri_sky/StuPort/stpc.htm)
- *Student Portfolios*, Delaware State Education Association (http://www.dmv.com/~dsea/profdevl/portintr.html)

- *Students Develop a Digital Portfolio,* Anaktuvuk Pass, Alaska (http://www.nsbsd.k12.ak.us/ARCHIVE/aste/digitalport.htm)
- *Technology-Supported Portfolio Development* (http://transition. alaska.edu/www/Portfolios/ElectronicPortfolios.html)
- *Using Portfolios in the Classroom* (http://www.migrant.org/data/ portfolio.html)
- *What the "Digital Portfolio Guide" Is* (http://www2.soc.hawaii. edu/com/CClab/Portfolio/Is.html)
- *Why Electronic Portfolios* (http://www.wallowa.k12.or.us/ wallowa/Tips/why.html)

14

Professional Publication in Cyberspace: Guidelines and Resources for Counselors Entering a New Paradigm

Marty Jencius and Michael Baltimore

In recent years there has been an explosion of interest around the infusion of technology into the counseling discipline. Cyberspace has become a new tool of the counselor who is well skilled in the resources that it can offer (Wilson, Jencius, & Duncan, 1997). Counselors have increasingly used the Internet for the purposes of e-mail, a service that has only been easily accessible for less than 10 years. In a similar fashion, counseling listservs (mailing lists) have become an accepted means of professional communication. Listservs like ICN for counselors, CESNET-L for counselor educators, and COUNSGRADS for counseling graduate students have become commonly referenced as resources for the counselor (Morrissey, 1998). Counselor preparation will include utilizing the Internet at an even greater capacity. This greater capacity includes using university department listservs, course web sites, virtual classes (Rotter, McFadden, Lee, & Jencius, 1999), and video conferencing as an adjunct to face-to-face supervision (Baltimore, Jencius, & Iris, 1999). The latest emergence from cyberspace is its use for scholarly publication.

This chapter first discusses scholarly publications on the Internet, comparing on-line publications and traditional journals and describing the movement toward acceptance of on-line publications. It next addresses the new thinking required for authoring on-line. The chapter then considers the format and design of h-journals, providing a description of a prototype and suggestions for authors writing in cyberspace.

SCHOLARLY PUBLICATIONS ON THE INTERNET

Scholarly digital publication runs the editorial continuum from moderated listservs to full multimedia web-based journals. Most listservs are unmoderated, allowing for any subscribed member of the listserv to post to the entire membership. Listservs can also be moderated where all posts go to the list owner, and the owner decides which posts are to be released to the entire group. In this way the information can be edited by the list owner as to appropriateness and content.

Another level of editorial responsibility comes into play in the case of e-journals, on-line journals, and h-journals. E-journals are journals available only in electronic form and distributed over the Internet usually without charge (Monty, 1997). *ACA eNews* (http://www.counseling.org/enews), for example, is an electronic news and practice bulletin of the American Counseling Association that follows the e-journal structure. The e-journal is created by ACA staff who provide and edit content. The e-journal is then distributed regularly to all subscribed members, via e-mail or is available on-line, but never appears in printed form.

On-line journals are journals that maintain an electronic existence parallel to a print counterpart and tend to be commercially produced (Langscheid, 1992). The ACA publication *Counseling Today* has its on-line counterpart in *CTOnline* (http://www.counseling.org/ctonline). In similar fashion, the Association for Adult Development and Aging (AADA) has its on-line presence (http://www.uncg.edu/ced/jada) and also includes a printed counterpart in *Adultspan*.

The next evolution in digital scholarly publication is the h-journal, or hypermedia journal. H-journals are web based and available to interested readers by going to the h-journal's web site with their Internet browser. The h-journal breaks away from the print journal organizational model by utilizing hypermedia capabilities of the medium (Sundaram, 1990). H-journals include hyperlinks to external sources and also include other document formats (graphics, audio, and video). The h-journal also supports user interactivity such as the ability to interact with the author of the article or publisher of the journal. The h-journal is considered the greatest level of evolution in electronic scholarly publication. The authors of this chapter are co-editors of the *Journal of Technology in Counseling* (*JTC*) (http://jtc. colstate.edu), an h-journal available in the counseling profession.

The publication which includes this chapter is a hybrid document. *Cybercounseling and Cyberlearning: Strategies and Resources for the Millennium* appears in paperbound form but references a separate cyberedition. The cyberedition, located at the ERIC/ CASS web site (http://www.cybercounsel.uncg.edu), contains articles not included in the paperbound form. These forms of Internet-published journals and other publications are part of the transition toward an increased use of cyberpublishing.

Traditional paper-based journals and cyberjournals have advantages and disadvantages for their readership. Functions for either remain similar, but the traditional functions of a scholarly journal should be kept in mind when considering the advantages and disadvantages of each. These essential functions of a scholarly journal, according to van Brakel (1995), are building a collective knowledge base, communicating information, distributing rewards (priority, recognition, and funding), and building scientific communities. *Building* a *collective knowledge* base means that the journal is serving a basic function for the counseling profession. Archives should be made available for interested scholars. The function of *communicating information* via text-based journals is rapidly being replaced by the quicker methods just described (e-mail and listservs). Journals do indirectly provide the function of *distributing rewards* in the form of establishing research priorities and inevitably leading to a scholar's success in, for example, applying for grant funding. Scholarly publication is also a large part of what is involved in successful granting of tenure for counseling faculty. Further, journals act to *build scientific communities* by making the scholarly community aware of who is doing what in particular areas of research. The advent of e-mail and other forms of cyberspace communication allows a ready means for scholars of similar interest miles apart to collaborate on similar interests.

Historic advantages that traditional journals have had over digital publication in scholarly publication include portability, consumer ease of use, and academic acceptance. Many professionals who are comfortable with text-based publications prefer to hold the document in their hand in lieu of reading the image on their monitor. A book or document can be dropped in a briefcase, taken home, and read in a more comfortable environment than computer screens allow. Consumer ease of use is an advantage that traditional publications have over h-journals. With a book there is no screen, mouse, browser, hyperlink, plug-in, software, or hardware. Paper-based journals have traditionally been accepted as a measure of scholarly success including faculty rank, promotion, and tenure.

On-Line Publications and Traditional Journals

The acceptance of on-line publications is hindered by the reluctance of a significant percentage of the counseling profession to use computers (Rosen & Weil, 1995). Beyond the personal level of discomfort with the electronic medium, there is an academic barrier that transcends its way into promotion and tenure activities. Peer-reviewed text-based journal publication is considered a more rigorous process by most tenure review committees (Langston, 1996) despite several studies that claim that electronic publishing is medium-neutral and that it is best to gauge the publication's rigor by other standards than its platform. Valauskas (1997) believed that the view of tenure committees is changing toward acceptance of electronic publication as a viable scholarly contribution based on factors that establish the publication as being sound. The advantages of portability, ease of use, and acceptance that traditional journals hold is loosing ground based on the advances in technology and movement to the digital paradigm. Computers are more compact and portable, interfaces are easier to use than they were in the past. Importantly, there is now an academic mandate to infuse technology throughout the counseling curriculum (Rotter et al., 1999).

As with the electronic medium, there are limitations for paper-based publications. Some of the limitations of traditional paper-based journals, as pointed out by van Brakel (1995), include ineffectiveness, high specialization—low circulation, declining revenue base, lack of timely feedback, and the process of reselling scholarly writings. The *ineffectiveness* in paper-based journals communicating scholarly information is that much of the information is already known by researchers prior to publication. Sources like professional conferences, listservs, and personal e-mail communicate immediately information that may take up to a year or more to get into paper publications. Because scholars are becoming more specialized, they are not often interested in many of the articles in a particular journal. In response to this, journals have become *more specialized* with declining interest and *lower circulation*. With lower circulation due to specialization, the revenue base from paper journals *declines*. Simultaneously, production costs increase and threaten the viability of paper journals. The largest limitation cited by van Brakel is the *lack of timely feedback* that is perpetuated by the cumbersome production process for paper journals. As an artifact of this process, the review process for articles is also cumbersome, preventing timely feedback to the author. If the work takes up to or over a year to get to press, the response by the scientific community takes additional years to appear back in paper form. As a final note, van Brakel pointed out the irony that the intellectual efforts of scholars are sold back to them by a publisher in the form of a journal or book.

Kubly (1996) pointed to some of the advantages of the h-journal web-based interface. First and foremost the web-based interface is simple to the end user but has powerful document keyword search and storage capabilities. In addition, because of the nature of indexing that goes on with the web, articles published to the web become self-indexing, but with limited accuracy as the number of web pages multiplies. Web-based journals also have direct links to other resources outside the bounds of the journal that permit the reader to further explore particular ideas from the document. The process of creating web-based documents has become easier so publishing can be learned very quickly. This simple process increases availability and reduces cost in that potential readership is unlimited and without the production costs of a paper journal. H-journals are not limited to font size or production dimensions but can for all purposes be unlimited documents not constrained by traditional physical limitations. Publication and peer review is faster and can essentially be done without paper. Components left out in traditional publications because of space and format limitations can be included in h-journals, adding a potential depth to data presentation. Primary materials like video, audio, and complicated graphics can be made accessible to a broader audience on the net. The document from an h-journal is available at anytime and in many locations rather then being restricted to a library shelf for access. Web-based h-journals can also be available to many people at the same time, unlike paperbound journals on library shelves. H-journals use less paper and less storage space than their paperbound counterparts but can also be printed out for user availability in print format.

Other proponents of web-based publication support the unique aspects web-based documents bring to the learning process. Ayersman (1993) used the prior work of Piaget, Kolb, Witkin, and others to support how cognitive learning is enhanced in a hypermedia environment. Harnad (1995) extolled that considering what we now know about the complex way in which the brain assimilates information, multimedia opens up utilizing the brain's many ways of organizing memory.

Despite these advantages of web-based publication over the paper-based publication, electronic journals do have issues surrounding them. Some of the issues are related to the reliability of the digital transmission of information over the Internet (Machovec, 1996). Internet connections are not always reliable and sometimes slow. Questions also arise as to who will maintain archives of articles. In traditional publication, this responsibility falls on the publisher. Machovec speculated that archiving responsibility for h-journals will also fall on the web publisher.

Copyright of electronically published material is an area that is having a difficult time keeping up with the advancement in technology (Okerson, 1991). The standard process now occurring is to apply the same concepts of copyright in text to the web environment, but this process has not been well tested in the courts. An issue mentioned earlier is the question of how tenure committees view scholarly publications on the Internet.

Harnad (1995) asserted that as publishers develop products on the web, print-based documents will become obsolete and refereed electronic journals will prevail. Despite the concerns with web-based publishing already noted, he suggested that the traditional system adopt an electronic peer-reviewed format in which the format can be modified to meet the needs of the publication and its readership.

MOVEMENT TOWARD ACCEPTANCE

Collins and Berge (1994) cited three major functions that must be adopted by electronic publishing for greater professional acceptance: credibility, accessibility, and permanence. *Credibility* refers to the publication's ability to advance thinking in the field. The publication should be supported by universities, professional associations, and peer interest in the publication. *Accessibility* refers to the need for the electronic publication to be able to be retrieved by the end user. The user should be provided adequate training to navigate the publication successfully. *Permanence* refers to the previously mentioned need for archiving and retrieval of past issues. The provision for archiving documents on the web is easily available to publishers and rivals archiving in a text-based publication format.

So how can the strength of an electronic publication be measured? Butler (1994) provided a familiar list that many h-journals in existence are able to accommodate. Scholarly criteria for journal publication include

- the contribution the journal makes to further scholarly dialogue;
- the ability of the publication to serve as an exclusive channel for initial dissemination;
- being known and respected through strict review policies and having a well-respected editorial board;
- quick publication of submitted materials so that authors may establish priority claims to new knowledge;
- sponsored by a well-respected institution;
- receiving good publication reviews from other publications in the same field;
- accessible through indexing and abstracting services; and
- retrievable by the scholarly community.

Butler claimed that this list can be used by authors and external reviewers to assess the scholarly viability of an electronic publication.

NEW THINKING IN WRITING AND RESEARCH DESIGN

Shifting writing style from traditional text-based publishing to authoring on a web-based platform requires a dramatic shift in the way we think about the authoring process. Text-based authoring is generally a linear process in which an author writes a structured outline that takes the reader from one point to another in a logical progression. Because of the flexibility of the web-based platform, the author has the freedom to start with a central subject and expand out from the center of an idea. The use of hyperlinks allows the reader to move outward from a central idea so the authoring of a web-based document can follow the same approach. Text-based authoring often requires a chronological progression of ideas as an organizing pattern. In the same way that the author is free from writing in a linear fashion with hyperlinks, the author is also free to write in a fashion that allows him or her to skip backward and forward chronologically. Traditional authoring has limits in the type of material the author can present (primarily text with a few tables, graphs, and illustrations). Web-based authoring requires the author to think more toward multimedia presentation of ideas. The transition may cause difficulty for some authors, but it appears to be a welcome one for many who present information better in a visually rich medium. The paradigm shift in authoring may be required to happen before an author picks up the keyboard to write. The way the ideas will ultimately be presented appears to have an impact on the strategy used for collecting data. The research process itself may undergo significant change due to the transitioning from paper to web-based research publication.

Whether the movement to publishing on the web is seen as a major shift in the way research is published is very much a debatable subject. For example, writers have suggested that a "paradigm shift" referenced to Thomas Kuhn's famous work on scientific revolution (1970) is occurring currently. Willis (1995) has suggested that, according to Kuhn, such shifts to a new paradigm occur over more than one generation and that there is much resistance to such a change. Given that some will embrace the new technological advances in publication and others will work against such change, the debate is sure to be an interesting one. Another question that is raised, of course, is What will be the impact of this change on the research process itself? Indeed, will this change cause repercussions in the gathering, collecting, and dissemination of research?

Given the added dimensions introduced by cyberpublishing, the impact on the research process comes under question. Are there additional or different expectations from the format so well established in presenting research material? What are the constraints or technological challenges for both researcher and publisher given this change in process?

The research process need not be changed or challenged by this new paradigm (Willis, 1995). The accepted format of printed research articles from the scientist-practitioner paradigm has existed for many years. The scientific research method provides researchers a format for presenting their findings to the scientific community. However, several issues new to the process must be considered. First, the advent of audio and video, in an on-demand medium, appears to be an important factor for researchers to consider. The *Journal of Technology in Counseling,* for instance, has established a format protocol for the inclusion of video and audio within research manuscripts that allows for new information to be disseminated. Researchers are asked to provide video and audio (other forms of media are also used) in the form of clips for publication along with the usual manuscript. This inclusion suggests that researchers are faced with additional expectations from the publishers. Readers hear and see footage from the researcher's perspective that provides additional and enhanced information. For example, researchers can discuss the origins of ideas, elaborate on the research question, detail interesting issues, describe research methodology, and add personal notes on the experience itself. These are a few examples of how the electronic journal and the use of interactive media presentation can impact the researcher.

Opportunities for researchers to present to the reader more than the typical design format and findings give rise to other points. One noticeable difference is in the planning stages of the research method. Anticipating a video discussion as part of the publication, the authors can record via videotape aspects of the study that are never seen by the reader of research. Events, actual demonstrations of techniques, and procedures can be captured during the research process and used to explain and advance the understanding of process and findings in a project. This idea alone appears to be an exciting opportunity and can lead to insight for reader and researcher.

FORMAT AND DESIGN OF H-JOURNALS

Publishing in electronic journals has begun to raise questions regarding formatting and style differences in how manuscripts are prepared. This presentation design or format allows for researchers, and readers of research, to maintain consistency, to guide writing, and to structure the research process itself as ideas and advances in the field occur. Comparison of research ideas and findings can thus be easily viewed. As noted, the scientific research method has provided researchers a format for presenting their findings to the scientific community. This format or design has not been challenged in any significant way. The onset and proliferation of the Internet and World Wide Web gives rise to an opportunity to add to the established paradigm.

At first glance, the established research design might transpose without variation into cyberspace and onto the computer screen. The traditional style of writing research manuscripts (American Psychological Association, 1994) will be alive and well long into the new era of Internet publishing. Similarly, paper and Internet journals are not radically different and indeed may be very similar. Valauskas (1994) presented several ideas concerning why differences in cyberspace and printed journals will not lead to an overthrow of the printed medium. First, establishment of scientific rigor and acceptance within the scientific community will continue. Peer review of published material and verification will continue to stand as a basis for judging the appropriateness and worthiness for publication of any study. Editing processes will change as manuscripts are submitted via e-mail or other process, but the editor's job will remain much the same. The review of journal submissions can be expedited through e-mail or entered via the web on submittable web-based forms.

Other issues for electronic journals have arisen that traditional journals have not faced. Evaluation and critique of the aforementioned video and audio clips embedded in the presentation of electronic-based manuscripts lead to new procedures. How does an electronic journal evaluate a video segment for inclusion in an elec-

tronic article? This is a question that has led to several new proto-
cols for such a task at the *Journal of Technology in Counseling*. Additionally, the education of authors for preparation of video and
audio has become an unexpected task. This shift in preparation of
manuscripts has led to a web-based design format page at the *JTC*
site (http://jtc.colstate.edu/proto/index.html) for new authors to
gauge their preparation of manuscripts prior to submitting.

The presentation of material on the Internet and the reader's perspective have also entered the debate. Reading on the Internet versus reading from the printed page is quite different. We read the
computer monitor more slowly than the printed page. The printed
page can hold more information in a given area than the monitor.
Too much text can be bothersome and cause eyestrain. Yet the
computer publication can present material in an interesting and
helpful manner. Most information can be printed from the web
page. Electronic citations can be instantly found and read. Pictures, video, and audio can enhance the experience, as already
mentioned.

These additional aspects from the development of the h-journal
will continue to impact traditional research standards and invoke
creative uses for a traditional venue. One such example of this publishing venue is the authors' journal for professional counseling and
the use of technology.

JTC as a Prototype for Counseling H-Journals

As noted earlier, the *Journal of Technology in Counseling*
(http://jtc.colstate.edu) is a production of the Department of Counseling and Educational Leadership of Columbus State University.
JTC was developed as a web-based peer-reviewed journal to address a need in the counseling profession to have a journal that supports the current trends in technology infusion. Because
technology infusion issues span many counseling orientations, it
was felt that such a journal could not emerge from the current divi-
sional organization of professional organizations like the American
Counseling Association. The development of a journal vehicle that
utilizes the whole capability of the Internet multimedia seemed to
establish the next level of Internet professional linkages. In addition, the use of a web-based format for a journal on the topic of

technology seemed appropriate. Because the technology field advances so quickly, added benefits of the web-based format are the capabilities of the journal to provide timely feedback to authors and to shorten the publication schedule. The journal's goal of advancing the professional discussion on the use of technology in counseling carries the message by using the medium.

The *Journal of Technology in Counseling* publishes articles on all aspects of practice, theory, research, and professionalism related to the use of technology in counselor training and counseling practice. The *JTC* accepts manuscripts that respond to the full scope of technology interests of its readers. Each edition of the journal contains articles from one or more interest areas. Manuscripts are solicited that respond to one or more of the journal's six areas of focus: professional exchange, newcomer's interest, theory, teaching, practice, and book/software reviews. *JTC* has an editorial board representative of counselor education professionals who have expertise in technology and diverse areas of counseling. The editorial board acts to guide the overall direction of the journal and to review manuscripts for the journal. Manuscripts are submitted electronically and are posted at a secure site that allows for reviewers to review the article on-line and submit their reviews electronically to the editors. Reviewers' comments are compiled, and reviews returned to the authors for consideration. Should the review require a rewrite and resubmission, the authors can elect to do so and resubmit. Because the entire submission/review rewrite process is on-line, the journal can maintain an aggressive production schedule. Authors are encouraged to use the full range of available web resources when submitting manuscripts including hyperlinks to other web resources, audio, graphics, video clips, and video streaming. Most authors, new to this medium, welcome guidelines for publication.

The *Journal of Technology in Counseling* measures up well using Butler's (1994) criteria for scholarly publication previously mentioned. *JTC* was developed to respond to a professional need to disseminate information on technology in an accurate and timely fashion, given the pace of change in the field. In that way it contributes to further scholarly dialogue (per Butler's criteria) around the infusion of technology in the field. *JTC* has established a respected editorial board made up of scholars in the field of counseling. The journal aims to reduce the production time and allow for quick publication of submitted material by creating a paperless submission and review process. Using electronic review and revision, the turnaround time for reviewing submitted articles is greatly reduced, a goal suggested by Butler. During any publication cycle, should there be a large number of approved-for-publication submissions, *JTC* is not physically limited to page number like paperbound journals. Another of Butler's conditions for scholarly h-journals is the use of an indexing system. *JTC* has established an ISSN number and is being catalogued as part of On-Line Computer Library Center (OCLC) Electronic Collections On-Line, and its editors will look to having *JTC* catalogued through other indexes.

SUGGESTIONS FOR AUTHORS WRITING IN CYBERSPACE

Print media provide guidance regarding general article preparation (Smaby, Crews, & Downing, 1999) that can be used with h-journals. In general, paper-based journal recommendations for manuscript preparation apply well to this new medium. Additional considerations for authors are as follows:

- **Know the journal you are writing for.** Look at other examples of work in the journal so that you can visualize how to present your ideas in a format that suits the journal's web site.
- **Consult with the editors whenever possible.** This is a new medium for scholarly publication, and with few examples around you may have to tap into the editor's vision for the journal until you develop your own digital vision.
- **Think differently** about how you can use the full qualities of the net to present your ideas. Glitzy is not necessarily better, and multimedia components should relate directly to the theme of your work.
- **Collaborate with someone who mirrors your weaknesses.** For those new to the digital realm, enhance your own cyberauthorship by coauthoring with colleagues who know the digital landscape. For those more comfortable with digital publishing and its capabilities, associate with colleagues who can help you in the content areas of your work.

- **Organize thematically not linearly.** Because digital articles use hyperlinks, authors are encouraged to think in themes that connect from a central idea rather than to think in terms of a linear development of ideas across one text.
- **Compartmentalize thinking; write in concise fashion.** Most text publications are too cumbersome for readers to waft through on a web site. Get your ideas out briefly; use multimedia to simplify complex ideas. Graphics are used liberally in cyberpublications compared to traditional text-only publications.

CONCLUSION

The advent of a new era in publishing has begun. The reach and scope of publishing on the web are not known but challenge us in unexpected ways. The impact of this new medium on the traditional paper-based publishing is also not known. We can predict that the transition to cyberpublishing will generate much discussion and lead us in new directions for writing and publishing, and even effect changes in the research process itself. Neither the h-journal on the Internet nor the traditional printed journal articles will become extinct. The possibilities and challenges wait as this paradigm shift continues. It has begun.

REFERENCES

American Psychological Association. (1994). *Publication manual of the American Psychological Association* (4th ed.). Washington DC: Author.

Ayersman, D. (1993, February). *An overview of research on learning styles and hypermedia environments.* Paper presented at the Annual Convention of the Eastern Educational Research Association, Clearwater, FL. (ERIC Document Reproduction Service No. ED 356756)

Baltimore, M., Jencius, M., & Iris, K. (1999, April). *Supervision and technology: Efficacy and uses for Internet video conferencing.* Paper presented at the American Counseling Association 1999 World Conference, San Diego, CA.

Butler, H. J. (1994). Where does scholarly electronic publishing get you? *Journal of Scholarly Publishing, 26*(4), 174–186.

Collins, M. P., & Berge, Z. L. (1994). IPCT Journal: A case study of an electronic journal on the Internet. *Journal of the American Society for Information Science, 45*(10), 771–776.

Harnad, S. (1995). The post Gutenberg galaxy: How to get there from here. *Information Society, 11*(4), 285–291.

Kubly, K. H. (1996, March–April). *The electronic journal on the Internet.* Paper presented at the Mid-South Instructional Technology Conference, Murfreesboro, TN. (ERIC Document Reproduction Service No. ED 400810)

Kuhn, T. S. (1970). *The structure of scientific revolutions.* Chicago: University of Chicago Press

Langscheid, L. (1992). Electronic journal forum: Column 1. *Serials Review,* 18(1–2), 131.

Langston, L. (1996, April). *Scholarly communication and electronic publications: Implications for research, advancement, and promotion.* Paper presented at a conference sponsored by the Librarians Association of the University of California, Santa Barbara, and Friends of the UCSB Library, Santa Barbara, CA. (ERIC Document Reproduction Service No. ED 403892)

Machovec, G. S. (Ed.). (1996). Electronic journals: Trends in World Wide Web (WWW) Internet access. *On-line Libraries and Microcomputers, 14*(6), 1–5.

Monty, V. (1997). Web journals and education. *Education Libraries, 20*(3), 11–17.

Morrissey, M. (1998). Student mentoring program via the Internet considered. *Counseling Today, 40*(9), 22–23.

Okerson, A. (1991). With feathers: Effects of copyright and ownership on scholarly publishing. *College and Research Libraries, 52*(5), 425–438.

Rosen, L. D., & Weil, M. M. (1995, Fall). Tips for mental health professionals to merge on-line. *Treatment Today,* pp. 48–49.

Rotter, J., McFadden, J., Lee, R., & Jencius, M. (1999, April). *The infusion of technology in counselor education programs.* Paper presented at the American Counseling Association 1999 World Conference, San Diego, CA.

Smaby, M. H., Crews, J., & Downing, T. (1999). Publishing in scholarly journals: Part 2—Is it an attitude or technique? It's a technique. *Counselor Education and Supervision, 38*(4), 227–235.

Sundaram, A. (1990). *Towards the design of a hypermedia journal.* Urbana: University of Illinois [On-line]. Available: http://alexia.lis.uiuc.edu/~sundaram/phd.

Valauskas, E. J. (1994). Reading and computers—Paper-based or digital text: What's best? *Computers in Libraries, 14*(1), 44–47.

Valauskas, E. J. (1997). Waiting for Thomas Kuhn: First Monday and the evolution of electronic journals. *First Monday* [On-line]. Available: http://www.firstmonday.dk/issue2_12/valauskas/index.html.

van Brakel, P. A. (1995). Electronic journals: Publishing via Internet's World Wide Web. *The Electronic Library, 13*(4), 389–396.

Willis, J. (1995, October). *Bridging the gap between traditional and electronic publishing.* Paper presented at the EDUCOM Conference, Portland, OR [On-line]. Available: http://www.coe.uh.edu/~brobin/Educom95/EducomJW/index.html.

Wilson, R. F., Jencius, M., & Duncan, D. (1997). Introduction to the Internet: Opportunities and dilemmas. *Counseling and Human Development, 29*(6), 1–16.

PART III

Outcomes, Achievements, and
Quandaries of Cybercounseling

15

The Subjective Experiences of Therapists in Face-to-Face, Video, and Audio Sessions

SUSAN X DAY AND PAUL SCHNEIDER

Most psychotherapists hold preconceptions about what it could be like to deliver services using distance technology. Some might say, "The physical presence of the client is absolutely necessary for a working alliance," and others might say, "The nonverbal cues I get from my clients are essential to my case conceptualization." Both comments suggest that remote contact is felt to be a poor substitute for face-to-face communication. The question of whether psychological contact over a distance is the same as a relationship built by people in the same room is vital in these days of teleconferences, e-mail friendships, and chat room romance (e.g., Kraut et al., 1998). Reactions to distance technology in counseling have been governed by guesses rather than by experience or research. However, a recent teletherapy project has provided insight into how remote systems of treatment actually are perceived. It is the only large, empirical project on the subject known to this chapter's authors.

This chapter first describes how the project—the Telehealth Project—was set up and implemented, and then examines six themes that emerged from analyses of the comments of participating therapists. Implications for clinical training and practice are briefly explored.

203

THE TELEHEALTH PROJECT

From 1997 to 1999, the authors of this chapter executed a research study to compare psychotherapy delivered face-to-face, over video teleconference (viewing each other on television monitors), and over audio-only conference (analogous to telephone) (Day, 1999; Schneider, 1999). We set up a clinic at which clients were assigned randomly to one of these technological conditions, and other variables were held constant: that is, the type of therapy delivered was mainly cognitive-behavioral; all clients attended five sessions; the same therapists did the counseling; a variety of client problems was accepted in each condition; and each condition involved the same physical setting—the Psychological Services Center at the University of Illinois at Urbana-Champaign. By June 1999, 26 or 27 clients in each condition had completed a five-session treatment at our clinic, well exceeding the median number of clients per group in psychotherapy research so far, which is 12.

In the case of the two-way video conference delivery mode, the setting consisted of two rooms, each with a video camera, one trained on the therapist and one on the client. Each of these cameras was then routed through VCRs in order to tape both the client and the clinician. From the VCRs the route continued to two 20-inch television monitors, one in each room displaying what went on in the other room. In the audio mode, each client used a hands-free audio system to connect and speak with the therapist. This therapy was delivered in the same rooms, using the same technology as the two-way video system. The only difference was that the video display was disabled for both the client and the clinician. Face-to-face dyads sat in one room together, with a video camera focused on each party. Therapists and clients in the video and audio modes never saw each other in the flesh at any time.

The study thus provided a unique group of clinicians who had delivered psychotherapy in all three conditions under closely comparable circumstances. Each of the therapists performed under all three conditions—face-to-face, video, and audio. The therapists were able to report on their perceptions of the three conditions and their subjective experiences of working with each. As each therapist left the project, he or she was interviewed on tape concerning subjective points of view on working in the three conditions. They were asked about their preferences, their perceptions of effectiveness, changes they saw in their techniques according to condition, their ideas about individual differences in responses to the technology, whether certain problems seemed better and worse for teletherapy, and so forth. The tapes were transcribed, and both authors of this chapter separately read the transcripts according to traditions of qualitative research, looking for common themes running through the therapists' experiences. These themes are the findings reported in this chapter.

The 10 therapists participating in the assessment and treatment of our clients were members of an advanced practicum group supervised by doctoral-level psychologists. All therapists were doctoral students in clinical or counseling psychology at the University of Illinois; cognitive-behavioral treatment is part of both curricula and was the suggested type of therapy delivered in our clinic. This type of therapy is understood to be empirically validated, especially in time-limited treatments (DeRubeis & Crits-Christoph, 1998). These student clinicians had completed practica at the master's level already; all had completed further practica at the doctoral level or had also held jobs as therapists. Their hours of practicum and on-the-job experience ranged from 1,250 to 3,200, including experience in community mental health centers, university counseling centers, the Illinois Department of Rehabilitation Services, Veteran Affairs medical centers, Latina Liaison, forensic clinic, rape crisis center, vocational advisement, and sexual harassment clinic. Thus they brought solid backgrounds of experience as touchstones for comparing their experiences on our project. Therapists participated at varying levels, seeing between 3 and 30 clients and staying with us for 3 to 24 months.

SIX THEMES

In analyzing the transcripts, we identified six themes that came up repeatedly. Contextual information is provided on each theme, and then the therapists speak for themselves on these matters through direct quotations from the interviews. This helps to capture the flavor as well as the content of their remarks.

THEME 1: EMOTIONAL CONNECTIONS: MIXED REACTIONS

Videotapes from all conditions were rated by a team of judges on a range of behaviors reflecting the working alliance between the therapist and the client. This alliance is often seen as the "active ingredient" in any treatment and as a necessity for success. The variables construed as representing the alliance were therapist exploration, client participation, and client hostility (inversely). A multivariate analysis of variance revealed no significant differences in any of these variables across face-to-face, video, and audio conditions. In other words, trained raters, who were practicing psychotherapists themselves, could not see any difference in the working alliance according to technological mode. This finding supports the idea that the emotional connection between client and therapist was not meaningfully impaired by technological intercession. Lombard and Ditton (1997) have provided theoretical support to the concept of *telepresence*, the ability to project and perceive social presence in technologically mediated communications.

Several therapists felt differently, however, no matter what outward appearances conveyed to raters.

- *Therapist:* All three modes could be useful for crisis management. When you are talking about deeper issues or are trying to work through stuff, the audio and the video had distance to them, and it's so hard to connect emotionally with the client. When you are face to face and having problems with someone, you lean forward or reach out and touch the person. When it's video, what can you do? When he's not looking at me in the TV, I can't move to show him that he's not looking at me.
- *Therapist:* With one client, she started crying and I just sat for a little bit. But the problem there is that I just felt so helpless like I wasn't there. I mean, I'm on a TV screen. There's no human contact or presence, and I think that's really important. I think that's one of the important pieces in the healing process and it wasn't there.
- *Therapist:* There's some sort of aspect that's kind of missing on the video . . . that wonderful, mythical presence.
- *Therapist:* It requires trust. That's a hard thing to develop if you haven't experienced it before. You have to have ego strength to be

able to withstand the kind of irony of it, you know, forming a relationship with someone who isn't really present, is there but is not there.

- *Therapist:* I had a client on video who was crying but I couldn't see it. When I finally realized that she was crying, I didn't know what to do. Usually if a client is crying in the session, I can sit there and wait for them to let it out or compose themselves, and I will usually hand them a box of tissues or something. But for me to speak over the video and say something felt intruding; I wanted her to feel my presence, but I didn't want to intrude.

Some therapists were surprised to find strong working alliances in spite of distance technology, and some thought the technology may even have enhanced the relationship:

- *Therapist:* The video, the only thing is that it's hard to tell sometimes if someone is tearing up or what the other nonverbals are. You can't see much beyond the face. So it's missing those sources of information, but I was really surprised how connected I felt with that client.
- *Therapist:* The client I had with the video was one of the strongest working alliances that I've ever developed with a client.
- *Therapist:* I got a sense that clients, once they got used to using the TV, that distance gave them a safeness. The clients compared to face-to-face didn't seem more rigid. They didn't sit up as straight, and they were more laid back, kind of like they were watching TV and doing this.
- *Therapist:* One client was real leery about being open about her issues, and so for her it was more comfortable being on video than being in the same room. She even said if she had been face-to-face she probably wouldn't have come or she would have dropped out. The flip side to the weakness of video, that distance I think, offers safety for some clients.

THEME 2: WORKING BLINDFOLDED

The lack of visual evidence in the audio mode was a frequent theme in the interviews, requiring changes in therapists' habitual patterns of interacting and thinking:

- *Therapist*: The audio, the problem was having to always remember not to just nod your head, making everything verbal that I wanted to express. Empathy is hard to constantly express verbally. You feel awkward saying "uh-huh" all the time. But maybe as I got more practice it would be no big deal.
- *Therapist*: Whenever I was thinking about my clients, I would always forget that audio client because I didn't have a visual picture in my mind.
- *Therapist*: I like to read people's body language. And I didn't have that. And I'm just used to when people are experiencing strong emotion or dealing with something painful it's typical to sit in silence, just be with them. How do you do that on video or audio? If you are silent, they can misinterpret that in so many ways. In audio I found myself talking a lot more, filling the silence because I wanted them to know I was there. The only way I could express my presence was to speak.
- *Therapist*: With audio, I felt more self-conscious about how I spoke and what things I said because that's all she had, so I felt I qualified things more so that she wouldn't misunderstand me. I tried to use more humor in how I was saying things to make her feel more at ease because she couldn't see me smiling, and she couldn't see me using my hands or whatever, and a lot of times I would say, "I'm listening, but I'm writing something down," or when there were moments of silence I would fill up those moments of silence by saying what I was doing so that she didn't feel like I just dozed off or whatever.
- *Therapist*: This one guy was so uncomfortable with his emotions and so scared of them that having me in the room with him would have made it a safer place and maybe he would have felt better about experiencing his emotions and I could be a container for him in a way [making sure that he wouldn't fly out of control]. But as far as video and audio goes, I wasn't a container at all. There wasn't a safe place created to experience emotions in that way. Especially on audio only, I don't think I pushed clients to do that, because I didn't feel comfortable doing it, at all. Because there was no way I could tell how far they'd gone or how in control they felt.
- *Therapist*: I had a client who I thought had an eating disorder—I never saw him so I was never able to judge how thin he was or if

he was gaining weight or losing weight or did he look healthy? I didn't have that benefit of being able to see him.

Conversely, our clinicians often found unforeseen benefits in the distancing effect of audio-only treatment:

- *Therapist:* I like the audio, too; I think that was really freeing for the client. The ones who used the audio, I think that they were more open. I think the fact that they didn't have somebody looking at them—they were able to open up a lot more and to disclose some pretty serious stuff. For example an audio client disclosed his abusive side.
- *Therapist:* The guys in audio gave me more feedback [on the therapy process] than the guys that were face-to-face. You know, in the other modes god forbid they might say something that might hurt my feelings.
- *Therapist:* At least for two of my clients that I had on audio I believe that it wouldn't have worked as well in a face-to-face situation or even a video situation. The gentleman I just finished up with, I think that anonymity of working with me and me not knowing who he was helped him talk about himself.
- *Therapist:* What surprised me was that audio was, I felt, just as effective as video or face-to-face. In some senses I feel that audio is something that should be used as a teaching tool because as I used audio I found myself being able to pay more attention to clients, not only what they said but how they said it. The fluctuation in their voices. I paid more attention to the silences, to pauses. With face-to-face or video there are things to distract you from that, because you're watching the person. It got to the point that I looked forward to working with a client in the audio mode.

Several therapists noted that their preconceptions did not operate as automatically when they could not see their clients:

- *Therapist:* I didn't find myself making as quick of judgments about the person as I might have if they had come in with a certain appearance and a certain problem. Then I might have jumped to some conclusions that I wasn't able to jump to. I probably wasn't taking therapy off in certain directions right away based on the way they appeared or the way they acted.

- *Therapist:* When you see the client, all the other factors that play into what you read into a client, you know, like how they dress, you may read in they weigh too much, or that socioeconomics are part of the problem because of the way they look. I got a sense that a lot of people prejudge a lot on appearance. What the audio does is it teaches you to listen. You know, we always talk about listening to the client. Audio puts it in your face; that's all you got.

One clinician pointed out that the subjective perception of the audio experience may be distorted by the absence of visual activity:

- *Therapist:* With one audio client, it was interesting when my supervisor was watching the tape and I was listening to it again [therapists weren't allowed to view tapes of their audio sessions]. I had felt in session like there were these hour-long pauses between what we were saying. I felt as though I was taking too long to respond and that I had a little less room to maneuver. It seemed very slow and felt very awkward and that I wasn't able to respond well. When I listened to it later I realized that the pauses were only half a second or a second, so all this time I felt like I was fumbling around and thinking about how to come up with the right response really wasn't that long, but it felt a lot longer because there wasn't any of the usual stuff going on in between.

THEME 3: THE INVISIBLE THERAPIST

We did not expect therapists to emphasize the advantages of being unseen themselves, but several did:

- *Therapist:* The audio was not only freeing for the client but for me too. I know if you see my videos in audio mode, I'm like totally relaxed. I had my feet up, so that was a nice mode for me too. I don't do that with face-to-face clients.
- *Therapist:* The most comfortable was probably audio, to a certain extent, because I didn't have eyes on me. I could just sit there and do my thing.
- *Therapist:* I learned that these restricting clothes [worn in face-to-face and video therapy] are not me. I do better work if I'm not

confined. I learned not to wear binding and constricting things. I'll be a California kind of therapist.

- *Therapist:* I was most comfortable in audio. Because I was more relaxed. When you're doing face-to-face I think you have got to have a certain posture. I think that most of the clients I had that way were more relaxed. They seemed like they liked the anonymity too.
- *Therapist:* In the audio I could be completely relaxed and focus only on what they were saying, and in some ways that helped them to be more honest because it wasn't face-to-face. So I didn't feel as embarrassed. I think they were more open about what they said and a little more free about the way they expressed themselves. I think audio was easier for me because I'm someone who enjoys talking on the phone. I tend to be more verbally expressive. So that was fine for me.
- *Therapist:* The audio was good because race never played into it, or me being in a wheelchair didn't play into it. It was just two people working without all those other areas popping up about if I was Black or if I was disabled. My face-to-face and video clients would eventually say, "You have it much more difficult than I do." They try to compare the situation they think I am in. In audio that never became an issue.

One of our therapists, however, found a communication problem due to being unseen:

- *Therapist:* When I'm in situations where I'm not especially comfortable or when I get nervous, I lose confidence in my English-speaking abilities since it is my second language. Usually I feel like I can kind of compensate for any misunderstandings in the way I speak by my body language and my demeanor. With audio, I felt that if I said something that didn't make sense, which I often do, I couldn't see the client give me that confused look.

THEME 4: APPROACHES TO PSYCHOTHERAPY

In our clinic, we encouraged clinicians to follow a five-session cognitive-behavioral model. However, for reasons of ecological validity, we allowed them to vary from this model according to their own judgment, just as a real-world therapist would. Most of the therapists had ideas about which orientations to treatment could work over which modes of delivery:

- *Therapist:* A psychodynamic therapist would do really well with the audio, especially psychoanalytic, because you don't look at your client anyway. But I'm more humanistic and interpersonal, like I use the relationship more and look at how it was similar to other relationships. You can do this in all the modes, which I did.

- *Therapist:* If you had your clients journaling or role-playing, things that are more interactive, that would be difficult. If it was video or audio, we had to make sure you had stuff xeroxed, and if you didn't, figure out how to deal with it. [At our clinic, before each session the site manager made copies of homework for the therapist in audio or video modes.] I thought in one situation about using the two-chair technique . . . I don't know how that would work in the audio because the movement is such a big part of it. In audio maybe the person would feel silly moving back and forth.

- *Therapist:* With the audio client, her therapy was exposure therapy to her fear of heights, and so normally under those circumstances I would have gone with her to experience some of the things that she was afraid of as part of the exposure therapy. We would have gone to the University Inn, right across the street, all the way to the top. I made up for the limitations by really concentrating on the homework and trying to play the homework out as much as possible during the session. A lot of imaginal in-session exposure. I can imagine that, for example, if a compulsive washer had to be exposed to dirt and all that stuff, that her doing it on her own would've been incredibly difficult, at least based on my experience with those problems.

- *Therapist:* In exposure therapy, just your physical presence and reassurance is important in doing certain tasks with them. If I had a client with a driving phobia I couldn't—well, I suppose we could talk on the phone while they are driving, but probably not such a good idea. Or I could talk to a friend of theirs or a spouse or someone and sort of get a support person who could then go and do these sorts of tasks with them.

THEME 5: CLIENT DIFFERENCES

Therapists had strong opinions about the types of problems that were suitable and unsuitable for the distance modes of treatment. (However, two therapists who treated eating disordered clients over audio had differing points of view on the effect of the mode, although both thought it increased client comfort.) Looking at all three types of treatment delivery, the idea of matching problem and delivery mode came up in almost every interview:

- *Therapist:* I had a client who was audio only who wanted to quit smoking. That was easily done, but we didn't deal with emotions. We didn't deal with other things in his life, just quitting smoking. But then I had another client who was eating disordered and was audio only, and I don't think it worked. For her, body image was a big issue and I never saw her. In some ways it may have made her feel more comfortable, but maybe she needed to be a little more uncomfortable. Then the video only played into another client whose issue was paranoia. He wanted to know if I really cared about him or if he was just being taped so others could watch him. He was paranoid that I was just a computer not a person, and the TV constantly reminded him that he was being taped. We just couldn't get past this because every time he looked at me he was reminded that I really wasn't there.
- *Therapist:* I would be real wary of seeing people who are severely depressed and suicidal and offering them video only. And someone who's schizophrenic working on video, that might be one of their main hallucinations, "People are talking to me on the TV set."
- *Therapist:* The woman I had in audio had issues about self-esteem and appearance, and since I couldn't see her I think that made a little bit of difference in how the therapy developed. The therapy went well with that client.
- *Therapist:* I had one client in video who had some issues with trying new things. She wanted to go out and do new things. I think that helped because she was doing something new in doing video therapy. She felt uncomfortable about it but when she decided *this* wasn't really a big deal. . . .
- *Therapist:* I had a client with OCD [obsessive compulsive disorder] that was audio, but I guess he was doing some ritual stuff,

but I could not see. So that might have been additional information that would have been helpful.

Besides matching for the type of problem, all the therapists also brought up matching other client characteristics with treatment mode. Background and personality, they felt, ideally would be taken into account when assigning clients to distance therapy:

- *Therapist:* One client had a very extensive background in counseling. Actually the audio was better for that client because it wasn't the same old thing. It changed it. She had to go by what I said and I had to go by what she said. With a sense of anonymity, she could be more emotional because she didn't feel as vulnerable as in typical counseling. I also had a man who had been a counselor for people who are drug abusers. He didn't really like being on the other side of the chair. This was video, so it gave him some distance, some space in the sense that it wasn't what he did. I mean it wasn't the same way he did it. I think in those two cases it helped a lot, the clients having to adjust to the situation and not be in the same old routine.
- *Therapist:* The limitations depend on the client. Like how comfortable do they feel? Are they the kind of person that has problems talking about how they feel? How do they express emotions? Are they very verbal? Do they make a lot of eye contact? Do they fidget a lot? So if the client doesn't make eye contact, has trouble talking, I would feel uncomfortable putting them in anything besides face-to-face. Because there is more of a demand on the client to talk more on audio. I still think you're losing information over the technical media. You may have to do a cost-benefit analysis.
- *Therapist:* There might be clients for whom audio is better, clients who wouldn't otherwise come to therapy. Clients who'd be concerned about being in the same room as the therapist. If it makes them more comfortable to be in their own space, if that will open it up to a lot more people, that would be great. And I don't think you can't do it. This has taught me that you can do it, that you can still do a good job of therapy over a different medium.
- *Therapist:* It seems like people who were more secure in themselves or more confident tended to do better in the audio and the

video. In clients who didn't have a lot of coping mechanisms, I had to do a lot more work in therapy, and it was harder to do that with video and audio.

- *Therapist:* I would screen ambivalent people into more face-to-face.
- *Therapist:* That audio client was an easy one. She had a very specific problem, and I felt like it was a good therapeutic relationship; but had it been a difficult client, I'm not sure what I would have done.
- *Therapist:* My video client was very amusing and very expressive, and she used her hands a lot, and her tone of voice was very marked, her intonations, and she was just very personable as a client. The other client that was through video was much more reserved and much more just quiet and not as open, and it took a long time for us to establish a rapport.
- *Therapist:* I think that a client that will benefit in audio has to be one of those learners who is relatively quick and can process a lot of verbal information and doesn't need those visual cues so much. But there aren't a lot of clients like that.
- *Therapist:* At first with this video thing, my client was like, "I don't like this. I don't like this. I don't feel I can feel close to my therapist," but then she really liked it. Then she loved it. I mean, those last two sessions she's like, "I think that this has been a wonderful experience because I felt that with the video I had more privacy and more personal space, that I didn't have somebody in my presence sharing with this, and it made me take responsibility for my emotions more." It was therapeutic for her because she felt like, well, one of her problems was she's just not taking enough responsibility for her life and her emotions, and this way it didn't allow for anybody to comfort her in a physical, like, in a presence way. Usually she would've become much more needy in a therapeutic relationship.
- *Therapist:* I think anything where there is going to be a lot of personal disclosure it is easier for the client to open up earlier [on audio]. Because they are more anonymous and I didn't know who they were.
- *Therapist:* One client, she's glad she doesn't have to be face-to-face. Because she likes to keep her distance from people, I think initially it made therapy easier for her.

- *Therapist:* If my client were in an audio mode, she would feel like she was revealing herself and not really know what's on the other side in some way. She might feel more exposed.

THEME 6: NATURAL ADAPTATIONS

When plainly asked their preferences, most therapists chose face-to-face (7 out of 10). Two therapists liked audio best, and one liked all modes equally. Interestingly, the three therapists *not* choosing face-to-face were also the three who did the most work in audio. This suggests that familiarity with the mode interacts with preference, and indeed many of the therapists choosing face-to-face said that their choice had mostly to do with familiarity.

Clients were given satisfaction rating sheets at the close of treatment. An analysis of variance showed that clients were very satisfied (an average rating of 5.97 on a 7-point scale) with their treatments, and there were no significant differences in satisfaction among the conditions. This is a provocative finding, in that clients in audio and video modes experienced the supposed disadvantages of distance treatment without the obvious advantages—that is, not having to travel far or being able to receive treatment at home. The fact that clients who finished treatment in the distance modes were just as satisfied as those in the traditional mode lends hope for the future of therapy over a distance. However, we must note that the highest dropout rate was among clients in the distance modes (though our dropout rate in general was very low, less than 14%: five clients in audio, four in video, and two in face-to-face). Therapists' satisfaction ratings averaged 5.67 on a scale of 1 to 7, with no significant differences among modes of delivery.

A major theme in all of the interviews was the ability of both therapists and clients to adjust to whatever situation they encountered:

- *Therapist:* I was expecting the audio to be the hardest because, as I said, I am such a visual person. That wasn't what happened.
- *Therapist:* I was mildly surprised about how well people responded to it, and some people actually made comments like, "You know, it's kind of cool to be on this video thing," and I didn't think it was going to work as well as it did.
- *Therapist:* I've learned that people are pretty adaptable and that when there's a need to learn to make allowances, they can do the

audio, they can do the video. I think I was more skeptical going into it. I thought they would be very resistant, and they weren't at all.

- *Therapist:* I think the client actually just adapts to the mode they're in, and so they might say to themselves, "Wow, you know, this video thing is good; if I were face-to-face this would be more uncomfortable," without really having any idea how face-to-face would have been. They just adapt.
- *Therapist:* You make adjustments: it's just like from client to client, from mode to mode you make the adjustments.

IMPLICATIONS FOR CLINICAL TRAINING AND PRACTICE

The thoughts and feelings of the clinicians in this research project may be taken to heart by pioneers in all kinds of distance therapy. A notable finding was that most of the nonconventional features of technologically mediated counseling entailed both the expected disadvantages and some surprising advantages. For example, although the lack of visual evidence in the audio mode frustrated therapists, some also found that it kept them from making judgments based on appearance and that it refined their listening skills. Both of these advantages reflect sound traditional practices, and the use of audio counseling in training programs is suggested. Our study highlights many areas where training for futuristic modes of delivery should focus: the matching of problem types and clients to delivery systems, the choice of treatment approaches considering media limitations, and making full use of the adaptability of each client and therapist pair, to name a few.

Another intriguing theme is the freeing nature of the physical separation in video and audio treatment, mentioned by many of the therapists. It seems to relate to an oft-heard claim that some people are more expressive and truthful in letters, over e-mail, or on the telephone than they are in person. In fact, one study found that people were more likely to admit alcohol abuse over the telephone than in a face-to-face interview (Kobak et al.,1997). If distance engenders honesty and feelings of safety, the new technologies may serve some groups better than face-to-face ever did. Social phobics, schizophrenics, agoraphobics, and the personality disordered are populations for whom subjectively "safe" treatment deliveries could be godsends. Distance modes could be used to ease such clients into treatment, followed by face-to-face contact, or could be used intermittently to maintain the therapeutic relationship through rough periods when otherwise these clients tend to drop out. Such possibilities should inspire further research.

CONCLUSION

Our research strongly suggests that technologically mediated treatment may be a substitute for, and in some cases an improvement upon, traditional face-to-face therapy. We found no barriers that were insurmountable, and we were impressed by the adaptability of both clients and therapists. Further research is needed on the best ways to train clinicians and work around the problems distance therapy presents. With the proper support and consultation as they make the transition, we believe that well-trained practitioners already hold the tools they need to send their touch through cyberspace.

REFERENCES

Day, S. X. (1999). *Psychotherapy using distance technology: A comparison of process in face-to-face, video, and audio treatments.* Unpublished doctoral dissertation, University of Illinois at Urbana-Champaign.

DeRubeis, R. J., & Crits-Christoph, P. (1998). Empirically supported individual and group psychological treatments for adult mental disorders. *Journal of Consulting and Clinical Psychology, 66,* 37–52.

Kobak, K. A., Taylor, L. vH., Dottl, S. L., Greist, J. H., Jefferson, J. W., Burroughs, D., Mantle, J. M., Katzelnick, D. J., Norton, R., Henk, H. J., & Serline, R. C. (1997). A computer-administered telephone interview to identify mental disorders. *Journal of the American Medical Association, 278,* 905–910.

Kraut, R., Patterson, M., Lundmark, V., Kiesler, S., Mudopadhyay, T., & Scherlis, W. (1998). Internet paradox: A social technology that reduces social involvement and psychological well-being? *American Psychologist, 53,* 1017–1031.

Lombard, M., & Ditton, T. (1997). *At the heart of it all: The concept of telepresence* [On-line]. Available: http://www.ascusc.org/jcmc/vol3/issue2/lombard.html.

Schneider, P. L. (1999). *A comparison of outcome variables in psychotherapy: Distance technology versus face-to-face.* Unpublished doctoral dissertation, University of Illinois at Urbana-Champaign.

16

Skills for On-Line Counseling: Maximum Impact at Minimum Bandwidth

KATHARINE R. COLLIE, DAN MITCHELL, AND LAWRENCE MURPHY

In July and August of 1999, Katharine Collie (KC) conducted an interview with Dan Mitchell (DM) and Lawrence Murphy (LM) on the topic of on-line counseling skills. The interview was done by e-mail so DM and LM could simultaneously describe and demonstrate skills they use in their e-mail counseling practice. The interview is reproduced here after a brief introduction in which the context for the interview is outlined, the people involved are introduced, and the key concepts that underlie the discussion are highlighted.

CONTEXT AND CONCEPTS

In on-line counseling, computers and the Internet are used to make it possible for counseling to occur without the counselor and client(s) being in the same physical place at the same time. On-line counseling falls into the general category of *telehealth*, that is, the use of telecommunications technologies to make health care available to anyone who, whether by choice or necessity, receives care without the physical presence of a caregiver.

The three authors of this chapter have been involved in the development of two forms of on-line counseling. Thus the comments in the interview are based on direct experience. DM and LM began an e-mail counseling and therapy practice in 1995 (Murphy & Mitchell, 1998) and are among the few people who have both practiced on-line counseling and published on the subject. Their approach is called therap-e-mail and embraces narrative (White & Epston, 1990) and solution-focused (de Shazer, 1994) perspectives on counseling. They also have been instrumental in developing ethical guidelines for on-line counseling (Bloom, 1998). KC has been involved in the collaborative development of computer-supported distance art therapy (Collie & Cubranic, 1999; Cubranic, Collie, & Booth, 1998), an art-based form of on-line counseling that uses synchronous speech communication and shareable hand-drawn computer art.

Both therap-e-mail and computer-supported distance art therapy are low bandwidth forms of on-line counseling. *Bandwidth* refers to the amount of electronic information that can be transmitted at once between networked computers. It is a measure not only of the maximum speed of transmissions but of the expense of using the system. When computers and the Internet are used to expand access to health care by making a service available to people in their own homes, it is advantageous to keep the bandwidth requirements low enough that the service can be used by people with standard home computers and dial-in access to the Internet. The lower the bandwidth requirements, the more people will be able to use the service.

There is some evidence that bandwidth limitations do not need to have a detrimental effect on the quality of communication. For example, in a study of pairs of people who used either video-conferencing systems or text-based chatlines with shareable drawing spaces to do collaborative architectural design, Vera, Kvan, West, and Lai (1998) found that the participants "implicitly compensated for the narrower bandwidth" (p. 503) so that there was no difference in the quality of the results achieved by the two groups. The low-bandwidth group compensated not by altering their design strategy but by focusing their attention on the crucial aspects of their tasks.

In counseling situations, there may be advantages associated with not being able to see the other person. Colón (1996) suggested that in on-line therapy there may be fewer emotional distractions. In a discussion of telephone communication, Rutter (1987) proposed that a lack of face-to-face contact may favor psychological proximity when the purpose of the encounter is to be personal, as is the case with counseling.

When discussing health care services that involve computers and the Internet, it is easy to let the technology be the main focus of the discussion, and to compare types of equipment rather than types of human interaction. However, the human aspects of computer-mediated communication may be as significant or more significant than the technological aspects. One of the most striking results of an initial evaluation of computer-supported distance art therapy (Collie, 1998) was that the particulars of the computer system seemed less important than guidelines and procedures for using the system. This suggests that success as an on-line counselor might depend on acquiring specific on-line communication skills.

DM and LM have developed a set of on-line counseling skills through their work as on-line counseling practitioners and researchers. These skills were developed for text-only on-line counseling; however, they address issues that pertain to many types of distance therapeutic communication. The e-mail interview that follows contains a discussion of these skills.

THE INTERVIEW

KC: Hello, Dan and Lawrence. It is a pleasure to have this opportunity to interview the two of you. Before we begin our discussion of on-line counseling skills, I wonder if one of you could briefly describe how your e-mail counseling practice works.

DM: Hi Kate. I'm very excited about this opportunity and want to thank you for the work you're putting into this chapter. Let me first prepare myself (explicitly, so you know how I do it) the way I do when replying to my clients. Before I type even my first keystroke, I have only one thing on my mind: express warmth and personal caring. If I were permitted only to say one thing in this interview, it would be that: express warmth and personal caring. To this end, even as I write at this moment, I have pulled up a chair for you and a chair for Lawrence, and placed them beside me. In a similar fashion, I would like to invite our readers to imagine the three of us sitting in chairs in front of them as if they were watching the interview. They may even choose to place three chairs in front of them. Kate, I'm imagining your warm smile and I feel a sense of anticipation about the insightful questions I know you're about to ask. So I'll begin by answering your first question.

New clients contact us through our web site http://www.therapyonline.ca, using an automated form that we receive by e-mail. The form asks for appropriate consents and demographic information. Once we receive a completed form, we send clients the Virtually Solve It™ (VSI) worksheet via e-mail. The VSI is comprised of a series of questions intended to help clients begin to externalize their problem(s) and to orient themselves for change. Clients fill out the VSI off-line at their convenience. When they have completed some or all of the worksheet, they e-mail it to us, and the process of exchanging therap-e-mail begins. To each e-mail sent by clients, we reply with therap-e-mail as soon as possible. Clients send us e-mails whenever it suits them. They usually only communicate with us via e-mail, but they can also ask for clarification via toll-free telephone.

KC: Dan, I am amazed. You certainly conveyed warmth and caring in your first paragraph – and your words changed my state of being. You "warmed me up." I mean, I was feeling very matter-of-fact and rational when I wrote the first question. I feel a closer rapport with you now, and I feel more inclined to speak from my heart.

Let me move on to my next question. Lawrence and Dan, you say in your article, "When Writing Helps to Heal: E-mail as Therapy," which appeared in the *British Journal of Counselling and Guidance* (Murphy & Mitchell, 1998), that your approach to on-line counseling is based on narrative therapy and solution-focused therapy. Can you describe briefly what the therapeutic goals might be within these perspectives?

LM: Hi Kate. I want to echo Dan's sentiments. It's a pleasure to be involved with you on this project, and after reading Dan's work on the first question I'm sitting here smiling with anticipation myself. The set of questions you've prepared is very engaging. Thank you so much for all the work you've done (and will have to do after we're done responding!).

To be brief, in the narrative approach what we are involved in is reauthoring the stories clients tell themselves about themselves. The idea, somewhat simplified, is that we all tell ourselves a story about ourselves that allows us to make sense of the world. This story is learned over time and is co-constructed by us, our families, our culture, and society. Race and gender and sexual orientation, intelligence and talent and family traditions all play a part in our story. As a therapist working in this tradition, I am interested in unpacking the influences of this story and helping clients to rework their story so that it is conducive to their mental health and to their continued healthy development.

In the solution-focused approach, again somewhat simplified, I am interested in learning what the client is doing that already works and helping him or her to do more of that. There are always things that clients are doing that reduce the power of the problem in their lives, or that give them brief glimpses of the experience they want to have all of the time (or at least more often). My goal then is to uncover these thoughts, feelings, actions, places, people, and what have you, and help clients orient themselves toward these aspects of their lives.

When we combine the two, we conceive of the existing solutions—the things that the client is already doing that are working—as an underlying story of ability and success that is covered over by the dominant problem-saturated story. In some sense, the solution-focused approach is the means to the end of helping clients reauthor their story.

KC: Thanks, Lawrence, for reducing complex concepts into a clear synopsis. I am struck by your use of the word *reauthoring*. In therap-e-mail, clients do the reauthoring by writing rather than by talking, and they produce a reauthored story they can keep and read later. I could guess that the writing process helps make the change process real and believable for the client.

LM: When clients tell me in a face-to-face interview of a success that they've had, it is very easy for them to retract their responsibility for that success the next week. This is not impossible when the evidence is in print, but it's that much more difficult. Further, once the evidence is in writing, the client can refer back to it, should the problem ever rear its ugly head again. One of our goals is to begin collecting such solution stories so that people who have been able to overcome adversity can share their successes with others. We believe that an on-line interactive network of such stories could be beneficial to clients and therapists alike in helping people to reauthor their lives.

KC: One of the issues that gets discussed in reference to on-line counseling is the lack of nonverbal cues. In a text-only form of counseling like e-mail counseling, there are even fewer nonverbal cues than there are in telephone counseling, where you hear a lot in the person's tone of voice, the silences, the speed of the speech, or if you are communicating with letters, where you can see the handwriting. The lack of nonverbal information is often assumed to be a serious drawback to on-line counseling (e.g., Colón, 1996). In your article, you agree that the lack of nonverbal cues presents a challenge. However, you claim that by using techniques that contextualize and enhance the meaning of therap-e-mail, it is possible to produce a therapeutic experience that rivals face-to-face interviews.

You have developed very specific on-line counseling skills for this. Three you mention in your article are emotional bracketing, descriptive immediacy, and the use of similes, metaphors, and stories. I am going to ask you to explain each of these and give examples of how you might use them, but first can you explain why contextualization and meaning enhancement are important in on-line counseling?

DM: Sure. It's like the difference between reading the newspaper and reading a novel that makes you cry. The former, while providing information, does nothing to attempt to personalize or make the stories relevant to your particular context. The novelist helps you become emotionally involved by bringing you into the presence of the characters, showing you the personal meaning and impact of events on the characters. Likewise, in therap-e-mail, intensification of what is relevant to the client's context and to the therapeutic relationship both personalizes and enhances the meaning of the interaction.

KC: Now for some specifics: What is *emotional bracketing?*

LM: I'll explain emotional bracketing and demonstrate it at the same time [feeling pleased that I thought of this]. This technique is used throughout therap-e-mails. When we thought about our face-to-face therapy experiences, it seemed obvious to us that the nonverbal element is [feeling unsure of the wording I want] in the background of our conscious awareness. It takes effort, and indeed training, to be aware of these elements. Once aware, we discover that the nonverbal dimension often communicates emotional material. Sometimes this is congruent with the person's words, sometimes not [now feeling very on track]. In therap-e-mail, we discovered that we could compensate for the lack of nonverbals by bracketing the emotional content behind the words. We place, and invite our clients to place, important emotional content (particularly emotional information that we couldn't otherwise glean from the text) in square brackets. Here is an example of what a client might write:

> I have reread your last therap-e-mail several times [feeling stupid again] and although I appreciate your words [can't believe you have such faith in me] I don't think I'm ever going to have a worthwhile relationship [very very sad]. Richard called again to say I'm an idiot [angry with myself]. He's so mean [actually I think I'm more angry with him]. But, hmm, now that I think about what you said again, I am actually feeling angry with him [Weird. I feel pretty good just now].

This accomplishes at least three things. First, it gives the therapist and the client more information about each other, in a way that is relatively simple to learn. Second, it encourages the client to be more deeply aware of his or her emotional content and thus more self-aware. Third, it creates a context in which clients are able to begin to externalize part of their conversation with themselves (and us). Many therapeutic traditions, from gestalt to narrative, use some form of externalizing to encourage change.

KC: And *descriptive immediacy*: What is it, and how and why would you use it?

LM: Descriptive immediacy is a technique that we use to deepen the connection between client and therapist. We also encourage clients to use it when they feel that it will give us important information. Here is an example of what a therapist might write:

> I have just finished reading your last therap-e-mail, Angie, and my smile is a mile wide. As I think about your successes over guilt, I find myself nodding my head and saying the words "you did it, you did it" smiling all the while. If you were here with me now you would see me shrugging my shoulders with my hands in the air, as if to say "well . . . looks like guilt's power is all burned out." Congratulations Angie.

> We use descriptive immediacy in several situations. First, we use it to highlight a moment of intense emotion, any situation in which a simple verbal response is not enough. This may be about a success, as in the example above, or it may be in response to a very painful disclosure. Second, we use it in situations where we might use immediacy face-to-face. An example would be a situation in which the client's words seem incongruent, or contradict a previous therap-e-mail. We would use descriptive immediacy to first deepen the intimacy between us before venturing to—even mildly—confront. However, the technique can be used any time the therapist feels that it would be helpful to deepen the bond with a client.

DM: I often use descriptive immediacy in greetings and closings. For example, when I receive the first e-mail from a client, I may reply with the following:

> Hello John,
>
> In my mind's eye, I'm stretching out my hand to you right now with a welcoming smile on my face saying, "I am very pleased to meet you." If I could, I'd offer you a nice cup of tea as well. . .

In a closing I might say:

> Laughing with you as you see through the empty threats of anxiety, Dan

Descriptive immediacy is one of a broader category of skills that Lawrence and I have called *presence techniques*. With therap-e-mail, we are not simply conveying thoughts, or even feelings via text. More than that, we strive to establish and maintain a therapeutic relationship in which we maintain a subtext of genuine warmth and caring for the client. We use presence techniques to bring clients into our presence, as I am doing by having the two empty chairs beside me. We also use presence techniques to make more vivid for our clients the experience of being present with us. The latter is the case with descriptive immediacy.

A subtle, but crucial thing happens when I use presence techniques: I find myself using language that implies that my client and I are face-to-face. When I receive e-mail from other counselors whom I have never met, I almost always begin my reply with, "It's a pleasure to meet you." I said something similar in my example of a greeting to a client a moment ago. Oh, I just did it again! [surprised at myself] "A moment ago" is not usually a phrase used in text. One normally writes, "In the example above . . . ," but "above" is not my own or my client's experience. "A moment ago" draws attention to the experience we just shared rather than to the text itself.

LM: One thing that I want to point out here is that we use presence techniques *and* teach them to our clients. Thus, clients are encouraged to be more aware of themselves, their experience, their behaviour, and their environment. Some therapists do not attempt such teachings in therapy because they prefer that the client be unaware of what his or her nonverbals are communicating. Others don't have the time. We have the luxury of unlimited time on the client's part because the time they take to compose their therap-e-mail is (apart from length) unrelated to the time we spend reading and responding. And we believe that the more tools we can give our clients, the better.

KC: In your article, you mention *the use of metaphorical language for meaning enhancement*. How does that work?

LM: Most fiction uses some form of metaphor or simile to communicate and deepen meaning. We believe that accessing the part of the brain that processes metaphorically allows us to access a deeper, nonverbal (perhaps preverbal) level of consciousness. In our face-to-face work we often invite clients to bring in symbols of their problems, or desired solution states, in order to access this part of themselves. In text, we can invite clients to describe their problems or desired states in metaphor. "The guilt is like a weight. It's like liquid concrete in a sack. It moves wherever I move, never lets me get out from under it." We have found that when clients share with us in this manner, it deepens the connection between us (this is also true in face-to-face therapy). It also helps clients to get a better idea of what they want and what they don't want, and why.

Such language can also be quite simple. "My heart feels like a weight inside my body as I write to you John. I am so sorry that your mother died." Or "Reading how happy you feel now that you're out of that damaging relationship, Carol, it was like my monitor itself was going to start laughing." Because a text-based interaction lacks some of the richness of a face-to-face interaction, therapists need to add richness to their writing. One doesn't need to be a Pulitzer caliber writer, but one has to enjoy writing, and be willing to become creative . . .

KC: . . . which will encourage clients to be creative in their writing and perhaps also in their lives.

Have you developed any other techniques since you wrote the *British Journal of Guidance and Counselling* article?

DM: Yes, we have! This is the part I find most exciting. Perhaps I can first focus on the appearance of the e-mail itself. Some clients write using 8-point fonts. Others use coloured text with special backgrounds. Still others use the defaults that come with their software. This creates for me something of a first impression—similar to the moment of having a client enter my physical office. From the appearance of the e-mail, I begin to form hypotheses about clients' stories.

Looking more closely at the text itself, I may notice that the client has used the lower case "i" to refer to himself. Could this client be a little bit shy? Possibly. Or I may notice that some words have been misspelled. Does that mean the client was in too much of a rush to check, or does it speak to the client's literacy level? A moment ago, I spelled the word *coloured* using Canadian spelling. If a client had done so, I would wonder whether he or she has British or Canadian origins.

Sometimes clients use ALL CAPS to emphasize a point or even to convey emotion that can be interpreted based on the context. For example, a client may write, "I took your advice and told my mother. I can't believe I ACTUALLY DID IT!" Clearly the client is showing excitement and pride in his or her accomplishment.

Naturally, I can use any of these observations therapeutically as well! For instance, perhaps it is important for me to take a one-down position with a client so that a certain intervention will be effective. i may choose to do so by using lower case "i" and by reducing the size of my font. Or I can use a dash—or a series of dots to denote a pause in my thought process . . . and thus intensify the point I'm making.

And of course I can use pseudo-words such as *hmmmm* or intentional misspellings such as *oooooohhh boy*. Were you able to hear that long *oooooohhh* in your head?

Hmmm. Stretching the length of words . . . Isn't that non-verbal communication? [Can you tell I'm feeling a little smug right now?]

Did I just notice a smile creeping over your face, Kate? . . . or was that my imagination?

Here I'm using spacing, presence techniques, and sequence to anticipate, and to some extent, even create your reactions.

Perhaps I should slow down and explain what I'm talking about. I used spacing to control the timing of delivery. Large spaces create an extended pause. In this case, where I was trying to bring in some levity, I used extra space to create a sense of delayed timing.

What did I mean by *sequence*? The nature of e-mail is that it is read sequentially. While reading, clients certainly cannot interrupt me as they can in a face-to-face situation. This allows me to develop a mood, or to set the stage for making a certain point, or to control the level of intensity.

Although e-mail is read sequentially, I suspect that it is rarely written completely sequentially. I can use the backspace key; I can cut, paste, reword; and so on. In fact, I'm doing that now. This allows me and, as our anecdotal evidence suggests (Mitchell & Murphy, 1998), clients to clarify thoughts and feelings more deeply. With e-mail, unlike any other form of communication, I can decide whether and where to interject my reply or comments. If I wanted to, I could reply to clients with a new, blank e-mail. Or I could place my entire reply at the beginning or at the end of clients messages. I rarely choose to do any of those. I find it much more personal to interject my comments and reactions where they best fit in the sequential context. The resulting document looks more like a transcript of a conversation, which, in fact, it is.

I'm sure that some of our readers will be wondering about the use of *emoticons*. Emoticons are strung-together keyboard symbols that, when turned 90 degrees clockwise, look like facial expressions. Here are some examples:

- :-)happy, pleased
- ;-)just kidding, a joke, (called a *winkie*)
- :-(sad, sympathetic, compassionate

I use these occasionally, especially when I want an informal tone. I find the winkie particularly useful for marking an attempt I've made to be humorous or to introduce some levity. I've found that humour sometimes doesn't come through very well in text. So I need to use special care to ensure that I convey the message I intend. Being explicit about the tone of voice I'm using and a winkie can help. Especially if it wasn't funny ;-).

The final technique that I want to talk about is *text-based externalization*. This is similar to the two-chair technique, using text instead of chairs. For example, if a client is deliberating about whether to leave her husband, I might invite her to explore each side of the internal struggle she is having. My invitation might go something like this:

> Janet, I know the battle that's going on inside you. It's like you're having this argument with yourself that never is resolved. One part of you says, "I can't take this! I have to leave." The other part of you loves him and can't bear to hurt him.
>
> I have an idea that may sound a bit weird at first but I know it can be helpful. Other clients have tried it, and I use it myself sometimes when I have an argument going on inside myself. It helps me "hear out" each side of the argument without having the other side interrupt.
>
> What I do is I name the two sides. Perhaps in your case it would be, "I'm leaving" and "I love him." (Name them with names you find fitting.) Then start writing purely from one side until you feel you've said your piece. Then switch your attention to the other side and write purely from that perspective. The conversation might go something like this:
>
> - *I'm leaving*: I can't stand the way he totally ignores what's going on around him . . . etc., etc.
> - *I love him*: Yeah, but he and I can be such good friends at times. He's so much fun . . . etc., etc.
>
> Let me know if this makes sense. It's a little difficult to explain, so I'd like you to ask me for clarification if you need to.

Text-based externalization also can be used to externalize problems and to give them a voice. Does all of that make sense?

KC: Yes, it does. And I see now that compensating for the lack of nonverbal cues is only part of what you address with the on-line counseling skills you have developed. You also have ways of compensating for the lack of shared physical presence.

I have noticed when reading about on-line counseling that physical presence and nonverbal cues often get lumped together as one thing. Maybe they shouldn't be: In the case of a blind person, there can be physical presence without visual cues and in the case of video conferencing there can be visual cues without shared physical presence. In the study of computer-supported distance art therapy I conducted with Davor Cubranic (Collie, 1998), lack of shared physical presence emerged as one of two very serious problems (along with the risk of technical failure), but not being able to see the other person was seen as a problem with many possible solutions and in some cases as a distinct advantage.

Are there other concerns that come into play with therap-e-mail that require special on-line skills?

LM: In circumstances in which a client's writing is different from my own, I can do what I would do in a face-to-face interaction. I can, respectfully and without parroting, adapt my style so that it reflects the client's. One takes the concepts concerning joining that one learns when one is first starting to do therapy, and one adapts them to a text-based medium. So my sentences can be longer or shorter, my vocabulary more or less complex, my metaphors computer based or religiously based, all depending upon the client's writing. I respond to the client's writing patterns in much the same way that I respond to a client's speech patterns.

I'll just note one other thing here that can be very troubling—and you note it above—which is technical glitches. E-mails do still get lost. Sometimes they get truncated. Systems fail, programs get infected, and ISPs have server troubles. It is extremely important, at the outset, to inform clients of such possibilities, and to have in place plans in case things go wrong. For example, there should be a window of time during which clients can expect a response. If they don't receive one, they are to write and tell us so. Thus a lost e-mail does not become a huge misunderstanding.

KC: When I was planning this interview and imagining how it might go, I didn't expect that you would have so many different skills and techniques to discuss! You have shown that there can be a large nonverbal dimension to text-only communication and that there are many ways not only to compensate for not being in the same room, but also to take advantage of opportunities that are available with on-line text communication.

   Would you say that the skills you have developed for on-line counseling have helped you in your work as face-to-face counselors?

LM: This is a great question. The answer is a very powerful yes. The very first thing I notice in doing therapy on-line is how critical it is to suspend judgments and assumptions about people. Because I can't see them, I need to ask quite a few questions about my clients in order to know who they are. When I then go to my office to do face-to-face therapy, I am sensitized to this. And what do you know? A client walks in who looks and talks and acts like me. His skin's the same colour, he's about the same age, and he wears a wedding ring. And I discover that there's a part of my brain that just assumes that I know who he is. Not entirely of course, but I discover that I'm less inclined to ask him the kinds of questions that I'd ask of someone different from myself. And yet when I do ask those questions of him, the answers often surprise me. I have come to believe that we make far too many assumptions about our clients when—or perhaps because—we see them face-to-face.

   Another thing that is critical in therap-e-mail is attention to the impact I'm going to make before I make it. As a result, I am now much more aware in face-to-face work of having a part of myself devoted to planning ahead how to phrase things. I have also found that I am more inclined to pause to reflect or to take time out from the conversation in order to collect my thoughts. This is something that I find very useful when I'm writing (I'm doing it now as I write this response), and I have found it equally useful in conversation.

As a result of our use of presence techniques in therap-e-mail, I have found myself sharing my inner thoughts and feelings with face-to-face clients more often, and to great effect. I believe that there is still a sense in the counseling world that we, as therapists, don't want to be too much ourselves for fear of contaminating the process (or dare I say it, of losing some power within the relationship). I am finding that the more I am genuinely myself, the better the process is for the client.

I also find myself doing more teaching within therapy; unpacking useful therapeutic techniques for clients so that they can use them themselves without my help. I find I do more explaining of what I'm doing and why, and of how we're going to get from where we are now to where the client wants to be. In the past, I suppose I assumed that the client would simply learn how to better tackle problems by watching me and mimicking me; learning by osmosis. But because there is more explaining that I feel needs to be done in a therap-e-mail, and because that has had such a positive impact, I have found myself doing it face-to-face.

KC: Lawrence, your answer underscores the notion that on-line counseling can be much more than a substitute for face-to-face counseling. I noticed on your therap-e-mail web site that you list many advantages of conducting counseling or therapy by e-mail. Convenience, privacy, schedule flexibility, the possibility of communicating thoughts and feelings right away rather than waiting until the weekly appointment, and the potential for leveling power imbalances are some of the advantages you describe. I wish we had space here to discuss your ideas about the therapeutic benefits of writing, but we have just about arrived at our page limit.

I have one more question. What advice would you give to someone who wants to begin acquiring on-line counseling skills?

LM: First, communicate with someone who has done it and who has experienced some measure of success. Second, it is absolutely essential that you put the client's well-being and thus the ethics of what you are doing before everything else. Third, make sure that you know the technology. You need to be as familiar with the computer as you are with empathy. And finally, be prepared for a period of transition. It is unlikely that you will be able to do the same kind of therapy that you have been doing face-to-face. In some instances, your whole perception of the process of change will be shaken. This approach is not for everyone, whether client or therapist. Doing therapy on-line requires a great deal of humility and a willingness to adapt and to be a student once again. Be prepared.

KC: This brings us to the end of our e-mail conversation. Dan and Lawrence, thank you for your thoughtful and informative answers. It has been a pleasure collaborating with you on this project, and I look forward to discussing readers' responses with you.

REFERENCES

Bloom, J. W. (1998). The ethical practice of web counseling. *The British Journal of Guidance and Counselling, 26,* 53–59.

Collie, K. (1998). *Art therapy on-line: A participatory action study of distance counseling issues.* Unpublished master's thesis, University of British Columbia, Vancouver, Canada.

Collie, K., & Cubranic, D. (1999). An art therapy solution to a telehealth problem. *Art Therapy: The Journal of the American Art Therapy Association,* 16(4), 186–193.

Colón, Y. (1996). Chatter(er)ing through the fingertips: Doing group therapy on-line. *Women and Performance: A Journal of Feminist Theory, 9,* 205–215.

Cubranic, D., Collie, K., & Booth, K. (1998). Computer support for distance art therapy. In *Summary of CHI'98* (pp. 277–278). Los Angeles: ACM Press.

de Shazer, S. (1994). *Words were originally magic.* New York: Norton.

Mitchell, D. L., & Murphy, L. M. (1998). Confronting the challenges of therapy on-line: A pilot project. *Proceedings of the Seventh National and Fifth International Conference on Information Technology and Community Health,* Victoria, Canada [On-line]. Available: http://itch.uvic.ca/itch98/papers/ftp/toc.htm.

Murphy, L. J., & Mitchell, D. L. (1998). *When writing helps to heal: E-mail as therapy.* British Journal of Guidance and Counselling, 26, 21–31.

Rutter, D. R. (1987). *Communicating by telephone.* Oxford, England: Pergamon.

Vera, A. H., Kvan, T., West, R. L., & Lai, S. (1998). Expertise, collaboration, and bandwidth. In *Proceedings of CHI'98* (pp. 503–510). Los Angeles: ACM Press.

White, M., & Epston, D. (1990). *Narrative means to therapeutic ends*. New York: Norton.

17

Technology-Delivered Assessment: Power, Problems, and Promise

JANET E. WALL

An explosion! An upheaval! A revolution! Those words are often used to describe the remarkable influence of technology on our lives. Bill Gates, in his most recent book, speaks of a web workstyle and web lifestyle to describe how technology has permeated all aspects of our lives (Gates, 1999). Education has been a prime beneficiary of technology's power. Computers used for instruction will grow to over 10 million by the beginning of the 1999–2000 school year (Anderson & Ronnkvist, 1999; Quality Education Data, 1998). More than 75% of classrooms are equipped with computers, with a majority having Internet access. As more technology becomes available, it becomes integrated more fully into the mainstream of the educational process (Market Data Retrieval, 1998).

Never before has so much information been available for individuals to learn, make decisions, and take actions. Counselors and educators who think technology is another passing fad are sorely out of step.

One role of counselors and educators is to use assessment in the service of the students and clients. Under the right conditions and with proper use, using technology to foster assessment is a great way to go. This chapter focuses on the use of technology as a tool for testing and assessment and emphasizes that to make proper use of technology tools for assessment, savvy counselors and educators need to

237

- understand the advantages and pitfalls of technology use, particularly as they relate to the use of assessment tools with clients and students;
- follow the assessment standards and policies of applicable professional associations;
- use the best practices suggested in this chapter to better assure good service to their clientele; and
- stay updated on topics related to assessment and technology.

This chapter thus presents cautions and capabilities related to the use of technology with assessment. Standards and policies on assessment that have been prepared and endorsed by various professional associations and organizations are provided, and various guidelines are outlined so that technology can be used with quality assessments for the purpose of aiding individuals in reaching for their goals and aspirations. The chapter also suggests ways of staying current within the field of assessment, particularly as it relates to technology.

UNDERSTANDING THE ADVANTAGES
OF ASSESSMENT VIA COMPUTER AND THE INTERNET

The tools of technology offer counselors and educators new capabilities and opportunities to add value to their services. These include

- **accessibility:** Various tests are increasingly available via the computer and over the Internet. Individuals can take various tests for many purposes including college entrance, course placement, certifications and licensure, career decision making, academic achievement, military selection and classification, personality assessment, and test preparation. Each year the list expands. The availability of locations where assessments can be taken range from the privacy of one's home to organized computer laboratories in colleges, high schools, and the private sector. Although there seems to be a disparity in the degree of access to technology, Bill Gates, in his book *The Road Ahead,* (1995), suggested that individuals who are "wired" have access to the same information. He proposed that virtual equity is achievable more easily than real-world equity.

- **immediate feedback:** The potential for immediate test scoring and feedback is a key advantage with technology-delivered assessment that can be a significant motivator for persons taking assessment instruments. Individuals can learn their status on assessments quickly and use that information to take immediate action. For example, information made available immediately on a college course placement test can assist both students and counselors in registering students for the appropriate level of mathematics class or language program. High school students can acquire immediate information on their performance on academic tests and plan their courses accordingly. Students taking an interest inventory can obtain their results promptly and immediately investigate occupations and job openings that fit their interest profiles.

- **ability to use new assessment theories:** The use of computer-adaptive testing, as opposed to computer-assisted testing, allows persons to take tests that are targeted more accurately to their ability levels (Heubert & Hauser, 1999). Use of technology in combination with the increasingly popular item response theory can determine an individual's performance level using fewer questions to perform this task. The time and money saved by using computer-adaptive testing can be substantial, particularly in large-scale assessment situations or when time is a critical consideration.

- **portfolio assessment:** The capability of placing one's work or educational history on a floppy disk and making that information available to those judging performance or capability is empowered by technology. Writing samples, art work, letters of recommendation, journals, test results, certificates and certifications, community service, club memberships, and project work can be saved electronically, transported easily (either physically or electronically), and evaluated by others to make decisions related to educational promotion, graduation, job entry, and other purposes.

- **ability to assess higher order skills:** Use of technology permits test developers to use techniques and create situations that are difficult or impossible to construct in regular paper/pencil assessments. Consequently, and with some creativity, the assessment can reflect more authentic conditions and may provide the capability of tapping into higher order cognitive skills than can be accomplished with a paper/pencil instrument. For example, test developers can construct situations that simulate the real world. Test items on computer can simulate events in biology or economics and ask students to take measurements, make observations, and analyze results, and then to propose a theory on how the world works in that subject area. A licensure test in architecture can simulate the tools an architect uses to create blueprints and engineering drawings, track what tools are selected and how they are used, and determine the design and structural quality of the final product. A technology-delivered foreign language assessment can use audio and video to simulate various situations that could be encountered in the foreign country to assess the students' verbal skills, knowledge of the vocabulary, and understanding of the culture and business environment. Using the Internet to obtain information on a particular topic and then to prepare an essay using that information can provide an indication of the individual's information-gathering techniques; ability to locate, analyze, and synthesize information; and skill in documenting the findings in a well-written and succinct document.

- **persons with disabilities:** A powerful use of technology in assessment is in the use of assistive technologies for persons with disabilities. Employment of audio can help persons with visual impairment gain access to testing situations. Persons with impaired physical ability can take advantage of voice recognition technology in answering test items, even to the point of dictating long responses to essay questions. Those who experience difficulty controlling fine motor skills can use a touch screen or smart board to respond to assessment items rather than complete a scannable answer sheet. Persons who are housebound and not able to travel to a test site can take a test over the Internet from their home. Computers are even being created that can respond to slight movements of the head or eyes.

- **outreach to others:** Technologies such as e-mail can provide the test taker with the prospect of reaching out to competent professionals to obtain further information, test interpretation advice, and the chance to discuss a particular situation or test result with an experienced and qualified professional.

Access to technologies such as video teleconferencing can enhance assessments though one-on-one interaction between a test administrator and a test taker. This technology can be used to refine assessments when it is important that the test taker been seen and heard. Some applications are to assess speaking skills, to test language capability by putting a student in touch with persons across the ocean to help critique language performance, or to determine a person's capabilities through interviews or oral exams. Video teleconferencing can have a powerful influence on test security by providing real-time monitoring of the test administration environment.

UNDERSTANDING THE PITFALLS OF ASSESSMENT VIA COMPUTER AND THE INTERNET

Counselors and educators should also be alert to the problems and limitations that can be encountered in using technology in assessment situations. Some potential disadvantages are

- **accessibility:** Some assessments are free and others can be obtained for a fee. Persons with limited resources, and especially those without computers, who may in fact be in more need of assessment services, could be blocked from using essential assessments due to resource restrictions. The Department of Commerce has shown in its most recent study that access to computers and the Internet is highly dependent on income, racial and ethnic group, and urbanicity (U.S. Department of Commerce, 1999).

- **test security:** A major concern about computerized testing and testing over the Internet is the issue of test security. Test items without suitable security can be compromised, resulting in unfair advantage to test takers who might obtain the questions prior to taking an exam. Also, there is the potential for individuals taking assessments via the Internet to acquire information from external sources to answer the test questions. Solutions to test security range from using removable hard drives to tracking or prohibiting access to certain universal resource locators (URLs; Internet addresses).

- **test taker identity:** Test users need to be sure that the person taking the assessment (especially via the Internet) is representing his or her identity accurately. Special care needs to be taken to ensure that the person answering a licensure test for credentialing, for example, is the actual person that is seeking this certification. Various measures can be taken to reduce the degree of uncertainty. Solutions can range from desktop video teleconferencing to fingerprint recognition systems.

- **privacy/confidentiality:** As with paper/pencil assessments, information about an individual's answers or test scores should be kept confidential and be made accessible only to those individuals who have a need to know. This concern is particularly critical for assessments of a delicate or sensitive nature that are answered over the Internet.
- **lack of information on the quality of the instrument:** Tests taken on computer or over the Internet may not match the quality of paper/pencil assessments. Because taking assessments via the tools of technology is often made to look easy, it can be mistakenly assumed that the test meets professional testing standards. Assuming quality just because a test is available is a potentially dangerous assumption. It is quite possible for a technology-delivered instrument to be deficient in possessing the requisite technical information necessary for a user or test taker to judge the quality and suitability of the instrument. Often little or no information is provided to verify if the instrument has been normed on an appropriate population, if the test results have any validity for decision making in the area in which the test taker intends to use the results, or if it is reliable in assessing a person's condition, status, or performance.
- **test comparability:** If an instrument is available in both paper/pencil and computer-delivered format, it can be mistakenly supposed that the test developers have produced a technology-delivered assessment that provides the same scores regardless of administration format. It is not unusual for some high-quality tests offered in the paper/pencil format to report different results when those same items are administered via computer or Internet. Without the assurance that the test scores are comparable, a test taker may have an advantage by using one format rather than the other. Decisions based on false or different outcomes may point a counselor's client in a wrong direction. Disparate results from noncomparable assessments can transpire for any number

of reasons including speededness, point size of the words, monitor resolution, use of color, comfort with the equipment, and response mode.

- **gender and racial and ethnic fairness:** That females, persons of color, or individuals of different ethnic backgrounds may be disadvantaged in certain testing situations has been a long-standing concern in paper/pencil testing. This can be exacerbated with tests delivered via computer or the Internet. If a particular group has disproportionate access to computers and technology, there could be disparity in the comfort level and familiarity with the use of technology. As a result, test scores could be influenced by the mode of administration in addition to the content.

- **reporting and interpretation:** Immediate feedback is clearly desirable. Without appropriate interpretation, though, there is danger that the test taker will take actions that are not warranted by the test results. The potential exists for interpretations to appear to be so definitive and persuasive that test takers fail to understand the lack of accuracy of the scores and the need for caution surrounding further actions and making decisions. Conversely, there are situations in which the feedback can be so extensive that the test results are overinterpreted to the point of paralyzing a person's actions, or that they are so like a horoscope as to be of little actual value.

- **lack of human contact:** With technology-delivered assessments, meaningful human contact and intervention to assist with test score interpretation and guidance may be lacking or unavailable. Without a skilled educator or counselor, it may be difficult for a test taker to sort out his or her results and use them in the context of other experiences.

FOLLOWING ASSESSMENT
STANDARDS AND PRACTICES

How do counselors and educators sort out the promise from the danger? They need to be aware of the various issues related to the construction, production, administration, and interpretation of tests delivered via the computer or Internet. No compromise should be made on the quality of a test administered to a client or student with either traditional or technology-delivered assessments. Various agencies and organizations have produced policy statements and standards for testing that are applicable to both paper/pencil and technology-delivered assessment. Counselors and educators should be cognizant of and familiar with the premises of these documents when considering the use of technology-delivered assessments. Applicable standards and policies are as follows.

- American Educational Research Association, American Psychological Association, and National Council on Measurement in Education. (2000). *Standards for Educational and Psychological Testing.* Washington, DC: American Educational Research Association.
- American Association for Counseling and Development. (1989). *Responsibilities of Users of Standardized Tests.* Alexandria, VA: Author
- American School Counselors Association and Association for Assessment in Counseling. (1998). *Competencies in Assessment and Evaluation for School Counselors.* Alexandria, VA: Author.
- Committee on Professional Standards and Committee on Psychological Tests and Assessment. (1985). *Guidelines for Computer-Based Tests and Interpretations.* Washington, DC: American Psychological Association.
- Dahir, C. A., Shelton, C. B., and Valiga, M. J. (1998). *Vision Into Action: Implementing the National Standards for School Counseling Programs.* Alexandria, VA: American School Counselor Association.
- Joint Committee on Testing Practices. (1988). *Code of Fair Testing Practices in Education.* Washington DC: National Council on Measurement in Education. This document is being reviewed and should be revised for publication in 2000 or 2001.
- Joint Committee on Testing Practices. (2000). *Test Takers' Rights and Responsibilities.*
- National Board for Certified Counselors. (1998). *Standards for the Ethical Practice of Web Counseling.* Greensboro, NC: Author.
- National Career Development Association. (1997). *NCDA Guidelines for the Use of the Internet for the Provision of Career Information and Planning Services.* Alexandria, VA: Author.
- U.S. Department of Labor Employment and Training Administration. (1999). *Testing and Assessment: An Employer's Guide to Good Practices.* Washington, DC: Author.

USING BEST PRACTICES FOR
TECHNOLOGY-DELIVERED TESTS AND ASSESSMENTS

This section identifies best practices that can be used by both test users and test takers to be more resourceful in evaluating and using technology-delivered assessments and to better ensure their appropriate use. The guidelines are consistent with professional standards and are categorized into considerations relevant to test administration, test quality, test developer credibility, test interpretation, and access to professionals. Adherence to these guidelines is of vital importance in reviewing, selecting, and using technology-delivered assessment instruments.

Test Administration

Best practices are as follows.

1. The test setting should be comfortable, quiet, and conducive to allowing the test taker to maximize performance. The arrangement of the computers should ensure privacy and comfort.
2. Testing equipment should be in good working order, and the software and/or Internet programs should be operating properly.
3. A site administrator should be available to troubleshoot problems that may occur due to equipment, software, or other technology failures.
4. Policies and procedures need to be established, explained to the test taker, and applied in cases of a technology failure. For example, if there is a computer crash or a power disruption, are the responses to the test items saved, or does the test taker need to begin the assessment again?
5. Test takers should be comfortable with the test format and use of keyboard or other equipment. If there is a question about the test takers' familiarity with the technology, practice exercises should be provided to enable them to become facile with the equipment in order to focus on the assessment rather than the mode of delivery.
6. Test items and answers must be protected from compromise. Security of the equipment and test items is critical to the fairness of current and future test administrations.

7. The identity of the test taker should be verified, particularly in high-stakes testing.

8. Tests must be administered according to the procedures specified by the test developer, particularly in cases where standardization is important.

9. Both test users and test takers need to know if individual score information is stored; and if so, where and for how long. Periodic purges of individual test results stored locally or centrally may be advantageous in maintaining privacy. It may be more desirable for an individual to save test results on a personal disk rather than on a server or local computer.

Test Quality

Best practices include the following.

1. The test content should match the purpose of the testing. Assessment items should cover, at least on the face, the areas that the test taker and user desire.

2. Clear and supportable statements should be provided by the test developer on what the test is intended to measure so that test users can better ensure that the constructs of the assessment match their intentions.

3. Evidence should be made available by the test developer and reviewed by the test user to determine if the assessment is appropriate for the test taker with regard to age, membership in a subgroup, educational level, disability, and language competence.

4. If the test can also be administered in a paper/pencil format, test results should be comparable to the technology-delivered version. There should be ample evidence that there is comparability in the test scores or that adjustments made to those scores are necessary and appropriate.

5. Evidence should be provided to indicate the conditions under which the test results have been found reliable. The strength of that reliability should be reported by the test developers and examined by the individual considering use of the test.

6. Test results should not be interpreted unless there is validity evidence to support that interpretation. Ample evidence should be presented on the validity of the assessment for particular uses. Care needs to be taken to ensure that the test users or test tak-

7. The identity of the test taker should be verified, particularly in high-stakes testing.
8. Tests must be administered according to the procedures specified by the test developer, particularly in cases where standardization is important.
9. Both test users and test takers need to know if individual score information is stored; and if so, where and for how long. Periodic purges of individual test results stored locally or centrally may be advantageous in maintaining privacy. It may be more desirable for an individual to save test results on a personal disk rather than on a server or local computer.

TEST QUALITY

Best practices include the following.

1. The test content should match the purpose of the testing. Assessment items should cover, at least on the face, the areas that the test taker and user desire.
2. Clear and supportable statements should be provided by the test developer on what the test is intended to measure so that test users can better ensure that the constructs of the assessment match their intentions.
3. Evidence should be made available by the test developer and reviewed by the test user to determine if the assessment is appropriate for the test taker with regard to age, membership in a subgroup, educational level, disability, and language competence.
4. If the test can also be administered in a paper/pencil format, test results should be comparable to the technology-delivered version. There should be ample evidence that there is comparability in the test scores or that adjustments made to those scores are necessary and appropriate.
5. Evidence should be provided to indicate the conditions under which the test results have been found reliable. The strength of that reliability should be reported by the test developers and examined by the individual considering use of the test.
6. Test results should not be interpreted unless there is validity evidence to support that interpretation. Ample evidence should be presented on the validity of the assessment for particular uses. Care needs to be taken to ensure that the test users or test tak-

1996). *Training Magazine* (Ganzel, 1997) reported that some form of distance learning occurs in over half of all organizations. Of course, this trend is replicated in nearly 100% of institutions of higher learning. Imel (1996) estimated that within 20 years the current models of learning and higher education will cease to exist.

High-tech supervision is in place at the University of Florida's counseling department (R. Myrick, personal communication, July 7, 1999). Students there communicate with faculty and classmates through e-mail, departmental listservs, and networks. Students have access to the Internet for research. Each is required to develop his or her own web page where assignments are posted. They also prepare multipurpose PowerPoint presentations targeting specific populations. These presentations may be revised and used again as resource pages.

In another high-tech example, Christie (1998) examined an integrated model for distance clinical supervision for counselors, which follows four interns for a semester. After the initial class meeting, and barring any emergency, all future contact with the professor was on-line. Christie paid careful attention to ethical and logistical issues in this study.

Professional associations and organizations are beginning to take leadership roles in creating basic standards and competencies for learners and, in some cases, their educators. The Association for Counselor Education and Supervision has taken a leadership position in development of technical competencies for counselor education students and guidelines for on-line instruction in counselor education (ACES, 1999a). These guidelines examine course quality and content, objectives, instructional support, faculty qualifications, evaluation, technological standards, and grievance procedures. ACES's Technology Interest Network has also developed a set of technical competencies counseling students should master before graduation (ACES, 1999b). (See Appendix 2.)

The National Board for Certified Counselors advocates for and offers continuing professional education through emerging technology (Leary, 1998). The Council for Accreditation of Counseling and Related Educational Programs is currently revising its standards to include technology and distance learning in preservice preparation (Bobby, 1998). The Association of College and Research Libraries

(ACRL) has also developed a draft of information literacy competency standards for higher education. The ACRL draft enumerates specific standards, performance indicators, and measurable outcomes for the information literate learner (ACRL, 1999).

Administrators need to recognize the impact of reordering priorities with faculty development, assessment, research time, and control of student learning environments (Breivik, 1998). Maddux (1998) agreed that

> university administrators at all levels need to recognize the need for information technology instruction in all disciplines. Merit plans for faculty must be structured to reward the integration of technology into all courses, and in-service programs must be instituted to help existing faculty develop needed skills and attitudes. (p. 9)

Administrators must solve the problems of hardware and time constraints. Technology is expensive, time consuming, and frequently outdated within 6 months. Learners are interested in convenience; but are they willing to pay for the increased cost? Educator recognition, technology integration throughout the curriculum, and professional collaboration are key points to consider.

RECOMMENDED ACTION STRATEGIES

The action strategies recommended in this section are based on the integration of technology in both preservice and professional development programs. Three major themes emerge: technology integration is multidisciplinary; technology use is viewed as valid, necessary, and worthy of merit; and education is learner driven.

UTILIZE AVAILABLE RESOURCES

Effective utilization of available resources requires consideration of organization-wide support, multidisciplinary approaches, community resources, resource development, technology across the curriculum, recognition, and national standards.

- **Organization-wide support:** Support should be on an organization-wide basis. This includes all administrators, educators, and staff in organizations. Breivik (1998) suggested that administrators take a four-pronged approach to garner support: move forward, make a commitment, develop a plan, and sell the vision. She also recommended that institutions and educators utilize more resource-based models of learning while insisting that new methods of delivery permeate the curriculum (1998). Organization-wide support must include financial and resource support as well.

- **Multidisciplinary approaches:** There are varying degrees of technological competence in most organizations. Existing resources can be used for cross training and support, and creative pooling of shared resources offers new solutions. Often neglected educational resources include computing and technology centers, libraries, centers for teaching and learning, campus web masters, and knowledgeable learners and faculty from other disciplines. Breivik (1998) recommended that education programs be willing to form academic partnerships with these various learner and educational services. This can be difficult. Often the technically competent resource persons (educators and learners) are in great demand and stretched thin.

  Learners themselves are the most frequently untapped resources. Many learners and practicing professionals are already highly skilled in the uses of technology. They could serve as peer tutors, mentors, and coaches. For instance, academic librarians are information and subject specialists who instruct classes; create on-line guides, tutorials, and bibliographies; and serve as consultants for faculty instruction and research. They develop web pages to support university curricula. At Wright State University, for example, the education and human services librarian has developed lengthy on-line research guides for counseling and education students and faculty (Reynolds, 1999a). Through these guides, faculty and students have remote access to the library catalog, multiple databases, full-text scholarly journals, and the Internet. Reynolds has also created a massive web site with categories supporting various interests and degree concentrations in WSU's Department of Human Services (Reynolds, 1999b). These and similar resources are widely used for student and faculty research and instruction.

- **Community resources:** Counseling, psychology, social work, rehabilitation, nursing, and education department and faculty web pages serve as models for those interested in developing resources on the Internet. Counseling and mental health listservs such as California State University Northridge's (1999) Counseling Discussion Groups or Robert Bischoff's (1999) ShrinkTank bulletin board service provide beginners with sounding boards as well as networking forums with colleagues. Other community resources geared to counselors include Behavior On-Line (Levin, 1999), the Counselor Education Resource Center at Florida Gulf Coast University (Sabella, 1999), World Counseling Network (http://www.CounselingNetwork.com), the Counseling Web (http://seamonkey.ed.asu.edu/~gail/resource htm), CounselorLink (Hutt, 1998), Dr. Bob's Mental Health Links (Hsiung, 1999), and John Grohol's PsychCentral (1999) and Mental Health Net (1999).

The Greater Dayton Area Health Information Network (http://www.gdahin.org) is an example of a community-wide effort that targets the health field. Members of the network include hospitals, universities, individuals, and organizations. Professional development efforts include training, resources, and education that are current and easily accessible.

Business and industry have been technology leaders for decades. Some provide continuing training not only to their staff by also to educational, civic, and service organizations. NCR, the giant, multinational corporation, has created NCR University (NCRU) for its staff and customers. NCRU's web page includes news and information about hundreds of courses it offers by location and topic (in classroom, CD ROM, audio/video, web-based, and video teleconferencing/downlink). NCR is committed to continued learning because acquiring, sharing, and using improved technical skills and knowledge gives a "competitive advantage" (NCR, 1999). Educators should look closely at this model. Its educational philosophy more closely matches the needs of today's learners than do most traditional higher education programs.

Lucent Technologies is another example of a large corporation making technological training and advanced education possible through its Center for Excellence in Distance Learning (CEDL). The CEDL works closely with universities that are recognized leaders in distance education learning (including Indiana University, Penn State University, and the University of Wisconsin-Extension). Through such collaborations, the diversity of distance learning resources is increased to business departments, employees, and customers as well as to university students, staff, and faculty (Lucent Technologies, 1999). The CEDL serves as a model for collaboration and shared resources.

- **Resource development:** Existing resources must be allocated to support technology initiatives across campus. Early on, administrators might use one-time start-up funds, university grants, competitive awards for excellence, or student technology fees to begin building the technology program. They may apply for resources from federal, state, local, and community organizations and agencies. The best start-up approach is to begin collaborating with colleagues and departments around campus. Identify those who share common interests. For example, at Wright State University, when the library needed a computer lab, the Computer and Telecommunications Services Department needed more space, and the Center for Teaching and Learning needed both labs and space, the three worked together to share resources. The computing department built a lab in the library classroom. Both units shared the space and equipment with the Center for Teaching and Learning, which, in turn, shared its instructional expertise with both. However, now that all this is in place, ongoing budgeting support must be maintained.

- **Technology across the curriculum:** All educational efforts must include learners' exposure to, and use of, technology in every course, workshop, internship, practicum, and continuing education and training program. This curricular immersion may range from use of technology as supportive educational resource to its mandatory use in classes, or as preferred method of information delivery to total distance learning with no on-campus (or on-site) contact required. Universities have successfully implemented similar sweeping curriculum changes in the past when they adopted "writing across the curriculum" guidelines in the 1980s and 1990s. The National Council for the Accreditation of Teacher Education (http://www.ncate.org) expects all courses to have a technological component infused in the curriculum.

- **Recognition:** Educators' involvement in technology should be encouraged and rewarded. They need time to create, develop, and design on-line classes, tutorials, and workshops. If they have work published in reputable, on-line journals or maintain significant counseling sites on the Internet, these efforts should be evaluated and valued along with their other scholarly and service activities. This recognition of merit must be included in their promotion and tenure process. In the near future, administrators and educators must also grapple with the issue of ownership of cyberspace resources. When educators create web-based courses, tutorials, and professional web sites, who owns the rights to the information, to the class, to the site? At most institutions in higher education, this is the subject of intense negotiation with many innovative models emerging. Although complicated, ownership and copyright will be clarified in time.

- **National standards:** Continued leadership by professional associations and organizations is essential. When they develop guidelines, standards, and basic competencies for technology use, they serve as models for all educational programs. Adoption of these guidelines is critical to professions. Learners and educators must support the cybereducation efforts of the American Counseling Association (http://www.counseling.org), the American Psychological Association (http://www.apa.org), Council for Accreditation of Counseling and Related Educational Programs (http://counseling.org/cacrep), ACES (1999a, 1999b), NBCC (http://www.nbcc.org), National Council for Accreditation of Teacher Education (http://www.NCATE.org), and the U.S. Departments of Health and Human Services (http://www.os.dhhs.gov) and Education (http://www.ed.gov). The many state associations, agencies, and interest groups also need professionals' support. They too can play a leadership role and act as models for the profession. In all cases, these associations and organizations provide invaluable resources to their members and to professions.

ADAPT EXISTING ON-LINE AND DISTANCE LEARNING RESOURCES

Although there are literally millions of resources on the Internet, professionals sometimes have difficulty knowing where to begin.

Books are a good place to start. Numerous Internet guides have been published that could be used as reference guides or textbooks. One of the best is Karger and Levine's (1999) *The Internet and Technology for the Human Services.* Grackenbach's *Psychology and the Internet: Intrapersonal, Interpersonal, and Transpersonal Implications* (1998) and Rheingold's on-line book *The Virtual Community* (1998) examine the psychology and sociology of cyberculture. Harrison's (1999) book offers very specific, step-by-step directions for the analysis, design, development, testing, and implementation of distance learning programs. Porter's (1997) book gives background and an overview of the issues surrounding distance education. Palloff and Pratt's (1999) book looks at defining and building communities in cyberspace. All of these books are important guides to both practical and theoretical concerns.

Resources for learners include *Internet Companion for Abnormal Psychology* (Hamel & Ryan-Jones, 1998), *Quick Guide to the Internet for Psychology* (Whitford, 1998), *Guide to the Internet in Educational Psychology* (Bissell & Newhoff, 1997), and *Psychology on the Internet: A Student's Guide* (Stull, 1997). Literature searches in databases like ERIC (http://www.uneg.edu/edu/ericcass) and PsycInfo (http://utcat.library.utoronto.ca:8002/pschi_deser.html) pull hundreds of articles about on-line instruction and distance learning. They too reflect the burgeoning interest in cybereducation. Journals of special interest to educators are *Computers and Education, Computers in Human Services, Computers in Teaching, Teaching of Psychology,* and the new electronic journal for educators and practitioners, the *Journal of Technology in Counseling* housed at Columbus State University in Georgia (http://jtc.colstate.edu).

Educators will find a multitude of distance learning resources on the Internet as well. Premier sites include the World Lecture Hall (http://www.utexas.edu/world/lecture/index.html), Globewide Network Academy (http://www.gnacademy.org), and, LibrarE (http://www.librare.com/li-fr3ac.htm). Other recommended sites with in-class exercises, projects, course syllabi, and relevant web links include Suler's (1999) *Teaching Clinical Psychology;* Krantz's (1999) *Psychological Tutorials and Demonstrations; Internet Guides, Tutorials, and Training Information* from the Library of Congress (1998); *Counseling Courses and Syllabi* (1999); and Internet Mediated Learning's (1999) *Resources to Use in Creating On-Line Web-Based Courses*. John Barnes (1998) at Pennsylvania State University (PSU) has also created a web site many educators could emulate: *Foundations of Chemical Dependency Counseling*. PSU also offers undergraduate, graduate, professional degrees, certification, and continuing professional education in other diverse areas through their World Campus Learning Community (http:www.worldcampus. psu.edu.8900/public/CNED4012/index.html).

Goldberg (1999), the executive director of the Global Institute for Interactive Media, has discussed a wide array of issues involved in offering on-line classes, including software selection, assignments, teaching approaches, and maintenance functions (such as on-line atmosphere and codes of civility). Ivanoff and Clarke (1996) also have examined issues surrounding the creation of a course web site for learners by questioning design, content, and intellectual property issues.

Focus on the Individual Learner

Though some learners prefer face-to-face interaction in traditional classes, technology can accommodate the learning styles, needs, and objectives of individual learners. It allows for the development of more self-paced, customized learning packages, and more individualized instruction. Again, though not absolute, technology allows professional education to be seamless, with no artificial separation between preservice learning and professional development. PBS's Adult Learning Service Online (http://pbs.bilkent.edu.tr/adultlearning/als) is a good example of a web site developed with adult learners in mind. Because it provides degree programs, workforce education, literacy instruction, and business training programs to adults, it supports their critical learning needs.

Utilize the Technology Continuum

Determine where the organization is on the technology continuum and consider moving beyond mid tech and toward total technological integration. Avoid using technology for the razzle dazzle. The most important questions raised here include Will on-line courses enhance or impede the learning process and delivery of information? Will on-line supervision during training and education offer the learners what they need? Technology is not an end in itself. It is a tool that allows many learners to maximize their learning potential. Professionals must continue to pose these questions as they move to the new millennium.

CONCLUSION

"Technology is a train that stops for no one. It keeps moving whether you get onboard or not" (Karger & Levine, 1999, p. 312). Some human service professionals have been slow to queue up to the train because they are fearful or overwhelmed by the challenges technology creates for them. When human service professionals examine technology closely, they find but another useful tool to add to their repertoire of skills. According to Karger and Levine (1999), the problem is not with the "potential of technologies but with the way they are implemented" (p. 312). Technology is a tool, not a panacea. In light of these new expectations, educators must reevaluate and redesign their programs and curriculums to help meet the educational needs of learners and practicing professionals alike. They can use roadmaps created by a variety of professions, such as business, medicine, and psychology, to chart their future course.

As competent professionals, we must take the lead in implementing technologies that save time and make our work more productive. We must also redefine who and what we are and the directions we wish to take our professions in the 21st century.

REFERENCES

Association for Counselor Education and Supervision, Technology Interest Network. (1999a). *Guidelines for on-line instruction in counselor education* [On-line]. Available: http://www.chre.vt.edu/f-s/thohen/acesweb.htm.

Association for Counselor Education and Supervision, Technology Interest Network. (1999b). *Recommended technical competencies for counselor education students* [On-line]. Available: http://www.chre.vt.edu/f-s/thohen/competencies.htm.

Association of College and Research Libraries. (1999). *Information literacy competency standards for higher education* (Draft) [On-line]. Available: http://www.ala.org/acrl/ilcomstan.html.

Barnes, J. (1998). *Foundations of chemical dependency counseling* [On-line]. Available: http://www.worldcampus.psu.edu:8900/public/CNED401 2/index.html.

Bischoff, R. (1999). ShrinkTank [On-line]. Available: http://www.shrinktank.com.

Bissell, J., & Newhoff, S. (1997). *Guide to the Internet in educational psychology* (2nd ed.). Madison, WI: Brown & Benchmark.

Bobby, C. (1998, Summer). If you're measuring student learning by the amount of time students spend sitting in their seats, are you not concerning yourself with the wrong end of the student? *The CACREP Connection*, pp. 7–8.

Breivik, P. (1998). *Student learning in the information age*. Phoenix, AZ: American Council on Education/Oryz Press.

California State University, Northridge. (1999). Counseling discussion groups [On-line]. Available: http://www.csun.edu/~hfedp001/counseling_listservs.html.

Casey, J. (1995). Developmental issues for school counselors using technology. *Elementary School Guidance and Counseling, 30*(1), 26–34.

Casey, J., Bloom, J., & Moan, E. (1994). Use of technology in counselor supervision (ERIC Digest). Greensboro, NC: ERIC Counseling and Student Services Clearinghouse.

Christie, B. (1998). *Distance clinical supervision in cyberspace: A qualitative study*. Unpublished doctoral dissertation, Oregon State University, Eugene.

Counseling courses and syllabi. (1997). [On-line]. Available: http://seamonkey.ed.asu.edu/~gail/courses.htm.

Ganzel, R. (Ed.). (1997, October). Distance training [Special section]. *Training Magazine, 34*, A1–A24.

Goldberg, E. D. (1999). *Some thoughts about how to offer a course over the Internet* [On-line]. Available: http://www.edgorg.com/course.htm.

Grackenbach, J. (Ed.). (1998). *Psychology and the Internet: Intrapersonal, interpersonal, and transpersonal implications*. San Diego, CA: Academic Press.

Grohol, J. M. (1999). *Mental health net* [On-line]. Available: http://mentalhelp.com.

Grohol, J. M. (1999). Psych Central [On-line]. Available: http://psychcentral.com.

Hamel, C. J., & Ryan-Jones, D. L. (1998). *Internet companion for abnormal psychology*. New York: Longman.

Harrison, N. (1999). *How to design self-directed and distance learning programs*. New York: McGraw-Hill.

Hirumi, A., & Bermudez, Z. (1996). Interactivity, distance education, and instructional systems design converge on the information superhighway. *Journal of Research on Computing in Education, 29*(1), 1–16.

Hsiung, R. (1999). Dr. Bob's mental health links [On-line]. Available: uhs.bsd.uchicago.edu/~bhsiung/mental.html.

Hutt, J.P. (1998). CounselorLink [On-line]. Available: http://www.counselorline.com.

Imel, S. (1996). *Distance education*. Columbus, OH: ERIC Clearinghouse, OSU.

Internet Mediated Learning. (1999). *Resources to use in creating on-line web-based courses* [On-line]. Available: http://www.cet.sfsu.edu/intmediated.html.

Ivanoff, G., & Clarke, J. (1996). *The use of the World Wide Web for teaching—Things to consider before putting materials on-line* [On-line]. Available: http://walton.uark.edu/disted.

Karger, H., & Levine, J. (1999) *The Internet and technology for the human services.* New York: Longman.

Krantz, J. (1999). *Psychological tutorials and demonstrations* [On-line]. Available: http://psych.hanover.edu/Krantz/tutor.html.

Leary, P. (1998, October). The changing face of continuing education, *Counseling Today*, p. 16.

Levin, G. (Ed). (1999). *Behavior on-line* [On-line]. Available: http://www.behavior.net/index.html.

Library of Congress. (1998). *Internet guides, tutorials, and training information* [On-line]. Available: http://lcweb.loc.gov/global/internet/training.html.

Lowther, D.T., Bassoppo-Moyo, T., & Morrison, G. (1998). Moving from computer literate to technologically competent: The next educational reform. *Computers in Human Behavior, 14*(1), 93–100.

Lucent Technologies. (1999). *Center for Excellence in Distance Learning (CEDL)* [On-line]. Available: http://www.lucent.com/cedl.

Maddux, C. (1998). Barriers to successful use of information technology in education. *Computers in Schools, 14*(3/4), 5–11.

Manning, P., & DeBakey, L. (1992). Lifelong learning tailored to individual clinical practice. *Journal of the American Medical Association, 268*(9), 1135–1136.

Masys, D. (1998). Advances in information technology: Implications for medical education. *Western Journal of Medicine, 168*(5), 341–347.

Miller, T. (1998). The psychologist with 20/20 vision. *Counseling Psychology Journal: Practice and Research, 50*(1), 25–35.

Myrick, R. (1997). Traveling together on the road ahead. *Professional School Counseling, 1*(1), 4–8

Myrick, R., & Sabella, R. (1995). Cyberspace: A new place for counselor supervision. *Elementary School Guidance and Counseling, 30*, 35–44.

NCR (1999). *NCR University* [On-line]. Available: http://www.ncru.ncr.com/about/philosophy.asp.

Palloff, R. M., & Pratt, K. (1999). *Building learning communities in cyberspace: Effective strategies for the on-line classroom.* San Francisco: Jossey-Bass.

Porter, L. R. (1997). *Creating the virtual classroom: Distance learning with the Internet.* New York: Wiley.

Reynolds, K. (1999a). *Research in counseling: Basic outline* [On-line]. Available: http://www.libraries.wright.edu/libnet/subj/cou/counseling_resguide.html.

Reynolds, K. (1999b). *Counseling and psychology resources: Meta sites and minutia on the Internet* [On-line]. Available: http://www.libraries.wright.edu/libnet/subj/cou/cpmeta.

Rheingold, H. (1998). *The virtual community* [On-line]. Available: http://www.rheingold.com/vc/book.

Sabella, R. (1999). Counselor education resource center [On-line]. Available: http://coe.fgcu.edu/faculty/sabella/cerc/index.htm.

Sampson, J., Kolodinsky, R., & Greeno, B. (1997). Counseling on the information highway. *Journal of Counseling and Development, 75*(3), 203–212.

Sattem, L. (1997). *Mandatory continuing professional education in an emerging field: A prospectus on the counseling profession.* Unpublished doctoral dissertation, Ohio State University, Columbus.

Sloane, A. (1997). Learning with the web: Experience of using the World Wide Web in a learning environment. *Computers and Education, 28*(4), 207–212.

Stull, A. T. (1997). *Psychology on the Internet: A student's guide.* Upper Saddle River, NJ: Prentice-Hall.

Suler, J. (1999). *Teaching clinical psychology* [On-line]. Available: http://www.rider.edu/users/suler/tcp.html.

Whitford, F. W. (1998). *Quick guide to the Internet for psychology.* Boston: Allyn & Bacon.

20

Technology and the Continuing Education of Professional Counselors

PAMELA S. LEARY

Continuing education for professional counselors is in a state of metamorphosis. How can professional associations, universities, institutes, trainers, and educators deliver high-quality continuing education to increasing numbers of credentialed counselors in diverse geographic areas? Similarly, how can counselors find high-quality continuing education when they are facing the challenges of remote location, family and job demands, financial constraints, illness, and other circumstances that make attendance at live conferences, workshops, and training programs very difficult? How can technology help us to answer these needs?

This chapter first discusses the history and trends in continuing education in the counseling profession, focusing on home study programs with particular attention to web-based continuing education. Web sites are then listed and briefly reviewed, and recommendations for those developing continuing-education-related-programs and services on the web are provided.

HISTORY

Since the beginning of education, the method of disseminating knowledge to the population of practicing professionals has been the conference or convention. Presenting papers and research findings at professional conferences has long been a rite of passage for most professionals. Add to that smaller workshops, training institutes, and seminars, and the picture of continuing education up until the early 1990s is complete.

The single factor most responsible for changing this picture is the growth of credentialing in our profession. With credentialing has come the need for continuing education hours for recredentialing. There are now 30,000 National Certified Counselors (NCCs) in the United States who "all need 100 hours of continuing education in every 5-year certification cycle" (Leary, 1998). There are also approximately 55,000 state licensed counselors, most of whom must accrue continuing education to maintain their professional credentials. Thus professional counselors consume somewhere in the neighborhood of 1,700,000 hours of continuing education every year. Counselors who live in remote areas, have heavy family or work demands, live with chronic or transitory illnesses, or are under financial constraints may find obtaining traditional continuing education a serious challenge.

Realization of these facts has led continuing education providers to develop ways for counselors to make continuing education more accessible and affordable than traveling to conferences or attending workshops or training programs.

> The new focus on accessibility and required hours created two significant changes in the world of continuing education. . . . The first was an increase in the number of workshops and training institutes. . . . In addition, there has been an explosion in the world of home study. (Leary, 1998)

The number of home study programs approved by the National Board of Certified Counselors (NBCC) has grown from about 20 in 1992 to over 150 in 1999. Most of these are books or audiotapes with quizzes. There are also videotapes with quizzes and one program that uses a compact disk. Since the late 1970s, live programs have been broadcast to remote locations for teleconferences via satellite or closed circuit television. The most logical next step for continuing education providers was to begin to offer continuing education over the Internet. According to Thomas J. Bacon, director of the North Carolina Areas Health Education Centers Program,

Technology can increase individualized contact, communication, and interaction with our traditional learners. Telecommunications and access to the Internet can also overcome barriers of geographic isolation, helping those in rural and underserved areas access information and education resources when and where they choose. (1998)

THE WEB: A NEW SOURCE
FOR CONTINUING EDUCATION

The NBCC received its first application for approval of an Internet-based continuing education program in early 1997. The company, Distance Learning Network (DLN), is still one of the more unique and specialized sites offering continuing education for counselors. DLN (www.dlnetwork.com) took the idea of the interactive teleconference and adapted it for the Internet.

Several other organizations have followed. In the spring of 1997, the NBCC affiliate, the Center for Credentialing and Education (CCE), made the decision to develop an on-line continuing education course. Thomas Clawson, executive director of both NBCC and CCE, has stated that "CCE wants to be on the cutting edge of continuing education delivery for professional counselors. We are committed to helping to set the standard for this new medium" (personal communication, May 14, 1999).

The Laurasian Institution was selected to develop the web site for CCE. Case studies were used as the basis for the program. Counselors read the case studies and then answer a series of questions about each one. If a counselor answers incorrectly, an explanation is given and the counselor is directed back to the part of the case that he or she has misunderstood. This continues until a correct answer is chosen. Because of this format, failure is impossible. The counselor can register, pay, take the program, and print out the certificate of completion all on-line. So far, according to Clawson, "The program has not yet had enough registrants to totally pay for its development, but we think that picture will improve as more counselors become computer literate and more aware of the opportunities for continuing education on the Internet" (personal communication, May 14, 1999).

WHAT IS OUT THERE?

As more counselors become comfortable with computers as learning instruments, and as they become familiar with the Internet, there will be increasing numbers of professionals looking for continuing education opportunities on the Internet. In an effort to discover the current picture, this chapter's author completed a search for on-line continuing education for counselors and other mental health professionals using ERIC (www.uncg.edu/edu/ericcass), Yahoo (www.yahoo.com), and Ask Jeeves (www.askjeeves.com) as search engines. The results of the search are the sites listed and described in this section. In considering the thousands of continuing education live events offered each year and the hundreds of traditional home study programs available on a continuous basis, it may be somewhat disappointing to see only 10 sites listed. There are certainly more sites available than those found by the search engines. The Associated Press, for example, has reported that "A study found that search engines . . . cover a diminishing fraction of web pages and take a long time to list new sites" ("Search Engines," 1999). A similar report on National Public Radio stated that search engines find only about 16% of the web sites on a particular topic. Therefore, the list of continuing education sites for mental health professionals that follows should not be thought of as complete but only as a starting place for further exploration.

- **Dimensions in Mental Health Practice** (www.dmhp.org): Sponsored by the Center for Credentialing and Education (CCE), an affiliate of the National Board for Certified Counselors (NBCC), this web site contains one NBCC-approved learning module:
  — Clinical Skills for Mental Health Professionals
  Registration and credit are available on-line. The course is a series of case studies with interactive quizzes after each one. Three hours of credit may be earned.
- **Trance*Sand*Dance Press** (www.psychceu.com): These NBCC-approved home study programs are available on the web site of this New Mexico organization. The web site is easy for the novice user to navigate and is visually pleasing as well. Two programs are available:

— Reweaving the Web: The Treatment of Substance Abuse; and
— Sandplay, The Sacred Healing: A Guide to Symbolic Process. Not all of the functions are on-line yet, but the developers are working to make all aspects of each program available on their site.

- **Mental Health InfoSource** (MHI) (www.mhsource.com): Awards include LA Times "Times Pick," Select Surf "Best of the Web," and Snap Search "Editor's Choice." The site is associated with the psychiatric profession and has these features:
  — *The Psychiatric Times* newsletter is on-line and available for 1 hour of CE credit.
  — One on-line course—Progress in Psychopharmacology: Psychotic Disorders Update—offers the quiz on-line and mails the certificate afterward. No cost!
  — Another on-line course—Clinical Puzzles for 18 hours credit—consists of case studies and an interactive posttest, plus viewing discussion between participants and an expert on a bulletin board.
  — Professionals can hear the entire recorded conference "Practical Psychopharmacology Update," view the transcribed text, and then take an interactive posttest for 16 hours of credit. Fours sessions are available at 4 hours each at $49 per session.
  — On-line registration for conferences worldwide is available.
- **American Association of Marriage and Family Therapy** (www.aamft.org): AAMFT has a full range of services and opportunities on this site. Features include
  — an on-line course, Brief Therapy: Essential Elements, Concepts, and Techniques, offered through the University of Colorado at Denver for three graduate credits. Registration is on-line as well.
  — registration forms available on-line as well as conference programs. Information on sessions, costs, and location is also available.
- **Behavior On-Line** (www.behavior.net): BOL has several NBCC-approved courses that are hosted on the audiopsyche site. BOL is responsible for awarding the NBCC-approved continuing education credit. There are four courses:

— Listening to Prozac;

— Cognitive Therapy for Personality Disorders;

— Complex PTSD and Incest/Child Sexual Abuse: Approaches to Treatment; and

— Mind-Body Mastery Over Surgery.

- **Distance Learning Network** (www.dlnetwork.com): The first web-based continuing education organization to be approved by NBCC to offer live programs broadcast over the Internet. These programs are similar to teleconferences and are auditory, visual, and interactive. Their site lists upcoming events and gives information for registration.

- **PsyBC, the Psy Broadcasting Corporation** (www.psybc.com): This award-winning, NBCC-approved site has a unique format. It sponsors four programs to which counselors subscribe. The topics of the programs are

— cognitive behavior therapy;

— psychoanalysis;

— group therapy; and

— psychopharmacology for psychotherapists.

Each month an expert in the field leads an on-line discussion through e-mail in which participants may read the comments as well as make comments or ask questions of their own. Printed copies of the articles discussed are available. Continuing education credit is earned monthly for those who wish to purchase it.

- **Institute for Behavioral Healthcare** (www.ibh.com): This organization is a division of the Institute for the Advancement of Human Behavior (IAHB), which is approved by the NBCC. However, the on-line programs offered by the Institute for Behavioral Healthcare have not been submitted to NBCC for approval. The IAHB site has a listing of their live workshops and on-line registration. The Institute for Behavioral Healthcare site has four on-line courses available for credit:

— The Ethical Way;

— Who Owns the Data?;

— Treating Childhood Depressive Illness; and

— Redecision Therapy.

- **Internet Guides Press** (www.virtualcs.com): This site, built by mental health professional David Lukoff, helps guide other professionals through Internet searches for information, products, and services that assist counselors and therapists in their work. One course is offered:
  — Navigating the Mental Health Internet.
  A page of helpful links is available, and purchasers receive a copy of the site author's book on the same topic.
- **CyberEd** (www.isg-cybered.com): This site is the on-line campus of the International Seminars Group. Features on the site include a calendar of live events, a library of materials, a bookstore, and two web-based continuing education programs entitled
  — Avengers, Conquerors, Playmates, And Lovers: Roles Played by Child Sexual Abuse Perpetrators; and
  — Assessing Violent Couples.
  Articles on these programs are available on-line along with the quiz, which then must be e-mailed to the sponsor. The fee must be mailed by regular post.
- **The Institute of Natural Sciences** (www.ccourses.com): This site has correspondence courses in various areas of study, including counseling, that are available in traditional correspondence format or by e-mail. The courses can be ordered and paid for on-line.
- **New York University** (www.scps.nyu.edu/): This site is sponsored by NYU's School of Continuing and Professional Studies. They have over 45 courses available on-line. This is a site found through Peterson's Publishing, which produces *Peterson's Guide to Distance Learning Programs* (www.petersons.com). Only one course is for human service professionals:
  — Introduction to HIV Mental Health: A Primer for Counseling.
  The site is easy to navigate and instructions for registering on-line are unusually clear. This is a very good site for the novice user.

WHAT DOES THE FUTURE HOLD?

As cybertechnology makes instant communication more common, possibilities that continuing education providers and credentialing boards should be considering as we move into the new millennium include

- methods for on-line and traditional continuing education providers to send continuing education credit directly to certification and licensing boards;
- more interactive courses allowing counselors to dialogue with one another as well as with experts in the field (see www.psybc.com);
- on-line record-keeping services for counseling professionals who wish to have electronic continuing education credit storage;
- more live conferences, seminars, and even training programs on the Internet with audio and visual capabilities (see www. dlnetwork.com); and
- Internet-based visual and auditory supervision of practicing counselors as well as counseling interns.

As Internet technology makes these and other possibilities become realities, leaders in our profession may question the effect this will have on the traditional forums for continuing education such as conferences, workshops, and training institutes. Because these events provide opportunities and services that the on-line world cannot, such as networking, purchasing professional products, spontaneous discourse with colleagues and leaders, and participation in the political process of the profession, it is logical to assume that the world of live meetings will not fade. However, it is also logical to assume that they will be shaped by the need to broadcast them live over the Internet. One speculation is that home-based conference attendees could as easily attend plenary sessions and committee meetings by computer as they can now via the conference telephone call.

RECOMMENDED ACTIONS AND START-UP STRATEGIES

This chapter's author encourages any continuing education provider who has home study programs to consider placing some or all of them on the web, if the format allows. Currently, the selection of on-line continuing education programs is rather small. Every year, several thousand counselors and other mental health professionals need to earn hours for recertification or relicensure. Every year, a certain number of counselors wait until the end of their certification/licensure period before they become aware that they need continuing education hours in very short order. Every year the NBCC recertification administrator grants extensions of time to NCCs who have experienced extenuating circumstances so that they may complete the continuing education requirements. The need is there. Now the profession must decide how to meet the need.

RECOMMENDATIONS

For any organization planning to launch an Internet-based continuing education program, the following recommendations are offered.

1. Surf the Web thoroughly before making any business decisions. Get help with this, if necessary, to ensure getting a real picture of what is already being done.
2. Contact others who have done similar projects. Most professionals are very willing to share their experiences.
3. Make it very clear what organization is the sponsor of the site and how to get in touch with that organization by phone, fax, e-mail, and ground mail.
4. Make the navigation instructions simple enough for the *most inexperienced user*. The last thing wanted is for those counselors who probably already have too much on their plates to feel frustrated by the site.
5. If the program is a small part of a very large operation, make it easy to move off the front page to the program site.
6. Unclutter the program site: the cleaner the better. See the Trance*Sand*Dance Press site at www.psychceu.com for a good example of a fledgling effort that is both elegant and rich. Only one program is up at this time, but the site is so easy to navigate that it seems sure that users will return to catch the second program as soon as it is available.

It is worth mentioning that the periodical *Association Management* (Cox & Chon, 1996) has an excellent article describing the initial effort of the American Occupational Therapy Association (AOTA) to create an on-line symposium for its members. Their pointers and cautions are well worth reading before venturing into the world of on-line continuing education. One excellent recommendation made by AOTA was to "thoroughly test the downloading process" before posting the program or event. This is especially important for programs that will feature large text files designed for the user to print.

For organizations that are considering web-based services to counselors, recommendations are as follows.

1. Surf the web thoroughly to find out if there are other similar services competing for the same constituency.
2. Speak to others who have done similar projects to determine how much staff time and funding this project may take over the long term.
3. Compare that information with current staff, their technological expertise, and their workload before making the decision to begin such a project.
4. Get some expert advice on the long-term viability of the service. It is important to consider whether or not the service will be antiquated in 3 years or 10 years.

CONCLUSION

The counseling profession is at the beginning of a growing trend to utilize computer technology for a widening variety of needs. One of the most important is for the delivery of accessible and affordable continuing education. Another need is for more on-line continuing education programs on a wider variety of topics. Transmission and storage of continuing education credit are also areas of need that are currently not being widely addressed. Increasing use of the Internet for continuing education purposes will not diminish the need for live conferences and training but may alter their format to accommodate the need for Internet transmission.

Guidelines for continuing education providers planning on creating continuing education programs on the Internet include surfing to determine what is currently being offered, clear identification, and simple instruction and navigation. Guidelines for continuing education services such as credit storage banks include researching for similar services, carefully gauging financial and staff resources, and getting expert advice on future trends.

As Thomas Clawson has stated, "there is beginning to be a shift from training for training's sake to training for better job opportunities and higher salary for human service professionals" (personal communication, May 14, 1999). Considering this fact, the world of continuing education in cyberspace can only gain importance in the never-ending effort to make human service professionals respected and competitive in the new millennium.

REFERENCES

Bacon, T. J. (1998, Fall). What has AHEC been doing for continuing education? *AHEC Review*, pp. 1–3.

Cox, J. B., & Chon, A. (1996, June). Continuing education goes on-line. *Association Management*, pp. 51–56.

Leary, P.S. (1998, October). The changing face of continuing education. *Counseling Today*, 41, 17.

Search engines lag behind web growth. (1999, July 8). *The Greensboro News and Record*, p. A8.

21

On-Line Instruction in Counselor Education: Possibilities, Implications, and Guidelines

M. Harry Daniels, J. Michael Tyler, and B. Scott Christie

The World Wide Web has become a ubiquitous component of American life. Television ads now provide web addresses to obtain information. Movie studios create elaborate web sites to promote their latest movie. Even school children are making the web a part of their routine. Web66 (1998) currently maintains a list of over 13,000 K–12 institutions that have their own web presence.

At the postsecondary level, 33% of all college courses use the Internet, with 22% of all courses using web pages for class materials (Green, 1998). An estimated 753,640 students formally enrolled in distance education courses in the academic year 1994–95 (National Center for Education Statistics, 1998). A growing number of large universities now offer complete master's degrees in business through the Internet. In short, the World Wide Web has created a new medium for distance education and new opportunities for place-bound learners. Counselor education programs have also been influenced by these trends, and a master's degree in human services with an emphasis in counseling is being offered in its entirety as an on-line program (Capella University, 1999).

A review of materials suggests that in the postsecondary classroom, the Internet is used in one of several ways. Some institutions are taking a minimalist approach where the only information available on-line is a brief course description, or perhaps a course syllabus. A few institutions have pushed to the other extreme and are working to provide entire courses, and in some cases entire programs, over the Internet. A third group is seeking out a midline position where courses are supported or enhanced by materials available on-line. Regardless of which approach an institution or counselor education program takes, the process is largely one of trial and error. As noted by Thyer, Artelt, and Markward (1998), "This use of technology is largely taking place in the absence of well-designed studies . . ." (p. 291).

Since 1995, a small group of studies have been published that represent an attempt to identify methods for teaching on-line. Unfortunately, these studies have not provided consistent results. Some authors (Thyer et al., 1998) have found that face-to-face teaching provided a better learning experience for students in which to learn and practice skills. Further, Thyer and Polk (1997) demonstrated that students preferred face-to-face teaching over distance approaches. These findings are supported by Tyler and Baylen (1998), who also found that students preferred and performed better in a face-to-face setting. However, Freddolino (1998) found no difference in the satisfaction level of students or in other learning outcomes between distance and traditional students. Similarly, Stocks and Freddolino (1998) found that students participating in an Internet-based research methods course had similar course outcomes to those in the face-to-face course.

In the absence of solid research that can be used to direct on-line instruction, assumptions may be made that educators can simply transfer their current practices to this new medium. However, research has demonstrated that alterations are necessary. For instance, Boling and Robinson (1999) have demonstrated that student groups engaged in cooperative learning tasks learn the most, while those using multimedia have a higher level of satisfaction. Findings such as these have resulted in attempts to create cooperative learning groups on-line. However, Scifres, Gundersen, and Behara (1998) found that team development is different when live versus virtual teams are compared. Virtual team members overall tend to be less satisfied with their project, and believe they give more individual effort in comparison to others on the team.

Due to these inconsistent research results, and because on-line teaching and learning result in dynamics that are different than those found in a traditional classroom, educators in general, particularly those involved in graduate education programs, need to be careful in their approach to on-line instruction (Council of Graduate Schools, 1998). Recognizing this need for caution as well as a need to provide counselor educators with direction, the Association for Counselor Education and Supervision Technology Interest Network established a work committee to develop a set of standards that could provide direction for students and educators interested in on-line instruction.

This ad hoc committee drafted a set of guidelines that were widely disseminated among interest group members for feedback and discussion. Working electronically, counselor educators, practitioners, and others provided the committee with input and direction over a period of months in 1998 and early 1999. A final set of standards was reviewed at the 1999 Annual Convention of the American Counseling Association and adopted by ACES in May 1999.

In all, 27 guidelines that inform counselor educators of critical issues that require careful consideration in the development of on-line courses were identified. The guidelines were then organized into sections that mirror the proposed Council for the Accreditation of Counseling and Related Educational Programs standards for traditional instructional practices (CACREP, 1997). The sections include course quality, course content/objectives, instructional support, faculty qualifications, instructor/course evaluation, technological standards, and grievance procedures.

The complete approved standards (ACES, 1999a) are represented in this chapter along with brief discussions to help counselor educators and others understand the intentions of the authors and contributors and to further promote quality practice in counselor education. Concerns related to guideline implementation and on-line course design are also presented.

GUIDELINES FOR ON-LINE INSTRUCTION IN COUNSELOR EDUCATION

COURSE QUALITY

1. The course must offer, at a minimum, an equivalent educational opportunity to that provided in a traditional course. This should

include equality in the domains of information, skill building, and course evaluation.

Discussion: Distance learning offerings should be held accountable to the same standards for quality as traditional courses. Objectives that cannot be maintained at the same level, and that cannot be reasonably modified or replaced with equivalent objectives, should be delivered in a traditional format.

2. Specific course content must be amenable to effective delivery in the manner proposed.

Discussion: Some courses may readily lend themselves to many distance learning formats. Other courses may lend themselves to only a limited range of formats, while some may not be appropriate for distance delivery. In deciding when and how to deliver instruction outside of a traditional framework, faculty should focus on specific objectives, and determine the best manner in which to meet each group of learning objectives.

3. Reasonable efforts must be taken by the institution to ensure that the student has been responsible for course work submitted.

Discussion: Some arrangement needs to be made to attempt to ensure that the registered student has completed the required course work. This does not necessarily mean that every course will require some direct meeting, but at some point a direct meeting where the identity of the student can be verified, and a thorough evaluation of all distance courses and student learning can be completed, should be included. One alternative may be to use proctored exams that can be administered at distance sites.

4. Distance learning courses must provide an opportunity for the students to be actively engaged in a learning process beyond simply reviewing text-based material, if the parallel traditional course provides opportunities beyond the review of text-based materials.

Discussion: Current learning theory suggests that appropriate education of adults involves opportunities to process information, formulate solutions to real-world problems, and apply abstract theoretical models to specific settings and situations. Traditional classrooms provide opportunity for student interaction, social construction of knowledge, and human contact that cannot be replicated simply by reviewing text materials. Distance learning offerings need to consider carefully how to replicate these experiences to provide a broad range of learning opportunity.

5. Distance learning courses should not be limited to a re-creation of a traditional face-to-face course but should be specifically designed to take advantage of educational opportunities provided by the medium used to deliver the course.

   Discussion: To provide the most effective educational opportunities available, instructors must fully utilize the tools available to them, and build upon the strength of each tool utilized. Advanced technology offers the opportunity to develop new approaches to learning that take full advantage of the technology to move beyond what has been done in the past.

6. The differential impact on student learning that is likely to occur to those students taught in a distance fashion must be considered, and any potential problems must be guarded against or steps for remediation provided.

   Discussion: It is unclear at the current time if distance education approaches are equal in all respects to more traditional instructional settings. In some cases, students may gain more, while in others they may gain less. To ensure appropriate educational standards, a range of potential outcomes should be assessed including skills, knowledge, attitudes, personal development, and professional orientation. Distance courses should meet the needs of students in each domain, or steps must be taken to ensure that student's needs in those domains not met through distance education are met in an alternative format.

7. In those cases where distance classes provide for a meeting opportunity for students, the meeting environment should be one that is supportive of and conducive to the educational process.

   Discussion: Not all physical environments meet the needs for educational meetings. If groups of students are meeting in a face-to-face setting, the physical space provided must be adequately designed and equipped to meet the specific needs of the learning group.

8. As in all courses at the university level, issues of equity and diversity should be addressed and promoted in a distance environment.

     Discussion: A variety of variables influence individual students' communication styles, learning needs, and behavioral patterns. Approaches to distance education may not meet the needs of all students, and the instructor and institution involved have a responsibility to monitor student behavior, learning, and communication to ensure that individual needs are met, and that individual differences are recognized as strengths and, as appropriate, built upon.

COURSE CONTENT/OBJECTIVES

9. Distance-based classes should be designed to meet a specific need.

     Discussion: Distance education opportunities should be judiciously and wisely chosen to meet a specific set of needs. The availability of technology does not dictate its use anymore than the availability of medication suggests it is the best response to all clients. By focusing on specific needs and working to meet these, institutions can ensure that distance offerings are beneficial.

10. Because counseling courses often involve the exchange of sensitive information about clients and students, security precautions need to be implemented and enforced that ensure appropriate protection of this information.

     Discussion: Client and student confidentiality will be maintained via methods such as, but not limited to, data encryption, pseudonym use, password protection on various access levels to the Internet and other communication programs, and a method of security for the verification of postal delivery of sensitive information.

11. If the objectives for a specific distance class are different than those for an on-campus class, then appropriate steps must be taken to ensure that every distance student receives appropriate remediation to meet all objectives.

> *Discussion:* Programs that provide opportunities for students to learn at a distance must ensure that the educational opportunities provided for all students are equivalent. In some cases, certain objectives may not be appropriately addressed through some distance modalities. In those cases, equivalent opportunities may be provided through alternative formats to ensure student success.

12. Appropriate procedures for evaluation of student learning must be implemented.

> *Discussion:* Counselor education addresses knowledge, skills, and attitudes in students. Evaluation procedures need to be devised that allow for assessment of growth in each of these areas. Additionally, procedures need to be implemented to ensure that the material submitted as documentation of student learning is genuine.

INSTRUCTIONAL SUPPORT

13. Students must have access to equivalent educational supports including library resources, tutorial assistance, and access to the course instructor.

> *Discussion:* The university experience expands beyond the walls of the individual classroom and the information provided in a text. A variety of support materials, ancillary contacts, and personal relationships are successfully combined in a well-balanced academic environment. Care must be taken to move beyond simply providing class lectures or reading material on-line to incorporating the entirety of the academic experience that the student otherwise would have in a traditional setting.

14. Students must be provided with the opportunity to receive complete training in the technology prior to being required to use the technology and should be provided with ongoing support throughout the educational experience.

> *Discussion:* Just as faculty cannot be expected to maintain currency in all aspects of technology, neither can students. Clear expectations should be established prior to enrollment in a course about the student's competencies in relation to the use of specific technology. If students who are enrolled

do not meet these competencies, then it is the responsibility of the institution to provide training and support to help students in those areas where skills and knowledge are lacking. If during the period of time that a student is receiving instruction the interface, technological demands, or other aspects of technology change, the institution must take reasonable steps to ensure that students are trained/retrained to handle these changes adequately. Institutions have a responsibility to provide adequate support services that can be readily accessed to resolve student difficulties that result from a lack of knowledge or skills, changes in software or equipment, software or equipment malfunction, or other circumstances over which the institution has control or responsibility.

15. Financial resources must be available to meet the needs of the distance learning activities.

    Discussion: Institutions should be aware prior to undertaking distance-based educational offerings that standard methods of calculating the institutions' financial commitment and needs may not be applicable to new modalities. In all cases, institutions must, in advance, make the necessary financial commitment to ensure that student needs are met.

16. Students must be provided with adequate access to faculty in a timely fashion.

    Discussion: This may occur through the use of specific electronic media as long as students have been provided the opportunity for appropriate training.

17. The specific purpose and outcomes of a distance delivery method is to be explained prior to the beginning of the course and included in the syllabus.

    Discussion: For most students, distance learning opportunities will be new. Prior to agreeing to participate in this environment, students must have adequate information about the course, procedures, and expectations to make an informed decision about the appropriateness of this modality in meeting their own learning goals.

18. Appropriate policies must be developed and disseminated concerning expectations for student attendance, time commitments, and other faculty expectations for performance.

Discussion: Many students will have no experience working in a distance learning setting. Because of this lack of exposure, and because distance learning approaches can vary substantially, students can be expected to have little accurate information concerning expectations for performance. It is incumbent upon faculty to ensure that students understand fully expectations for performance prior to enrollment in distance education whenever possible, or as early in the process as is practicable.

19. Courses need to reflect sound pedagogy, and where appropriate, opportunities for student interaction and collaboration on specific course materials must be provided.

    Discussion: Traditional approaches to education may not translate easily into a distance environment. It is the responsibility of the faculty member to ensure that the pedagogy employed is valid and appropriate based on the needs of the students and objectives of the course.

20. Support resources, such as books, videos, and computer software, must be made available to students in a manner that is reasonable for those students who have enrolled in an on-line or distance class.

    Discussion: If services are anticipated to be provided to students at a long distance from the main campus, then reasonable steps must be taken to provide those students with access to support materials at distance sites, or the students must be fully informed in advance that they will not have access and that there will be portions of the learning opportunity that will not be available to them.

FACULTY QUALIFICATIONS

21. Faculty instructing distance education courses should be of equivalent experience and eligible for academic rank in the same manner as their on-site counterparts.

    Discussion: Faculty involved in distance learning opportunities need to be fully involved in all aspects of the academic program, just as they would be if they were involved in more traditional offerings. Although some distinctions in qualifications may be appropriate in terms of knowledge of technology or other specialty areas, the breadth and degree of training and experience should be as extensive as that of any other faculty member.

22. Faculty must be fully trained in all aspects of the technology that is used to deliver the course, and continuous ongoing support must be provided by the educational institution.

    Discussion: The faculty member delivering instruction needs to have the requisite skills necessary to implement successfully the effective use of whatever teaching tools are used in the delivery of material. However, faculty outside of computer-oriented disciplines cannot be expected to stay current in the rapidly evolving field of computers and related technology. Therefore, institutions that use advanced technology as a delivery tool must be prepared to provide the support necessary to ensure that these tools are used appropriately. This must include support in the design, delivery, student access, and updating of on-line or computer-based materials.

23. In those cases where appropriate, qualified mentors or discussion leaders are required, the same standards must exist for determining quality and ability of these support personnel as would be used in a traditional setting.

    Discussion: In all cases, equivalency of quality should be sought between on-line and traditional settings.

24. Faculty assignment to distance education courses must reflect the actual faculty involvement, including adequate time and resources for faculty training, course preparation, and technology adaptation.

    Discussion: Faculty who undertake to teach classes at a distance are substantially increasing their responsibilities in ways that many institutions are unprepared to understand and acknowledge. Institutions are responsible to monitor faculty behavior and involvement, to assist faculty in transitioning to new modalities of teaching, and to compensate faculty adequately for the additional time necessary to succeed in this new arena.

INSTRUCTOR/COURSE EVALUATION

25. Course/instructor evaluations for distance classes must be implemented to be commensurate with procedures used for eval-

uation of classes taught through traditional methods. Students participating in distance classes must be given the opportunity to provide course/instructor evaluations anonymously (e.g., by returning evaluations via the U.S. Postal Service).

TECHNOLOGICAL STANDARDS

26. Technological problems will occur that will require appropriate back-up and/or face-to-face technologies.

    Discussion: These back-up technologies should be designed to maintain the integrity of the course in a manner that provides as little disruption to student learning as possible. If student learning is disrupted or a student cannot complete a course due to technological issues that are the responsibility of the educational institution, then the institution is responsible for providing the student with alternative means that will meet his or her specific needs in relation to the original learning contract.

GRIEVANCE PROCEDURES

27. Procedures to address grievances of the student must be implemented.

    Discussion: These procedures must be responsive to the needs of students "at a distance." If a student population is developed and instructional programs maintained that do not require on-campus activities for learning, then students cannot be burdened with expectations of on-campus activities for administrative dealings such as filing a complaint against an instructor.

ON-LINE COURSE DESIGN: IMPLEMENTING THE GUIDELINES

Counselor educators are ultimately concerned with educating counselors-in-training; thus the primary concern associated with implementing on-line instruction is how it will affect students' learning as well as their understanding of counseling skills, processes, and practices. At present, little is known about how on-line instruction influences counselor trainees' learning or skill acquisition. Yet it seems relatively certain that administrators and institutions will continue to encourage (i.e., expect) faculty and programs to design and deliver courses on-line. And counselor educators must position themselves to respond to such expectations. The guidelines presented here represent the range of concerns that counselor educators who are interested in developing on-line learning environments must be prepared to address. No single guideline is seen as being necessarily more important than any of the others, although some have argued that if the first two guidelines are not satisfied, the remaining issues are rendered moot.

Place-bound counselor education students will expect faculty and programs to use computer technology and make professional preparation programs more available and convenient to complete. They will also be concerned about the quality of the instruction that they receive. From their perspective, any course that is delivered on-line should satisfy the instructional standards that the department requires of courses that utilize the traditional face-to-face format. In short, place-bound students want assurances that their program will prepare them to fulfill their professional aspirations and responsibilities. The guidelines presented here can be used to develop on-line courses that will address students' needs and expectations.

Recognizing that counselor educators and place-bound students share an interest in and concern for the quality of on-line instruction, this chapter's authors offer the following sequence of steps for designing an on-line course.

- **Step 1: Identify instructional goals for on-line instruction.** Adoption of the guidelines will influence the manner in which the instructional goals of the program will be implemented. Because a variety of different stakeholders (e.g., students, faculty, staff, and administrators) have an interest in such a decision, it is important to identify the goals of each stakeholder and determine how these goals relate to the on-line course and program goals. One question to ask is, How might the technology, on-line course work, or the on-line process minimize or enhance the overall goals of the program and participants?
- **Step 2: Determine technological competence of instructors and students.** Traditional instructional methods place little or no emphasis on the technological competence of either faculty or students. On-line instruction introduces dramatic

changes into the instructional milieu by altering some elements of the space and time relationships that link students with faculty, with other students, or with facilities that are commonly found on a campus (American Council on Education, 1996). For on-line instruction to work, both faculty and students must be prepared to manage these changes because serious gaps in domains of technical competence will seriously limit the utility of an on-line course. Thus it is important to assess the technological competence of instructors and students both prior to and during the development and delivery of on-line instruction. The ACES-recommended technical competencies (ACES, 1999b; Appendix 2) could serve as a basis for conducting an initial assessment.

- **Step 3: Provide relevant learning opportunities for faculty and students.** Successfully completing an on-line course means that both the instructor and the learner have to co-exist with technology without it becoming a barrier to instruction. In order to enhance instruction, it will be important to eliminate as many technological barriers as possible. This goal can be achieved by providing relevant learning opportunities to all participants. This training process could be applied to all of the components of a distance learning environment including, but not limited to, e-mail communication, real-time conferencing, videotape supervision, and telephone/conference call applications.

CONCLUSION

The expansion of on-line instruction in higher education has been very rapid, and its popularity among administrators and institutions is expected to grow. Given its popularity among campus administrators, it is expected that various methods of on-line instruction will either be blended with or replace the traditional instructional strategies that are most commonly used in higher education programs, including counselor education. At present, most counselor educators are just beginning to explore the possibilities of using on-line instruction. Nonetheless, the transition from the exclusive use of traditional methods to the adoption of on-line instructional strategies has begun. As counselor educators become more familiar with on-line instruction, the rate of the transition will, in all likelihood, increase until sometime soon every graduate of a counselor preparation program will have completed a portion of his or her program on-line.

This transition from face-to-face to on-line instruction also illustrates the need for guidelines that can be used to guide the development of courses that will be substantially equivalent in terms of content, quality, instructional support, and faculty qualifications. The guidelines presented here represent an initial response to that need. As more becomes known about on-line instruction and what does and does not work for students in counseling programs, or as technological advances enhance the quality of and possibilities for on-line instruction, it will be important to revisit and modify these guidelines. For now, this chapter's authors believe that the guidelines can be used to inform the profession's discussion about this critical issue.

REFERENCES

American Council on Education. (1996). *Guiding principles for distance learning in a learning society*. Washington, DC: Author.

Association for Counselor Education and Supervision. (1999a). *Guidelines for on-line instruction in counselor education* [On-line]. Available: http://www.chre.vt.edu/f-s/thohen/ACESWEB.htm.

Association for Counselor Education and Supervision. (1999b). *Recommended technical competencies for counselor education students* [On-line]. Available: http://www.chre.vt.edu/f-s/thohen/competencies.htm.

Boling, N. C., & Robinson, D. H. (1999). Individual study, interactive media, or cooperative learning: Which activity best supplements lecture-based distance education? *Journal of Educational Psychology, 91*, 169–174.

Capella University. (1999, August 6). *The on-line master's of science in human services* [On-line]. Available: http://www.CapellaUniversity.com/9/.

Council for the Accreditation of Counseling and Related Educational Programs. (1997). *The 2001 standards: Draft 1*. Alexandria, VA: American Counseling Association.

Council of Graduate Schools. (1998). *Distance education: Opportunities and challenges for the 21st century* [On-line]. Available: http://www.cgsnet.org/DISTANCE2.html.

Freddolino, P. (1998). Building on experience: Lessons from a distance education M.S.W. program. *Computers in Human Services, 15*, 39–50.

Green, K. (1998). *Colleges struggle with IT planning: 1998 Campus computing survey* [On-line]. Available: www.campuscomputing.net.

National Center for Education Statistics. (1998, January 18). *Statistical analysis report: Distance education in higher education institutions* [On-line]. Available: http://nces.ed.gov/pubs98/distance/index.html.

Scifres, E., Gundersen, D. E., & Behara, R. S. (1998). An empirical investigation of electronic groups in the classroom. *Journal of Education for Business, 73,* 247–50.

Stocks, J. T., & Freddolino, P. P. (1998). Evaluation of a World-Wide-Web-based graduate social work research methods course. *Computers in Human Services, 15,* 51–69.

Thyer, B. A., Artelt, T., & Markward, M. K. (1998). Evaluating distance learning in social work education: A replication study. *Journal of Social Work Education, 34,* 291–295.

Thyer, B. A., & Polk, G. (1997). Distance learning in social work education: A preliminary evaluation. *Journal of Social Work Education, 33,* 363–368.

Tyler, J. M., & Baylen, D. (1998). Exploring factors that moderate learning and teaching in a web-based course. In J. A. Chambers (Ed.), *Selected papers from the 9th International Conference on College Teaching and Learning.* Jacksonville, FL: Center for the Advancement of Teaching and Learning.

Web66. (1998). *Web66: A K–12 World Wide Web Project* [On-line]. Available: http://web66.umn.edu/.

PART V

Ethical and Professional
Challenges in Cybercounseling

22

Cybercounseling and Regulations: Quagmire or Quest?

ROSEMARIE SCOTTI HUGHES

You log on to the Metanoia (Ainsworth, 1996–99b) web site, click to the introduction, and then proceed to an audio welcome from Dr. Frasier Crane, from his radio show on the popular TV series *Frasier*. "I'm listening," he tells you. You have several links to explore, ranging from information about therapy over the Internet to lists of therapists and their credentials, verified by Metanoia (Metanoia & Mental Health Net, 1997–99), for a fee to the therapist. You also read, "Using the Internet, professional counselors are forming effective helping relationships with people like you." What do you do next? Are you about to enter into cyberspace, lay out your problems to someone you will never meet, and in the process part with some of your cash in exchange for what Metanoia claims is "an effective alternative" to traditional therapy? You are warned that "on-line counseling is not appropriate for everyone." You keep going, clicking through screens, and come to a key phrase: ". . . if something goes wrong, the legal system is probably not going to be able to do anything about it." You are told that you must take responsibility for your on-line work, and you read further that "as far as I can tell" the therapists listed on this site are responsible and accountable professionals. By now, your personal antennas should be sending off some clear signals. How can this be "effective"? Despite Frasier Crane's reassurance, it is hard to believe that confidence is instilled in the potential client.

We are in the midst of exciting times, when technology is expanding faster than our ability to learn how to use it ethically and competently. Is regulation of cybercounseling a quagmire or a quest? Will the profession become bogged down, in unresolvable quandary, entangling itself into a muddy morass over this issue? Or will the profession rise to the occasion, use the opportunity for exploration and adventure, not to pursue some unattainable Golden Fleece or Fountain of Youth, but to use technology to promote well-being and health, and growth and development of individuals, families, and organizations? Hopefully, this book is an attempt to achieve the latter.

A myriad of ethical, legal, and regulatory issues surround cybercounseling, however. Few structures and precedents exist. This chapter explores elements bogging down counseling on the Internet, and those that make it worth pursuing, by exploring telemedicine and implications for counseling, central ethical issues in counseling, state regulation of cybercounseling, and strategies for the future. It is significant to note that most of the research for this chapter occurred through web sites, various search engines, electronic databases, e-mail, and faxes.

THE FIELD OF TELEMEDICINE IN ITS PRESENT STATE: IMPLICATIONS FOR COUNSELING

If you have ever used the telephone to counsel a client or to consult with a colleague, if you have looked up mental or physical health information on a web site, you have, in the broadest sense, been a user or participant in telemedicine. The field of medicine as a whole has been using telemedicine since shore stations were linked by radio to ships at sea for medical emergencies in the 1920s (Butt, Zimmerman, & Ziob Ro, 1996). Medicine has been far ahead of the counseling profession in its use of technology and in examining the benefits and pitfalls of its use. A number of circumstances came together in the 1990s to speed the adoption of telemedicine. They were the development of available technology; the lack of doctors and specialists in rural areas; federal, state, and private sector grant money; and Medicaid payments (Health Care Financing Administration, 1998; National Rural Health Association, 1999; U.S. Department of Health and Human Services,

1998). State networks have been established, and uses include radiology, dermatology, psychiatry, fetal monitoring, nursing visits, remote surgery, and interactive examinations. These networks flourish because of the availability of grant money, but programs expire when funds are gone (Butt et al., 1996; Council on Competitiveness, 1996a, 1996b; World Health Organization, 1997).

TELEMEDICINE DEFINITION

Although many call all medical efforts using electronic means telemedicine, there are further distinctions in definitions. *Telemedicine* is using electronic communication networks for the transmission of information and data related to the diagnosis and treatment of medical conditions. The issues in this chapter related to ethics and regulation of cybercounseling most often fall under this category. *Telehealth* is using electronic communication networks for transmission of information and data focused on health promotion, disease prevention, and the public's overall health, including patient/community education and information, data collection and management, and linkages for health care and referrals. Telehealth is also included in this chapter, specifically information web pages and distance education. A *telecommunity* is created through telecommunications and becomes a virtual community without physical boundaries within a region, an institution, or consortia. A telecommunity can range from being a self-help peer group that meets in a chat room to a formal network of providers of services (World Health Organization, 1997).

REGULATION AND TELEMEDICINE

There are very few regulatory problems when telemedicine is practiced within closed systems, such as intrastate networks, institutions, Indian Health Service, the military, corrections, and the Veterans Administration. Most states have a broad enough definition of the practice of medicine to allow telemedicine within the state. However, the very nature of the Internet allows the instant crossing of geographic borders, and when state and, in some cases, national lines are crossed, regulatory issues emerge. The most common issues arising from telemedicine across state lines are confidentiality of records, patient privacy, definition of *consultation*, jurisdiction, patient complaint mechanisms, and credentials and license of the doctor. Although each state has a definition of the practice of medicine that is somewhat similar, similarities end when deciding how to allow doctors from out of state to consult electronically within the state. Twenty-two states in 1999 have a liberal definition of the consultant exemption, but over half have no exemption at all or are severely limiting (Butt et al., 1996; Reid, 1996; Telemedicine Law Update [http://www.mbc.com/telemed/sum.html]).

CRITICAL CONCERNS AND BENEFITS OF TELEMEDICINE

Although each state regulates medical practice, other issues emerge regardless of whether borders are crossed. Lack of rigorous research on effectiveness of telemedicine, a high technology learning curve for practitioners, cost, and scant case law for precedence for ethical issues are concerns (Reid, 1996; Telemedicine Law Update [http://www.mbc.com/telemed/sum.html & http://www.mbc.com/telemed/federal.html]).

RELATIONSHIP TO COUNSELING

The field of counseling has a much younger history of being licensed than does medicine. Licensure for doctors began in 1870 (Whelan & Wood, 1996). Counseling at the master's level is not yet licensed in all 50 states. The profession as a whole is still looking for national recognition. Many people practice counseling under various licenses. In some states, psychologists are also licensed at the master's level, while others license psychologists at the doctoral level only. Also, psychiatrists counsel people, although psychiatric services have been included under telemedicine grant projects and are generally considered to be under the aegis of medicine in general. However, for this chapter, especially when speaking of ethics and regulation, *counselor* is always used to denote those persons licensed by the state at the master's level specifically for the practice of counseling.

The occupation of medical doctor is recognized worldwide, no matter the specialty. The occupation of counselor is not: some countries only recognize psychologists. Also, the title of *counselor* is used with an adjective in many trades—such as financial counselor, weight-loss counselor, travel counselor—and does not necessarily carry even the requirement of having a bachelor's degree. The profession itself is not yet unified, with its many specialty areas competing with one another on the state level for specific licenses. As evidenced by the inability of the states to agree on who should be allowed to practice medicine from out of state, counseling will have no easier time than medicine in trying to regulate who should be allowed to cybercounsel in each state. In the federal telemedicine grants, very few networks were developed within states for mental health services, some exceptions being California, Georgia, Hawaii, and Virginia.

CENTRAL ETHICAL ISSUES IN CYBERCOUNSELING

Telemedicine and cybercounseling both use technology, but there are significant differences. Telemedicine, especially in the fields of radiology and electronic monitoring of patients, deals with hard data, such as blood counts, blood pressure, heart rate, and other vital signs of the body. Counseling, however, deals in few if any hard data and relies on the client's definition of the problem. Of course, medical practice is also subject to patient report and doctor subjectivity to some degree. Although telemedicine was used in psychiatry in Nebraska in the 1950s (Hilty, Servis, Nesbitt, & Hales, in press), the first discussion is whether cybercounseling really is counseling.

Is it Counseling?

At an ethics committee meeting of the American Association of State Counseling Boards (AASCB) in January 1999, a discussion was held as to whether counseling over the Internet is actually counseling. The majority decision from that group was that it was not, but the committee decided that the matter warranted further discussion and kept it on the agenda for the future. The central issue that emerged from that discussion was that without face-to-face encounters, counseling could not actually occur.

Cybercounseling, or web counseling as it is called by the National Board for Certified Counselors, is defined by the NBCC (1998; see Appendix 5) as "the practice of professional counseling and information delivery that occurs when client(s) and counselor(s) are in separate or remote locations and utilize electronic means to communicate over the Internet." This definition seems to include web pages, e-mail, and chat rooms but not telephone calls and faxes. The NBCC also stated that it does not advocate for or against web counseling. Of those who say that cybercounseling is not counseling, some are therapists who already have web sites available to people. Most of the web sites have some kind of disclaimer, such as that this is advice, e-therapy, information and education, or a supplement to therapy. In contrast to popular perception, the field of cybercounseling is not really flourishing at this time (Rice, 1997), and few licensed therapists are doing cybercounseling. In addition, there is no large federal grant initiative on the horizon for cybercounseling services to spur its development. Insurance companies are not providing reimbursement for cybercounseling. These two factors alone are disincentives for this new venture to flourish.

One of the counseling profession's main concerns will be for those persons who are unlicensed but promote themselves as competent Internet counselors. When a counselor is unlicensed, a state has no regulatory authority, unless there is a law in that state that allows prosecution as a criminal act for practicing counseling without a license or that gives the board regulatory authority. Unlicensed cybercounselors are almost legally untouchable, especially those with a disclaimer statement that says what they are doing is not therapy.

The NBCC *Standards for the Ethical Practice of Web Counseling* (1998; see Appendix 5) are specific and give the impression this is an area that one does not enter lightly, without careful thought and consideration of implications and possible effects. Despite disclaimers on web sites that a counselor is only giving advice, or education/information, the expectation of the client is a key factor that courts and regulatory boards will consider in determining whether or not a counseling relationship exists (Childress, 1998; Rice, 1997). Some legal commentators have stated that with on-line services, if the client agrees to pay for the services of a licensed counselor, a therapeutic relationship exists (in Stricker, 1996).

Specific Ethical Issues

Beyond the issues of whether cybercounseling is actually counseling and equivalent to the traditional office visit, several additional issues are salient. These include truth in advertising, confidentiality, duty to warn, competence, and dual relationships.

Truth in Advertising

What would a client expect from Concerned Counseling (http://www.concernedcounseling.com), which has 24-hour on-line and telephone service and claims to have licensed professional counselors available? "No matter what you're going through, our counselors are here to help you. . . . There is no subject that is taboo . . . . we are here for you," says this advertisement. The word *therapy* is never used, but *counseling* is, many times, which could lead people to believe that counseling will actually occur. The site does add a disclaimer that Concerned Counseling may not be appropriate for everyone, in contradiction to prior statements. In addition, Concerned Counseling states that "if you are seriously considering suicide, please log off your computer [why?] and call the police or emergency medical services for assistance." However, this statement appears at the bottom of the site's second page.

Confidentiality

As in telemedicine, confidentiality is a central ethical concern (Sampson, Kolodinsky, & Greeno, 1997). The NBCC recommends encryption methods; however, the process is not always a simple one, and a client in crisis is unlikely to be concerned about encryption before contacting a counselor via the Internet. Privacy is a related issue. The counselor has no way of knowing who is in the room with the client when either sending or receiving e-mail. Clients could be at risk without the counselor's knowledge. For example, if an abused woman's batterer has access to her e-mail and can read the interactions of counseling, what is the potential for harm? What if a client accidentally sends a message to her boss that was meant for her therapist, and then because the message was about abuse, commits suicide or is fired? This chapter's author once received a message that a student thought that she sent to her parents and that contained sensitive information. Student and professor discussed the e-mail, thankfully with an outcome significantly better than the previous example. People may use their work sites for web counseling, not being aware that the employer has the right to all e-mail of employees. A therapist could violate confidentiality by using transcriptions of sessions in a research report or conference presentation and fail to get consent of the client because of ease of printing out the sessions (Polauf, 1998).

Duty to Warn

The lack of identity of the client can be problematic. What is the counselor's obligation to a client who has suicidal or homicidal ideation, especially if the client gives no identifying information? Following a duty-to-warn mandate by the licensed counselor's state is difficult if not impossible without identifying information. If that client harms self or another, the family or the client, if from another state than the counselor, has little chance of legal recourse. Cybercounseling that crosses national borders can further complicate the issue. For example, the Samaritans, a group of volunteers in England that provide emotional support to any person who is suicidal or despairing (http://www.samaritans.org), promise, unlike crisis hotlines in the United States, complete confidentiality to any caller. If someone threatens suicide the Samaritans do nothing. They do not have the same issues of taking precautions as do U.S. counselors (Holmes, 1997).

Related to identity is how lack of physical presence influences the dynamics of a cybercounseling. In face-to-face counseling, the physical presence of the client provides audio and visual cues. The counselor knows the client's identity. However, on the Internet using text, the client may take on another persona. The counselor does not know age, gender, or appearance. Conducting a therapeutic session could be limited. In addition, therapeutic modalities in which the counselor is well versed may not be appropriate for cybercounseling (Childress, 1998). A related problem of identification is in chat groups. A group of female sexual abuse victims could be infiltrated by a male abuser who has potential to cause harm without warning (White, 1998).

Competence

Problems can also exist in the identity of the counselor. An example is a web site that offers *Your Confidential Sexual Issues Report* (Goldman, n.d.). On this site, Arlene Goldman, PhD, claims 20 years of experience as a sex therapist but does not list any license. The $69.95 report carries a disclaimer that it is for "informational and educational purposes only." At the same time it offers "A personalized review of your assessment, including the options and alternatives available to you, answers to your specific question, and what the therapist has suggested to clients with similar issues." Although this chapter's author has not participated in Dr. Goldman's assessment, the web site does not instill confidence sufficient to submit personal information to her for "a consultation with a professional." The lines between therapy and consulting and education/information seem rather tenuous.

Issues of competency and referral are also raised. How does a counselor become qualified to use the Internet for counseling? What kind of training is necessary? Outside of established state networks funded through grant money, no Internet counselor that this chapter's author was able to locate on the web is using video teleconferencing (VTC), with two-way video/audio. One of the NBCC standards speaks to explaining to clients what misunderstandings can occur from cybercounseling and how to cope with them. Misunderstandings are rife in even face-to-face counseling, so the potential is far greater in cybercounseling. When cybercounseling a client in another state or country, or perhaps even in a distant city in the same state, the counselor will not have access to good referral sources for that person. How does one go about finding a "counselor-on-call" as recommended by NBCC when state boards can only tell who holds current licenses, not where and if they are practicing?

Dual Relationships

The largest category of ethical violations dealt with by regulatory boards is dual relationships. Is there potential for an Internet counseling situation to become a dual relationship? If the counselor uses explicit language that offends a client, whether intentionally or not, will the client have a basis for complaint? What if the Internet relationship leads to a phone or face-to-face encounter? Will a predatory therapist be able to claim that he or she was never in a counseling relationship at all with the client, but only giving advice by Internet, especially if the client is from another state?

OTHER ETHICAL ISSUES

Other ethical concerns in cybercounseling include verifying validity of software assigned as homework to clients; inadequate counselor prescreening of clients for suitability for cybercounseling; lack of counselor awareness of conditions, events, and cultural issues that may affect the remote client (Sampson et al., 1997); and lack of clarity whether communication using the Internet is covered by therapist/client privilege (Childress, 1998). The underserved, who telemedicine has targeted for services, are the least likely to be technologically savvy; cybercounseling clients are likely to be more of the YAVIS (young, attractive, verbal, intelligent, successful) model. One has to be highly verbal, have access to a computer with modem, be able to write well, and have keyboard skills even to access cybercounseling (Martin, 1997). Even explicitly information-only sites can prove dangerous. Dubovsky (1997) pointed out that InterPsych (IP), which is a international organization of electronic mental health forums, can be risky. Although IP is one of the "best organized and most influential" groups, Dubovsky witnessed international leaders in pyschopharmacology jumping on the weight-loss drug phen/fen's wagon quickly, without reviewing adequate research data. He believed that the boundary between fact and opinion became blurred because of the speed of the information disseminated through the Internet.

The Ethics Committee of the American Psychological Association (APA) has issued *Services by Telephone, Teleconferencing, and Internet* (APA Ethics Committee, 1997). This statement is not specific to cybercounseling but points to existing APA standards that are particularly relevant and indicates that in the future task forces may or may not be adding more guidelines.

There have been some self reports of client satisfaction using Internet services (Callahan, Hilty, & Nesbitt, 1998). However, perhaps individual service providers are less satisfied. For example, D. I. Sommers, who began his Mental Health Cyberclinic web site November 1995, placed a statement on his site (http://www.nicom.com/davids/pageone.htm) saying that, as of June 21, 1999,

This site is closed insofar as offering any sort of on-line consultation via e-mail. Problems and concerns around issues of ethics, fees, confidentiality, and legalities need to be resolved before going forward with this work. Feel free to enter and look around for historical interest only.

The site had recorded 10,639 hits since February 1, 1996.

STATE REGULATION OF CYBERCOUNSELING

As with telemedicine, the issues of licensure and jurisdiction arise, except that counseling boards have not begun to address the problem. A client who obtains counseling services via the Internet from a counselor licensed in the same state has recourse to that state's regulatory board for any violations against either the state code or standards of practice. If the counselor is licensed in another state, to which state does the client register a complaint? As indicated earlier, state medical boards have addressed this issue, but not in a uniform manner.

CURRENT GUIDELINES

The Federation of State Medical Boards (FSMB) produced model legislation regarding telemedicine. This proposal is less than helpful as a guide, as the main responsibility for who can or cannot practice telemedicine in the state is left to each state (Orbuch, 1997). The Health On the Net Foundation (n.d.) has provided a *Code of Conduct for Medical and Health Web Sites* that might be a guide to those counselors who have web pages, but counseling is not specifically mentioned in any of the code's eight principles. The International Society for Mental Health Online has said in its *Mission Statement* (1999) that the society was formed in 1997 "to promote the understanding, use, and development of on-line communication, information, and technology for the international mental health community." However, the principles included in the statement are broad and not concerned with the nature of regulation. The American Telemedical Association (1999) has developed a policy that is a compromise between having a national medical license and restrictive state regulation. It proposed that the state should not restrict "virtual travel" of its patients to seek medical advice outside of the state. It also has stated that a non-face-to-face encounter by a patient with a physican in another state is regulated by the physician's home state.

DISTANCE EDUCATION

Regulation of cybercounseling is at present a quagmire, with no workable models for regulation. No state has a regulation that specifically permits cybercounseling. Neither have boards made progress in recognizing education by Internet. Distance education falls into the realm of both telehealth and telecommunity definitions, and is expanding exponentially in all fields. In preparation for writing this chapter, a phone survey was conducted of all of the state regulatory boards that license counselors to determine whether or not distance education courses would be acceptable toward meeting the educational requirements of the licensure law. Of the boards that responded, 9 would not accept courses; 17 said yes, but there were conditions, such as the program had to be CACREP, or have other accreditation; 12 said it was a board decision, case by case; and 4 said they had no policy. Not all boards are represented because of either problems obtaining a correct phone number or waiting for the boards to fax materials. A corresponding regulatory issue concerns distance supervision and continuing education. It seems that a first step for the NBCC is to address the burgeoning field of distance education with the setting of some kind of standards for acceptance of courses and CEUs. CACREP will be addressing distance education in its new standards, currently in progress.

LICENSURE

The next step, then, will be making a decision as a state whether or not to allow cybercounseling to be part of the definition of counseling within that state. However, not saying anything about cybercounseling may already allow it. States could follow the example of the Telemedicine Development Act (Orbuch, 1997) and spell out, in detail, how reimbursement, confidentiality, informed consent, and licensure specifically apply to electronic communications. As opposed to individual Internet therapists, some of the more credible counseling services are received through established intrastate networks, formed from telemedicine grants, as mental health centers network with referrals from primary physicians. In these cases, there are no questions of credentials or licensure, or client protection from ethics violations because all are under the same state's regulation and often use video teleconferencing. These networks, in some cases, are also eligible for Medicaid reimbursement (Health Care Financing Administration, 1998).

Some states are requiring that doctors must be licensed in that particular state, even if holding license in the state of residence, to practice telemedicine. Credentials, length and type of postgraduate experience, exams, and fees vary substantially by state. If counseling were to follow this model, holding licenses in several states could mean multiple exams, extra courses, and expensive fees that could all serve as deterrents and drive the counselor out of cybercounseling. The counselor could be liable to differing standards of practice if licensed in two or more states, and could possibly have differing procedures regarding the reporting of abuse, billing issues, keeping records, and other standards of conduct (Whelan & Wood, 1996).

STRATEGIES FOR THE FUTURE

The state of the art in technology will drive cybercounseling at any given point in time. Within the next 5 years, bandwidths will be significantly increased, so that current computer users may all have video teleconferencing. Within 10 years all may have this capability via cable TV stations. Picture phones could be as common an option as call waiting and call forwarding are now. With technology developing so that clients can sit in their homes and see and hear the therapist and vice versa, what does the profession need to do now to insure capability, ethics, and responsibility in cybercounseling?

UNDERSERVED POPULATIONS

The professional organizations could come together, not only in each state, but on a national and perhaps international basis. If the main benefit of telemedicine and cybercounseling is to reach remote and underserved populations, only a unified, combined effort will include counseling services. Counselors should be proactive in these efforts. Linking with established telemedicine networks is one possibility. Urban areas have not been addressed. An inner-city, low-income, or disadvantaged person could also benefit from telemedicine. In a similar fashion to the availability of ATM machines, health information and resource kiosks, with limited interactive features, could be established in schools, clinics, and shopping malls.

STATE WEB SITES

Each state should develop information web sites with both general and professional information. The Georgia Mental Health Network (Adams & Grigsby, 1995; Lee, Grigsby, Dennison, & Vought, 1999) offers a database of over 500 mental health-related web sites searchable by topic. There is also a resource database, which allows users to locate agencies in Georgia, and these include advocacy, legal assistance, support groups, and workshops. The on-line bulletin board includes mental heath, mental retardation, and substance abuse organizations that post news items, meetings, and services. Consumers from anywhere in the world can post questions that are answered by professionals. Inquiries range from concerns about relatives in prison, runaways, and the elderly mentally ill to requests for information when making a decision of what services are available for people moving to Georgia.

Each state could list, on its web page, all licensed counselors, and also show those counselors who are under sanction by the state. In addition, state boards could develop a listserv and e-mail their newsletters and announcements to all licensed counselors and counselor educators who subscribed. Substantial savings in printing and posting could result. Educators could forward the information to students immediately via e-mail.

PROFESSIONAL ASSOCIATIONS

NBCC, CACREP, the Ethics Committee of ACA, and the AASCB should work together to develop a draft of standards for acceptable cybercounseling standards and practices and address Internet-based distance education courses for counselor licensure. National standards, endorsed by these organizations, might prevent disparity among state boards regarding cybercounseling. A byproduct of allowing distance education could be to familiarize students with Internet use and contribute to their skill in communicating in that medium, which could transfer into working with clients in cybercounseling, as recommended by Sampson (1998). CEUs over the Internet could allow counselors to keep current and updated, (Grohol, 1998) and perhaps could result in fewer ethical violations.

Supplemental Cybercounseling

Counselors can develop a mind-set that goes beyond the either-or mentality of using cybercounseling, and consider text cybercounseling as a supplement to face-to-face therapy (Childress, 1998). Almost all counselors use the telephone to supplement in-office sessions, handle emergencies, consult, and follow up clients. Text cybercounseling can be used in the same manner, and the counselor may find it less time consuming to reply to clients via e-mail. Of course, emergencies should always be handled in the quickest manner, and we should never abandon those procedures that we now have in place for clients.

Malpractice Insurance

NBCC has advised counselors to be aware of all legal issues in cybercounseling. If counselors are practicing across state lines, some kind of national legislation is needed to set a uniform cap on malpractice damage awards. Clients have been known to go "forum shopping" for the state in which to file claims, looking for which state will pay the largest damages (California Telehealth/Telemedicine Coordination Project, 1997).

CONCLUSION

Regulation is a complex issue. In telemedicine, some have advocated an international worldwide license. The hurdles are many, such as accommodating the variety of educational standards and legal codes, not to mention determining who would administer this license. The American Nursing Association is exploring a multistate license (Kincade, 1998). It seems that a start might be a national counselor certificate in cybercounseling, with states accepting that certificate and thus allowing their already licensed counselors to participate in cybercounseling, with the counselor subject to the jurisdiction of the state of license.

Cybercounseling in one form or another is upon us (Lee, 1998). To dismiss it is unrealistic. We cannot ignore it, for to do so is to allow it to progress unregulated and open to charlatans, with the result of diminishing the profession of counseling. To change the quagmire into a quest will require risk takers who are willing to be forward thinkers, to embrace technology as having the possibility to positively affect the profession, and thus to bring well-being to a greater number of people.

REFERENCES

Adams, L. N., & Grigsby, R. K. (1995). The Georgia State Telemedicine Program: Initiation, design, and plans. *Telemedicine Journal, 1*(3), 227–235.

Ainsworth, M. (1996–99a). *ABCs of Internet therapy: Is there legal support if something goes wrong?* [On-line]. Available: http://www.metanoia.org/imhs/legal.htm.

Ainsworth, M. (1996–99b). *ABCs of Internet therapy: Talk to a therapist on-line* (Consumer guide) [On-line]. Available: http://www.metanoia.org/imhs.

American Psychological Association Ethics Committee. (1997). *Services by telephone, teleconferencing, and Internet* (Statement) [On-line]. Available: http://www.apa.org/ethics/stmnt01.html.

American Telemedicine Association. (1999). *News and events* [On-line]. Available: http://www.atmeda.org/news/060199a.html.

Butt, A. Y., Roman, J. K., Zimmerman, A. S., Ziob Ro, S. M. (1996). *Telemedicine networks and physician licensure* (Paper) [On-line]. Available: http://www.spp.umich.edu/courses/744/writing/paper/telemedicine.html.

California Telehealth/Telemedicine Coordination Project. (1997). *Taking distance out of caring* [On-line]. Available: http://catelehealth.org/cont.html.

Callahan, E. J., Hilty, D. M., & Nesbitt, T. S. (1998). Patient satisfaction with telemedicine consultation in primary care: Comparison of ratings of medical and mental health applications. *Telemedicine Journal, 4*(4), 363–369.

Childress, C. (1998). *Potential risks and benefits of on-line psychotherapeutic interventions* (White paper) [On-line]. Available: http://www.ismho.org/issues/9801.htm.

Council on Competitiveness. (1996a). Transforming U.S. health in the information age. In *Highway to Health* (Executive summary) [On-line]. Available: http://nii.nist.gov/pubs/coc_hghwy_to_hlth/exec_summ.html.

Council on Competitiveness. (1996b). Transforming U.S. health in the information age. In *Highway to Health* (chap. 2) [On-line]. Available: http://nii.nist.gov/pubs/coc_highway_to_hlth/chp2.html.

Dubovsky, S. L. (1997). Balancing the risks and benefits of clinical consultations on the internet. *PsychNews International, 3*(1) [On-line]. Available: http://mentalhelp.net/pni/pni31b.htm.

Goldman, A. (n.d.). *Your confidential sexual issues report* (Advertisement) [On-line]. Available: http://www.on-linepsych.com/vendors/200/csia.htm.

Grohol, J. M. (1998). *The state of mental health on-line* [On-line]. Available: http://www.behavior.net/column/soapbox/sb980412.html.

Health Care Financing Administration. (1998). States where Medicaid reimbursement of services utilizing telemedicine is available (Report). *Federal*

Register, 63(119), 33882–33890 [On-line]. Available: http://www.hcfa.gov/medicaid/telelist.htm.

Health On the Net Foundation. (n.d.). *Code of conduct for medical and health web sites. HONcode principles* [On-line]. Available: http://www.courses.has.vcu.edu/students/cbryce/651/honcode.htm.

Hilty, D. M., Servis, M. E., Nestbitt, T. S., Hales, R. E. (in press). The use of telemedicine to provide consultation-liaison services to the primary care setting. *Psychiatric Annals.*

Holmes, L. (1997). *Suicide on the Internet* [On-line]. Available: http://www.mentalhealth.about.com/library/weekly/aa101397.htm?pid=2791& cob=home.

International Society for Mental Health on-line. (1999). *Mission statement* [On-line]. Available: http://www.ismho.org/mission.htm.

Kincade, K. (1998) Nurses take leadership role in developing telepractice guidelines. *Telehealth Magazine, 4*(1), 11 [On-line]. Available: http://www.telemedmag.com/topics/licen3.htm.

Lee, C. (1998). Counseling and the challenges of cyberspace. *Counseling Today* [On-line]. Available: http://www.counseling.org/cton-line/sr598/lee498.htm.

Lee, R., Grigsby, K., Dennison, L., Vought, R. (1999, June 10). *Georgia Mental Health Network: A web-based supplement to telepsychiatry services with Georgia.* Poster presentation.

Martin, R. (1997). *The influence of technology on the helping profession.* Atlanta: Georgia State University. (ERIC Document Reproduction Service No. ED 412 461)

Metanoia & Mental Health Net. (1997–99). Credential check (Service) [On-line]. Available: http://mentalhelp.net/check.

National Rural Health Association. (n.d.). *Universal service: Alive but not kicking* (Report) [On-line]. Available: http://www.nrharural.org/dc/a10.html.

National Board for Certified Counselors. (1998). *Standards for the ethical practice of web counseling* [On-line]. Available: http://www.nbcc.org/ethics/wcstandards.htm.

Orbuch, P. M. (1997). A Western states' effort to address telemedicine policy barriers. *North Dakota Law Review, 73*(1) [On-line]. Available: http://wga-internet.westgov.org/wga/publicat/NDLRART.HTM.

Polauf, J. (1998). *Psychotherapy on the Internet: Theory and technique* [On-line]. Available: http://www.nyreferrals.com/psychotherapy/index.htm.

Reid, J. (1996). *A telemedicine primer.* Billings, MT: Innovative Medical Communication.

Rice, V. (1997). *Cyberpsychology: Therapy for the 1990s* [On-line]. Available: http://www.zdnet.com/zdtv/thesite/0597w5/life/life179_052997.html.

Sampson, J. P. (1998). The Internet as a potential force for social change. In C. C. Lee, & G. R. Walz (Eds.), *Social Action* (pp. 213–225). Alexandria, VA: American Counseling Association.

Sampson, J. P., Kolodinsky, R. W., & Greeno, B. P. (1997). Counseling on the information highway: Future possibilities and potential problems. *Journal of Counseling and Development, 75,* 203–212.

Stricker, G. (1996). Psychotherapy in cyberspace. *Ethics and Behavior, 6*(2), 169–177.

U.S. Department of Health and Human Services. (1998). Health Care Financing Administration, 42 CFR Pts. 410, 414 (Report). *Federal Register, 63*(119), 33882–33890 [On-line]. Available: http://www.access.gpo.gov/su_docs/aces/aces140.html.

Whelan, L. J., & Wood, M. B. (1996). Unresolved issues snarl licensure laws. *Telehealth Magazine, 2*(8), 33 [On-line]. Available: http://www.telemedmag.com/topics/licen5.htm.

White, R. (1998, September). *LPCS and Internet counseling—Ethical considerations* [On-line]. Available: http://www.tmhca.org/ethics.htm.

World Health Organization. (1997, December 23). *Telehealth and telemedicine will henceforth be part of the strategy of health for all* (Press release). Geneva, Switzerland: Stroote, Philippe [On-line]. Available: http://www.who.int/archives/inf-pr-1997/en/pr97-98.html.

23

Cybercounselors v. Cyberpolice

JEFFREY S. LOVE

Do cybercounselors practicing interstate risk arrest, prosecution, and conviction in their clients' home states for counseling without a local license? That is the primary legal issue facing cybercounselors who practice nationwide.

One example of a state that warns all providers of Internet services to state residents that they must comply with all state laws is Minnesota. Minnesota is also an example of a state that has prosecuted on-line providers of some goods and services, such as gambling bookies, for violating state law. The Minnesota attorney general's web site states

WARNING TO ALL INTERNET USERS AND PROVIDERS

THIS MEMORANDUM SETS FORTH THE ENFORCEMENT POSITION OF THE MINNESOTA ATTORNEY GENERAL'S OFFICE WITH RESPECT TO CERTAIN ILLEGAL ACTIVITIES ON THE INTERNET.

PERSONS OUTSIDE OF MINNESOTA WHO TRANSMIT INFORMATION VIA THE INTERNET KNOWING THAT INFORMATION WILL BE DISSEMINATED IN MINNESOTA ARE SUBJECT TO JURISDICTION IN MINNESOTA COURTS FOR VIOLATIONS OF STATE CRIMINAL AND CIVIL LAWS.

The following discussion sets out the legal basis for this conclusion. Minnesota's general criminal jurisdiction statute provides as follows:

A person may be convicted and sentenced under the law of this state if the person: (1) Commits an offense in whole or in part within this state; or (2) Being without the state, causes, aids, or abets another to commit a crime within the state; or (3) Being without the state, intentionally causes a result within the state prohibited by the criminal laws of this state. It is not a defense that the defendant's conduct is also a criminal offense under the laws of another state or of the United States or of another country. Minnesota Statute Section 609.025 (1994).

This statute has been interpreted by the Minnesota Supreme Court. In State v. Rossbach, 288 N.W.2d 714 (Minn. 1980), the defendant appealed his conviction for aggravated assault. The defendant, standing inside the border of an Indian reservation, had fired a rifle across the boundary line at a person outside the border. The defendant claimed that Minnesota courts did not have jurisdiction because his act took place off of Minnesota lands. Applying Minnesota Statute Section 609.025 and the common law, the Minnesota Supreme Court affirmed the conviction, holding that the intentional impact within Minnesota land created jurisdiction. Id. at 715-16.[1]

The web site includes press releases on enforcement actions against Internet crimes, such as the following:

LANDMARK MINNESOTA DECISION DECLARES THAT STATES CAN ADDRESS LAWBREAKING ON INTERNET
Humphrey's Case Against Cyber-Bookie First To Establish State Jurisdiction Over 'Net

Attorney General Hubert Humphrey III today lauded a state trial court's landmark decision finding that his office has jurisdiction to enforce Minnesota's false advertising and consumer fraud laws against a Las Vegas company offering gambling services over the Internet.

"In the eyes of the law, it's the behavior that matters, not the medium," Humphrey said. "Whether a company solicits using the telephones, the mails, television, or the Internet, the rules against fraud and illegal conduct are the same. There is no 'Internet exception' in our consumer protection laws."

Humphrey filed a consumer fraud and false advertising suit in July 1995 against Granite Gate Resorts and its president, Kerry Rogers, in Ramsey District Court. The lawsuit alleges that the defendants operate a web site on the Internet which advertises illegal sports betting and information services. The lawsuit charges that by falsely claiming that these services are legal, the defendant's advertisements violate Minnesota's consumer protection laws. The defendants asked the court to dismiss the state's lawsuit, claiming that they are not subject to Minnesota's laws because they are based in Las Vegas.

In finding the state can enforce its laws against the defendants, Ramsey County District Judge John S. Connolly relied on evidence showing that defendants actively targeted Minnesota residents. For example, the court found that during a 2-week period in February and March of 1996, at least 248 Minnesota computer users viewed the defendants' gambling web site. The court also noted that two Minnesotans were on a list kept by the defendants of the top 500 computer users accessing the defendants' web sites.[1]

Minnesota is not alone in its desire to regulate the on-line provision of goods and services, including health care services. State and federal officials are tightening laws against telemedicine practitioners[2] and on-line pharmacists.[3] State psychology and counseling boards are considering proposals expressly to restrict on-line counseling. It is only a matter of time before some state enforces its licensing laws against out-of-state cybercounselors. Because it is unrealistic to expect cybercounselors to become licensed in every state, such enforcement of local licensing laws could destroy interstate cybercounseling as a viable profession for experienced and responsible counselors. Even now, uncertainty regarding the legality of interstate cybercounseling has undoubtedly deterred many conscientious and qualified counselors from starting an on-line practice. What defenses could a cybercounselor raise to a charge of practicing without a local license in a client's home state? This chapter discusses three potential defenses for cybercounselors and then presents recommendations for interstate practice. The defenses are that

1. the counselor and client agreed that the services were not subject to the licensing laws of the client's state;
2. the client's state has no right to arrest and extradite a counselor who was physically present in another state at the time the services were being provided; and
3. the counselor has a constitutional right to practice cybercounseling without a license under the free speech clause of the First Amendment of the U.S. Constitution and free speech provisions of some state constitutions.

Most potential legal defenses to a charge of unlicensed practice are premised on the contention that state and federal legislators and state licensing boards have failed to enact laws clearly and unequivocally prohibiting all forms of cybercounseling. If such laws were enacted, those defenses would disappear. The only defense discussed in this chapter that could survive a concerted attempt by lawmakers to outlaw cybercounseling is the freedom of speech defense based on the First Amendment of the U.S. Constitution and similar provisions of some state constitutions. That constitutional defense is unique. It raises issues of personal freedom and individual rights that go beyond the question of whether cybercounseling is an effective and safe form of therapy. It contends that, even if cybercounseling is demonstrably less safe and less effective than in-person counseling and other psychotherapies (such as drugs and electric shock therapy), it is nevertheless a type of activity that the public has a right to choose.

The dangers associated with speech and the communication of ideas are ones that our country chose to embrace in the Bill of Rights, the Fourteenth Amendment, and many state constitutions. This choice was made in part to avoid potentially greater dangers associated with empowering government officials to regulate freely what people may say and hear, and the means through which they may communicate it. Efficacy, cost, and safety may be the sole relevant grounds for deciding whether to legalize or outlaw particular psychotherapeutic drugs. But should they also be the sole grounds for deciding whether to outlaw particular forms of talking therapies?

Consider the issue at its logical extreme. If some studies found that psychotherapeutic drugs were safer, less costly, and more effective than all talking therapies, should those be the sole grounds for deciding whether to outlaw all talking therapies in favor of psychotherapeutic drugs? Or would issues of individual rights and freedom of speech then be appropriate considerations? Would any rights of preeminent importance be lost—beyond the loss common to the prohibition of any potentially therapeutic activity or drug—if the public were prohibited from obtaining private, professional counseling altogether?

Counselors are in the best position to determine whether talking therapies in general, and cybercounseling in particular, promote any values that the First Amendment was intended to protect, such as freedom of thought and intellectual growth. If so, then issues of individual rights and freedoms should be considered by counselors, counseling boards, and legislators in determining whether to outlaw cybercounseling, or how closely to regulate it. Although these issues are discussed in this chapter only in the context of a potential legal defense to a charge against a cybercounselor of violating a state's practice act, they are relevant to the broader issue of whether and how cybercounseling should be regulated.

FIRST POTENTIAL DEFENSE: THE CLIENT AGREED THAT LOCAL LAWS DID NOT APPLY

Counselors' agreements with clients often include limitations on or disclaimers of legal obligations. Cybercounselors' web sites often address topics such as the following (the examples are provided for illustration only, and are not intended as recommendations):

- **choice of law:** For example, "Oregon law applies to any disputes or claims arising out of this counseling service."
- **choice of venue:** For example, "Any lawsuit arising out of these services may be filed and tried only in the State of Oregon."
- **arbitration:** For example, "Either party may compel arbitration of any claims or disputes arising out of these counseling services under the following terms and conditions: . . . . "

- **location of services:** For example, "Users agree that these counseling services shall be considered for all legal purposes to be provided in the State of Oregon only."
- **limitations on the nature and scope of the services:** For example, "Important differences between cybercounseling and face-to-face psychotherapy limit the responsibilities assumed by counselors on this web site. Although psychotherapy includes elements of both treatment and educational processes, cybercounseling is almost exclusively an educational process. During psychotherapy, counselors are responsible for the treatment of the patient and exercise substantial control over the therapeutic process. This is only possible in the face-to-face environment of traditional psychotherapy. During cybercounseling, users are responsible for their own treatment. Users control completely the information received by the counselors, and the interventions applied (if any). Cybercounselors provide information based on the users' statements but cannot provide users with significant emotional support. For these reasons, cybercounseling is not a substitute for traditional psychotherapy. It is self-help in which users completely control the treatment."[4]
- **limitations on damages:** For example, "Users agree that in any lawsuit arising out of these services, consequential damages, emotional distress damages, and punitive damages shall not be recoverable. Damages awarded shall not exceed the fees paid for these services."
- **limitations on side agreements and oral modifications:** For example, "Users agree that the terms stated on this web site comprise the entire agreement governing these services. No other agreement or representation governs these services. Modifications of these terms are not effective unless agreed to in writing."
- **indemnity:** For example, "Users agree to indemnify and hold harmless the counselors providing these services from any and all liability, costs, attorney fees, and other legal expenses arising out of these services, to the maximum extent allowed by law."

Courts enforce client agreements to waive or limit legal rights, unless courts find that it would undermine an overriding public policy. For example, courts often enforce agreements to arbitrate disputes, or to apply a certain state's law or use a certain state's courts (so long as that state has some connection to the dispute). But courts sometimes refuse to enforce disclaimers purporting to strip consumers of a convenient remedy in their home states for consumer fraud on the ground that overriding public policies against fraud or malpractice are at stake. In short, in suits brought by clients, sometimes disclaimers help and sometimes they don't.

Although clients can waive their own legal rights, they cannot waive the rights of state officials (such as district attorneys and state licensing boards) to file civil or criminal actions against cybercounselors for practicing without a license. Disclaimers bind only the contracting parties. State officials are not parties to any agreements between cybercounselors and their clients. Thus even if clients are bound by their agreements on arbitration, choice of venue, choice of law, and limitations on damages, state prosecutors and counseling boards are not.

Client agreements on the scope of legal services can, however, be used as evidence that the cybercounselor's services are outside the definitions of *counseling* or *psychology* in state licensing laws. Cybercounselors might defend a charge of unlicensed practice by arguing that state law requires a license only for mental health "treatment," and the cybercounseling agreement states that only "education" (or spiritual advice or personal consulting) and "not treatment" is being provided. That defense has been raised by some unlicensed therapists in response to charges of unlicensed practice. It is comparable to an argument by on-line psychics that their services are not fraudulent because their web sites state that the services are "for entertainment purposes only." The issue of whether all counseling is necessarily "therapy" is fairly debatable.[5]

Agreements with clients can also support an argument that licensing laws of the client's state do not govern counselors in other states. Many state licensing laws do not specifically address counseling provided by counselors in another state, whether by telephone, mail, or computer. State legislatures did not have those practices in mind when they enacted the licensing laws, and so the laws do not expressly address them. This often creates ambiguities or vagueness in the laws that cybercounselors can use to argue that a license in their client's home state is not necessary. For example, the Mississippi attorney general has issued an official opinion that out-of-state physicians treating patients in Mississippi on-line are not subject to Mississippi's licensing requirement. The Mississippi State Board of Medical Licensure disagrees, but the attorney general determined that the state definition of *practicing medicine* does not include an out-of-state physician practicing telemedicine across state lines.[6] In a comparable dispute involving out-of-state counseling, a disclaimer stating that the services shall be considered for all purposes to be provided only in the counselor's home state, and shall be governed by the law of that state only, could help persuade a judge that the law of the client's state does not apply.

Client agreements can also help avoid or defend against a charge that the cybercounselor's web site includes false, misleading, or deceptive statements. Note that the Minnesota attorney general's press release quoted earlier identifies the charge against the on-line bookie as false advertising ("The lawsuit charges that by falsely claiming that these services are legal, the defendant's advertisements violate Minnesota's consumer protection laws"). Such a charge could be avoided by a disclaimer stating that the legality of on-line services is unclear, and that some states may contend that a license in their state is necessary.

Disclaimers are more likely to be enforced by courts if they are conspicuous, comprehensible, accurate, and reasonable. Often they are not. Legal disclaimers on cybercounselors' web sites vary widely in content, length, placement, comprehensibility, and style. Some are simply unintelligible, and read as if they were largely copied from contracts on other matters. Because cybercounseling is a novel practice, there are no "form disclaimers" that have been tested over the years in the courts. Disclaimers should be tailor-made and should specifically address the practitioner's views on the nature and scope of the services being provided and the manner in which any disputes should be resolved. The best disclaimers are simply written, are conspicuous, and contain helpful information about the services being provided. The counselors probably spent many hours helping to draft them. Significant work by the counselors on the content of legal disclaimers helps ensure that they are clear, accurate, and reasonable.

SECOND POTENTIAL DEFENSE: STATES
HAVE NO RIGHT TO EXTRADITE COUNSELORS

What gives officials in one state the right to arrest and extradite cybercounselors in another state for services performed by the counselor entirely in that other state? Extradition arguably should not be available, especially because the charge of violating state licensing laws is often merely a technical violation and not a felony or other serious crime.

Extradition is addressed by the United States Constitution at Article IV, Section 2, clause 2, which provides

> A Person charged in any State with Treason, Felony, or other Crime, who shall flee from Justice, and be found in another State, shall on demand of the executive Authority of the State from which he [or she] fled, be delivered up, to be removed to the State having Jurisdiction of the Crime.

This is supplemented by a federal extradition law, 18 U.S.C. 3182, which provides, in part,

> Whenever the executive authority of any State or Territory demands any person as a fugitive from justice, of the executive authority of any State . . . to which such person has fled, and produces a copy of any indictment found or an affidavit made before a magistrate of any State . . . charging the person demanded with having committed treason, felony, or other crime, . . . the executive authority of the State . . . to which such person has fled shall cause him [or her] to be arrested and secured . . . to be delivered to such agent [of the demanding State] when he [or she] shall appear. . . .

The words *felony, or other crime* in those laws arguably require that the charge be for violating a serious criminal law. Because misdemeanors and licensing law violations are not specifically mentioned, arguably cybercounselors cannot be extradited for violating such laws. However, the U.S. Supreme Court has rejected the argument that the crime must be serious, and has held that a person may be extradited on charges of violating any state law, including a misdemeanor.[7]

The words *fugitive* and *flee from justice* arguably require that the person have been in the charging state at the time the crime was allegedly committed. That argument has been accepted by the U.S. Supreme Court. A person not within a state at the time the crime was allegedly committed cannot be deemed a fugitive for purposes of those laws, and so cybercounselors cannot be extradited under those federal laws.[8]

The states have enacted their own uniform extradition laws, however. The Uniform Criminal Extradition Act expressly provides for the extradition of any person charged

> with committing an act in this state, or in a third state, intentionally resulting in a crime in the state whose executive authority is making the demand; . . . notwithstanding that the accused was not in that state at the time of the commission of the crime and has not fled therefrom. (ORS 133.767)

The language is quoted from an Oregon statute, but most other states' laws are similar. The word *intentionally* may seem to offer a defense to cybercounselors who subjectively "intended" to practice under only their home state's laws, and who may be unaware of the laws of their clients' states. But in general, ignorance of the law is no excuse. Only the "result" need be intended, not the legal violation. So long as cybercounselors intend to offer services to people residing in other states, the "intent" requirement is probably satisfied.

The intent requirement is arguably not satisfied by a cybercounselor who intends to counsel only clients in the counselor's home state. This intention can be proved by a statement to that effect on the counselor's web site, and a requirement that each client disclose the client's home state. Under such circumstances, ignorance of the fact that the client truly lives in another state may be a defense. If the counselor unintentionally counseled someone from another state due to the client's misrepresentation of his or her residence, the counselor could argue that the intent required for extradition is lacking.

In general, however, cybercounselors can be arrested and extradited for trial in their clients' home states under the Uniform Criminal Extradition Act on charges of counseling clients without a license. The primary barrier to arrest and extradition is a practical one. It is costly for states to extradite people from one state to another, costly to try them, and costly to enforce any criminal penalties. Administrative approval for those expenses must be obtained. It is unlikely that states will approve such expenses unless the state has made the issue a law enforcement priority, or the counseling is connected to some more serious crime (such as a murder or suicide committed by a client who had forewarned the counselor).

State officials may also bring a civil action against out-of-state cybercounselors for practicing without a license without extraditing the counselor, usually by merely hiring someone to personally hand the counselor a copy of a summons and complaint. In a civil action, the state is limited to seeking a money judgment for past violations and a court order prohibiting future violations. The state cannot seek a criminal conviction or jail sentence. But because civil proceedings are less expensive than criminal proceedings, the risk that state officials will file civil charges against out-of-state cybercounselors is greater.

A state court's power to enter judgment, civil or criminal, against a resident of another state is limited by the due process clause of the Fourteenth Amendment to the U.S. Constitution, which provides in relevant part, "No State shall . . . deprive any person of life, liberty, or property, without due process of law. . . ." If a nonresident counselor is sued in a state with which the counselor has no contacts whatsoever, the court should dismiss the lawsuit for lack of personal jurisdiction. The counselor must raise this defense promptly or it will be waived. For the state court to deny a counselor's timely motion to dismiss for lack of personal jurisdiction, the person prosecuting the lawsuit (whether that person is a state official or a private plaintiff) must at a minimum prove that the suit does not violate the counselor's constitutional right to due process.

[D]ue process requires that in order to subject a defendant to a judgment . . . , if he [or she] be not present within the territory of the forum, he [or she] have certain minimum contacts with it such that the maintenance of the suit does not offend "traditional notions of fair play and substantial justice." (*International Shoe v. Washington*, 326 US 310 [1945])

The court must find that the counselor's conduct and connection with the state is such that the counselor should reasonably anticipate having to defend a lawsuit there. (See *World-Wide Volkswagen Corp. v. Woodson*, 444 US 286, 297 [1980]). The Supreme Court has held that wire communications alone may suffice to establish this, so long as the communications are purposefully directed toward residents of the state and other factors make the assertion of jurisdiction fair:

> Although territorial presence frequently will enhance a potential defendant's affiliation with a state and reinforce the reasonable foreseeability of suit there, it is an inescapable fact of modern commercial life that a substantial amount of business is transacted solely by mail and wire communications across state lines, thus obviating the need for physical presence within a state in which business is conducted. So long as a commercial actor's efforts are "purposefully directed" toward residents of another state, we have consistently rejected the notion that an absence of physical contacts can defeat personal jurisdiction there. . . . Once it has been decided that a defendant purposefully established minimum contacts within the forum state, these contacts may be considered in light of other factors to determine whether the assertion of personal jurisdiction would comport with "fair play and substantial justice." (*Burger King Corp. v. Ruzdewicz*, 471 US 462, 476 [1985])

The U.S. Supreme Court has yet to decide whether on-line counselors or other service providers may fairly be sued in their clients' home states based solely on their provision of on-line services. Most lower courts that have considered the issue of jurisdiction based on web sites have held that a merely passive web site alone does not subject its owner to out-of-state lawsuits,[9] but an interactive web site directed at out-of-state residents for the purpose of doing on-line business with them does make it fair for courts in the customers' home states to proceed with lawsuits against the web site's owner related to that on-line business.[10]

Courts probably will hold that cybercounselors who direct their web sites at out-of-state residents for the purpose of providing ongoing on-line counseling for a fee should fairly anticipate being sued in their clients' home states over disputes arising out of those services. State officials probably can prosecute civil or criminal lawsuits against nonresident cybercounselors based solely on their on-line counseling activities without violating the counselors' constitutional right to due process of law.

THIRD POTENTIAL DEFENSE: CYBERCOUNSELING IS PROTECTED BY THE FIRST AMENDMENT

At least one state has declared that counselors have the "right" to practice their skills freely and the public has the "right" to choose any counselor. The state of Washington's counselor registration law provides that

> . . .The legislature recognizes the right of all counselors to practice their skills freely, consistent with the requirements of the public health and safety, as well as the right of individuals to choose which counselors best suit their needs and purposes. . . . (RCW 18.19.010).

Washington's law protects these rights by allowing counselors of any "therapeutic orientation, discipline, theory, or technique" to register with the state and practice professionally so long as they follow reasonable ethical constraints and disclose to their clients their qualifications, training, and orientation. (See RCW sections 18.19.020, 18.19.060, and 18.19.090.) Colorado has a similar registration law for unlicensed psychotherapists: C.R.S. Title 12 (Professions and Occupations), Article 43 (Mental Health), section 12-43-702.5 (see also sections 12-43-214 and 12-43-222 to 224).

What is the source of these rights? Comparable rights are not mentioned in Washington's laws for other professions, such as law, medicine, and accounting. What makes counseling different?

Counseling is different from most professions in part because it consists entirely—or almost entirely—of pure speech. Counselors communicate with individuals about their personal problems and aspirations for the purpose of helping them. This suggests one possible source of a right to engage in professional counseling. As stated by one philosophical counselor and psychoanalyst,

While wanting to be mindful of the potential for harming the vulnerable, I wish to champion the legitimacy of applied philosophy and of philosophical counseling, down to and including much that might be popularly understood as "psychotherapy." This is partly because I genuinely believe that the extensive study of philosophy is very practical in many ways. . . . Partly, it is because I believe very strongly in freedom. This is about freedom of speech. The sort of "psychotherapy" I am interested in is a matter of talking. No one should need a license to talk.[11]

The First Amendment to the U.S. Constitution provides in relevant part that "Congress shall make no law . . . abridging the freedom of speech . . . ." By its terms the First Amendment applies only to Congress. However, in the 1920s the U.S. Supreme Court held that freedom of speech is a fundamental liberty protected against state abridgment by the due process clause of the Fourteenth Amendment. Even broader free speech provisions are found in some state constitutions. Arguably, state licensing laws that unreasonably prevent residents from obtaining on-line counseling from nonresident cybercounselors violate the free speech rights of the residents and cybercounselors.

Although state licensing laws punish only counselors and not clients for unlicensed practice, as a practical matter the laws still greatly restrict clients' ability to speak with the counselors of their choice. States justify licensing laws by the need to protect clients from unqualified practitioners, but they apply the laws to the counseling of all clients regardless of whether the clients need or want such protection. Thus the issue is not just whether cybercounselors have a right to practice. The issue is also whether clients have a right freely to choose their counselor. See *Monteiro v. The Tempe Union High School District*, 158 F2d 1022, 1027 and n 5 (9th Cir 1998) ("the right to receive ideas is a necessary predicate to the recipient's meaningful exercise of his [or her] own rights of speech, press, and political freedom"); *Stanley v. Georgia*, 394 U.S. 557, 564 (1969) (it is "now well established that the Constitution protects the right to receive information and ideas"); *Procunier v. Martinez*, 416 U.S. 396, 408-409 (1974) ("Whatever the status of a prisoner's claim to uncensored correspondence with an outsider, it is plain that the latter's interest is grounded in the First Amendment's guarantee of freedom of speech. . . . [T]he addressee as well as the sender of direct personal correspondence derives from the First and Fourteenth Amendments a protection against unjustified governmental interference with the intended communication").

The concern of state officials over possible adverse reactions of clients to the unlicensed advice of cybercounselors is not by itself a reason for courts to deny all First Amendment protection to cybercounseling. The U.S. Supreme Court has repeatedly held that state "regulations that focus on the direct impact of speech on its audience" are subject to strict scrutiny under the First Amendment— *Boos v. Barry*, 485 U. S. 312, 321 (1988). See also *Forsyth County v. Nationalist Movement*, 505 U. S. 123, 134 (1992) ("Listeners' reaction to speech is not a content-neutral basis for regulation"), and *Reno v. ACLU*, 521 US 844, 868 (1997) ("the purpose of the CDA is to protect children from the primary effects of 'indecent' and 'patently offensive' speech [on the Internet], rather than any 'secondary' effect of such speech. Thus the CDA is a content-based blanket restriction on speech and, as such, cannot be 'properly analyzed as a form of time, place, and manner regulation'").

The fact that cybercounseling is provided over the Internet does not mean that states are free to regulate it. The Supreme Court recently held that on-line speech is as fully protected under the First Amendment as off-line speech—*Reno v. ACLU*, 521 US 844 (1997).

The fact that cybercounselors usually charge a fee for their services does not mean that states are free to restrict it. "It should be remembered that the pamphlets of Thomas Paine were not distributed free of charge. . . . Freedom of speech, freedom of the press, freedom of religion are available to all, not merely to those who can pay their own way"—*Murdock v. Pennsylvania*, 319 U.S. 105, 111 (1943); see also *Spiritual Psychic Science Church v. Azusa*, 39 Cal.3d 501, 508, 217 Cal. Rptr. 225, 228-29 (1985). The United States Supreme Court has repeatedly held that speech does not lose protection under the First Amendment merely because a fee is charged.[12] The practices of professional musicians, authors, stage and movie theater owners, public speakers, and private tutors are all protected by the right to freedom of speech, even though they charge fees. State courts in Oregon and California have held that professional fortune telling and palm reading are protected by the free speech clauses in the Oregon and California state constitutions. Their rationale is straightforward: laws prohibiting those professions are unconstitutional because the professions consist entirely—or largely—of speech for the purpose of communicating ideas (as opposed to speech that is merely an incidental tool for accomplishing some activity, such as the purchase of a business, making of a will, or surgery).[13]

A federal trial court in San Francisco recently rejected the argument that psychoanalysis is protected speech under the First Amendment. California's Psychology Licensing Law requires a license to practice psychoanalysis (or counseling), but does not offer a license in psychoanalysis (or counseling, except for marriage and family therapy). A national association of psychoanalysts and several individual analysts filed suit alleging that California's Psychology Licensing Law is an unconstitutional restriction on their and their prospective clients' rights to freedom of speech. The court held that the therapeutic purpose of psychoanalytic discussions strips them of all First Amendment protection:

> Psychoanalysis may very well rely heavily on speech . . . [but] the key component of psychoanalysis is the treatment of emotional suffering and depression, not speech. . . . That psychoanalysts employ speech to treat their clients does not entitle them, or their profession, to special First Amendment protection.[14]

The court's opinion does not explain why a therapeutic purpose should strip speech of First Amendment protection. The U.S. Supreme Court has held that the First Amendment protects even speech and expression intended or known to cause emotional suffering, such as marches by neo-Nazis through Jewish neighborhoods, hateful public speeches and literature, flag burning protests, antiabortion protests, antiabortion "street-counseling" of patients approaching abortion clinics, vulgar parodies and caricatures of public figures in magazines and other media, publication of embarrassing and defamatory facts, personal insults and obscenities, and harsh and mean spirited criticisms. Why would, or should, courts deny protection to speech intended to relieve emotional suffering? The reason is hardly obvious.

The psychoanalysts have appealed the trial court's decision to the Ninth Circuit Court of Appeals. If the Ninth Circuit determines that psychotherapy is protected by the First Amendment, that decision will provide cybercounselors with a powerful defense to any charge of practicing without a license brought by states within the Ninth Circuit (California, Oregon, Washington, Alaska, Hawaii, Arizona, Nevada, Idaho, and Montana). It will also be a helpful precedent in defending against such charges brought by other states. Ultimately, whether cybercounselors have a constitutional right to practice in states where they are not licensed is an issue that can be finally resolved only by the U.S. Supreme Court, and the supreme courts of those states (such as Oregon and California) whose constitutions provide even broader free speech rights than the U.S. Constitution.

If cybercounselors have a First Amendment defense to prosecution under state licensing laws, the First Amendment still may not be a successful defense to prosecution under less burdensome laws. First Amendment rights are not absolutes. For example, the First Amendment clearly protects the rights of counselors and other professionals to advertise their qualifications and lawful services truthfully. Courts have declared laws unconstitutional that purport to restrict therapists from truthfully advertising their services as psychotherapy and psychological counseling and using the title psychotherapist and (for master's-level psychologists) the title psychologist.[15] But those same laws do not violate the First Amendment when applied to therapists who falsely claim that they are licensed psychologists or licensed counselors.

If states can prove that restrictions on free speech rights are no more burdensome than is reasonably necessary to protect a significant or compelling government interest, the restrictions are not unconstitutional. See *Madsen v. Women's Health Center*, 512 US 753, 761-65, 781 (1994) (e.g., "the First Amendment protects the speaker's right to offer 'sidewalk [antiabortion] counseling' to all passersby. That protection, however, does not encompass attempts to abuse an unreceptive or captive audience"—Opinion of Justice Stevens, concurring in part and dissenting in part). The problem with licensing laws is that states are unlikely to be able to demonstrate their necessity,[16] especially as applied to cybercounselors who are highly educated, experienced, nationally certified, and licensed in another state.

In contrast, states should be able to prove the reasonableness and necessity of counselor registration and disclosure laws,[17] such as those in Washington and Colorado (discussed earlier), even as applied to cybercounselors. Such laws offer a level of protection to the public that Washington and Colorado[18] have found adequate, without imposing the much more burdensome requirements for obtaining a state license. Although cybercounselors cannot reasonably be expected to obtain a license in every state and country in which they do business (at least, not until reciprocity provisions become more prevalent), they can reasonably be expected to comply with registration and disclosure laws in each state and country in which they do business. Corporations are expected to register in each state and country in which they do a substantial amount of ongoing business, and readily comply with those laws. State registration requirements for cybercounselors are comparable.

In sum, the First Amendment may be a valid defense to a charge that cybercounselors are violating state licensing laws. It is not a defense to a charge that cybercounselors are engaged in false or misleading advertising. It is probably not a defense to a charge of providing counseling to residents of states with registration and disclosure laws, such as Colorado and Washington, if the cybercounselor fails to comply with those laws.

RECOMMENDATIONS

Cybercounselors practicing interstate should

- include thorough, reasonable, and accurate legal disclaimers and descriptions of services on their web sites;
- promptly consider the defenses discussed in this chapter (disclaimers, lack of personal jurisdiction, improper extradition, and the free speech protection of the First Amendment and state constitutions) if charged or threatened by officials in another state with violating that state's licensing laws;
- comply with counselor registration and disclosure laws in states such as Washington and Colorado; and
- encourage all states to enact counselor registration laws. Although not intended as cybercounseling laws, registration laws

are a simple and reasonable means of both protecting the public by regulating on-line counseling in a manner that counselors can be expected to follow, and assuring cybercounselors that their services are lawful if they do.

CONCLUSION

The future of cybercounseling will be greatly affected by state efforts to regulate it. Cybercounseling probably will be found by some courts to violate state licensing laws. The risk of prosecution under those laws is substantial, and undoubtedly has already stunted the growth of cybercounseling in the United States. The threat is real. States have the power to arrest and extradite out-of-state cybercounselors for providing counseling to residents without a license (although usually the incentive for states to do so will not justify the costs involved). States also generally have the power to serve cybercounselors with a summons and complaint on civil (rather than criminal) charges of practicing without a license, seeking monetary damages and injunctions (as opposed to a jail sentence). Civil charges are the more likely threat because they cost less than criminal charges for the state to prosecute.

Few if any state licensing laws expressly address on-line counseling, so arguments can be made that state laws currently do not prohibit it. These arguments may succeed in some states, and will be helped by carefully worded legal disclaimers and descriptions of services on cybercounselors' web sites.

Cybercounselors may be able to defend themselves from charges of practicing without a license by raising a free speech defense. Cybercounselors can argue that their discussions with clients are protected speech under the First Amendment to the U.S. Constitution and the free speech provisions of some state constitutions. Whether psychotherapy is constitutionally protected speech is only now being tested in the courts. It will be years before the issue is finally decided. Even if psychotherapy is constitutionally protected speech, state regulation of psychotherapy that is demonstrably reasonable and necessary will still be enforceable. Washington and Colorado provide a working model of demonstrably reasonable regulations of the professional practice of psychotherapy. Those states supplement their licensing laws for psychologists, social workers, and counselors with registration and disclosure laws for unlicensed psychotherapists. This provides substantial protection to the public, without unnecessarily burdening the rights of counselors to practice their profession and the rights of the public freely to choose their counselor.

Whether the First Amendment essentially requires states to follow the Washington and Colorado model is an issue of importance not just to professional psychotherapists but also to the public at large. This is not an issue for just counseling experts to decide. Although experts are in the best position to measure the risks of unlicensed cybercounseling, they are not in a superior position to weigh those risks against the opposing values of having the freedom to speak with the counselor of one's choice. Nor is this an issue just for legislatures. Although legislatures are well positioned to weigh the aggregate risks and benefits of state laws, they are not well positioned to weigh the impact of those laws on individual rights and freedoms. That is why individual freedoms are protected from state legislatures by the federal and state constitutions. Cybercounseling can be a highly personal, educational, spiritual, emotional, and expressive activity. Arguably, it strongly implicates individual rights and freedoms.

State legislatures and law enforcement officials have the power virtually to eliminate cybercounseling as a viable practice for responsible professionals. Counselors, the public, and the courts all have a strong interest in seeing that they use that power responsibly, with due regard for the individual rights and freedoms at stake.

NOTES

[1] www.ag.state.mn.us/home/consumer/consumernews/On-lineScams/memo.html.
[2] See *Findings and Recommendations of the Center for Telemedicine Law Licensure Task Force.* (1997, February 12). ("The difficulties telemedicine practitioners face in meeting differing state licensure requirements have been compounded by recent state actions. During the last two and a half years, at least 11 states have modified their state licensure requirements. In general these states have (1) narrowed the consultation exception; and (2) required all out-of-state physicians to possess a license in a state in order to provide diagnostic or therapeutic services directly on a regular and ongoing basis to patients located in the state.")

[3]See Stolberg, S. (1999, July 31). Officials struggle to regulate on-line sale of prescription drugs. *New York Times*, p. A28. ("The Food and Drug Administration announced steps today to curb the illegitimate sale of prescription drugs over the Internet, while officials at another agency, the Federal Trade Commission, asked Congress to require electronic pharmacies to post detailed on-line information about their licenses and the doctors who write the prescriptions they fill. . . . Now doctors are prescribing pills on line to patients they have never met, in states where they are not authorized to work. Pharmacies are shipping pills across state lines without the requisite licenses. Regulatory authorities have disciplined some doctors and pharmacies, but the work is slow and difficult because the ownership of web sites is so hard to track. . . . Mr. Hubbard, of the F.D.A., said his agency would immediately begin trying to identify each site and learn where it is registered, so the authorities in those states could be alerted.")

[4]A similar limitation on the scope of services was found at www.headworks.com, an on-line counseling web site highly rated by Mental Health Net (www.metanoia.org).

[5]See Russell, J. M. (1998, April). Philosopher as personal consultant. *The Philosopher's Web Magazine* [On-line]. Now archived, but available: this chapter's author's web page at http://members.aol.com/jmrussell/index.htm.

[6]Scott, J. S. (1996, December). *State responses to telemedicine licensing issues. HEALTHCARE FIN. MGMT.*, at 46.

[7]See Ex parte Reggel, 114 US 642 (1885); Appleyard v. Massachusetts, 203 US 222 (1906).

[8]See Hyatt v. People, 188 US 691 (1903); Munsey v. Clough, 196 US 364 (1905).

[9]See, e.g., Cybersell, Inc. v. Cybersell, Inc., 130 F3d 414 (9th Cir 1997); Bensusan v. King, 937 F Supp 295 (SDNY 1996); and McDonough v. Fallon McElligott, Inc., 1996 WL 753991 (SD Cal 1996).

[10]See, e.g., CompuServe v. Patterson, 83 F3d 1257 (6th Cir 1996); Minnesota v. Granite Gate Resorts, Inc., 568 NW2d 715, 719-720 (Minn. Ct. App. 1997), affirmed 576 NW2d 747 (Minn. 1998); and Zippo Manufacturing v. Zippo Dot Com, Inc., 952 F Supp 1119 (WD Pa 1997).

[11]Russell, J. M. (1998, October 24; 1999, May 7). *Philosophical counseling is not a distinct field.* Paper presented to the Southern California Philosophy Conference at UCI; revised and presented to the Group Meetings on Philosophical Counseling of the American Philosophical Association, Western Division, New Orleans [On-line]. Available at this chapter's author's web page at: http://members.aol.com/jmrussell/index.htm.

[12]See, e.g., Board of Trustees, S.U.N.Y. v. Fox, 492 US 469, 482 (1989); Virginia State Bd. of Pharmacy v. Virginia Citizens Consumer Council, Inc., 425 U.S. 748, 761 (1976); Time, Inc. v. Hill, 385 U.S. 374, 397 (1967); New York Times Co. v. Sullivan, 376 U.S. 254, 266 (1964); Burstyn v. Wilson, 343 U.S. 495, 502 (1952).

[13]See Spiritual Psychic Science Church v. Azusa, 39 Cal.3d 501, 217 Cal. Rptr. 225 (1985); Marks v. City of Roseburg, 65 Or App 102, 670 P2d 201 (1983), rev den 296 Or 536.

[14]See National Association for the Advancement of Psychoanalysis, et al. v. California Board of Psychology Members et al., USDC ND Calif. Civ. No. C-97-3913, Memorandum Decision and Order filed January 7, 1999, at page 14.

[15]See Abramson v. Gonzalez, 949 F2d 1567 (11th Cir 1992); Eckles v. Oregon State Bd. of Psychologist Examiners, USDC Oregon Civ. No. 92-945 (1994).

[16]See Hogan, D. B. (1979). *The regulation of psychotherapists* (Vol. 1, pp. 368–370). Cambridge MA: Ballinger. ("Psychotherapy does not meet the criteria for licensing through laws that restrict a person's right to practice. . . . If one looks at the available empirical evidence, current licensing laws . . . are difficult to defend. First of all, psychotherapy . . . does not appear to be gravely dangerous. . . . Assuming, however, that psychotherapy represents a significant public danger, the lack of consensus as to what causes the danger and how to measure it should prevent the enactment of laws restricting a person's right to practice. The existing empirical evidence suggests that licensing efforts to date have focused on the wrong variables. No evidence exists that possession of academic credentials protects the public. Instead, the findings indicate that personality factors may be the most influential in determining whether a therapist is competent to practice.") See also Grohol, J. M. (1998, March 1). *Why don't current psychotherapy licensing regulations work? A review and suggestions for change* [On-line]. Available: http://mentalhelp.net/archives/editor29.htm; and Schmitt, K. (1995, May). *An analysis of complaints Filed Against Mental Health Professionals in Colorado* (Report). Available from the Colorado Department of Regulatory Agencies, Mental Health Professions.

[17]See Hogan, D. B. (1979). *The regulation of psychotherapists* (Vol. 1, p. 371). Cambridge, MA: Ballinger. ("As a method of regulation, registration has much to recommend it. Entry into the field is not restricted, utilization of paraprofessionals is not inhibited, and the cost of services is not artificially increased. In fact, a system of registration produces few of the negative side effects created by traditional licensure. Registration recognizes that a consensus does not exist as to what standards and criteria are appropriate for measuring therapist effectiveness. Perhaps most important, rather than having the state make decisions for the consumer, registration laws allow the state to provide clients with relevant information and encourage the potential consumer of services to use careful judgment in selecting a professional.")

[18]See Schmitt, K. (1995, May). *An analysis of complaints filed against mental health professionals in Colorado* (Report, pp. 36–37). Available from the Colorado Department of Regulatory Agencies, Mental Health Professions. Among findings were that a smaller percentage of unlicensed psychotherapists—20%—than licensed psychologists—21%—had complaints filed against them, with a comparable percentage of nondismissed cases—5% and 4%—respectively.)

24

Understanding the Implications of Distance Learning for Accreditation and Licensure of Counselor Preparation Programs

CAROL L. BOBBY AND LUCIEN CAPONE III

Despite the recent flurry of activity and attention given to distance learning, the concept itself is not new. Traditional correspondence and home-study courses have been used worldwide for years. The United States military has been particularly active in making distance learning accessible to men and women in uniform for decades through the Defense Activity for Nontraditional Education Support, better known as DANTES (http://voled.doded.mil/dantes/dl/). The U.S. Navy has experimented with floating college degree programs, which include on-board instructors as well as courses beamed to ships in remote parts of the world by satellite. Nor is the idea of accreditation and licensure of distance learning a new concept. For example, the Distance Education and Training Council (DETC) (1998), formerly called the National Home Study Council, has been in operation since 1926. The primary change has been in the technology for delivery of distance education courses and programs. Television, computers, and the World Wide Web have made distance learning far more accessible to a broader market of potential consumers of postsecondary education. Additionally, the demographic profile of higher education students has changed dramatically in the last decade with a growing percentage of nontraditional students, that is, students coming back to college after spending time in the workforce rather than straight out of high school. Distance education is attractive to these students because of the increased flexibility it offers for scheduling study sessions around job obligations. A recent study prepared by the Institute for Higher Education Policy (Phipps, Wellman, & Merisotis, 1998) reports that an estimated 753,640 students enrolled in distance education courses in academic year 1994–95.

As institutions of higher education scramble to compete for these students, accreditation and licensure issues are becoming more conspicuous. The distance learning phenomenon is causing a major shift in the paradigms of how higher education is delivered to students, how students interact with faculty and with each other, how learning occurs and is measured, how faculty are assessed, and how education is funded. As a measure of quality in higher education, accreditation standards that have been built around the traditional classroom paradigm for delivery of higher education must shift radically to accommodate the use of new distance learning technologies. Furthermore, the movement from teacher-centered to learner-centered environments results in a need for the accreditation and licensure paradigms to be reevaluated in order to (1) remain relevant, (2) carry out their original functions of accountability, quality assurance, and consumer protection, and (3) not impede the development of distance learning programs.

This chapter first explores basic definitions of distance learning, accreditation and licensure, and outcomes assessment. It then addresses the question of how accreditation and licensure of educational programs will have to change to insure quality in both traditional and distance learning environments, discusses how the law may impact that change, and provides recommendations to insure that accreditation remains relevant.

WHAT IS DISTANCE LEARNING?

There are nearly as many definitions of distance learning as there are organizations that work with the concept. For example, the United States Distance Learning Association (1999) has defined distance learning as the "acquisition of knowledge and skills through mediated information and instruction, encompassing all technologies and other forms of learning at a distance."

According to Virginia Steiner (1995) of the Distance Learning Resource Network (DLRN), "Distance education is instructional delivery that does not constrain the student to be physically present in the same location as the instructor. Historically, distance education meant correspondence study. Today, audio, video, and computer technologies are more common delivery modes."

Perhaps the most comprehensive definition is the one given by the University of Idaho Engineering Outreach staff (1995) in their *Guide to Distance Education at a Glance*:

> What is distance education? At its most basic level, distance education takes place when a teacher and student(s) are separated by physical distance, and technology (i.e., voice, video, data, and print), often in concert with face-to-face communication, is used to bridge the instructional gap.

The two key concepts that seem to be common to all of these definitions are (1) physical separation of the student from the content provider by either place or time (also referred to as *asynchronous teaching*) and (2) a delivery system. Part of the problem with current discussion regarding distance learning is a tendency to focus too narrowly on the delivery system due to the glitz and glamour of computer-mediated technologies. At least for accreditation and licensure purposes, the focus should be on content and outcomes. The primary importance of the delivery system is the extent to which it facilitates or impedes the transfer of knowledge and the development of skills.

Just as there are a number of different definitions of distance learning, there are also a number of different terms used to describe the concept. Distance learning is variously referred to in terms such as *distance education, distributed education,* and *computer-mediated learning*. To some extent these are just differences in semantics and the terms are often used interchangeably. However, each term has a slightly different focus of emphasis. *Distance education* places stress on the delivery system. *Distance learning* focuses on the student and is more outcomes-oriented. Or, in the words of Virginia Steiner (1995), "Distance learning is the result of distance education." These are critical differences for accreditation and licensure purposes because they drive the formulation of standards along with design of the methods and instruments used to measure the extent to which a program meets those standards.

The administrative structures that are engaged in the creation, procuring, and delivery of distance learning are as varied as the definitions and terms used to describe it. Those structures can generally be grouped into three broad categories. The first category is composed of traditional colleges and universities that offer their own courses or degree programs through distance learning technologies. The second category might be called *virtual universities* in that they have no physical campus or classroom facilities but consist primarily of administrative offices and computer rooms. These virtual universities are content providers in that they own or contract for the creation of a set of courses, which are then provided by the virtual university to its students. The Jones International University, the first accredited cyberuniversity (http://www.jonesinternational.edu), is a good example of this second type. The third category might be called *brokerage agencies* in that they do not create or own the course content, but rather locate it for their students (Goldstein, 1991). Brokerage agencies may help the student design a program by drawing upon courses from several different sources. The brokerage agency may actually grant a degree to the student who has successfully completed the program of study. Western Governors University (WGU) is the prime example of this third type. WGU (http://www.wgu.edu/wgu/index.html) advertises itself as a "competency" rather than a clock-hour based institution in that it will "certify competency [for degree granting purposes] on the basis of assessment of what learners know and are able to do, not on the basis of a learner's accumulation of credit hours from prior learning."

ACCREDITATION AND LICENSURE

At its heart, accreditation is a quality assurance process. Additionally, to the extent that someone is paying for education, be it the student, taxpayers, or donors, accreditation performs a critical role in providing public accountability. In a very real sense, it is higher education's counterpart to consumer protection regulations. However, unlike consumer protection regulations, which are externally imposed upon business entities, accreditation is generally viewed as a self-regulatory process involving a cooperative effort between the institution and the accrediting body. The process typically begins with a self-study using the accrediting body's standards as a guide, followed by a team visit and then a judgment by the accrediting body about the extent to which the institution has met the standards. The self-study is often an educational process in and of itself as the institution learns about itself in a systematic fashion and, ideally, voluntarily undertakes corrective action where deficiencies are noted. The accrediting body's team of visitors, and the accrediting body itself, not only review the institution's compliance with standards but also often will make recommendations for improvement. In the words of the Council for Higher Education Administration (CHEA) ("What Is," 1996), "Accreditation in higher education is a collegial process based on self and peer assessment for public accountability and improvement of academic quality." Accreditation may either apply to an entire institution or may focus upon a particular academic program such as law, counselor education, engineering, and other professional preparation programs. Institutional accreditation is comprehensive and typically encompasses governance, financial status, student services, learning, and achievement. Professional or specialized accreditation has traditionally focused upon the ability of an academic program to train competent professionals.

Licensure of educational institutions and programs (versus licensure of individuals) is usually conducted through legislative mandate on a state-by-state basis. There is nothing collegial about it. At its best, licensure serves to protect the public from fly-by-night educational programs that have not gone through a legitimate accreditation process. At its worst, licensure serves an anticompetitive purpose by keeping outsiders away from the state institutions' market. Although licensing laws prescribe "standards," these differ from accreditation standards in that they are less outcome oriented and more focused on amenability to legal process, fiscal accountability, and compliance with state and federal law.

The lines between accreditation and licensure have become somewhat blurred because many licensing laws may require accreditation by a recognized accrediting body as a condition of licensure. Additionally many governmental bodies that provide financial aid to students and grants to institutions set accreditation as a condition for receipt of funds. For example, see *Chicago School of Automatic Transmission, Inc. v. Accreditation Alliance of Career Schools & Colleges* (1994); and 20 U.S.C. § 1141(a)(5) (1999).

INPUTS VERSUS OUTCOMES ASSESSMENT

Accreditation standards have traditionally evaluated identifiable physical facilities, faculty-to-student ratios, library holdings, support staff, and budgets as well as course syllabi, faculty credentials, history of graduates, and the like. These types of standards are sometimes collectively referred to as *inputs assessment* and tend to measure the capacity of an institution or program to carry out its educational mission. A movement began in the 1980s among some accreditors to shift from inputs assessment to *outcomes assessment* standards that evaluate the success of the institution or program in accomplishing that mission, that is, how well the institution or program does in transferring knowledge and skills to it students.

There has been resistance to this shift for a number of reasons, however, and progress has been tortuous at best. First, it is harder to do. It is much easier to count the number of faculty, the number of clock hours, and review budget figures than it is to determine if those inputs are leading to successful outcomes. Second, some view inputs standards as vehicles for protecting faculty lines, workloads, and resources—a position that at least annoys, if not infuriates, higher education administrators. Third, outcomes assessment has been viewed as the province of agencies that certify or license individuals to practice. But these objections are based on an unnecessarily narrow view of outcomes assessment that, if done correctly, can perform the critical function of letting an institution or program know whether changes are needed in the inputs. Additionally, there is growing pressure from the U.S. Department of Education (1997) and the Council for Higher Education Accreditation (1998), the nongovernmental body that recognizes accrediting agencies, to require the validation of standards in terms of relevancy to outcomes. Ironically, the Department of Education's own regulations defining the criteria for recognizing accreditation agencies are highly proscriptive and inputs oriented. However, in fairness to the Department of Education, much of what appears in the regulations is required by Congress' enabling legislation (20 U.S.C. § 1099b). Further, as will be discussed in the next section, distance learning defies the application of many traditional input assessment standards, and is likely to drive accreditors in the direction of outcomes assessment.

A good example of the kind of outcomes assessment standards referred to may be found in Section VI of the Council for Accreditation of Counseling and Related Educational Programs (CACREP) standards (CACREP, 1994). Standard VI.A. requires that

> Program objectives are reviewed and revised through self-study on a regular schedule based on student learning outcomes with input from program faculty, current and former students, and personnel in cooperating agencies, and are developed in accord with pertinent professional organization positions and perspectives.

And Standard VI.C. requires that

> Programs must be evaluated at least every 3 years. The formal evaluation [must] include, but not be limited to, the following:

> 1. review by program faculty of programs and specializations, curricular offerings, professional trends, and types of students seeking admission;
> 2. follow-up studies of graduates of the program to assess their perceptions and evaluations of the major aspects of the program; and
> 3. assessment of perceptions about the program among employers of program graduates, field placement supervisors, and personnel in cooperating and associated agencies.

Another good example of outcomes-based standards can be found in the August 1998 accreditation standards of the Commission on Collegiate Nursing Education (CCNE). The standards begin by requiring the applicant to demonstrate that "the mission, philosophy, and goals/objectives of the program [are] congruent with those of the parent institution, . . . reflect professional nursing standards and guidelines, and . . . consider the needs and expecta-

tions of the community of interest." Once that mission is determined, other standards are tied to demonstrating how the defined
goals and objectives are being met. For example, Standard IV requires that the program provide evidence that it

> is effective in fulfilling its mission, philosophy, goals/objectives,
> and expected results. Satisfactory student performance [must]
> reflect achievement of the expected results by the students in
> congruence with the mission, philosophy, and goals/objectives of
> the program as well as with professional nursing standards and
> guidelines. Alumni satisfaction and the accomplishments of
> graduates of the program [must also] attest to the effectiveness
> of the program. Faculty accomplishments in teaching, scholar-
> ship, service, and practice are congruent with the mission,
> philosophy, and goals/objectives of the program and with profes-
> sional nursing standards and guidelines. Program effectiveness
> reflects ongoing improvement.

Specifically, the program must accomplish the following:

1. Describe how faculty and students are involved in the evaluation of individual student performance. Describe how the
   evaluation of student performance is communicated to
   the students and how it is used to foster improved performance.
2. Demonstrate how the results of aggregate student performance are used to change or improve the curriculum.
3. Describe the student and graduate performance measures
   that are utilized by the program to indicate success in meeting
   the program mission, philosophy, and goals/objectives.
4. Describe the process for evaluating faculty performance in
   teaching, scholarship, service, and practice. Describe how the
   results of evaluations are communicated to individual faculty
   members and, in an aggregate sense, how they are used to foster ongoing improvement.
5. Provide evidence that professional growth and development
   are supported by the program and parent institution so that
   faculty can be expected to contribute effectively to the mission, philosophy, and goals/objectives of the program.

6. Describe how alumni, employers, and graduates evaluate the program and explain how results are used to improve the program.
7. Describe the process of the review and maintenance of records of student satisfaction and formal complaints.

THE IMPLICATIONS OF DISTANCE LEARNING FOR ACCREDITATION AND LICENSURE

ACCREDITATION

Distance learning stands the traditional accreditation paradigm of inputs assessment on its head. For example, one of the three critical steps in most accreditation processes is the site visit; however, in the case of a virtual university, there is no site to visit unless the accreditor wants to look at a few office spaces full of humming and whirring computer disk drives. Faculty-to-student ratios may have little meaning when any number of students can pursue an on-line course free of time and place constraints. There also may be no library to visit if access is provided either to computerized databases or to a number of libraries in different locations by way of the Internet.

Because the traditional classroom delivery of higher education is no longer the only way that learning opportunities are provided to students, accreditors can no longer rely solely on input standards to measure quality. Accreditors must ask questions regarding what constitutes quality education when learning occurs via alternative delivery methods. Then they must review their existing standards against these questions and, if necessary, revise the standards to insure quality within the new learning paradigm. Such questions include the following:

- First and foremost, what is being accredited? Is it an institution, a program of study, a delivery system, or something else?
- Who are the faculty? (This may not be an easy question to answer because distance learning courses are more and more frequently being created by teams of experts in multiple fields and disciplines.)
- Who are the students?
- How are transfer credits to be handled?

- How do students interact with faculty, and what is the appropriate response time?
- What instructional designs best fit with the mode of education delivery being offered by the program?
- How is student advising conducted?
- How are students and student progress evaluated?
- How are labs and clinics conducted?
- How are student services and financial aid provided?
- What faculty qualifications are desired when education is delivered at a distance?
- What types of support are provided to faculty to engage in distance learning activities?
- What library facilities are available?
- Is the delivery system accessible to disabled students?
- How is security assured in terms of privacy of student data, verification of student identity, and protection of intellectual property?

Once the fundamental questions have been answered, standards should be examined to determine if they adequately assess the appropriate factors in a way that does not constrain innovation in the development and implementation of delivery systems. For example, rather than requiring a set faculty-to-student ratio, the standard might require the institution to "Provide [a] rationale to support the adequacy of number and qualifications of faculty to accomplish the mission, philosophy, goals/objectives, and expected results of the program" (CCNE, 1998).

In revising its standards, the Council for Accreditation of Counseling and Related Educational Programs has asked questions such as those just listed. Each one of current 1994 standards has been examined to determine if it impedes programs from incorporating distance learning technologies. As a result of this review, CACREP has determined that some of its standards require revision. For example, CACREP has asked itself whether a library with set hours of operation is an appropriate measure of quality. The committee recommending revisions has suggested that revised wording of the standards should instead determine if there is appropriate access to information and services, regardless of mode. Furthermore,

CACREP is considering a much heavier emphasis on standards relating to program mission and objectives along with program requirements to regularly and systematically assess and evaluate how well the mission and objectives are being met. One recommended revision to the CACREP standards is that programs be required to submit a report showing how the results of evaluations are being used for necessary program modifications. In addition, the standards revision process has affirmed the need for the CACREP standards to be a single set of standards for all types of program delivery. CACREP has decided that standards as measures of quality should not be differentially defined according to varying educational delivery modes.

LICENSURE AND REGULATION

The regulation of higher education is a prerogative that has been reserved to the states since the formation of the nation (Goldstein, 1998). As a result, there are at least 51 different regulatory schemes (including the District of Columbia's) with which a distance learning program may have to contend just to operate within the United States alone. In addition, the federal government imposes a huge number of regulatory requirements on postsecondary education programs that receive federal funds or award federal financial aid to students. This multiplicity of regulations presents a number of difficult and perilous problems for distance learning programs desiring to offer courses across jurisdictional lines. Identification of the applicable regulations, time and effort that must be devoted to the application process, payment of multiple fees, and periodic audits and reporting to each jurisdiction are just a few of the more salient obstacles that must be overcome (Western Governors Association Design Team, 1996).

Simply getting to first base, that is, identifying a state's regulations, is a daunting task. First, most states make no mention of distance learning in their regulations. Reference must be had to broader statutes or rules governing out-of-state or nonpublic educational institutions. Second, some states have a very formal set of statutes (e.g., the North Carolina Higher Education Act, 1999) or regulations, while others opt for a simple delegation of authority to a board or commission (e.g., the Kentucky Higher Education Act, 1999).

Even after the relevant set of regulations has been identified, it is by no means clear that those regulations will actually apply to a given distance learning program. The majority of states take the position that the institution must have some physical presence within the state before the requirements come into play. But the definition of *physical presence* varies widely. Many states exercise jurisdiction only if there are live bodies in the form of faculty or administrative personnel operating within the state (Goldstein, 1998). Others exercise jurisdiction if the institution grants academic credentials to residents within the state. A few, such as Georgia, attempt to exercise jurisdiction if instruction is given to state residents "whether such instruction . . . [is] provided in person or by correspondence or by telecommunications or electronic media . . ." (Georgia Postsecondary Education Act, 1999). However, such an expansive approach to regulatory jurisdiction raises interesting questions under the Due Process and Interstate Commerce Clauses of the United States Constitution that are beyond the scope of this chapter. For example, see *Cybersell, Inc. v. Cybersell, Inc.* (1997) and *Thompson v. Handa-Lopez, Inc.* (1998) for cases reaching opposite conclusions about whether posting advertisements or material on a web site in one state creates "sufficient minimum contacts" to legally justify the assertion of jurisdiction over the author by another state whose citizens access that web site.

The scope of regulation varies just as much, ranging from simple registration of the institution and its programs at the low end to requiring that highly specific standards be addressed and a complex application process be completed at the other. An example of the latter is Florida, which requires a four-step process beginning with temporary licensure, moving to "provisional level one," to "provisional," and finally to "regular" licensure. Temporary licensure is an enforced period of planning during which an institution may not recruit, advertise, or conduct any educational business. At the provisional one level the institution may begin accepting students and offering courses, but may not offer degrees. At the provisional level, degrees may be granted. In order to receive regular licensure the institution must have shown a "history of stability." This process may take more than a year to complete and may cost nearly $12,000 for fees alone. Thereafter there is an annual review. The materials sent to this chapter's authors from Florida were nearly an inch thick and were accompanied by a letter stating that

> There are two licensing boards for private postsecondary education in Florida. If you plan to give an Associate of Arts, an Associate of Science, or higher degree, you will have to be licensed by [the State Board of Independent Colleges and Universities]. If you plan to offer only a specialized associate degree, or a diploma or certificate, you will have to be licensed by the State Board of Independent Postsecondary, Vocational, Technical, Trade, and Business Schools. If you plan to offer both types of credentials, you will have to be licensed *by both boards.*

Licensing requirements such as Florida's can only increase the cost of the programs—a cost that will undoubtedly be passed on to consumers, that is, the students.

Another problem posed by licensing laws for distance learning programs is the potential that they will be misused for anticompetitive purposes or to further peripheral agendas. An example of this appeared in *The Chronicle of Higher Education* in an article headlined, "N.J. Professors Seek to Stymie Expansion Plans of U. of Phoenix" (1998). Several faculty representatives attended a meeting of the New Jersey Commission on Higher Education demanding that the state block licensure for the University of Phoenix and "expose [it] for what it is."

Concerns about inconsistent, duplicative, and costly licensing requirements led the Western Governors Association to identify state policies on institutional licensure and authorization as one of the most significant barriers to setting up the WGU (Western Governors Association Design Team, 1996). Accreditation could provide a particularly valuable service in reducing these regulatory burdens if licensing agencies were willing to accept accreditation as satisfaction of most currently existing licensing requirements. For example, the Texas Education Code (1999) has specifically exempted institutions that are "fully accredited" by a "recognized accrediting agency" such as the Southern Association of Colleges and Schools (SACS). This approach could pare down those requirements to such things as providing the address of a registered agent for service of process, proof of insurance, and other such legal needs to ensure adequate legal and public accountability.

The downside of this approach is that it transfers a great deal of authority to accreditors who are already being accused of heavy-handedness by many higher education administrators. Additionally, although state governments are exempt from federal antitrust laws, accreditors are not (*Massachusetts School of Law at Andover, Inc. v. American Bar Association*, 1997). As regional and specialized accreditors come together to "standardize" their standards and enter into cooperative agreements to reduce the duplication of efforts, the threat of antitrust challenges increases. However, if distance learning is to thrive, rather than be crushed by the weight of multiple accreditation and licensure requirements, a cooperative approach must be the answer. A model already exists in the Inter-Regional Accrediting Commission (IRAC), an organization formed by four regional accreditors in cooperation with the Western Governors Association (http://www.westgov.org) with the purpose of coordinating standards and avoiding the necessity of duplicative self-studies for programs crossing regional accreditation boundaries.

RECOMMENDATIONS

Although many challenges have been created by the onslaught of distance learning technologies and environments, the historical reason for developing systems of accreditation and licensing in the United States has not changed. In fact, the need for these systems is as great today as ever. That need focuses on having quality assurance systems that can provide information to the public to keep them from being duped by fly-by-night diploma mills. With that need still in place, accreditors should be empowered to think creatively, as well as cooperatively, so that their standards and processes not only remain relevant in the new world but also will foster the development of quality distance learning programs.

There are three major recommendations that can be made to insure that accreditation remains relevant and insures quality as distance learning environments become more common.

1. **Review and rewrite accreditation standards to make them outcomes versus inputs oriented.** Accreditors should

conduct a comprehensive review to determine whether their standards may unnecessarily impede innovation in the design and implementation of nontraditional delivery systems. Where possible, standards should be written with a view to determining outcomes rather than inputs. Institutions and programs should be encouraged to define their mission and to create ways of assessing mission accomplishment. Accreditors should gear standards toward determining that multiple assessment tools are being used by institutions to measure mission accomplishment, and that the feedback from those assessment tools is not being ignored but is being used to make appropriate changes and improvements in program content and delivery.

2. **Educate the public on what questions are being asked to evaluate quality educational offerings in the new learning paradigm.** As the Internet makes it easier for fraudulent diploma mills to prey on the public (Guernsey, 1997), accreditors must recognize that the ever-increasing demand for information is not going to go away. Accreditors have a responsibility to educate the public about their standards and quality assurance processes. The public should know what questions the accreditors are asking to insure quality as well as be informed on questions they should be asking.

3. **Reduce duplication of effort by educational programs by encouraging cooperation and collaboration between and among accrediting agencies and licensing authorities.** Accreditors and licensing agencies should be encouraged to cooperate for the purpose of reducing duplication of effort by educational programs that cut across regional or programmatic boundaries. Licensing laws could be rewritten to allow satisfaction of most requirements other than those relating to assurances of legal responsibility by providing evidence of accreditation from the appropriate nationally recognized accreditors.

CONCLUSION

Because the paradigm for delivery of higher education is shifting so markedly in the distance learning environment, accreditors and licensure authorities will face new challenges in determining what constitutes quality education. Standards that have traditionally quantified inputs are slowly being altered to measure student learning outcomes. Knowing where, when, and how to alter standards is not always easy. Accreditors and licensing authorities have had little time to prepare for changes or to define what constitutes good practices and standards when examining distance learning programs. However, it is imperative that accreditors and licensing authorities begin to work together immediately to create a quality assurance system that is relevant to new learning environments and protective of the public's interest.

REFERENCES

Commission on Collegiate Nursing Education. (1998, August). *Standards for accreditation of baccalaureate and graduate nursing education programs* (Amended). Washington, DC: Author [On-line]. Available: http://www.aacn.nche.edu/accreditation/standrds.htm.

Council for Higher Education Accreditation. (1998, September 28). *Recognition of accrediting organizations: Policy and procedures.* Washington, DC: Author. (Available from CHEA, National Center for Higher Education, One Dupont Circle, NW, Suite 510, Washington, DC 20036-1135)

Chicago School of Automatic Transmission, Inc. v. Accreditation Alliance of Career School & Colleges, 44 F.3d 447,449 (7th Cir. 1994).

Council for Accreditation of Counseling and Related Educational Programs. (1994). *Accreditation standards and procedures manual.* Alexandria, VA: Author. (Available from CACREP, 5999 Stevenson Avenue, Alexandria, VA 22304)

Cybersell, Inc. v. Cybersell, Inc., 130 F.3d 414 (9th Cir 1997).

Distance Education and Training Council. (1998, February 2). *Facts about DETC* (Fact sheet.) (Available from DETC, 1601 18th Street, NW, Washington, DC 20009-2529)

Georgia Postsecondary Education Act, GA. Code §§ 20-3-250.19 (West 1999).

Goldstein, M.B. (1991). Keynote address: Distance learning and accreditation. In M. P. Lenn (Ed.), *Distance learning and accreditation* (pp. 7–17). Washington, DC: Council on Postsecondary Accreditation.

Goldstein, M. B. (1998, June). *Regulatory implications of distance learning: The external environment.* Paper presented at the annual conference of the National Association of College and University Attorneys, Philadelphia, PA.

Guernsey, L. (1997, December 19). Is the Internet becoming a bonanza for diploma mills? *The Chronicle of Higher Education*, pp. A22–A24.

Kentucky Higher Education Act, K.R.S. § 164-947 (West 1999).

Massachusetts School of Law at Andover, Inc. v. American Bar Association, 107 F.3d.1026 (3d Cir.), *cert denied*, 118 S.Ct. 263 (1997).

North Carolina Higher Education Act, N.C. Gen.Stat. § 116-15 (West 1999).

N.J. professors seek to stymie expansion plans of U. of Phoenix. (1998, July 10). *The Chronicle of Higher Education.*

Phipps, R.A., Wellman, J.V., & Merisotis, J.P. (1998, April). *Assuring quality in distance learning: A preliminary review* [Report]. Washington, DC: Council for Higher Education Accreditation.

Steiner, V. (1995, October 10). *What is distance learning?* [On-line]. Available: http://www.wested.org/tie/dlrn/distance.html.

Texas Education Code, Title 3, Chapter 61, Subchapter G. Section 61.303 (West 1999).

Thompson v. Handa-Lopez, Inc., 998 F.Supp. 739 (W.D.Tex. 1998).

20 U.S.C. § 1141 (a)(5) (1999).

20 U.S.C. § 1099b (1999).

United States Distance Learning Association. (1999, May 10). *Definition.* Watertown, MA: Author [On-line]. Available: http://www.usdla.org/Pages/define.html.

University of Idaho Engineering Outreach Staff. (1995, October). *Distance education at a glance: Guide No. 1.* Boise, ID: Author [On-line]. Available: http://www.uidaho.edu/evo/dist1.html.

U.S. Department of Education Procedures and Criteria for the Recognition of Accrediting Agencies, 34 C.F.R. §§ 602.20-.30 (1997).

Western Governors Association Design Team. (1996, July). *The policy environment for implementing the Western Governors University.* Denver, CO: Author [On-line]. Available: http://www.wgu.edu/wgu/about/policy_environ.html.

What is accreditation? (1996). *The CHEA Chronicle, 1*(2).

25

Cyberpaths to
Ethical Competence

Elizabeth DuMez

By its nature, ethics is principally a shared discipline. Any solitary aspect has only to do with plumbing the depths of conscience. The realization of an ethical professional life has everything to do with cooperation, critique, and conformity. Ethics scholars study and evaluate human conduct in light of moral principles that reflect community consensus. Applied ethicists seem to subscribe to both the intuitionists' view that conscience is innate and instigates moral action, and empiricism that suggests ethical behavior is a byproduct of experience. As all disciplines—both their scholarly evolution and their applications—soar on cyberwings, the exercise of the ethical professional life can best be informed by ready consultation.

A simple but insightful conceptualization of the need for consultation is found in a slender volume of parables, *Jacob the Baker,* by Noah BenShea (1989). Having discovered that their fellow villager, the baker, has profound answers to all manner of questions pondered by his neighbors, two men approach Jacob. One states, "I know what is right." The other asserts, "I know what is wrong." Jacob responds, "Together you make one wise man" (p. 26).

This chapter first considers a conceptual floor for ethics consultation on the Internet and discusses directions and detours as well as redressing ethical infractions. It then provides examples and innovations in ethics consultation, describes anticipated perils and advantages, and presents frameworks for decision making. The chapter has two appendixes, one containing vignettes of ethical dilemmas and the other questions for decision making.

A CONCEPTUAL FLOOR FOR THINKING ABOUT INTERNET ETHICS CONSULTATION (BUT THE SKY'S THE LIMIT)

Virtue, traditionally the domain of moral philosophy, pertains to making judgments and thus choices. Although moral virtue is a necessity, it is not sufficient for the achievement of a good life. Mortimer Adler (1984) discussed the phenomenon of engagement in order to achieve favorable external circumstances. He stated, "Habits consist of potentialities for action . . . but these are acquired, not innate, potentialities . . ." (p. 93). Further, ". . . knowing and understanding rules of any sort that prescribe the right acts and proscribe the wrong ones do not form habits. Habits are formed by acting repeatedly in accordance with the rules . . ." (p. 96). The virtue of prudence is knowing how to judge well and make good decisions regarding conduct. Only in the context of effects on others and information by which to interpret effects can good judgment be achieved.

> There would appear to be rules that should be followed in order to develop prudence, which consists in knowing how to form a sound judgment and reach the right decision about the means to be chosen. These rules include taking counsel, deliberating about alternatives and weighing their pros and cons, and being neither precipitate or rash on the one hand, nor obstinately indecisive on the other hand. (pp. 108–109)

The exercise of prudence clearly has dialogic underpinnings.

In Burton L. Visotzky's (1996) earthy interpretation of Genesis, he pointed out that ethics requires some agreement on the underlying philosophical systems. Once that is accomplished, working out the rules by which ethics are served is a communal task. Indeed, the development of codes of ethics and the adjudication of grievances alleging infractions are undertaken by practitioner peers. Does not logic suggest that the interpretation and application of the ethical standards should also be an interactive endeavor? Visotzky directed the reader to "ask hard questions, listen to one another. . . . In questions and in listening lie the keys to the formation of enduring communities and to moral development." (p. 210). We may read *ethical development* as well.

Turn then to consider the implications of interactive ethical decision making. The obvious contemporary means for this endeavor is, of course, the Internet. Robert Watkins (1994) hypothesized that

- the Internet is a way to strengthen the human services professions by developing a stronger professional community; [and]
- the Internet is a way to facilitate the spread of information relevant to the professions. (p. 59)

He postulated that the key to the development of any community is, logically, communication, "be it of knowledge or attitudes or values." Unless these are shared, there can be no community. One of the hallmarks of a profession is, of course, shared knowledge, attitudes, and values. Watkins believed mediated communication can develop and strengthen professional identity. For many months he monitored Internet discussion lists and observed the process of what he described as "community development." One example was a 2-week-long discussion about confidentiality on the Internet that generated a range of ideas. Another example could be the development of electronic peer review journals, he suggested, which could make professional information available worldwide with time, cost, and distance relatively meaningless. Watkins also observed that there is an underlying humanism among the helping professions and a general desire to help others, which suggests a cooperative spirit of community—auspicious for collegial consultation perhaps.

Traditionally, consultation has referred to an interactional helping process. Kadushin (1977) pointed to a series of sequential steps "…taken to achieve some objective through an interpersonal relationship." One of the participants in the transaction, in his conceptualization, has greater expertise, knowledge, and skill in performing professional functions. It is a problem-solving process that relates to a difficulty or dilemma encountered in professional practice (pp. 25–26). The possibility emerges that there may be at least three formats for ethics consultation: (1) the identification of ex-

pert guidance in resolving ethical dilemmas, (2) a Socratic method
of dialogue, and (3) a discussion group approach in which ideas are
paramount in a free-for-all environment.

The idea of consultation is beginning to appear in many formats
of discourse. A recent letter in the Letters (1999) section of *The
Economist* stated, "Sensitivity and a wider consultative process are
needed. . . ." A second letter noted that ". . . people tend to rely less
and less on 'self-selected wise men' to make decisions for them"
(p. 6). The context was unrelated to behavioral health professions
but suggested broad-based attention to the validity of consultation
in problem-solving processes.

In 1996, the United States social workers' code of ethics (National
Association of Social Workers [NASW], 1996) was substantially re-
vamped. For the first time, it included an articulation of the foundation values and principles that undergird the standards for
professional behaviors. The code explicitly encouraged consultation:
"For . . . guidance, social workers should consult the relevant literature on professional ethics and ethical decision making and seek appropriate consultation when faced with ethical dilemmas" (p. 3).
Further, "If a reasonable resolution of (a) conflict does not appear
possible, social workers should seek proper consultation before making a decision" (pp. 3–4). And, most specific to the point, standard
2.05(a) under Social Workers' Ethical Responsibilities to Colleagues
stated, "Social workers should seek the advice and counsel of colleagues whenever such consultation is in the best interests of
clients." In addition—and this concept will have more poignancy as
we delve deeper into the question of the propriety and practicality of
Internet ethics consultation—standard 2.05(b) stated, "Social workers should keep themselves informed about colleagues' areas of expertise and competencies. Social workers should seek consultation
only from colleagues who have demonstrated knowledge, expertise,
and competence related to the subject of the consultation" (p. 16).
How to ascertain that an Internet correspondent has sufficient expertise to consult on an ethical conundrum is an important question.

SOME DIRECTIONS AND DETOURS ON
THE BYWAYS OF ETHICS CONSULTATION

Professional codes of ethics differ both because of variations in
the missions of the disciplines and because of disparate emphases

in the professions. Consider the colloquial version of the Hippocratic oath, "Do no harm," which is perhaps the most universal foundation concept, and which is derived from the elements of the medical code historically attributed to Hippocrates. Each professional practitioner who has achieved standing by virtue of education and credentials must subscribe to his or her profession's relevant code. Heightened ethical consciousness has brought to the forefront a new realm of problem solving for professionals. Traditionally, problem solving addressed client psychosocial conditions. More recently, service delivery systems have been the focus of analysis and experimentation. The value conflicts reflected in ethical dilemmas are not new, but increasingly, professional practitioners are learning to resolve them through systematic analysis and applications of codes of ethics (NASW, 1998).

The commonalities in standards for mental health care on the Internet were identified by a representative group of professionals in January 1998. A Forum on Internet Mental Health Practice was convened in Bethesda, MD, at the invitation of the National Board for Certified Counselors. Twenty-one representatives of mental health professional membership associations as well as individuals from key federal agencies attended. From these discussions emerged a set of core principles—a beginning attempt to address ethical issues, behavioral health, and the Internet. So superimposed on professions' particular codes of ethics, there may be a set of common principles necessary for self-regulation in the pursuit of protection of clients and assurance of standards for professional activity on the Internet. The core principles drafted by group members, whose work continued for a time as an Internet discussion group, included the following:

I. The basic standards of professional conduct governing each mental health care profession are not altered by the use of Internet technologies to deliver mental health care, conduct research, or provide education. Developed by each profession, these standards focus in part on the practitioner's responsibility to provide ethical and high-quality care.

II. A mental health care system or mental health care practitioner cannot use the Internet as a vehicle for providing services that are not otherwise legally or professionally authorized.

III. Services provided via the Internet must adhere to basic assurance of quality and professional mental health care in accordance with each mental health care discipline's clinical standards. Each mental health care discipline must examine how Internet mental health practice impacts and/or changes its patterns of care delivery and how this may require modifications of existing clinical standards.

IV. The use of Internet technologies does not require additional licensure.

V. Each mental health care profession is responsible for developing its own processes for assuring competencies in the delivery of mental health care through the use of Internet mental health practice.

VI. Practice guidelines and clinical guidelines in the area of Internet mental health should be developed based on empirical evidence, when available, and professional consensus among all involved mental health care disciplines. The development of these guidelines may include collaboration with government agencies.

VII. The integrity and therapeutic value of the client-mental health care practitioner relationship should be maintained and not diminished by the use of Internet mental health technology.

VIII. Confidentiality of client visits and client mental health records is essential to the integrity of information in a mental health care information system.

IX. Documentation requirements for Internet mental health services must be developed that assure documentation of each client encounter with recommendations and treatments, communication with other health care providers as appropriate, and adequate protections for client confidentiality.

X. All clients directly involved in an Internet mental health encounter must be informed about the process, attendant risks and benefits, and their rights and responsibilities, and must provide adequate informed consent.

XI. The safety of clients and practitioners must be ensured. Safe hardware and software, combined with demonstrated user competency, are essential components of safe Internet mental health practice.

XII. A systematic and comprehensive research agenda must be developed and supported by government agencies and mental health care professions for the ongoing assessment of Internet mental health practices. (Bloom & Sampson, 1998)

An addendum to standard II that might be considered could require that professional identification and sanctioning credentials must be made known in standard terms (e.g., psychologist, marriage and family therapist, professional counselor, nurse).

In the absence of a system of professional review or accountability, standards remain, however, in the realm of guidelines. State regulatory (e.g., licensure) boards are generally charged with administering systems of review of complaints. The statutes among the states are extremely varied, and not all states regulate all the behavioral health professions. Therefore, no consistency of quality control is assured regardless of whether these boards would even entertain complaints of conduct that related to the Internet. Perhaps the threshold question is whether a practitioner who allegedly committed an ethical infraction could even be identified. Some practitioners will, of course, mete out opinion or advice via their web sites. Others may enter the fray only pseudonymously.

REDRESSING ALLEGED ETHICAL INFRACTIONS

The *NASW Code of Ethics* (1996) has articulated a social worker's obligation to take action against unethical conduct by any other member of the profession. The responsibility is generally construed to apply to representatives of sister disciplines, such as counselors, psychologists, nurses, and psychiatrists, as well.

2.11 Unethical Conduct of Colleagues

(a) Social workers should take adequate measures to discourage, prevent, expose, and correct the unethical conduct of colleagues.

(b) Social workers should be knowledgeable about established policies and procedures for handling concerns about colleagues' unethical behavior. Social workers should be familiar with national, state, and local procedures for handling ethics complaints. These include policies and procedures created by NASW, licensing and regulatory bodies, employers, agencies, and other professional organizations.

(c)   Social workers who believe that a colleague has acted unethically should seek resolution by discussing their concerns with the colleague when feasible and when such discussion is likely to be productive.

(d)   When necessary, social workers who believe that a colleague has acted unethically should take action through appropriate formal channels (such as contacting a state licensing board or regulatory body, an NASW committee on inquiry, or other professional ethics committees).

(e)   Social workers should defend and assist colleagues who are unjustly charged with unethical conduct. (p. 8)

All professions that promulgate codes of ethics must have enforcement methods. Most professional associations offer some form of peer review of complaints regarding their members' conduct. Most states regulate the behavioral health professions, albeit with mixed effectiveness. The purpose of state statutes, however, is to protect the public, that is, clients. Many professional codes have developed standards that extend practitioner ethical responsibility to colleagues and employing organizations as well. Professional activity on the Internet will undoubtedly be tested in these forums of review. As codes of ethics are updated by the professions, they are bound to contain standards specifically pertinent to the virtual relationships of the Internet.

Remarkably, the New York State Education Department Office of Professional Discipline includes its complaint form on its web site inviting complaints to be submitted either by fax or e-mail (http://www.nysed.gov/prof/complain.htm) to the Office of Professional Discipline. The form states that, when received, the complaint will be assigned to an investigator. The form requires authorization for the professional complained about to release information "about the treatment or the services rendered to you" (i.e., the complainant). The resources required for investigation are beyond many professional organizations, which typically require that complainants provide all necessary documentation or evidence in behalf of their cases. Arguably, justice can best be served by open access to such review systems. However, many entities could be overwhelmed or bureaucratically paralyzed by an open market for complaints, some proportion of which would be unjustified or unfounded.

In research into 10 years of adjudication cases processed by the National Association of Social Workers, Kimberly Strom-Gottfried reviewed nearly 900 ethics complaints (her study included the universe of cases of adjudicated ethics violations from 1986 to 1997). Less than half of the complaints received met the criteria for acceptance and went to hearing. Of that number, less than 30% resulted in findings of violation of the *NASW Code of Ethics* (Strom-Gottfried, 1998a). With this perspective, one might argue for the necessity of a direct contact with a representative of a review body in order to discuss the nature of a prospective complaint and whether the particular board or professional association is the appropriate venue of review.

Consultation is an explicit ethical responsibility for social workers and is addressed in six standards of the social workers' code of ethics. Models of supervision and consultation have long been established in the professions. These standards not only socialize new members to a profession and guide their behavior but also can serve as the basis by which professionals can be held accountable for actions in contravention to a code. Strom-Gottfried (1998b) stated, "clearly those crafting and enforcing the Code of Ethics consider supervision and administration to be forms of practice, subject to standards of conduct in the same way direct practice is" (p. 3). In her research into adjudicated personnel disputes, Strom-Gottfried found that the most commonly occurring violation involved the provision of poor supervision. Although there may not be a direct application of her findings to the field of consultation, certainly the parallels raise cautionary concerns. Two of 31 adjudicated cases had findings of incompetent practice, "in that the respondents were judged to have carried out their supervisory or managerial functions without application of appropriate knowledge or skills" (p. 10). Could Internet consultations subject a practitioner to the risk of having a professional complaint lodged against him or her? Over one third of all ethics complaints filed with the National Association of Social Workers between 1986 and 1997 were made by co-workers.

NASW processed a complaint brought by a professional practitioner against another with allegations of collegial misconduct, including violations of confidentiality and disrespectful treatment on the Internet. Personal information was allegedly conveyed by one about the other along with disparaging comments, all in the context of professional roles. In fact, the peer review panel concluded that an ethical infraction had occurred.

Increasingly, Internet practitioners may eschew traditional symbols and allegiances of professionalism. If one can make a living by offering unsanctioned services, whither accountability? What remains to be seen is whether parallel structures of standards, credentialing, peer review, and disciplinary action can be built into the dynamic metamorphoses of cybercommunication.

ETHICS CONSULTATION: EXAMPLES AND INNOVATIONS

In this section are some models, roughly construed to be consultative, that have been proposed or developed for use on the Internet. Consultation-cum-education models are ripe for development.

ELECTRONIC ETHICS NETWORKING CONSORTIUM

In a competitive proposal process, a National Association of Social Workers' chapter submitted a proposal for a dialogic process with the purpose of identifying, documenting, and assisting with ethical issues and dilemmas (NASW, Pennsylvania Chapter, 1998). In describing the proposed project (which ultimately was not awarded the grant and thus not implemented), the chapter pointed to its desirability as evidenced by

- practitioners working in significantly different settings than were prevalent at the time the 1966 *NASW Code of Ethics* was developed (for which, presumably, dialogue would serve to update practitioners and hone skills); and
- growing interest in ethics training as evidenced by larger-than-expected numbers of practitioners at continuing education events.

The learning goals included:

- training in adherence to confidentiality while using an electronic networking medium (with applications to other aspects of one's practice);

- expanding information about ethical concerns and dilemmas affecting practitioners in (discrete) geographic areas or particular practice settings;
- sharing information about resolution of ethical concerns and dilemmas; and
- providing experience in identifying appropriate ethical standards for application in particular problem situations. (p. 2)

The model proposed a subscriber list to link electronically interested practitioners connected to the chapter's web site. A cadre of experts were to be available to address the issues and questions presented. Further, the chapter could use the data that emerged for developing continuing education conferences based on demonstrated needs. The protocol was to include confidentiality guidelines for all those connected. The experts were to monitor the project, copying, coding, and organizing the incoming data and responses for use in analysis and discussion as well as content for the continuing education events. The chapter proposed to develop a satisfaction survey tool to determine the effectiveness of the service (pp. 3–4).

VERITABLE ANALYSIS

A companion book to the *NASW Code of Ethics* (1996), *Current Controversies in Social Work Ethics* (NASW, 1998), was prepared by the committee that drafted the new *Code*. In the companion book, vignettes of ethical dilemmas derived from actual ethics consultations provide a content base distinguished by its validity. Committee members developed commentaries on the vignettes to highlight the ethical considerations. Many of the scenarios may be typical of problems addressed by disciplines other than social work. The vignettes, therefore, could be used as case examples. (Two samples from the book are provided in Appendix A.)

Various learning strategies present themselves:

1. In a dialogue with an Internet learner, the ethical standard and situation solely could be presented with an invitation for discussion. The consultant should ascertain whether the essential points in the analysis are identified. And does commentary provided raise additional issues?

2. An Internet learner could be presented with the situation and be asked to identify the relevant code standard(s) from that practitioner's professional code of ethics and to develop a course of action including the justification.

3. An Internet learner or consultee could be directed to summarize his or her dilemma of the moment, to identify relevant code sections from that practitioner's code of ethics, and to write up the available courses of action with the likely consequences in a format similar to the commentaries that appear in Appendix A.

CASES AND COMMENTS

The Santa Clara University (1999) web site includes an exercise in its *Ethics Connection* section titled "Cases and Comments" (www.scu.edu/SCU/Centers/Ethics/dialogue/candc/cases). Although the exercise gives examples of contemporary societal ethical issues and provides a forum for dialogue on cases, the design should be readily adaptable to professional practice ethics cases. Cases are presented in summary form with a focusing question. The site includes a message board for each case where accumulated ideas and comments can be collected.

DIALOGUES

Another exercise sponsored by Santa Clara University, also an option from its web site and potentially adaptable to professional ethics subject matter, is dialogic in nature (www.scu.edu/SCU/Centers/Ethics/practicing/focusareas/education/character.shtml). On various subjects, two versions of response to an ethical dilemma are presented, one an ethical course of action, the other not. The Internet learner is expected to identify the "principles and virtues" that apply. Presumably, such an undertaking could then be posted for discussion by cohorts.

DEBATE AND DISCUSSION

A true dialectic experience can be achieved through structured debate—especially if it permits rejoinder to each debate partner's position. Gambrill and Pruger's (1997) collection of debates about practice, the use of coercion, self-regulation of a profession, professional education and training, and special client populations is a fine print example. The manager of a discussion group could readily identify profession-specific questions or more general ones, pertinent to a variety of disciplines and "sign up" individuals who self-identify to take up one side or the other. General discussion could be invited to follow.

This model could stimulate more critical thinking for participants and could include some identification of foundation theoretical material and underlying values. Gambrill and Pruger (1997) adapted a "Code of Conduct for Effective Rational Discussion" (pp. xv–xvi) and encouraged its application in order to achieve well-reasoned ethical decisions:

- the fallibility principle;
- the truth-seeking principle;
- the burden of proof principle;
- the principle of charity;
- the clarity principle;
- the relevance principle;
- the acceptability principle;
- the sufficient-grounds principle;
- the rebuttal principle;
- the resolution principle;
- the suspension of judgment principle; and
- the reconsideration principle.

ANTICIPATED PERILS, OBVIOUS ADVANTAGES FOR INTERNET ETHICS CONSULTATION

No one should embark on the opportunistic journey of ethics decision making reliant on Internet guidance without due caution and a well-examined protocol in place. Weighing the merits and pitfalls of Internet ethics consultation, in whatever form, parallels the conundrums of ethical dilemmas themselves.

Conflicts are inevitable among both code standards in the assignment of their relative powers and the competing sources of authority or colliding values that ordinarily conjure a dilemma. Each individual is responsible under the unique standards of the code to which she or he subscribes. Therefore, cross consultation among professionals of various orientations will inevitably pose some difficulties. One seeking consultation can, and perhaps should, challenge a correspondent to identify the basis of an assertion grounded in that individual's professional code of ethics. The reconciliation of priorities among the various professions and primacy of certain values—that may indeed differ, hierarchically—requires a dialogic process and critical skill. May an instinct to find common ground among divergent points of view undermine the achievement of a truly just and justifiable decision?

Hazards of Internet communication have been broadly documented. In the instance of ethics consultation some issues to be considered include the following:

- Distinctions must be made between peer consultation, in which professional practitioners might engage in dialogue and raise crucial issues but have no established expertise or special knowledge, and consultation with experts who have demonstrable qualifications. Further, an employing agency or institution can be held accountable for the action or inaction of an employee. The concept of vicarious liability in supervision (clearly not an absolute parallel to consultation) is discussed in *Prudent Practice* (Houston-Vega & Nuehring, 1998, pp. 139–140).

- Posting an interpretation or opinion based on information conveyed—possibly biased or partial—could expose the consultant to liability if action were taken by the consultee based on the misperception or misinterpretation of the guidance proffered.

- Case law illustrates the liability risk of alleged negligence when a professional does not refer a client to a specialist for consultation or fails to consult an organization for advice (e.g., failure to consult a child protection agency when neglect or abuse is suspected). Documented consultation could demonstrate the reasonableness of one's intentions (Reamer, 1994). Peterson, Murray, and Chan alluded to the legal and ethical ramifications of improper use of Internet therapy, suggesting the possibility of malpractice suits based on (a) negligent rendering of services, (b) negligence that leads to suicide, and (c) improper supervision of a disturbed client (1998, p. 203).

- If a central source for consultation were established, perhaps it might have to be profession-specific because of remaining differences in function among the behavioral health disciplines.

- Face-to-face interaction between a consultant and consultee enhances the data available, the basis on which each might have a more fruitful response. Mentoring and role modeling, valid forms of teaching, are difficult to accomplish without personal contact. And problems that require critical thinking, abstraction, and active processing and synthesis of information may not lend themselves to other than direct human interaction (Peterson et al., 1998).
- A single source of consultation within a discipline might be absent a diversity of perspectives that could be essential for legitimate ideas or opinion to be generated on a broad array of subjects. Interdisciplinary consultation, by the same token, could be devoid of depth of information about the roles of practitioners and their typical client problems and situations.
- Demands of time and timeliness for an expert could be unduly burdensome.

On the crest of the wave of the future, however, it is also important to recognize the unlimited potential and inevitable pervasive supplanting of traditional interchanges by Internet communication, both informal and formal. Many advantages are evident:

- The conferencing techniques allow groups of individuals to confer simultaneously through text, ideally with one person serving as moderator (Peterson et al., 1998). The dynamism of class learning can be vicariously captured. Although a practitioner may still choose to have a primary practice consultant, the breadth of discussion available in Internet exchanges will inevitably expand a professional's thinking and range of options.
- The immediacy and accessibility of discussion on the Internet is a potentially powerful mediating dynamic in the prevention of unethical conduct, both advertent and inadvertent. For most practitioners in the near future, the pipeline to a world of ideas and problem solving may be available in the next room. Mistakes born of desperation and passion may be avoided. Intuitive or emotion-based initiatives in the face of difficult clients or scarce resources, as well as the succumbing to the fulfillment of personal needs that represent boundary violations, can be readily prevented.

- Supervision (akin to consultation) via the Internet has been noted as particularly useful for sharing professional ideas and information with supervisees (or consultees) in remote and distant geographic areas. Similarly, peer supervision can be accomplished (Peterson et al., 1998).
- "Cultural competence" was a hallmark of the expansion of the social workers' code of ethics in the 1996 edition. Yet some practitioners have limited exposure to ethnic and social diversity, may be culturally biased, or may be confronted with culturally based client issues for which they are ill-equipped. Discussion or consultation could be enlightening. Reamer (1998) noted that

An important element of [the code] concerns social workers' obligation to recognize the strengths that exist in all cultures. Practitioners need a solid understanding of various cultural groups' positive and functional coping patterns, traditions, and customs. Social workers must understand that cultural practices that are different from those of the majority culture are not, by definition, counterproductive or dysfunctional. Rather, differences among cultural groups should be celebrated and accounted for in [professional] practice. (p. 42)

- For those who choose to keep it, a verbatim record exists of the Internet communication that may support decision making that is later questioned.

FRAMEWORKS FOR DECISION MAKING

Most authors who have written in the field of ethics have presented problem-solving methodologies or decision-making paradigms. Reamer (1997) summarized by listing the typical elements:

- identifying the individuals, groups, and organizations who are likely to be affected by the ethical decision;
- exploring possible courses of action and likely risks and benefits;
- considering relevant ethical theories, principles, and guidelines, codes of ethics, and personal values (and their interactions);
- consulting with colleagues and appropriate experts;
- making the decision; and
- monitoring and evaluating the decision. (p. 172)

Models appear on the Internet and in many sources of professional literature. The Markkula Center web site, for example, features *Thinking Ethically: A Framework for Moral Decision Making* (Velasquez, Andre, Shanks, & Meyer, 1999), which briefly describes five approaches in addressing moral issues: the utilitarian, rights, fairness/justice, common-good, and virtue approaches. Once facts of a situation have been established, a participant is directed to ask a prescribed set of questions. (See Appendix B.)

Elsewhere on the same web site (www.scu.edu/SCU/Centers/Ethics/practicing/decision/framework.shtml) is *A Framework for Ethical Decision Making* that also poses questions in the following categories:

- get the facts;
- evaluate the alternative actions from various moral perspectives;
- make a decision; and
- act, then reflect on the decision later.

The *Framework for Ethical Decision Making: Version 4 Ethics Shareware* is presented by Michael McDonald (1999) at www.ethics.ubc.ca/mcdonald/decisions.html. His directives include

- identify the problem;
- specify feasible alternatives;
- use your ethical resources to identify morally significant factors in each alternative;
- propose and test possible resolutions; and
- make your choice. (pp. 1–2)

Each area also entails provocative questions and guidance.

A University of Oregon (1999) site (http://jcomm.uoregon.edu/~tbivins/j495/Worksheet.html) represents another alternative, titled *Worksheet for Ethical Decision Making*, and stimulates the participant to articulate

- the issue;
- relevant facts;
- claimants;
- claimants' assumed preferences;
- options (with consideration of harm, ideals, and rules);
- ethical guidelines;

- decision; and
- defense. (pp. 2–4)

CONCLUSION

Reverberating aspirations in the unfolding dimensions of cyber-space are our inevitable future. Being a professional practitioner requires a good deal of wisdom—a necessity in weighing and choosing among the inevitable choices that one's practice presents. The steps along a path to wisdom, according to Visotzky (1996), require exposure to varying opinions, debate, and discussion. In the midst of our frenetic workdays, we must all afford the luxury of (or exercise a personal commitment to) thoughtful discourse on difficult issues.

Every practitioner grapples with ethics dilemmas, consciously (which is cause for rejoicing) or unconsciously. Mortimer Adler (1984) reminded us that a means and methodology for working through those dilemmas can become a habit. But—there is always the matter of choice. A moral philosophy or a code of ethics that relies solely on obedience to the rules it sets forth is unpragmatic. Being virtuous is wholly within our power, he challenged. It is a result of exercising freedom of choice. The journey need not be a lonely one.

REFERENCES

Adler, M. J. (1984). *A vision of the future.* New York: Macmillan.

BenShea, N. (1989). *Jacob the baker.* New York: Villard Books.

Bloom, J. W., & Sampson, J. P., Jr. (1998). *Core standards for Internet mental health practice* [On-line]. Available: http://www.career.fsu.edu/techcenter/standards.html.

Gambrill, E., & Pruger, R. (Eds.). (1997). *Controversial issues in social work ethics, values, and obligations.* Needham Heights, MA: Allyn & Bacon.

Houston-Vega, M. K., & Nuehring, E. M. (1998). *Prudent practice.* Washington, DC: National Association of Social Workers.

Kadushin, A. (1977). *Consultation in social work.* New York: Columbia University Press.

Letters. (1999, August 28–September 3). *The Economist,* p. 6.

McDonald, M. (1999). *Framework for ethical decision making: Version 4 ethics shareware* [On-line]. Available: www.ethics.ubc.ca/mcdonald/decisions.html.

National Association of Social Workers. (1996). *NASW code of ethics.* Washington, DC: Author [On-line]. Available: http://www.naswdc.org/CODE.HTM.

National Association of Social Workers. (1998). *Current controversies in social work ethics: Case examples.* Washington, DC: Author.

National Association of Social Workers, Pennsylvania Chapter. (1998). *Ethics education proposal.* Harrisburg, PA: Author.

Peterson, D. B., Murray, G. C., & Chan, F. (1998). Ethics and technology. In R. R. Cottone & V. M. Tarvydas (Eds.), *Ethical and professional issues in counseling* (pp. 196–235). Columbus, OH: Merrill.

Reamer, F. G. (1994). *Social work practice and liability.* New York: Columbia University Press.

Reamer, F.G. (1997). Does professional education adequately prepare students to resolve ethical problems of practice? In E. Gambrill & R. Pruger (Eds.), *Controversial issues in social work ethics, values, and obligations.* Needham Heights, MA: Allyn & Bacon.

Reamer, F. G. (1998). *Ethical standards in social work.* Washington, DC: National Association of Social Workers.

Santa Clara University, Markkula Center for Applied Ethics. (1999). *Ethics connection* [On-line]. Available: www.scu.edu/SCU/Centers/Ethics/dialogue/candc/cases & www.scu.edu/SCU/Centers/Ethics/practicing/focusareas/education/character. shtml.

Strom-Gottfried, K. (1998a). Oral presentations. Presented to the National Association of Social Workers National Committee on Inquiry.

Strom-Gottfried, K. (1998b). *When colleague accuses colleague: Adjudicating personnel matters through the filing of ethics complaints.* Unpublished manuscript.

University of Oregon (1999). *Worksheet for ethical decision making* [On-line]. Available: www.comm.uoregon.edu/~bivias/j495/Worksheet.html.

Velasquez, M., Andre, C., Shanks, T., & Meyer, M. (1999). *Thinking ethically: A framework for moral decision making* [On-line]. Available: www.scu.edu/SCU/Centers/Ethics/practicing/decision/thinking.shtml.

Visotzky, B. L. (1996). *The genesis of ethics.* New York: Crown.

Watkins, R. L. (1994). *An exploratory study of the use of the Internet by members of the helping professions: With implications for social work.* Unpublished manuscript, Southern University at New Orleans.

Appendix A
Vignettes of Ethical Dilemmas

These examples are purposefully devoid of references to the *NASW Code of Ethics* (1996) in order to illustrate that many problem situations are typical to various professional disciplines. In each vignette and commentary, the term *social worker* is replaced by *practitioner* in order to generalize the examples. The examples are just 2 among 78 in the book, *Current Controversies in Social Work Ethics: Case Examples* (NASW, 1998).

Vignette 1

Ethical standard: Practitioners should not take unfair advantage of any professional relationship or exploit others to further their personal, religious, political, or business interests.

Situation: An independent case manager for senior citizens in a small town recently received notice that her apartment had been sold and she must move. One of her clients owns an apartment complex and has mentioned that there is a vacancy. The practitioner is considering transferring the client to a local nonprofit agency that provides case management services similar to hers, thus freeing her to rent the apartment without an appearance of conflict of interest.

Commentary: A practitioner may find that a client has access to a valuable resource; in this instance, the practitioner could benefit from the client's ownership of an apartment complex. Although it may be tempting to take advantage of a client's access to such a resource and the client's largess, the practitioner must avoid engaging in this kind of dual relationship, in which services are terminated to pursue a business relationship with a client because of the potential harm (disadvantage) to the client.

There are several possible risks. First, the dynamics in the clinical relationship are likely to change in a way that could be detrimental (not optimally in the client's best interest) to the client. The practitioner and client would need to relate to each other in the context of a business relationship, which may interfere with the client's ability to take full advantage of the therapeutic relationship. This may result in part because the client could begin to view the practitioner as a tenant as well as a counselor; similarly, the practitioner could begin to view the client as a landlord as well as a client. Second, the practitioner's decision to refer the client to another service provider may not be to the client's advantage. The break in continuity of service could affect the extent to which the client benefits from the services. Moreover, the client may feel some pressure to consent to this arrangement because of the client's dependence on the practitioner. Finally, the relationship between the client and practitioner could be undermined if the practitioner's new apartment is somehow defective or unsatisfactory. Addressing this problem could complicate the practitioner-client relationship in a way that is not in the best interests of the client as a client. (p. 24)

VIGNETTE 2

Ethical standard: **Practitioners should respect clients' right to privacy. Practitioners should not solicit private information from clients unless it is essential to providing services or conducting practitioner evaluation or research. Once private information is shared, standards of confidentiality apply.**

Situation: A clinical practitioner meets weekly for therapy with a 15-year-old female client. During a session, the client reports that she is dealing drugs and has begun seeing a boyfriend who just completed a 6-month jail sentence for selling drugs. The client's parents have forbidden contact between their daughter and her boyfriend and have asked the practitioner to inform them if their daughter reported that she is seeing the boy again. The practitioner believes that his client trusted him not to pass on this information to anyone else and that disclosure might permanently impair the trust in their relationship. However, the practitioner told his client when they first began their sessions that he could not promise to keep confidential any statements that indicate a threat to harm self or others. The practitioner is concerned for his client's safety with the boyfriend but also is far more concerned about her illegal involvement in the sale of drugs and the dangers she may face from the drug trade.

Commentary: The practitioner must struggle among obligations to his primary client, a minor; to her parents, who are inevitably part of the client system; and to society, whose laws are intended to protect. He can seek to work with the client toward the goal of achieving consent to bring the parents into active work as a family unit. The practitioner could endeavor to support the client and work toward accomplishing consent to reveal the relationship but with the goal of establishing a growing alliance with her parents. Or he can weigh the dangers to the client of the renewed relationship with her boyfriend plus the betrayal of the collateral clients' (the parents') expectations for the protection of their daughter and decide that revealing the information to them constitutes a compelling exception to confidentiality. If he decides on the latter course of action, the primary client (the daughter) must be informed in advance of the disclosure. (p. 36)

Appendix B
Questions for Decision Making

The five approaches of Velasquez, Andre, Shanks, and Meyer (1999) suggest that once facts have been ascertained, five questions should be posed in trying to resolve a moral issue:

1. What benefits and what harms will each course of action produce, and which alternative will lead to the best overall consequences?
2. What moral rights do the affected parties have, and which course of action best respects those rights?
3. Which course of action treats everyone the same, except where there is a morally justifiable reason not to, and does not show favoritism or discrimination?
4. Which course of action advances the common good?
5. Which course of action develops moral virtues?

According to Velasquez et al.,

This method, of course, does not provide an automatic solution to moral problems. It is not meant to. The method is merely meant to help identify most of the important ethical considerations. In the end, we must deliberate on moral issues for ourselves, keeping a careful eye on both the facts and on the ethical considerations involved. (pp. 4, 5)

PART VI

Envisaging the Future of Cybercounseling

26

Summing Up

GARRY R. WALZ WITH CONTRIBUTIONS FROM JOHN W. BLOOM,
JAMES SAMPSON, WAYNE LANNING, AND ROBERT CHAPMAN

I t is always a challenge to know how to construct a summary and conclusion. Traditionally, a summary should not contain new material but be a concise statement of what has been said previously. A conclusion, however, should logically follow ideas presented in the document itself. New ideas or discussions not driven by the previous narrative are typically considered inappropriate.

But what of a situation where you have approximately 30 authors each with his or her own ideas—many of the ideas well developed, but others only just introduced? Clearly, a traditional writing model does not fit this publication. It both poses a horrendous task for the reviewer/writer and forces fitting ideas into a cumbersome format that imperils creative and dissonant thinking. Because this publication, in many ways, challenges the existing status quo of counseling, why not adopt a format or means of communication between the writers and readers that places a premium on expressing and examining key ideas rather than adhering to a traditional format?

That is exactly what has been done: the separate and disparate ideas of the different writers are woven together into a mosaic of knowledge generalizations that spring from the ideas and writings of the authors. It is not, however, in most cases, a direct translation of the thinking of any one writer. Therefore, what has been produced is a *summing up* that is a series of freestanding knowledge generalizations. Each of the generalizations speaks in a targeted and succinct manner to a cogent concept or idea that has been distilled from a wide array of the ideas presented. Wherever possible, individuals whose thinking is reflected in the statements are identified. However, in many cases, there are no clear originators, and attributions are difficult, if not impossible, to make. In these cases, the concepts are constructed as best as possible, and the responsibility for fallacious thinking or inadequate representations is this chapter's authors alone.

The term *knowledge generalization* is used as a device for conveying cogent ideas in a succinct and readily understandable manner. It provides a useful way to focus thinking and discussion on each significant concept. It is also a way of preventing other ideas and thoughts from unduly interfering with a full digestion of the inherent merit of each generalization. The blending of the generalizations into a striking tapestry of ideas can be achieved at the end by the reader. The purpose of this summing up is to serve as a springboard for new dialog and discussion, not to close them down.

KNOWLEDGE GENERALIZATION ONE

Cybercounseling is an idea whose time has come, but we as counselors are not yet ready to say with conviction what it really is or how it should be employed. We need continued interest and enthusiasm for its use, but for now, use should be experimental!

There are many gaps in our knowledge of cybercounseling, yet it is being written about with an authority and assurance that hardly seem justified by the available research. It is one thing to say that cybercounseling is a fact of the contemporary counseling scene (it is being used, and it does have its enthusiastic proponents); but it is quite another matter to say that cybercounseling has shown itself to be a viable counseling entity based upon appropriate research. There are promising initial results that are intriguing and provide good reason for further research, but cybercounseling has yet to earn the mantle of a validated and effective counseling intervention.

Notably, distance learning, which might be thought of as cybercounseling's precursor, has itself recently been the subject of numerous discussions questioning the claims made for its effectiveness. Again, distance learning does have many enthusiastic proponents, but the enthusiasm may have dimmed the critical faculties of those extolling its virtues. From a research standpoint, there is still much to be done and learned before claims can be made as to its efficacy. As to whether it is a valid learning entity with comparable outcomes to face-to-face learning, the jury is still out. It seems that at least as much caution and reservation for the claims for distance learning should be applied to cybercounseling. Though there are important differences between the two (cybercounseling and distance learning), both are essentially learning processes, and many facets of the learning are common to both. It is improbable that one would prove to be highly effective while the other would not.

KNOWLEDGE GENERALIZATION TWO

The Internet will play an increasing role in how persons learn and behave. We need to take greater responsibility for insuring that they hone their Internet learning skills and become sharp learners, not dull ones.

We must acknowledge in designing and using the basic cybertool for counseling, the Internet, that it is essentially an end user's medium where what is learned when and how is determined by the learner and not by the instructor/counselor.

The Internet is the Wild West of learning where the individual may roam at will. There is much to be gained and learned, and it beckons with a glittering array of information resources and opportunities unthinkable even a few years ago. But the end user learning culture can be harsh like the West itself. The unwary can be seduced and misled by distortion, misinformation, conflicting claims, and outright fraud. The naïve learner can pay a heavy price for the fool's gold of enticing learning opportunities, "guaranteed" outcomes, and quick fixes for whatever ails her or him.

In some quarters, the call of an earlier era for the young and adventuresome to "Go West" has been replaced by a new breed of pulp fiction writers who offer a vision of the Internet as a field of dreams and the place to go to prospect for whatever is needed. Though many starry-eyed learners are disillusioned by the enormity and uncertainty of the Internet landscape, the intermittent reinforcement by those enthralled with their discoveries keeps the dream alive. But the fact remains that for every learning prospector who discovers his or her vein of riches, there is a growing army of dull-eyed, disillusioned prospectors who expected much and gained little.

The belief that the New West of learning and resources is a reality and offers untold benefits should not be squelched. However, the new prospector needs to learn prospecting—and to remember that in the old West it was those who sold the shovels rather than those who *used* them who prospered. To navigate the Internet successfully our clients need to be equipped with the right tools. Information filtering and scanning, informed decision making, critical thinking, and logical inference drawing are just some of the higher level skills that the end user learning culture revolution rewards. Yet these very skills are the ones that repeated national assessments have shown to be low among contemporary students. These skills also seem resistive to improvement without concerted efforts.

It, therefore, seems imperative that as counselors and educators we assume responsibility for preparing the end user for informed and skillful use of an increasingly important learning resource—the Internet. We should not pay less attention to how our clients learn about themselves and their world than we do to how they learn about careers.

The Internet is a fantastic resource for clients to learn about themselves as well as the world in which they must function. It certainly behooves us, through individual and group counseling both off-line and on-line, to sharpen the skills of our clients in using the most ubiquitous of all learning resources.

KNOWLEDGE GENERALIZATION THREE

The augmentation of traditional counseling with different cybercounseling features will benefit the efficacy of present day counseling and contribute to increasing the experience and research base of knowledge regarding the efficacy of cybercounseling and its different features.

There is a propensity in writing and thinking about cybercounseling to view it as an either/or proposition with no in-between position. (You are a cybercounselor and use it, or you are not a cybercounselor and do not use it.) Nevertheless, there appears to be an attractive middle ground where counselors use cybercounseling and/or some of its components as an augmentation of traditional counseling.

The augmentation approach seems attractive for several reasons. First, a counselor need not make an either/or commitment but can ease into it (or out of it) by experimentation with different facets of cybercounseling. Using the Internet for test giving and interpretation (Sampson), for maintaining a previously established face-to-face relationship with a client, and for conducting counselor-moderated group sessions with clients with similar types of problems are just some of the augmentations that even Internet-dubious counselors could experiment with. Use of augmentation could also result in both more intensive and extensive experimentation, which is exactly what is needed for greater validation of the methodology.

KNOWLEDGE GENERALIZATION FOUR

Insuring that all clients are skilled in information searching is the greatest gift of all. It is a skill that can be acquired irrespective of age, gender, race, geography, or finances. Counselors should make it a critical priority in their counseling.

Contemporary nonfiction and professional literature is replete with references to the magnitude and importance of the information revolution. Notably, however, there is a scarcity of discussion as to what a person needs to do to become "information smart" or as to how one should acquire and use information in this information age.

The old adage that "he who has the gold rules" could well be updated to read "searching well results in living well." The last decade has probably generated more information than any previous generation in the history of the world. Being able to access and use that information is critical to how well a person copes in contemporary society—personally and professionally. "Knowledge is power," another old adage, is truer now than ever before. Human resources development researchers are now saying that knowing how to learn and how to acquire information is a more important characteristic of job seekers than experience, because experience is retrospective, that is, it looks backward at what a person has done. Skill in accessing information is prospective, that is, learning what will be.

Whatever the truth of these generalizations, it is indubitably true that persons who cannot use the new electronic tools of the Millennium are left behind. The digital divide does operate for many reasons to separate people who can cope in cyberspace from those who cannot. Clearly counselors who wish to empower their clients cannot find a more potent skill for empowerment than competence to search, retrieve, evaluate, and apply information from disparate sources—on-line and off-line. It involves using a computer effectively, but it is much more than that. It is concerned with knowing where to go to find different types of information and, more importantly, with knowing how to evaluate the information critically, separating the substantive from the superficial. It requires that a person be able to focus on how to use the information that he or she has carefully distilled from the myriad sources available, and how to convert information into knowledge and knowledge into personal action strategies. Counselors can be a big help in all of this!

Many counselors estimate that only a quarter or so of their peers regularly and skillfully use computers for themselves. Even fewer use them in working with clients at other than rudimentary data processing levels. If counselors were able to impart to counselees the means to become information smart, counselors could give to counselees the greatest gift of all that Whitney Houston sings about—self-esteem. But, actually, they would not be giving them self-esteem; they would be teaching them the means by which to attain self-esteem.

KNOWLEDGE GENERALIZATION FIVE

Basic to this generalization is the need for counseling to acquire an elan for moving out of the box, pushing the envelope, and putting our money and our future where it counts—outcomes. We should be known for what we bring about and not what we are called, the processes we use, or the standards we abide by. Controversial? Probably so! Bad? Probably not!

The major difference between perception and reality is that reality changes. The world changes, but we continue to see it as it was. A major challenge to us all is to stop using traditional thinking to deal with nontraditional events and resources.

Wayne Lanning is deeply concerned that we not try to fit such nontraditional developments as cybercounseling into a traditional mold. Cybercounseling should not be judged by traditional criteria of what counseling is. Rather it should be viewed and judged by what it contributes to a cognitive learning process and behavioral change. If it works, fix the title, not the idea. If we need to call cybercounseling something other than counseling because it does not fit the criteria of a face-to-face relationship, then change the title. The actual title is not important, but the process, the intervention, is. Let us do what contributes to the desired outcome and the title be damned!

KNOWLEDGE GENERALIZATION SIX

Cybercounseling and cyberlearning go together and are mutually reinforcing. They are a seamless process—one that appropriately expands the counseling field. In practice, it means a broader playing field with more opportunities for the counselor to score.

Cybercounseling and cyberlearning are highly interrelated. Many generations of Americans have enjoyed humming or singing to themselves the popular refrain of *Love and Marriage*, particularly the part about ". . . go together like a horse and carriage. You can't have one without the other." This maxim definitely applies to cybercounseling and cyberlearning. John Bloom, in the early phases of designing and titling this book, suggested that both cybercounseling and distance learning must be included. During labors over the contents, his suggestion proved to be highly prophetic. One could not be had without the other!

Particularly in moving toward giving more attention to counselor education and to broadening the perspective of cybercounseling, it became clear how important it was to cover both. The *cyber* in cybercounseling reflects the fact that we live in a life space without walls; and breaking out of the walls of the counselor's office to reach clients and students wherever they might be is our goal. Depending upon your learning style, you are either reading this summing up in a traditional manner, at the end, or non-traditionally, as the first chapter you read. In either case, but especially for those who have read the full text, it is abundantly clear that the articles and discussions have, in their focus, moved out of the counselor's office and into cyberspace. Clearly this is what was needed—and wanted. Also wanted was to coin a new word—*cyberlearning*—so as to make the point that this publication is not talking about just any kind of learning, but a learning that is relevant to learning and behaving in a cyberage.

KNOWLEDGE GENERALIZATION SEVEN

Even a minimal listing of the present and potential benefits of cybercounseling suggests that it is much more than a passing fad.

Even a cursory accounting of present and potential future benefits indicates that cybercounseling and cyberlearning have roots that will help them weather future challenges. Among the foreseeable benefits are

- the unification of people from around the world (both caregivers and care recipients) who, as a result of their cyberinteractions develop a greater appreciation of similarities and differences;
- a demystification of the counseling process so that more people can see the benefits and seek counseling assistance;
- judicious use of technology at a time when the relevance and worth of a helping service is judged by the extent to which and how well it uses technology; and
- increasing interaction with and learning from related professions as regards the effective use of both technology and the characteristics of "impactful" helping interventions. Clearly counselors are both sharing their insights and learning from the insights of therapists and other helpers.

KNOWLEDGE GENERALIZATION EIGHT

The existing support structures for cybercounseling suggest that the actual form it will take is uncertain, but indubitably, it is a delivery system for counseling that will very likely be with us in the future.

Overall, there is good reason to believe that cybercounseling will continue to expand in use with increasing support from research, professional caregiver participation, public support, and its increasing relevance in a technological era. But perhaps most of all, optimism regarding its future development and position within the helping professions relates to cybercounseling's capacity to reach more people in need with viable sources of assistance at comparably lower cost than any other discernible helping service presently available or even remotely on the horizon.

An eloquent perspective on the development of cybercounseling is provided by John Bloom:

This volume is a testament to the ability of the behavioral health professionals to rise up and be proactive in the face of evolving technologies. Rather than be victimized by nay-saying professionals or sensationalizing media representatives, the behavioral health (and the medical) professions have very rapidly and very wisely developed standards and codes to guide the evolution of this phenomenon. In less than 5 years licensure boards, membership organizations, and certification bodies have responded to the unknown and provided novice and professional alike the information necessary to proceed down the cyber road with appropriate caution.

OVERARCHING KNOWLEDGE GENERALIZATION

We should be fully committed to, but only half sure of, cyber-counseling.

Without commitment to it, we will not undertake the rigorous further development it needs. Being half sure will help us to reserve judgment until we have more information on which to make our judgment.

As visionaries, we should be optimistic and excited; and as behavioral scientists, we need to undertake continuing exploration and examination.

PART VII

Web Site Resources

27

Introducing the
Cybercounseling and
Cyberlearning Web Site
(cybercounsel.uncg.edu)

GARRY R. WALZ AND JOHN W. BLOOM

O ur vision from the start of this endeavor to develop *Cyber-counseling and Cyberlearning: Strategies and Resources for the Millennium* has been to create two distinct products: one a hard copy publication to include the most up-to-date writings about current practices in cybercounseling and cybereducation; the other a more dynamic and fluid publication with a home on the World Wide Web. The second product grew from our certain knowledge that we would be faced with a constant flow of new knowledge on a daily basis, and that fitting all that is happening in the cyberworld into one hard copy publication was as likely as controlling the explosion of knowledge on the World Wide Web.

What follows is a table of contents for the web product. It provides a glimpse of the many and varied cybercontributions already available. By the time this hard copy publication has reached readers early in the new millennium, we anticipate that additional material will have been added to the web product and that the table of contents will have expanded.

HOW TO VISIT THE SITE

To visit the *Cybercounseling and Cyberlearning* web site use the URL, cybercounsel.uncg.edu. It will take you to the resources that are briefly described in the table of contents, which follows. Have a rewarding visit!

CYBERCOUNSELING AND CYBERLEARNING WEB SITE
TABLE OF CONTENTS

WEB SITE CHAPTER 1: CYBERSUPERVISION: CLOSE
ENCOUNTERS IN THE NEW MILLENNIUM,
BY DIANE COURSOL AND JACQUELINE LEWIS

This chapter introduces the concept of cybersupervision that integrates innovative desktop video conferencing technology to revolutionize the counseling supervision process. Cybersupervision allows faculty supervisors to "cybercommute" over the information highway to provide quality supervision with their student counselors at geographically distant sites in real time.

WEB SITE CHAPTER 2: THEORETICAL TENETS OF
CYBERSUPERVISION: IMPLICATIONS AND OUTCOMES,
BY B. SCOTT CHRISTIE

This chapter addresses the nature of supervisees' experiences in a distance clinical supervision environment. The on-line, Internet-based supervision course was utilized by four students in a master's level internship course in counseling at Oregon State University. One finding suggests that the attitudes, prior experiences, and social expectations influenced participant experiences and participants' interest in technology. Other findings and their implications are presented.

WEB SITE CHAPTER 3: FROM A BUG IN THE EAR TO
A BYTE IN THE EYE, BY H. LORI SCHNIEDERS AND A. COLIN RALPH

Counselor educators increasingly face supervising intern counselors in diverse settings ranging from on-campus sites to sites cross-county and sites across the country. Technological advances have created a multitude of opportunities and challenges for counselor supervisors, and this chapter explores distance supervision using WebCam. Types of hardware and software necessary as well as the Murphy's Law aspects of the project are described along with legal and ethical implications.

WEB SITE CHAPTER 4: DEVELOPMENT OF WEB-BASED
COUNSELOR EDUCATION, BY ROBERT SLENCAK

This is a basic introduction to web-based authorware. The growth of the Internet and the advent of web-based instruction led to the development of software packages that aid instructors in converting traditional courses to web-based courses that improve interactivity among course participants. Characteristics of a web-based course-authoring package and examples are provided.

WEB SITE CHAPTER 5: INTERNET COUNSELING
OVER THE INTERNET: BENEFITS AND CHALLENGES IN
THE USE OF NEW TECHNOLOGIES, BY R. J. SUSSMAN

This is a discussion of the new Internet technologies such as cable modems, DSL lines, satellite communication, and software/hardware improvements that await us in the new millennium, and an exploration of implications for the provision of counseling over the Internet.

WEB SITE CHAPTER 6: A CAREER EDUCATIONAL
WEB SITE: CYBERSPATIAL SNAPSHOT, BY MARC VERHOEVE

As cybercounselors and educators move into the next millennium, it becomes apparent that there is a need for career and educational web sites that can be utilized as virtual professional tool kits as well as client and student resources sites. Verhoeve demonstrates the street-level power of such a career educational web site and includes a PowerPoint presentation graphically showing the site's usefulness.

WEB SITE CHAPTER 7: CAREER CYBERCOUNSELING:
RIPPLES ON THE GLOBAL POND, BY MARC VERHOEVE

The author describes several ripples on the pond, including his work as author of a web-based column entitled Cybercounsellor in his role as information technology liaison for the Ontario School Counselors Association. Also presented is his work as a member of the design team for the Career Development Practitioner Program sponsored by Conestoga Community College, which has produced 10 web-based courses that are available through WebCT, a web-course server program.

WEB SITE CHAPTER 8: ELECTRONIC COUNSELING
PORTFOLIOS: SIMPLE AND EFFECTIVE, BY THOMAS J. KELLER

The development of individual portfolios by teacher education graduates to summarize and demonstrate their knowledge, their experiences, and their dispositions is not a new idea, but in the counselor education program at Butler University in Indianapolis, Indiana, applying this concept to counselor education graduates is! Taking this concept to the next level, developing electronic portfolios for the faculty tenure and review process, is also discussed.

WEB SITE CHAPTER 9: TECHNOLOGY COMPETENCE IN
COUNSELOR EDUCATION: RESULTS OF A NATIONAL SURVEY,
BY JANE MYERS AND DONNA GIBSON

The Association for Counselor Education and Supervision (ACES) has developed and endorsed 12 technology competencies for counselor educators and counseling students. A survey was developed and disseminated through the ACES Spectrum and provided in an on-line web form to determine results of self-assessments of competence in these 12 areas. Implications for counselor education and research are presented.

WEB SITE CHAPTER 10: MENTORING WITHOUT WALLS:
USING CYBERSPACE TO ENHANCE STUDENT-FACULTY GUIDANCE
BY JUANITA LYNN HART

Graduate students can benefit from the mentoring relationship when mentors support the personal and professional development and growth of their mentees. Cyberdimensions of mentoring are explored.

Check the ERIC/CASS Cybercounseling web site at cybercounsel. uncg.edu for the most recent updates. For information on submitting new resources contact the cybercounseling web master at (800) 414-9769 or (336) 334-4114.

Appendixes

The following appendixes are included here as valuable resources for the counseling profession.

1. American Counseling Association. (1999). *Ethical Standards for Internet On-Line Counseling.*

2. Association for Counselor Education and Supervision. (1999). *Recommended Technical Competencies for Counselor Education Students* [On-line]. Available: http://www.chre.vt.edu/f-s/thohen/competencies.htm.

3. Hartman, K. (1999). *Technology Standards for School Counselors.*

4. Jencius, M. (1999). *Technology Competencies Matrix* [On-line]. Available: http://ccp.colstate.edu/jencius/matrix.htm.

5. National Board for Certified Counselors. (1998). *Standards for the Ethical Practice of Web Counseling* [On-line]. Available: http://www.nbcc.org/ethics/wcstandards.htm.

6. National Career Development Association. (1997). *NCDA Guidelines for the Use of the Internet for Provision of Career Information and Planning Services* [On-line]. Available: http://ncda.org/polweb.html.

Appendix 1

Ethical Standards for Internet On-Line Counseling of the American Counseling Association

(Adopted October 1999)

These guidelines establish appropriate standards for the use of electronic communications over the Internet to provide on-line counseling services, and should be used only in conjunction with the latest ACA *Code of Ethics and Standards of Practice.*

CONFIDENTIALITY

A. PRIVACY INFORMATION

Professional counselors ensure that clients are provided sufficient information to adequately address and explain the limitations of (i) computer technology in the counseling process in general and (ii) the difficulties of ensuring complete client confidenitality of information transmitted through electronic communications over the Internet through on-line counseling. (See A.12.a., B.1.a., B.1.g.)

1. Secured Sites

To mitigate the risk of potential breaches of confidentiality, professional counselors provide one-on-one on-line counseling only through "secure" web sites or e-mail communications applications which use appropriate encryption technology designed to protect the transmission of confidential information from access by unauthorized third parties.

2. Nonsecured Sites

To mitigate the risk of potential breaches of confidentiality, professional counselors provide only general information from "nonsecure" web sites or e-mail communications applications.

3. General Information

Professional counselors may provide general information from either "secure" or "nonsecure" web sites, or through e-mail communications. General information includes non-client-specific, topical information on matters of general interest to the professional counselor's clients as a whole, third-party resource and referral information, addresses and phone numbers, and the like. Additionally, professional counselors using either secure or nonsecure web sites may provide "hot links" to third-party web sites such as licensure boards, certification bodies, and other resource information providers. Professional counselors investigate and continually update the content, accuracy, and appropriateness for the client of material contained in any hot links to third-party web sites.

4. Limits of Confidentiality

Professional counselors inform clients of the limitations of confidentiality and identify foreseeable situations in which confidentiality must be breached in light of the law in both the state in which the client is located and the state in which the professional counselor is licensed.

B. INFORMATIONAL NOTICES

1. Security of Professional Counselor's Site

Professional counselors provide a readily visible notice that (i) information transmitted over a web site or e-mail server may not be secure; (ii) whether or not the professional counselor's site is secure; (iii) whether the information transmitted between the professional counselor and the client during on-line counseling will be encrypted; and (iv) whether the client will need special software to access and transmit confidential information and, if so, whether the professional counselor provides the software as part of the on-line counseling services. The notice should be viewable from all web site and e-mail locations from which the client may send information. (See B.1.g)

2. *Professional Counselor Identification*

Professional counselors provide a readily visible notice advising clients of the identities of all professional counselor(s) who will have access to the information transmitted by the client and, in the event that more than one professional counselor has access to the web site or e-mail system, the manner, if any, in which the client may direct information to a particular professional counselor. Professional counselors inform clients if any or all of the sessions are supervised. Clients are also informed if and how the supervisor preserves session transcripts. Professional counselors provide background information on all professional counselor(s) and supervisor(s) with access to the on-line communications, including education, licensing and certification, and practice area information. (See B.1.g.)

3. *Client Identification*

Professional counselors identify clients, verify identities of clients, and obtain alternative methods of contacting clients in emergency situations.

C. CLIENT WAIVER

Professional counselors require clients to execute client waiver agreements stating that the client (i) acknowledges the limitations inherent in ensuring client confidentiality of information transmitted through on-line counseling and (ii) agrees to waive the client's privilege of confidentiality with respect to any confidential information transmitted through on-line counseling that may be accessed by any third party without authorization of the client and despite the reasonable efforts of the professional counselor to arrange a secure on-line environment. Professional counselors refer clients to more traditional methods of counseling and do not provide on-line counseling services if the client is unable or unwilling to consent to the client waiver. (See B.1.b.)

d. Records of Electronic Communications

Professional counselors maintain appropriate procedures for ensuring the safety and confidentiality of client information acquired through electronic communications, including but not limited to encryption software, proprietary on-site file servers with fire walls; saving on-line or e-mail communications to the hard drive or file server computer systems; creating regular tape or diskette back-up copies; creating hard copies of all electronic communications; and the like. Clients are informed about the length of time for, and method of, preserving session transcripts. Professional counselors warn clients of the possibility or frequency of technology failures and time delays in transmitting and receiving information. (See B.4.a., B.4.b.)

e. Electronic Transfer of Client Information

Professional counselors electronically transfer client confidential information to authorized third-party recipients only when (i) both the professional counselor and the authorized recipient have "secure" transfer and acceptance communication capabilities, (ii) the recipient is able to effectively protect the confidentiality of the client confidential information to be transferred, and (iii) the informed written consent of the client, acknowledging the limits of confidentiality, has been obtained. (See B.4 e, B.6.a, B.6.b.)

ESTABLISHING THE ON-LINE COUNSELNG RELATIONSHIP

a. The Appropriateness of On-Line Counseling

Professional counselors develop an appropriate intake procedure for potential clients to determine whether on-line counseling is appropriate for the needs of the client. Professional counselors warn potential clients that on-line counseling services may not be appropriate in certain situations and, to the extent possible, inform the client of specific limitations, potential risks, and/or potential benefits relevant to the client's anticipated use of on-line counseling services. Professional counselors ensure that clients are intellectually, emotionally, and physically capable of using the on-line counseling services, and of understanding the potential risks and/or limitations of such services. (See A 3.a, A 3.b)

B. COUNSELING PLANS

Professional counselors develop individual on-line counseling plans that are consistent with both the client's individual circumstances and the limitations of on-line counseling. Professional counselors shall specifically take into account the limitations, if any, on the use of any or all of the following in on-line counseling: initial client appraisal, diagnosis, and assessment methods employed by the professional counselor. Professional counselors who determine that on-line counseling is inappropriate for the client should avoid entering into or immediately terminate the on-line counseling relationship and encourage the client to continue the counseling relationship through an appropriate alternative method of counseling. (See A.11.b, A.11.c)

C. CONTINUING COVERAGE

Professional counselors provide clients with a schedule of times during which the on-line counseling services will be available, including reasonable anticipated response times, and provide clients with an alternate means of contacting the professional counselor at other times, including in the event of emergencies. Professional counselors obtain from, and provide clients with, alternative means of communication, such as telephone numbers or pager numbers, for backup purposes in the event the on-line counseling service is unavailable for any reason. Professional counselors provide clients with the name of at least one other professional counselor who will be able to respond to the client in the event the professional counselor is unable to do so for any extended period of time. (See A.11.a.)

D. BOUNDARIES OF COMPETENCE

Professional counselors provide on-line counseling services only in practice areas within their expertise and do not provide on-line counseling services to clients located in states in which professional counselors are not licensed. (See C.2.a., C.2.b.)

e. Minor or Incompetent Clients

Professional counselors must verify that clients are above the age of minority, are competent to enter into the counseling relationship with a professional counselor, and are able to give informed consent. In the event clients are minor children, incompetent, or incapable of giving informed consent, professional counselors must obtain the written consent of the legal guardian or other authorized legal representative of the client prior to commencing on-line counseling services to the client.

LEGAL CONSIDERATIONS

Professional counselors confirm that their liability insurance provides coverage for on-line counseling services, and that the provision of such services is not prohibited by or otherwise violate any applicable (i) state or local statutes, rules, regulations, or ordinances; (i) codes of professional membership organizations and certifying boards; and/or (iii) codes of state licensing boards.

Professional counselors seek appropriate legal and technical assistance in the development and implementation of their on-line counseling services.

Appendix 2

Technical Competencies for Counselor Education Students: Recommended Guidelines for Program Development

ACES Technology Interest Network
(Endorsed by ACES Executive Council, April 1999)

At the completion of a counselor education program, students should

1. be able to use productivity software to develop web pages, group presentations, letters, and reports;
2. be able to use such audiovisual equipment as video recorders, audio recorders, projection equipment, video conferencing equipment, and playback units;
3. be able to use computerized statistical packages;
4. be able to use computerized testing, diagnostic, and career decision-making programs with clients;
5. be able to use e-mail;
6. be able to help clients search for various types of counseling-related information via the Internet, including information about careers, employment opportunities, educational and

training opportunities, financial assistance/scholarships, treatment procedures, and social and personal information;

7. be able to subscribe, participate in, and sign off counseling-related listservs;
8. be able to access and use counseling-related CD-ROM databases;
9. be knowledgeable of the legal and ethical codes that relate to counseling services via the Internet;
10. be knowledgeable of the strengths and weaknesses of counseling services provided via the Internet;
11. be able to use the Internet for finding and using continuing education opportunities in counseling; and
12. be able to evaluate the quality of Internet information.

(It is recommended that these competencies be reviewed and updated every 3 years.)

ACES Technology Interest Network Members: Thomas H. Hohenshil (Chair), Annette Albrecht, Ed Butler, Robert J. Chapman, Scott Christie, Harry Daniels, David Delmonico, Gary Goodnough, Grafton Eliason, Hildy Getz, Cary Houseman, Keith Iris, Marty Jencius, Wayne Lanning, David Lundberg, Jane Myers, Theresa M. O'Halloran, Patrick B. Romine, Russ Sabella, Holly Stadler, Michael Tyler, and Larry Tyson.

Appendix 3

Technology Standards for School Counselors

KENNETH E. HARTMAN

School counselors must be able to

1. understand and be conversant in the current and emerging state of technology in education;
2. possess basic computer literacy skills, demonstrating technology fluency;
3. comprehend and employ all major Internet components in guidance activities;
4. articulate the implications and opportunities of technology;
5. act as an educated and objective consumer of technology;
6. grasp the ethical and legal implications of technology;
7. construct group and "virtual" guidance activities using technology;
8. use relational databases to monitor and articulate student progress;
9. contribute to the development of their school's/district's technology plan; and
10. identify national, state, and private funding for technology.

Comments or questions can be directed to ken.e.hartman@widener.edu.

Appendix 4

Technology
Competencies Matrix

MARTY JENCIUS

Statements 1.1 through 3.5 are the International Society for Technology in Education (ISTE) *Recommended Foundations in Technology for All Teachers*.
Mastery Levels are noted as follows:

CK = Core Knowledge
IM = Identification Mastery
BM = Basic Mastery
AM = Active Mastery
TM = Teaching Mastery

1.1 Operate a computer system and install software packages

- CK = Receive training in basic concepts.
- IM = Be able to start up and shut down personal computer.
- BM = Know system commands for the specific platform.
- AM = Distinguish between operating systems, perform file management, and install software.
- TM = Teach basic concepts in stand-alone training or course topic area.

1.2 Use terminology related to computer technology appropriately in written and oral communication

- CK = Receive training in basic concepts.
- IM = Survey terminology related to computer technology appropriately in written and oral communication within a course.
- BM = Demonstrate terminology related to computer technology appropriately in written and oral communication within a course.
- AM = Incorporate terminology related to computer technology appropriately in written and oral communication within a course.
- TM = Teach basic concepts in stand-alone training or course topic area.

1.3 Describe and implement basic troubleshooting techniques

- CK = Receive training in basic concepts.
- IM = Be able to change toner cartridges, inkjet packs, etc.
- BM = Be able to complete basic diagnostic procedures such as isolating hardware from software problems and use a utility program to repair and optimize hardware.
- AM = Be able to resolve problems with driver/hardware conflicts.
- TM = Teach basic concepts in stand-alone training or course topic area.

1.4 Use imaging devices; scanners, digital cameras, etc.

- CK = Receive training in basic concepts of digital imaging (scanner and digital camera use) and graphic editing.
- IM = Use a scanner and a digital camera. Use text recognition software to edit and reformat a scanned selection of text.
- BM = Use graphic editor to manipulate images between formats and incorporate them into a document and/or presentation.
- AM = Demonstrate complete use of application incorporating digital cameras, scanned images, text recognition, and graphic editing.
- TM = Teach basic concepts in stand-alone training or course topic area.

1.5 Demonstrate knowledge of computers in business and industry

- CK = Receive training in basic concepts.
- IM = Survey (within discipline) knowledge of computers in business and industry.
- BM = Demonstrate (within discipline) knowledge of computers in business and industry.
- AM = Incorporate into course work knowledge of computers in business and industry.
- TM = Teach basic concepts in stand-alone training or course topic area.

2.1 Use productivity tools for word processing, database management, and spreadsheet applications (statistics packages)

- CK = Receive training in basic concepts of one of the three software packages (word processing, database management, and spreadsheet applications).
- IM = Demonstrate use of one of the following: word processing software, database management software, or spreadsheet software.
- BM = Receive advanced level training in one of the three application areas; or demonstrate ability to integrate two of the three software packages from one application to the other.
- AM = Demonstrate the ability to integrate and convert the three application areas by creating a document or presentation.
- TM = Teach basic concepts in stand-alone training or course topic area.

2.2 Apply productivity tools for creating multimedia presentations

- CK = Receive training in basic concepts.
- IM = Prepare a multimedia presentation for classroom instruction or a conference presentation.
- BM = Integrate the use of editing functions to customize (import) a multimedia presentation for classroom instruction or a

conference presentation. This would include using other software applications embedding in the presentation.

- AM = Demonstrate the ability to convert multimedia presentations into other formats and to integrate them completely into course content. This would include converting the multimedia into HTML and creating a series of modules to covert the course content areas.
- TM = Teach basic concepts in stand-alone training or course topic area.

2.3 **Use computer-based technologies including telecommunications to access information and enhance personal productivity**

- CK = Receive training in basic concepts.
- IM = Use a modem/LAN to connect with the Internet and use a variety of search engines.
- BM = Use a modem/LAN to connect with the Internet and FTP a resource file and use that resource file.
- AM = Use a modem/LAN to connect with the Internet and use chat software within the classroom framework.
- TM = Teach basic concepts in stand-alone training or course topic area.

2.4 **Use computers to support problem solving, data collection, information management, communications, presentations, and decision making**

- CK = Receive training in basic concepts.
- IM = Survey the use of computers to support problem solving, data collection, information management, communications, presentations, and decision making.
- BM = Demonstrate the use of computers to support problem solving, data collection, information management, communications, presentations, and decision making.
- AM = Incorporate into course work the use of computers to support problem solving, data collection, information management, communications, presentations, and decision making.
- TM = Teach basic concepts in stand-alone training or course topic area.

2.5 **Demonstrate awareness of resources for adaptive assistive devices for students with special needs**

- CK = Receive training in basic concepts.
- IM = Survey assistive devices within your discipline and include in course work.
- BM = Demonstrate assistive devices within your discipline within course work.
- AM = Incorporate into the course work the students' use of assistive devices within your discipline.
- TM = Teach basic concepts in stand-alone training or course topic area.

2.6 **Demonstrate knowledge of equity, ethics, legal, and human issues concerning the use of computers and technology**

- CK = Receive training in basic concepts.
- IM = Provide students in course work knowledge of equity, ethics, legal, and human issues concerning the use of computers and technology.
- BM = Demonstrate to students in the context of a course, knowledge of equity, ethics, legal, and human issues concerning the use of computers and technology.
- AM = Incorporate activities for students in the context of a course that engage knowledge of equity, ethics, legal, and human issues concerning the use of computers and technology.
- TM = Teach basic concepts in stand-alone training or course topic area.

2.7 **Identify computer-related technology resources for facilitating lifelong learning and emerging roles of the learner and educator**

- CK = Receive training in basic concepts.
- IM = Survey in coursework the use of computer-related technology resources for facilitating lifelong learning and emerging roles of the learner and educator.
- BM = Demonstrate in coursework the use of computer-related technology resources for facilitating lifelong learning and emerging roles of the learner and educator.

- AM = Incorporate into student learning activities computer-related technology resources for facilitating lifelong learning and emerging roles of the learner and educator.
- TM = Teach basic concepts in stand-alone training or course topic area.

2.8 **Observe demonstrations or uses of broadcast instruction, audio/video conferencing, and other distant learning applications and uses when appropriate**

- CK = Receive training in basic concepts.
- IM = Participate in a class session using video conferencing format.
- BM = Instruct a class session using video conferencing format.
- AM = Set up and instruct a class session using video conferencing format.
- TM = Teach basic concepts in stand-alone training or course topic area.

3.1 **Explore, evaluate, and use computer/technology resources including applications, tools, educational software, and associated documentation**

- CK = Receive training in basic concepts.
- IM = Survey discipline-associated educational software and include in course work.
- BM = Demonstrate discipline-associated software within a course.
- AM = Incorporate student use of discipline-associated software into course work.
- TM = Teach basic concepts in stand-alone training or course topic area.

3.2 **Describe current instructional principles, research, and appropriate assessment practices as related to the use of computers and technology resources in the curriculum**

- CK = Receive training in basic concepts.
- IM = Survey in course work of current instructional principles, research, and appropriate assessment practices as related to the use of computers and technology resources in the curriculum.

- BM = Demonstrate in course work current instructional principles, research, and appropriate assessment practices as related to the use of computers and technology resources in the curriculum.
- AM = Incorporate into course work student activities that integrate current instructional principles, research, and appropriate assessment practices as related to the use of computers and technology resources in the curriculum.
- TM = Teach basic concepts in stand-alone training or course topic area.

3.3 Design, deliver, and assess student learning activities that integrate computers/technology for a variety of student group strategies and for diverse student populations

- CK = Receive training in basic concepts.
- IM = Design student learning activities that integrate computers/technology for a variety of student group strategies and for diverse student populations.
- BM = Deliver student learning activities that integrate computers/technology for a variety of student group strategies and for diverse student populations.
- AM = Assess student learning activities that integrate computers/technology for a variety of student group strategies and for diverse student populations.
- TM = Teach basic concepts in stand-alone training or course topic area.

3.4 Design student learning activities that foster equitable, ethical, and legal use of technology for students

- CK = Receive training in basic concepts.
- IM = Provide guidelines to students in course content which give examples of student learning activities that foster equitable, ethical, and legal use of technology for students.
- BM = Demonstrate in course work student learning activities that foster equitable, ethical, and legal use of technology for students.
- AM = Incorporate in the context of a course student learning activities that foster equitable, ethical, and legal use of technology for students.

- TM = Teach basic concepts in stand-alone training or course topic area.

3.5 Practice responsible, ethical, and legal use of technology, information, and software resources

- CK = Receive training in basic concepts.
- IM = Survey responsible, ethical, and legal use of technology, information, and software resources.
- BM = Demonstrate responsible, ethical, and legal use of technology, information, and software resources.
- AM = Incorporate responsible, ethical, and legal use of technology, information, and software resources.
- TM = Teach basic concepts in stand-alone training or course topic area.

Resources used in the development of this matrix:

- Mastery Levels based on *Intentional Interviewing and Counseling: Facilitating Client Development in a Multicultural Society* (4th Ed.), by A. Ivey and M. B. Ivey, 1999, Pacific Grove, CA: Brooks/Cole.
- ISTE standards based on *ISTE Recommended Foundations in Technology for All Teachers*, International Society for Technology in Education [On-line]. Available: http://www.iste.org/Standards/index.html.
- An on-line version (in Table Format) of the Technology Competencies Matrix can be found at http://ccp.colstate.edu/jencius/tcm.htm.
- Comments or questions can be directed to Jencius_Marty@colstate.edu.

Appendix 5

Standards for the Ethical Practice of Web Counseling of the National Board for Certified Counselors

The relative newness of the use of the Internet for service and product delivery leaves authors of standards at a loss when beginning to create ethical practices on the Internet. This document, like all codes of conduct, will change as information and circumstances not yet foreseen evolve. However, each version of this code of ethics is the current best standard of conduct passed by the NBCC Board of Directors. As with any code, and especially with a code such as this created for an evolving field of work, NBCC and the Center for Credentialing and Education (CCE) welcome comments and ideas for further discussion and inclusion.

Further, the development of these web counseling standards has been guided by the following principles:

- These standards are intended to address practices which are unique to web counseling and web counselors;
- These standards are not to duplicate non-Internet-based standards adopted in other codes of ethics;

- Recognizing that significant new technology emerges continuously, these standards should be reviewed frequently;
- Web counseling ethics cases should be reviewed in light of delivery systems existing at the moment rather than at the time the standards were adopted;
- Web counselors who are not National Certified Counselors may indicate at their web site their adherence to these standards, but may not publish these standards in their entirety without written permission of the National Board for Certified Counselors; and
- The **practice of web counseling** shall be defined as "the practice of professional counseling and information delivery that occurs when client(s) and counselor are in separate or remote locations and utilize electronic means to communicate over the Internet."

In addition to following the NBCC Code of Ethics pertaining to the practice of professional counseling, web counselors shall:

1. Review pertinent legal and ethical codes for possible violations emanating from the practice of web counseling and supervision.

   Liability insurance policies should also be reviewed to determine if the practice of web counseling is a covered activity. Local, state, provincial, and national statutes as well as the codes of professional membership organizations, professional certifying bodies, and state or provincial licensing boards need to be reviewed. Also, as no definitive answers are known to questions pertaining to whether web counseling takes place in the web counselor's location or the web client's location, web counselors should consider carefully local customs regarding age of consent and child abuse reporting.

2. Inform web clients of encryption methods being used to help insure the security of client/counselor/supervisor communications.

   Encryption methods should be used whenever possible. If encryption is not made available to clients, clients must be informed of the potential hazards of unsecured communication on the Internet. Hazards may include authorized or unauthorized monitoring of transmissions and/or records of web counseling sessions.

3. Inform clients if, how, and how long session data are being preserved.

Session data may include web counselor/web client e-mail, test results, audio/video session recordings, session notes, and counselor/supervisor communications. The likelihood of electronic sessions being preserved is greater because of the ease and decreased costs involved in recording. Thus, its potential use in supervision, research, and legal proceedings increases.

4. In situations where it is difficult to verify the identity of web counselor or web client, take steps to address impostor concerns, such as by using code words, numbers, or graphics.

5. When parent/guardian consent is required to provide web counseling to minors, verify the identity of the consenting person.

6. Follow appropriate procedures regarding the release of information for sharing web client information with other electronic sources.

   Because of the relative ease with which e-mail messages can be forwarded to formal and casual referral sources, web counselors must work to insure the confidentiality of the web counseling relationship.

7. Carefully consider the extent of self-disclosure presented to the web client and provide rationale for web counselor's level of disclosure.

   Web counselors may wish to ensure that, minimally, the web client has the same data available about his or her service provider as would be available if the counseling were to take place face-to-face (i.e., possibly ethnicity, gender, etc.). Compelling reasons for limiting disclosure should be presented. Web counselors will remember to protect themselves from unscrupulous users of the Internet by limiting potentially harmful disclosure about self and family.

8. Provide links to web sites of all appropriate certification bodies and licensure boards to facilitate consumer protection.

9. Contact NBCC/CEE or the web client's state or provincial licensing board to obtain the name of at least one counselor-on-call within the web client's geographical region.

   Web counselors who have contacted an individual to determine his or her willingness to serve as a counselor-on-call (either in person, over the phone, or via e-mail) should also ensure that the web cient is provided with local crisis intervention hotline numbers, 911, and similar numbers in the event that the counselor-on-call is unavailable.

10. Discuss with their web clients procedures for contacting the web counselor when he or she is off-line.

   This means explaining exactly how often e-mail messages are to be checked by the web counselor.

11. Mention at their web sites those presenting problems they believe to be inappropriate for web counseling.

   While no conclusive research has been conducted to date, those topics might include sexual abuse as a primary issue, violent relationships, eating disorders, and psychiatric disorders that involve distortions of reality.

12. Explain to clients the possibility of technology failure.

   The web counselor

   — *gives instructions to web clients about calling if problems arise;*

   — *discusses the appropriateness of the client calling collect when the call might be originating from around the world;*

   — *mentions differences in time zones; and*

   — *talks about dealing with response delays in sending and receiving e-mail messages.*

13. Explain to clients how to cope with potential misunderstandings arising from the lack of visual cues from web counselor or web client.

   For example, suggesting the other person simply say, "Because I couldn't see your face or hear your tone of voice in your e-mail message, I'm not sure how to interpret that last message."

Appendix 6

National Career Development Association Guidelines for the Use of the Internet for Provision of Career Information and Planning Services

(Approved by the NCDA Board of Directors, October 1997)

INTRODUCTION

Based on readily available capabilities at the time of this writing, the Internet could be used in four ways for the purpose of providing career counseling and/or career planning services to clients. These are

1. to deliver information about occupations, including their descriptions, employment outlook, skills requirements, estimated salary, etc., through text, still images, graphics, and/or video. In this event, the standards for information development and presentation are the same as those for print materials and audiovisual materials as stated in NCDA's documents on these matters.

2. to provide on-line searches of occupational databases for the purpose of identifying feasible occupational alternatives. In this event, the standards developed by NCDA and the Association of Computer-based Systems for Career Information (ACSCI) apply.

3. to deliver interactive career counseling and career planning services. This use assumes that clients, either as individuals or as part of a group, have intentionally placed themselves in direct communication with a professional career counselor. Standards for use of the Internet for these purposes are addressed in this document.

4. to provide searches through large databases of job openings for the purpose of identifying those that the user may pursue. Guidelines for this application are included in this document.

GUIDELINES FOR USE OF THE INTERNET FOR DELIVERY OF CAREER COUNSELING AND CAREER PLANNING SERVICES

Career planning services are differentiated from *career counseling* services. Career planning services include an active provision of information designed to help a client with a specific need, such as review of a resumé; assistance in networking strategies; identification of occupations based on interests, skills, or prior work experience; support in the job-seeking process; and assessment by means of on-line inventories of interest, abilities, and/or work-related values. Although career counseling may include the provision of the above services, the use of the term implies a deeper level of involvement with the client, based on the establishment of a professional counseling relationship and the potential for dealing with career development concerns well beyond those included in career planning.

Multiple means of on-line provision of career planning or career counseling services currently exist, the most common of which are e-mail, newsgroups, bulletin boards, chat rooms, and web sites offering a wide variety of services. Telephone or audiovisual linkages supported by the Internet exist in their infancy, and will likely grow in potential as the technology improves and the costs decline.

1. Qualifications of Developer or Provider

Web sites and other services designed to assist clients with career planning should be developed with content input from professional career counselors. The service should clearly state the qualifications and credentials of the developers not only in the content area of professional career counseling but also in the development of interactive on-line services.

2. Access and Understanding of Environment

The counselor has an obligation to be aware of free public access points to the Internet within the member's community, so that a lack of financial resources does not create a significant barrier to clients accessing counseling services or information, assessment, or instructional resources over the Internet.

The counselor has an obligation to be as aware as possible of local conditions, cultures, and events that may impact the client.

3. Content of Career Counseling and Planning Services on the Internet

The content of a web site or other service offering career information or planning services should be reviewed for the appropriateness of content offered in this medium. Some kinds of content have been extensively tested for on-line delivery due to the long existence of computer-based career information and guidance systems. This includes searching of databases by relevant search variables; display of occupational information; development of a resumé; assessment of interests, abilities, and work-related values and linkage of these to occupational titles; instruction about occupational classification systems; relationship of school majors to occupational choices; and the completion of forms such as a financial needs assessment questionnaire or a job application.

When a web site offers a service which has not previously been extensively tested (such as computer-based career guidance and information systems), this service should be carefully scrutinized to determine whether it lends itself to the Internet. The web site should clearly state the kinds of client concerns that the counselor judges to be inappropriate for counseling over the Internet, or beyond the skills of the counselor.

4. Appropriateness of Client for
Receipt of Services via the Internet

The counselor has an ethical and professional responsibility to assure that the client who is requesting service can profit from it in this mode. Appropriate screening includes the following:

a. a clear statement by clients of their career planning or career counseling needs; and

b. an analysis by the counselor of whether meeting those needs via Internet exchange is appropriate and of whether this particular client can benefit from counseling services provided in this mode. A judgment about the latter should be made by means of a telephone or videophone teleconference designed to specify the client's expectations, how the client has sought to meet these through other modes, and whether or not the client appears to be able to process information through an Internet medium.

5. Appropriate Support to the Client

The counselor who is providing services to a client via the Internet has ethical responsibility for the following:

a. periodic monitoring of the client's progress via telephone or videophone teleconference;

b. identification by the counselor of a qualified career counselor in the client's geographic area should referral become necessary. If this is not possible, the web counselor, using traditional referral sources to identify an appropriate practitioner, should assist the client in the selection of a counselor; and

c. appropriate discussion with the client about referral to face-to-face service should the counselor determine that little or no progress is being made toward the client's goals.

6. Clarity of Contract With the Client

The counselor should define several items in writing to the client in a document that can be downloaded from the Internet or faxed to the client. This document should include at least the following items:

a. the counselor's credentials in the field;

b. the agreed-upon goals of the career counseling or career planning Internet interchange;

c. the agreed-upon cost of the services and how this will be billed;

d. where and how clients can report any counselor behavior which they consider to be unethical;

e. a statement about the degree of security of the Internet and confidentiality of data transmitted on the Internet and about any special conditions related to the client's personal information (such as potential transmission of client records to a supervisor for quality-control purposes, or the collection of data for research purposes);

f. a statement of the nature of client information electronically stored by the counselor, including the length of time that data will be maintained before being destroyed;

g. a statement about the need for privacy when the client is communicating with the counselor, e.g., that client communication with the counselor is not limited by having others observe or hear interactions between the counselor and client; and

h. if the service includes career, educational, or employment information, the counselor is responsible for making the client aware of the typical circumstances where individuals need counseling support in order to effectively use the information.

7. Inclusion of Linkages to Other Web Sites

If a career information or counseling web site includes links to other web sites, the professional who creates this linkage is responsible for assuring that the services to which his or hers are linked also meet these guidelines.

8. Use of Assessment

If the career planning or career counseling service is to include on-line inventories or tests and their interpretation, the following conditions should apply:

a. The assessments must have been tested in computer delivery mode to assure that their psychometric properties are the same in this mode of delivery as in print form; or the client must be informed that they have not yet been tested in this same mode of delivery.

b. The counselor must abide by the same ethical guidelines as if he or she were administering and interpreting these same inventories or tests in face-to-face mode and/or in print form.

c. Every effort must be exerted to protect the confidentiality of the user's results.

d. If there is any evidence that the client does not understand the results, as evidenced by e-mail or telephone interchanges, the counselor must refer the client to a qualified career counselor in his or her geographic area.

e. The assessments must have been validated for self-help use if no counseling support is provided, or that appropriate counseling intervention is provided before and after completion of the assessment resource if the resource has not been validated for self-help use.

PROFESSIONAL AND ETHICAL GUIDELINES RELATED TO THE USE OF THE INTERNET FOR JOB POSTING AND SEARCHING

1. The posting must represent a valid job opening for which those searching on the Internet have an opportunity to apply.
2. Job postings must be removed from the Internet database within 48 hours of the time that the announced position is filled.
3. Names, addresses, resumés, and other information that may be gained about individuals should not be used for any purposes other than provision of further information about job openings.

UNACCEPTABLE COUNSELOR BEHAVIORS ON THE INTERNET

1. Use of a false e-mail identity when interacting with clients and/or other professionals. When acting in a professional capacity on the Internet, a counselor has a duty to identify him- or herself honestly.
2. Accepting a client who will not identify him- or herself and be willing to arrange for phone conversation as well as on-line interchange.

3. "Sharking" or monitoring chat rooms and bulletin board services, and offering career planning and related services when no request has been made for services. This includes sending out mass unsolicited e-mails. Counselors may advertise their services but must do so observing proper "netiquette" and standards of professional conduct.

NEED FOR RESEARCH AND REVIEW

Since the use of the Internet is new for the delivery of career planning and counseling services, it is mandatory that the career counseling profession gain experience with this medium and evaluate its effectiveness through targeted research. The capabilities of Internet delivery of services will expand rapidly as the use of sound and video becomes more feasible. These early guidelines will need constant monitoring and revision as research data become available and additional capabilities become cost-feasible.

Guidelines developed by members of the NCDA Ethics Committee: Richard Pyle (Chair), David Caulum, Don Doerr, Pat Howland, Spencer Niles, Ray Palmer, David Reile, James Sampson, and Don Schutt.

Index

A

ACA eNews, 186
accessibility
    assessment technology and, 238, 241
    in electronic publishing, 191
accreditation and licensure for
    distance learning, 364–66
addiction, computer, 23–24
Adler, Mortimer, 380, 396
adult learning. See cyberspace education and lifelong learning for professionals
Adult Learning Service Online, PBS's, 286
African Americans
    Internet access of, 75, 85
    time-dependent resource on, 76
All Tech Investment Group, 17
America Online
    loss and grief support groups for teens, 107
    response to Columbine High School shootings, 105
    training of on-line hosts, 104
American Association for Counseling and Development, 244
American Association of Marriage and Family Therapy (AAMFT), 295
American Association of State Counseling Boards (AASCB), 325
American Counseling Association (ACA), 195
    ACA eNews, 186

Code of Ethics and Standards of Practice, 90
    Counseling Today, 186
    CTOnline, 186
    cybercounseling issues, 74, 334
    cybereducation efforts, 284
    development of standards for quality web sites, 46
    digital libraries, 155
    Ethical Standards for Internet On-Line Counseling, 421, 423–28
    expansion of ethical guidelines, 45–46
    Journal of Counseling and Development, 130
    site links for, 151
    standards for on-line instruction, 305
    web site, 131, 249
    web-related presentations at ACA annual conferences, 138
American Educational Research Association, 244, 249
American Federation of Teachers, 144
American homes, percentage with access to the Internet, 39–40, 75, 85
American Nursing Association, 335
American Occupational Therapy Association (AOTA), 299–300
American Psychological Association (APA)
    assessment standards, 244

American Psychological Association (APA)—*continued*
cybereducation efforts, 284
Ethics Committee, 330
Services by Telephone, Teleconferencing, and Internet, 330
web site, 131, 249
American School Counselors Association (ASCA)
assessment standards, 244
digital libraries, 155
site links for, 151
American Speech Language Hearing Association, 249
American Telemedical Association, 331
America's Career Kit, 60
America's CareerInfonet, 60
America's Job Bank, 60, 149
America's Learning Exchange, 60
America's Talent Bank, 60
Andre, C., 395, 401
anonymity breaches in on-line support groups for loss, 107–8
Artelt, T., 304
artificial intelligence (AI) systems
artificial intelligence computer programs, 9, 12
expert systems technology in, 255, 261–62
Asians/Pacific Islanders, Internet access of, 75
assessment, accreditation standards and inputs vs. outcomes, 366–69
assessment instruments, availability in computer-administered/scored formats, 7
assessment, technology-delivered, 237–38, 250–51
access to professionals, 248–49
credibility of the developers, 247
following assessment standards and practices, 243–44
staying current, keeping updates, 249–50
test administration, 245–46
test interpretation, 247–48

test quality, 246–47
understanding the advantages of assessment via computer and the Internet, 238–41
understanding the pitfalls of assessment via computer and the Internet, 241–43
using best practices for technology-delivered tests and assessments, 245–29
Associated Press, 294
Association for Adult Development and Aging (AADA), 186
Association for Assessment in Counseling, 244, 249
Association for College and Research Libraries (ACRL), 279–80
Association of Computer-Based Systems for Career Information (ACSCI), 118
Association for Counselor Education and Supervision (ACES)
cybercounseling on-line course guidelines, 74
digital libraries, 155
Guidelines for On-Line Instruction in Counselor Education, 62–63
Recommended Technical Competencies for Counselor Education Students, 73, 421, 429–30
standards for distance learning, 57
technical competencies, 279, 315
Technology Interest Network, 73, 74, 279, 305
Association Management, 299
asynchronous communication, 144
audio
audio/video counselor-client interactions, 45
face-to-face, video and audio sessions, 203–18
using audio in web-based courses, 132
authoring process, 192
suggestions for authors writing in cyberspace, 197–98
Ayersman, D., 190

B

Baby Boomers, 33
Bacon, Thomas J., 292
Baltimore, M. L., 172
bandwidth forms of on-line counseling,
    220
Barnes, John, 286
Barton, Mark, 17
BASIC (programming language), 4
Bateson, Gregory, 256
Baylen, D., 304
Behara, R. S., 304
Behavior-On-Line (BOL), 282, 295
behavior therapy, use of computers in,
    7
BenShea, Noah, 379
Berge, Z. L., 191
Besser, Howard, 23–24
Beyond Chalk: Teaching with Technology
    (Morse and Layne), 76
biofeedback, use of computers in, 7
Bissell, J., 285
BlackBoard, Inc., 145
Blackboard.com, 57–58, 145
Bloom, John, 412–13
Boling, N. C., 304
books on web-based course design, 140
Boolean logic, web searches and, 139,
    168
Boomer Echoes, 33
Boos v. Barry, 353
Breivik, P., 277, 280–81
Brief Family Therapy Center (BFTC),
    257–58
brief therapy approach, 256–59, 271
Brief Therapy Center (BTC), 256–57
BRIEFER I/BRIEFER II (computer-
    based expert systems), 260
*British Journal of Counseling and
    Guidance*, 222, 228
British Open University, 152, 155, 157
brokerage agencies, 364
Brosnan, M., 75
*Building Learning Communities in
    Cyberspace: Effective Strategies
    for the On-Line Classroom*
    (Palloff and Pratt), 140

Burdette, A. P., 76
Bureau of Labor Statistics, 34, 59
business and industry, continuing pro-
    fessional education by, 282–83
Butler, H. J., 191, 196, 197

C

California State University Northridge,
    Counseling Discussion Groups,
    282
California's Psychology Licensing Law,
    354
Cameron, C., 75
career counseling in middle and
    secondary schools, interactive,
    115, 124–25
    adolescent career exploration,
        116–17
    career planning for the 21st century,
        116–18
    current resources in use, 117–18
    implementing Career Explorer,
        122–24
    Internet access through Career
        Explorer, 118–20
    school counselor as coordinator/
        consultant, 121–22
    student access, 120
    teacher involvement, 120–21
    web sites for career information, 127
career development
    NOICC Exploring Career Develop-
        ment Interactive CD-ROM, 76
    web sites for, 59–61, 127
    See also electronic delivery of career
        development university courses
career development laboratory, virtual,
    60–61
Career Explorer program, 115, 118, 121
    implementing, 122–24
    Internet access through, 118–20
Career Key, 60
career portfolio, 173–74
Carlson, Burt, 165
Carney, J. A., 172
carpel tunnel syndrome, 23
Carr, J., 116

Casey, J., 277, 278
CD-ROMs
  as time-independent/place-
    dependent digital resources, 76
  use in web-based courses, 132
cell phone users, 24
Center for Credentialing and
    Education (CCE), 293, 294
Center for Quality Assurance in Inter-
    national Education (CQAIE),
    29, 30
Chamber of Commerce, U.S., 34
Chamness, B., 98
Chan, F., 392
*Change: Principles of Problem Formula-
    tion and Problem Resolution*
    (Watzlawick, Weakland, and
    Fisch), 257
chat rooms
  Internet chat rooms as time-
    independent/place-dependent
    resources, 77
  using, 79
*Chicago School of Automatic Transmis-
    sion, Inc. v. Accreditation
    Alliance of Career Schools &
    Colleges,* 366
children, loss and grief on-line support
    groups for, 106–7
CHOICES (computer-based career
    information system), 118
Christie, B., 279
Christie, Scott, 418
Chronicle of Higher Education, 373
Chrysler Corporation, 30–31
Clarke, J., 286
Clawson, Thomas, 293, 301
clinical skills portfolio, 173
*Code of Conduct for Medical and
    Health Web Sites,* 331
*Code of Ethics and Standards of
    Practice* (ACA), 90
*Code of Fair Testing Practices in
    Education,* 244, 249
cognitive psychotherapy, use of
    computers in, 7
Colby, K. M., 4
College Board, 144

Collie, Katharine, skills for on-line
    counseling, 219, 220, 221–35
Collins, M. P., 191
Colón, Y., 220
Columbine High School shootings, 105
Columbus State University, Depart-
    ment of Counseling and Edu-
    cational Leadership, 195
Commission on Collegiate Nursing
    Education (CCNE), 367–68
community audit, equal access to
    cybercounseling and
    performing a, 91
competencies
  ISTE competency standards, 74,
    433–40
  *National Career Development Com-
    petencies for Middle/Junior and
    High Schools* (NOICC), 117,
    119, 122, 123
  *Recommended Technical Competen-
    cies for Counselor Education
    Students* (ACES), 73, 421,
    429–30
  technology, 73–74
*Competencies in Assessment and Evalu-
    ation for School Counselors,* 244
competency issues in cybercounseling,
    ethical concerns on, 328–29
computational time, 3
computer addiction, 23–24
computer-aided instruction (CAI), 4,
    5–6
  computer-aided instruction
    programs, 4
  WWW and, 12
computer-assisted guidance systems, 7
computer-assisted instruction, 10
Computer Education Research
    Laboratory (CERL), 5
computer presentations in web-based
    courses, 132
computer-simulation training pro-
    grams, 9
Computer Supported Assessment and
    Treatment Consultation for
    Emotional Crises (CATCEC),
    9–10

"Computers in Counselor Education: Four Years After a Special Issue" (Lambert), 10–11
Computers and Education, 285
Computers in Human Services, 285
Computers in Teaching, 285
Concerned Counseling, 327
confidentiality and anonymity
  anonymity breaches in on-line support groups for loss, 107–8
  ethical concerns on confidentiality in cybercounseling, 327–28
  privacy/confidentiality in assessment technology, 242
Connolly, John S., 341
Consortium for Equity in Standards and Testing, 249
continuing professional education, 291–93
  the web as a new source for, 293
  what does the future hold?, 297–300
  what is out there?, 294–97
  See also cyberspace education and lifelong learning for professionals
Control Data Corporation, 5
copyright of electronically published material, 190
Council for the Accreditation of Counseling and Related Education Programs (CACREP)
  accreditation standards, 370–71
  cybercounseling standards, 334
  cybereducation eforts, 284
  distance education, 154, 279, 332
  outcomes assessment standards, 367
  performance assessment portfolios, 174
  standards for on-line instruction, 305
Council for Exceptional Children, 249
Council for Higher Education Administration (CHEA), 365
counseling
  defined, 19
  See also skills for on-line counseling
Counseling Graduates (COUNSGRADs), 11, 185

counseling intervention and service management, microcomputers in, 6–8
counseling therapy computer programs, early, 4–5
Counseling Today, 186
Counseling Web, 282
counselor education
  microcomputers and supervision applications in, 8–11
  See also electronic portfolios in counselor education; on-line instruction in counselor education; technology and the continuing education of professional counselors
counselor education curriculum
  challenge of changing, 46–47
  funding for revision of, 48
counselor education programs, preservice, 143
Counselor Education and Supervision, 8, 10
counselor educator, odyssey of a technologically challenged, 51–64
Counselor Educator and Supervision Network (CESNET), 11, 139, 185
counselor training programs
  in-service training of counselors, 47–48
  offering of specialty in technology-enhanced counseling, 47
CounselorLink, 282
CourseInfo system, 145
COURSEWRITER (programming langauage), 5
Coursol, Diane, 418
Cramer, S. H., 116, 117, 121
credentialing, 292
credibility in electronic publishing, 191
Cross, W. E., 68
Crowder, Norman, 4
Crutchfield, L., 172
CTOnline, 186
Cubranic, Davor, 232

cultural competence, developing,
67–68, 77, 81–82
converging paradigms, 73–77
premises of the stylistic model,
70–73
structure for stylistic counseling,
68–70
using chat rooms, 79
using e-mail, 77–78
using listservs, 77–78
using newsgroups, 78
using video conferencing, 80–81
using web sites, 80
*Current Controversies in Social Work
Ethics* (NASW), 389,
398–400
Cybercounseling and Cyberlearning
web site, 417
how to visit the site, 417
table of contents, 418–20
cybercounseling and empowerment,
85–86, 92
cybercounseling and the promise of
human empowerment, 87–90
guidelines for cybercounseling and
ensuring equal access, 90–92
tradition of mental health professionals and issues of power and
access, 86–87
cybercounseling and regulations,
321–22, 335–36
central ethical issues in
cybercounseling, 325–31
malpractice insurance, 335
professional associations, 334–35
state regulation of cybercounseling,
331–33
state web sites, 334
strategies for the future, 333–35
supplemental counseling, 335
telemedicine, 322–25
underserved populations, 333–34
cybercounselors vs. cyberpolice,
339–43, 357–58
first potential defense: client agreements and legal obligations,
343–46
recommendations, 356–57

second potential defense: extradition
of cybercounselors, 347–51
third potential defense: First
Amendment protection of
cybercounseling, 351–56
CyberEd, 297
cyberjournals and paper-based
journals, 187–88
cybernetics movement, 255, 256, 259
Cybersell, Inc. v. Cybersell, Inc., 372
cybershorthand and symbolic expression of emotions, 100
cyberspace education and lifelong
learning for professionals,
275–76, 287
adapting existing on-line and
distance learning resources,
284–86
focusing on the individual learner,
286
high-tech content and delivery,
278–80
low-tech content and delivery, 277
major concepts, 276–77
mid-tech content and delivery,
277–78
recommended action strategies,
280–87
the technological continuum, 277–80
utilization of available resources,
280–84
utilizing the technology continuum,
286–87

D

Dahir, C. A., 244
Daimler Benz, 30–31
day trading, 17
de Shazer, Steve, 257–58, 259, 260,
261
death and grieving. *See* loss and grief
through on-line support groups
decision-making paradigms, ethics
and, 394–96
questions for decision making, 401
Defense Activity for Nontraditional
Education Support (DANTES),
361

Department of Commerce, U.S., 75, 85, 241

Department of Education, U.S., 163, 284, 366–67

Department of Health and Human Services, U.S., 284

Department of Labor, U.S., 59, 115, 244

descriptive immediacy, 226–27

Diagnostic and Statistical Manual of Mental Disorders, 8

Dictionary of Occupational Titles (DOT), 117, 119

digital content, stylistic dimensions of, 72

Digital Diploma Mills: The Automation of Higher Education (Noble), 153

digital divide, 156, 157

Digital Equipment Corporation, 4

digital libraries, 155–56

Dimensions in Mental Health Practice, 294

disabilities, persons with, assessment technology and, 240

disclaimers on cybercounseling, 345, 346

disclosure laws, counselor registration and, 356

DISCOVER II (computer-based career information system), 118

distance education, 54

    distance education learning resources, 282–83, 284–86, 297

    and face-to-face instruction, 144

    landmark documents on, 144

    state regulation of cybercounseling, 332

    studies on, 153–58

    web-based, 4

Distance Education and Training Council (DETC), 361

distance learning, 54, 61

    standards for, 57

    using the web for, 129–41

distance learning for accreditation and licensure, implications of, 361–62, 369–74, 375–76

    accreditation, 369–71

    accreditation and licensure, 364–66

    inputs vs. outcomes assessments, 366–69

    licensure and regulation, 371–74

    recommendations, 374–75

    what is distance learning?, 362–64

Distance Learning and the Demise of the Professoriate (Van Nuys), 22

Distance Learning Network (DLN), 293, 296

Distance Learning Resource Network (DLRN), 363

Ditton, T., 206

Dozier-Henry, O., 76

Dr. Bob's Mental Health Links, 282

dual relationships, ethical concerns in cybercounseling on, 329

Dubovsky, S. L., 330

due process, right to, 349

Duncan, D., 77

Durndell, A., 75

E

e-journals, 186

e-mail

    sequence, 230

    therap-e-mail, 219–35

    using, 20, 24, 53, 77–78

    using e-mail for Career Explorer program, 120

Echterling, L. G., 258

eCollege.com, 145

Economist, The, 382

education

    equal access to cybercounseling and, 91

    See also cyberspace education and lifelong learning for professionals; electronic portfolios in counselor education; technology and the continuing education of professional counselors

Education Commission of the States, 249

electronic delivery of career development university courses, 143–45, 158–59

electronic delivery of career
development university
courses—*continued*
announcements, 146
assignments, 149
communications, 149–50
course documents, 148–49
course information, 146
external links, 151
guidance from two studies, 153–58
sample course folder contents,
147–48
staff information, 146
student tools, 151
understanding the long-term
possibilities, 151–53
understanding the near-term
possibilities, 145–51
electronic journals, 130, 186–98, 285
electronic portfolios in counselor
education, 171–72, 180
applications of, 173–74
concept of the electronic portfolio,
172–73
development and organization of the
electronic portfolio, 174–75
electronic portfolio resources, 182–83
implications for the new
millennium, 180
learning implications of the electronic portfolio, 179–80
model for infusing electronic
portfolios into the curriculum,
176–79
technological requirements, 175–76
ELIZA (counseling therapy program), 4
emoticons, 100, 230–31
emotional bracketing, 225–26
emotions, cybershorthand and symbolic expression of, 100
employee benefits, decreased, technology's limitations and, 22
empowerment. *See* cybercounseling
and empowerment
Encarta Africana (Microsoft), 76
encryption, 180, 327
ENIAC, 3
Epston, D., 259

equal access, guidelines for cybercoun-
seling and ensuring, 90–92
ERIC, 161–62, 294
Clearinghouse on Assessment and
Evaluation, 249
Counseling and Student Services
Clearinghouse, 249
ERIC databases, 60, 161
ERIC Digests, 162
ERIC Thesaurus, 161
literature searches on, 285
ERIC/CASS, 11, 59, 161, 186, 420
and development of virtual counseling libraries, 162–64
See also International Career Development Library
Erickson, Milton, 256
ethical guidelines
expansion of, 45–46
*Standards for the Ethical Practice of
Web Counseling* (NBCC), 74,
244, 326, 421, 441–44
ethical issues in cybercounseling, 325,
379–80
competence, 328–29
confidentiality, 327–28
dual relationships, 329
duty to warn, 328
electronic ethics networking
consortium, 388–89
ethics consultation, 382–85
ethics consultation, examples and
innovations, 388–91
frameworks for decision making,
394–96
Internet ethics consultation,
380–82, 391–94
is it counseling?, 325–26
other ethical issues, 330–31
questions for decision making, 401
redressing alleged ethical
infractions, 385–88
specific ethical issues, 326–27
truth in advertising, 327
vignettes of ethical dilemmas,
398–400
ethical and legal concerns in on-line
support groups for loss, 110–11

Ethical Standards for Internet On-Line Counseling (ACA), 421, 423–28
evolution of the relationship between computers and counseling, 3, 12–13
computer-aided instruction, 5–6
counseling therapy computer programs, 4–5
Internet access, 11–12
mainframes, minis, and computer as therapist, 3–6
microcomputers, 6–11
expert computer systems, 9, 255–56, 271–72
algorithms for solution-focused therapy, 259–61
an expert system design for resolution counseling, 264–71
evolution from cause to resolution in counseling, 256–59
evolution from general problem solvers to knowledge-based systems in artificial intelligence, 261–62
expert system design and implementation, 263–64
expert system feasibility, 262–63
explanation subsystem in expert computer systems, 264
EXSYS Professional (software), 272
extradition, 347

F

face-to-face instruction
distance education and, 144
video and audio sessions and, 203–18
Falling Through the Net: Defining the Digital Divide (study), 75
federal extradition law, 347
Federation of State Medical Boards (FSMB), 331
feedback, assessment technology and immediate, 239
felony crimes, 347
First Amendment, U.S. Constitution

First Amendment protection of cybercounseling, 351–56
outlawing cybercounseling and freedom of speech issue, 342, 343
Fisch, Richard, 256, 257
Florida Gulf Coast University, Counselor Education Resource Center, 282
form disclaimers, 346
Forsyth County v. Nationalist Movement, 353
Forum on Internet Mental Health Practice, 383
Foundations of Chemical Dependency Counseling (web site), 286
Foundations of Globalization of Higher Education and the Professions, The (Lenn and Miller), 30
Fourteenth Amendment, U.S. Constitution, 342, 349, 353
Framework for Ethical Decision Making: Version 4 Ethics Shareware, 395
Frasier (tv series), 321
Freddolino, P. P., 129, 304
funding methods
for the development of high-quality web sites, 48
for support of revising counselor education curriculum and research, 48

G

Galas, John, 61
Gambrill, E., 390, 391
Gates, William, 40, 237, 238
gender and racial and ethnic fairness, assessment technology and, 243
Generation X, 33
George, J. D., 172
Georgia Mental Health Network, 334
Gergen, K. J., 19, 20
Gibson, Donna, 420
Gilbert, J. P., 4
Gingerich, W. J., 260
Gladieux, L. E., 144, 156–58

Global Alliance for Transnational Education (GATE), 30
global credentialing, 33–34
Global Institute for Interactive Media, 286
globalization of professions, 29–33, 36–37
  checklist for customizing globalization to a profession, 35–36
  customizing globalization to professions, 33–35
Globewide Network Academy, 285
Goldberg, E. D., 286
Goldman, Arlene, 328–29
gopherspace, 130–31
governmental advocacy, equal access to cybercounseling and, 91–92
Grackenbach, J., 285
graphics in web-based courses, 132
Great Therapists Program, 9
Greater Dayton Area Health Information Network, 282
grief counseling. *See* loss and grief through on-line support groups
guidance, defined, 19
Guide to Distance Education at a Glance (University of Idaho), 363
Guide to the Internet in Educational Psychology (Bissell and Newhoff), 285
Guidelines for Computer-Based Tests and Interpretations (APA), 244
Guidelines for On-Line Instruction in Counselor Education (ACES), 62–63
Guidelines for the Use of the Internet for Provision of Career Information and Planning Services (NCDA), 121–22, 244, 421, 445–51
Gundersen, D. E., 304

H

h-journals, 186–87
  criteria for publication of, 191
  format and design of, 194–97
  JTC as a prototype for counseling, 195–97

web-based, 190
web-based interface, 189
Hamel, C. J., 285
Hannum, W., 55, 56, 57, 61
Hargitai, J., 138–39, 140
Harnad, S., 190
Harrison, N., 285
Hart, Juanita Lynn, 420
Hartman, Kenneth, 421, 431
Health on the Net Foundation, 331
health problems, technology's limitations and onset of, 22–23
Herr, E. L., 116, 117, 121
Hickson, J., 172
Hippocrates, 383
Hispanics, Internet access of, 75, 85
Hohenshil, Tom, 61
home study programs, 292, 294
hosts, on-line, 100, 103–4
  training for, 104
Houston, Whitney, 410
Houston-Vega, M. K., 392
Humphrey, Hubert, III, 340–41
hyperlinks, 80
hypermedia journals, 186–87
Hyperstudio (multimedia software), 175

I

Iacocca, Lee, 31
ILLIAC (computer-aided instruction program), 4
Indiana University, 283
inference engine in expert computer systems, 263, 264
Institute for the Advancement of Human Behavior (IAHB), 296
Institute for Behavioral Healthcare, 296
Institute for Higher Education, 144
Institute for Higher Education Policy, 362
Institute of Natural Sciences, 297
Inter-Regional Accrediting Commission (IRAC), 374
interactive teaching in web-based courses, 132

International Association of Educational and Vocational Guidance (IAEVG), 45
International Business Machines (IBM), 5
International Career Development Library (LCDL), 59, 60, 64, 161–62, 169–70
design and implementation of the, 164–69
Document Submission section, 167
features of the, 165–67
future development of the, 167–69
Member Services section, 166–67
Papers and Commentary section, 166, 168
Reference Room, 166
Search section of, 165
Training Center section, 166
What's New section, 167
International Counseling Network (ICN), 11, 139, 185
International Seminars Group, 297
International Society for Mental Health Online, 331
International Society for Technology in Education (ISTE)
competency standards, 74, 433–40
Internet, 39, 49
assessment technology and the, 238–43
challenges, 43–45
continuing education over the, 292
cultural access differences to the, 75–77
expectations about the use of the, 39–41
globalization of professions and the, 30, 36, 37
guides, 285
impact in 1990s and beyond, 11–12
Internet access through Career Explorer, 118–20
Internet addiction, 23
Internet chat rooms as time-independent/place-dependent resources, 77

Internet ethics consultation, 380–85, 391–94
possible solutions, 45–48
questions and concerns for counselors about the, 42–43
scholarly publications on the, 185, 186–94
security issues on the, 179–80
seeking counseling through the, 20
social impacts of the, 23–24
stylistic framework of the, 72–73
why the Internet has not improved education more, 278
Internet Companion for Abnormal Psychology (Hamel and Ryan-Jones), 285
Internet Guides Press, 297
Internet Guides, Tutorials, and Training Information (Library of Congress), 285
Internet portals, 98
Internet service providers (ISPs), 98
violators of ISP Terms of Service agreement, 110
Internet and Technolgy for the Human Services, The (Karger and Levine), 285
InterPsych (IP), 330
Iowa State University (ISU), 54
Ivanoff, G., 286

J

Jacob the Baker (BenShea), 379
Jencius, M., 73, 77, 421, 433–40
Job Hunting Online, 60
job insecurity, technology's limitations and loss of, 21
job search process, electronic portfolio development for, 179
John Grohol's PsychCentral, 282
Joint Committee on Testing Practices, 244
Jones International University, 364
Journal of Counseling and Development, 130
Journal of Technology in Counseling (JTC), 187, 193, 285

Journal of Technology in Counseling (JTC)—continued
  as a prototype for counseling h-journals, 195–97
journals, traditional
  of interest to educators, 285
  on-line publications and, 188–91
  paper-based journals and cyberjournals, 187–88

K

Kadushin, A., 381
Kaplan, Roberta, 165
Karger, H., 285, 287
Keating, A. B., 138–39, 140
Keller, Thomas J., 419–20
knowledge base in expert computer systems, 264
knowledge-based systems, 262
knowledge engineers, 261
knowledge generalization, 406–13
Knox, A., 75
Kotecki, J., 98
Krantz, J., 285
Krumboltz, J. D., 118, 124
Kubly, K. H., 189
Kuhn, Thomas, 192
Kvan, T., 220

L

laggerts, 277
Lai, S., 220
Lambert, M., 10–11
Lanning, Wayne, 410
Laurasian Institution, 293
Layne, R. G., 76
legal issues in cybercounseling. *See* cybercounselors vs. cyber-police; state regulation of cybercounseling
leisure, decreased, technology's limitations and, 24–25
less skilled workers, technology's limitations and, 21–22
Lester, Juliette, 164
Levin, A. S., 118, 124
Levine, J., 285, 287

Lewis, Jacqueline, 418
Lewis, Richard, 152
LibrarE, 285
licensure
  and accreditation for distance learning, 361–76
  and state regulation of cybercounseling, 332–33
lifelong learning. *See* cyberspace education and lifelong learning for professionals
linking in web-based courses, 132
listservs, 11, 185
  counseling and mental health, 282
  moderated and unmoderated, 186
  as time-independent/place-dependent resources, 77
  using, 78–79
Liszt search engine, 78–79
locus of control, use of technology and internal, 25
Lombard, M., 206
loss and grief through on-line support groups, 95–96, 111–12
  benefits of on-line support groups for loss, 105–7
  grief and healing, 96–97
  immediate response to grief on-line, 104–5
  inside an on-line support group for loss, 99–104
  limitations of on-line support groups for loss, 107–11
  on-line support, 97–99
  three aspects of grief, 96–97
Love and Marriage (song), 411
Lucent Technologies, Center for Excellence in Distance Learning (CEDL), 282–83
Lukoff, David, 297

M

McDonald, Michael, 395
McFadden, J., stylistic model, 67, 68–69, 70–71
Machovec, G. S., 190
McKee, J. E., 258

Maddux, C., 278, 280
Madsen v. Women's Health Center, 355
mainframe computers, during the
    1950s, 3–4
malpractice insurance for
    cybercounseling, 335
managing technology wisely, 17–18,
    25–27
    awareness of technology's benefits,
        19–20
    awareness of technology's
        limitations, 20–25
    developing awareness, 19–25
Manpower (temp agency), 22
Markward, M. K., 304
Mental Health Cyberclinic, 330–31
Mental Health InfoSource (MHI), 295
Mental Health Net, 282
mental health services, ideal consumer
    of, 86–87
Merisotis, J., 144, 153–56
meta search engines, 80
Metanoia web site, 321
metaphorical language, 228
Meyer, M., 395, 401
Meyers, Jane, 420
microcomputers
    counseling intervention and service
        management, 6–8
    counselor education and supervision
        applications, 8–11
    during 1970s and 1980s, 6–11
Microsoft's Encarta Africana, 76
Miller, T., 276
minicomputers, during 1960s, 4
Minnesota State University, Mankato,
    Department of Counseling and
    Student Personnel, 176
Mitchell, Dan, skills for on-line
    counseling, 219–20, 221–35
Mitchell, K. E., 118, 124
Molnar, A., 259, 261
*Monteiro v. The Tempe Union High
    School District*, 352
moral virtue, 380
Morse, L. C., 76
MORTON computer program, 7
movies in web-based courses, 132

multicultural counseling,
    competencies in, 73
multitasking, 25
Murdock v. Pennsylvania, 353
Murphy, Lawrence, skills for on-line
    counseling, 219–20, 221–35
Murray, G. C., 392

N

NASDAQ, 25
National Assessment of Educational
    Progress, 250
National Association of School
    Psychologists, 250
National Association of Social Workers
    (NASW)
    Code of Ethics, 382, 385–86, 387,
        389
    *Current Controversies in Social Work
        Ethics*, 389, 398–400
    electronic ethics networking
        consortium, 388–89
    ethics complaints filed with, 387–88
    web site, 131
National Association of Test Directors,
    250
National Board for Certified
    Counselors (NBCC), 44, 45
    CCE affiliate, 293, 294
    Code of Ethics, 74
    continuing professional education,
        279
    on cybercounseling is counseling
        issue, 325–26
    cybercounseling standards, 334
    distance education, 332
    Forum on Internet Mental Health
        Practice, 383
    home study programs approved by,
        292, 294
    Internet-based continuing education
        program, 293
    *Standards for the Ethical Practice of
        Web Counseling*, 74, 244, 326,
        421, 441–44
National Career Development
    Association (NCDA), 44, 45

National Career Development Association (NCDA)—*continued*
digital libraries, 155
Guidelines for the Use of the Internet for Provision of Career Information and Planning Services, 121–22, 244, 421, 445–51
site links for, 151
National Career Development Competencies for Middle/Junior and High Schools (NOICC), 117, 119, 122, 123
National Center for Education Statistics, 250
National Center on Educational Outcomes, 250
National Center for Higher Education, 30
National Center for Research on Evaluation, Standards, and Student Testing (CRESST), 250
National Certified Counselors (NCCs), 292
National Council for the Accreditation of Teacher Education (NCATE), 74, 283, 284
National Council on Measurement in Education, 244
National Defense Education Act, 48
National Education Association, 144
National Home Study Council, 361
National Institute for Occupational Safety and Health, 23
National Occupational Information Coordinating Committee (NOICC), 119
ERIC/CASS and NOICC design and implementation of ICDL, 164–65
Exploring Career Development Interactive CD-ROM, 76
National Career Development Competencies for Middle/Junior and High Schools, 117, 119, 122, 123
site links for, 151
SOICC and, 117–18
National Organization for Competency Assurance (NOCA), 33

National Public Radio, 294
National Telecommunications and Information Administration (NTIA), 75
NCR, 282
NCR University (NCRU), 282
New York Stock Exchange, 25
New York University, 297
Newhoff, S., 285
newsgroups
as time-independent/place-dependent resources, 77
using, 78, 131
Nobel, Alfred, 20
Noble, David F., 153
North Carolina Areas Health Education Centers Program, 292
North Carolina schools, Career Explorer program in, 118, 119, 121
North Carolina State Occupational Information Coordinating Committee (NCSOICC), 122
Nuehring, E. M., 392

O

O*NET, 61
obsessive compulsive behaviors and addictions, 23
occupational information
NOICC Exploring Career Development Interactive CD-ROM, 76
web sites for, 59–61, 127
Occupational Outlook Handbook, 60, 117, 120
Occupational Outlook Quarterly, 34
On-Line Computer Library Center (OCLC) Electronic Collections ON-Line, 197
on-line instruction in counselor education, 303–5, 315–16
course content/objectives, 308–9
course quality, 305–8
faculty qualifications, 311–12
grievance procedures, 313
guidelines for, 305–13

instructional support, 309–11
instructor/course evaluation, 312–13
on-line course design, implementing
    the guidelines, 313–15
technological standards, 313
on-line journals, 186
On-Line Psych, 107
on-line publications and traditional
    journals, 188–91
on-line resources, 284–86
    ACES cybercounseling on-line
        course guidelines, 74
    *Guidelines for On-Line Instruction in
        Counselor Education* (ACES),
        62–63
    for occupational information, 59–61
    on-line support groups for loss and
        grief, 95–112
    textbook publishers on-line, 139–40

P

Palloff, R. M., 140, 285
paper-based journals and
    cyberjournals, 187–88
partnerships, equal access to cyber-
    counseling and, 91
PASCAL (programming language), 4
PBS's Adult Learning Service Online,
    286
PC programs, 152–53
Pennsylvania State University, 283, 286
performance assessment portfolio, 174
permanence in electronic publishing,
    191
Person Centered Therapy, 4
personal information, electronic port-
    folios and security of, 179–80
personality testing, use of computers
    for, 7
Peterson, D. B., 392
*Peterson's Guide to Distance Learning
    Programs,* 297
Phipps, R., 144, 153–56
PLATO (computer-aided instruction
    program), 4, 5, 6
PlatoDCS computer program, 6–7
Polk, G., 304

Porter, L. R., 285
portfolio assessment, 239
portfolios, electronic. *See* electronic
    portfolios in counselor
    education
PowerPoint (presentation software), for
    electronic portfolios, 175, 176,
    177
Pratt, K., 140, 285
Presbury, J. H., 258
presence techniques in therap-e-mail,
    227–28, 230, 234
privacy/confidentiality in assessment
    technology, 242
Procunier v. Martinez, 352
professional development portfolio,
    173
professional organizations. *See* global-
    ization of professions
professional standards
    accreditation standards, 370–71
    assessment standards and practices,
        243–44
    for distance learning, 57
    *Ethical Standards for Internet
        On-Line Counseling* (ACA),
        421, 423–28
    information literacy competency
        standards for higher education,
        280
    national standards, 284
    for on-line instruction, 305
    professional associations and cyber-
        counseling standards, 334–35
    for quality web site development,
        43–44, 46
    *Standards for the Ethical Practice of
        Web Counseling* (NBCC), 74,
        244, 326, 421, 441–44
    technology competencies, 73–74
    technology standards for school
        counselors, 431
program languages, computer
    for CAI, 5
    during 1950s and 1960s, 3–4
programmed instruction, development
    of, 4
ProShare® (software), 54, 63

Prudent Practice (Houston-Vega and Nuehring), 392

Pruger, R., 390, 391

Psy Broadcasting Corporation (PsyBC), 296

PsychCentral, 282

Psychiatric Times, The, 295

psychoanalytic free association, counseling therapy computer programs using, 4

psychological benefits of technology, 19–20

Psychological Tutorials and Demonstrations (Krantz), 285

Psychology on the Internet: A Student's Guide (Stull), 285

Psychology and the Internet: Intrapersonal, Interpersonal, and Transpersonal Implications (Grackenbach), 285

PsycInfo, 285

publications, professional, 185–86, 198
  format and design of h-journals, 194–97
  movement toward acceptance, 191
  new thinking in writing and research design, 191–94
  on-line publications and traditional journals, 188–91
  scholarly publications on the Internet, 186–94
  suggestions for authors writing in cyberspace, 197–98

Q

Quick Guide to the Internet for Psychology (Whitford), 285

R

Ralph, A. Colin, 418

Reamer, F. G., 394

Recommended Technical Competencies for Counselor Education Students (ACES), 73, 421, 429–30

registration and disclosure laws, counselor, 356

regulations. *See* cybercounseling and regulations

Reno v. ACLU, 353

repetitive stress injuries, 22–23

reporting and interpretation, assessment technology and, 243

research and its impact on cyberpublishing, 192–94

research program, external funding for cybercounseling, 48

resolution counseling, 256–59, 264–65
  an algorithm for conducting a resolution counseling first session, 265
  example: how influencing behaviors are selected in a resolution session, 267–71
  the interface—what is on the screen, 265–66
  the rule base—what is in the computer, 266–67

Resources to Use in Creating On-Line Web-based Courses, 285

Responsibilities of Users of Standardized Tests, 244

Rheingold, H., 285

Riley Guide, 60

Road Ahead, The (Gates), 40, 237, 238

Robinson, D. H., 304

Roblyer, M. D., 76

Rogers, Carl, 4

Rogers, Kerry, 341

rural areas, Internet access in, 75, 85

Rutter, D. R., 220–21

Ryan-Jones, D. L., 285

S

Samaritans (volunteer group), 328

Sampson, J. P., 7, 334

Santa Clara University, 390

Schmidt, J. J., 116–17

Schnieders, H. Lori, 418

school career development programs, 115–27

school shootings, on-line support groups for, 104–5

Scifres, E., 304

search engines, 80, 294
Liszt search engine, 78–79
sequence, e-mail, 230
*Services by Telephone, Teleconferencing,
and Internet* (APA), 330
Shanks, T., 395, 401
Shelton, C. B., 244
ShrinkTank bulletin board service, 282
skills for on-line counseling, 219
context and concepts, 219–21
the interview, 221–35
Skinner, B. F., 4
Slencak, Robert, 418–19
Sloane, A., 276–77
Smith, C., 179
social workers' code of ethics, 382
Social Workers' Ethical Responsi-
bilities to Colleagues, 382
solution-focused therapy, 257–58, 259
algorithms for, 259–61
Sommers, D. I., 330–31
Southern Association of Colleges and
Schools (SACS), 373
Spinney, L., 110
*Spiritual Psychic Science Church v.
Azusa*, 353
*Standards for Educational and Psycho-
logical Testing*, 244
*Standards for the Ethical Practice of
Web Counseling* (NBCC), 74,
244, 326, 421, 441–44
Stanford University, 5
Stanley v. Georgia, 352
state occupational information coordi-
nating committees (SOICCs)
NOICC and, 117–18
North Carolina, 122
state regulation of cybercounseling, 331
current guidelines, 331
distance education, 332
licensure, 332–33
See also cybercounselors vs.
cyberpolice
state web sites, 334
Steiner, Virginia, 363
Stevenson, C., 116
Stocks, R., 75
Stocks, T. J., 129, 304

Stom-Gottfried, Kimberly, 387
stress, 23
student skills, use of computers in
developing counselor trainees,
8–11
StudyWeb Excellence Award, 164
Stull, A. T., 285
stylistic model for transcultural
counseling, 67, 68
premises of the stylistic model,
70–73
structure for stylistic counseling,
68–70
suicide ideation
ethical concerns in cybercounseling
on duty to warn issue, 328
and on-line support groups for loss,
109
Suler, J., 285
SuperShrink program, 9
supervision, microcomputers for counselor education and supervision
applications, 8–11
support groups, traditional support
groups for loss and grief, 97
support groups for loss and grief,
on-line, 95–96, 111–12
anonymity breaches, 107–8
benefits of, 105–7
cyberconnections/increased access
to support, 106
differing stages of group development and phases of grief,
108–9
difficulties in crisis management,
109
ethical and legal concerns, 110–11
hoaxes, 109–10
immediate response to grief on-line,
104–5
inside an on-line support group for
loss, 99–104
limitations of, 107–11
limited feedback, 110
on-line support, 97–99
specialized on-line support groups,
106–7
universality as a curative factor, 107

Supreme Court, U.S.
on communications toward state
residents, 350
First Amendment protection of
cybercounseling, 353, 355
state extradition issue, 347, 348
Sussman, R. J., 419
Swail, W. S., 144, 156–58
synchronous communication, 144

T

Teaching Clinical Psychology (Suler),
285
Teaching of Psychology, 285
technogap, the, 21
Technology Competencies Matrix
(Jencius), 421, 433–40
technology and the continuing education of professional counselors,
291, 300–301
history, 291–93
recommended actions and start-up
strategies, 298–300
the web as the new source for continuing education, 293
what does the future hold?,
297–300
what is out there?, 294–97
technology-related disorders, 24
technology. *See* managing technology
wisely
*Technology Standards for School
Counselors* (Hartman), 421, 431
technostress, 23
teens and children, loss and grief on-
line support groups for, 106–7
telecommunity, 323
telecommuting, 24
telehealth, 323
Telehealth Project, 203, 204–5, 218
implications for clinical training and
practice, 217–18
six themes, 205
theme 1: emotional connections,
mixed reactions, 206–7
theme 2: working blindfolded,
207–10

theme 3: the invisible therapist,
210–11
theme 4: approaches to
psychotherapy, 211–12
theme 5: client differences, 213–16
theme 6: natural adaptations,
216–17
telemedicine, 322–23
critical concerns and benefits of,
324
definition, 323
regulation and, 323–24
relationship to counseling, 324–25
Telemedicine Development Act, 332
Telemedicine Law Update, 324
temporary workers, technology's
limitations and, 21–22
test comparability, assessment
technology and, 242–43
test security, assessment technology
and, 241
test taker identity, assessment
technology and, 241–42
Test Takers' Rights and Responsibilities,
244
testing, use of computers for, 7
*Testing and Assessment: An Employer's
Guide to Good Practices*, 244
tests. *See* assessment, technology-
delivered
Texas Education Code, 373
Texas Instruments, 4
text-based authoring, 192
text-based externalization, 231–32
textbook publishers on-line, 139–40
themes in web-based courses, 132
therap-e-mail, 219–35
therapeutic games, use of computers
in, 7
*Thinking Ethically: A Framework for
Moral Decision making*
(Velasquez et al.), 395, 401
Thompson v. Handa-Lopez, Inc., 372
Thyer, B. A., 304
time-independent/place-dependent
resources, 76–77
Training Magazine, 279
Trance*Sand*Dance Press, 294–95

truth in advertising, ethical concerns on, 327
Tyler, J. M., 304
Type A behaviors, 23, 25

U

Uken, J., 98
Uniform Criminal Extradition Act, 348–49
United States Distance Learning Association, 362
United States and globalization of professions, 29–37
United States Open University, 152
university courses. *See* electronic delivery of career development university courses
University of Florida, 279
University of Idaho, 363
University of Illinois at Urbana-Champaign, Psychological Services Center, 204, 205
University of North Carolina at Chapel Hill, School of Education, 53–54, 55, 62
University of North Texas (UNT)
    Ethical, Legal, and Professional Issues in Counseling course, 135
    University Library, 130
    use of distance education, 129, 131
    web course development policies at, 136–38
University of Oregon, 395
University of Phoenix, 278
University of South Carolina, Career Development Training Institute (CDTI), 76
University of Tennessee, 157
University of Wisconsin-Extension, 283
urban areas, Internet access in, 75, 85
U.S. Navy
    CATCEC program, 9–10
    distance learning concept, 361
Usenet, 131
user interface in expert computer systems, 263, 264

V

Valauskas, E. J., 188, 194
Valiga, M. J., 244
van Brakel, P. A., 187, 188, 189
Van Nuys, David, 22
Velasquez, M., 395, 401
Vera, A. H., 220
Verhoeve, Marc, 419
video
    face-to-face, video and audio sessions, 203–18
    using video in web-based courses, 132
video conferencing
    distance learning and, 54
    using, 80–81
    video conferences as time-independent/place-dependent resources, 77
video counselor-client interactions, 45
video teleconferencing (VTC), 329
Virginia Tech, 157
virtual career development laboratory, 60–61
Virtual Community, The (Rheingold), 285
virtual libraries, 161–62, 169–70
    development of the counseling, 162–64
virtual universities, 364
Virtual University and Educational Opportunity, The (Gladieux and Swail), 144, 156–58
Virtually Solve It (VSI) worksheet, 222
virtue, 380
Vision Into Action: Implementing the National Standards for School Counseling Programs (Dahir, Shelton, and Valiga), 244
Visotzky, Burton L., 380–81, 396
vocational guidance, use of computers for, 7
voice recognition technology, 240
Volti, R., 20

W

Wanbil, L., 75

Watkins, Robert, 381
Watt, J. B., 4
Watzlawick, P., 257
Weakland, John H., 257
Web66, 303
web-authoring/web-based authoring,
     12, 192
  suggestions for authors writing in
     cyberspace, 197–98
web-based distance education, 4
web-based instruction, 129, 140–41
  advantages and disadvantages of,
     130–35
  developing a web class, 135–40
web-based journals, 189–90
web-based training
  advantages of, 55–56
  designing web-based training
     courses, 58–62
  disadvantages of, 56–57
  distance learning and, 54
web counseling standards, 74
web course development, 135–36
  100% web course, 135–36
  policies affecting, 136–38
  recommendations for preparing to
     develop a web course, 138–40
web for distance learning, using the,
     129–30, 140–41
  advantages and unique features of
     web courses, 130–34
  developing a web class, 135–40
  disadvantages of web courses,
     134–35
web searches, 139
web sites
  assessment technology, 249–50
  Cybercounseling and Cyberlearning
     web site, 417–20
  electronic portfolio resources, 182–83
  funding methods for the develop-
     ment of high-quality, 48
  for loss and grief, 98, 99
  for occupational information/career
     development, 59–60, 127
  of professional organizations, 131
  professional standards for quality web
     site development, 43–44, 46

state, 334
textbook, 140
truth in advertising, 327
using, 80
web-based training, 59
web-page development, 138
Weinberg, N., 98
West, R. L., 220
West Virginia University (WVU), 54
Western Governors Association, 373,
     374
Western Governors University (WGU),
     364
  Design Team, 373
What Color Is Your Parachute?, 60
*What's the Difference? A Review of
     Contemporary Research on the
     Effectiveness of Distance Learn-
     ing in Higher Education*
     (Phipps and Merisotis), 144,
     153–56
"When Writing Helps to Heal: E-mail
     as Therapy" (Murphy and
     Mitchell), 222
White, M., 259
Whitford, F. W., 285
Wiener, Norbert, 255
Willis, J., 192
Wilson, R. F., 77
Wired Professor, The (Keating and
     Hargitai), 140
Wizenbaum, Joseph, 4
Woods, James, 164
worker security, technology's limita-
     tions and loss of, 21
Worksheet for Ethical Decision Making
     (University of Oregon), 395
World Campus Learning Community,
     286
World Counseling Network, 282
World Lecture Hall, 285
World Wide Web (WWW)
  access to, 130, 131
  career development/information
     sites on, 155, 156
  counselor education programs on,
     303
  culture-based resources on, 80

external links for career development university courses, 151
globalization of professions and,
  29–30, 34, 37
impact of the Internet and, 11–12
as the new source for continuing
  education, 293
PC programs on, 152
search engines, 78–79
time-independent/place-dependent
  resources on, 77
Wright State University (WSU), 278,
  281, 283

Y

Yalom, I., 98
Young, K. S., 23
young-attracive-verbal-intelligent-
  successful (YAVIS) client,
  86–87, 330
Your Confidential Sexual Issues Report
  (Goldman), 328–29

Z

Zimmerman, D., 108